The Architecture of Historic Nantucket

The Architecture
of Historic Nantucket

by Clay Lancaster

Introduction by James C. Massey
Director of the Department of Historic Properties,
The National Trust for Historic Preservation
Former Chief of the
Historic American Buildings Survey,
National Parks Service

McGraw-Hill Book Company
New York: St. Louis: San Francisco: London: Sydney: Toronto

© 1972 McGraw-Hill, Inc. All rights reserved. Printed in the United States of America. No part of this publication may be reproduced, stored in a retrieval system, or transmitted, in any form or by any means, electronic, mechanical, photocopying, recording, or otherwise, without prior written permission of the publisher.

Library of Congress Catalog Card Number: 72-37747
First Edition
SBN: 07-036120-7

The editor of this book was Walton Rawls, the designer was Martin Stephen Moskof, and its production was supervised by Frank Matonti and Suzanne Lan Franchi.

This book was set in Garamond by University Graphics, Inc. It was printed by Halliday Lithograph Corporation and bound by A. Horowitz & Son.

for
JAMES HUNT BARKER
whose kindness and hospitality
made this study possible

Introduction

For the off-islander there is mystery to the persuasive harmony of Nantucket Island: a wholeness of nature and man, of landscape and man's creativeness. It pervades the unique appeal of Nantucket's historic architecture, and evokes in today's generation a reawakened environmental consciousness. This sense of environmental harmony tells us much about Nantucket and provides an awareness of the rhythmic balance between harbor and fish house, moor and cottage, beach and cabin, landscape and town. It is a fortunate corroboration, enriching man rather than ravishing him, and it is our fortune that this gem lives today amid a discordant and thoughtless world. Certainly the separation of Nantucket from the mainland contributes to its unique character and the integrity of its historic district, and in our automobile-oriented age what pleasure it is to find a retreat the tourist cannot drive to. Yet other islands and their historic settlements lack the enriched environment of Nantucket.

Nantucket Island is rich in history and tradition, and these qualities add dimension to the architecture; thoughts of whaling, sailing ships, the busy life of a port town, the great families, and self-reliance during the long decline from prosperity, all contribute to our wonder at this urban townscape so concordant with its setting. To walk in the quiet lanes in the early morning is to become a part of the richness of historic Nantucket, to enjoy an interwoven fabric of townscape, of street and land, rather than of individual buildings. Not pretentious masterpieces clamoring for attention, but each quietly adding to the other, to create in a cohesive unity one of the largest and finest historic districts in the United States. It is a singular cultural patterning we enjoy; plain houses, at ease with each other, mark the Nantucket scene, and reflect the traditional life of the Island. Simple in form and based on a few basic types, the Nantucket house is close to the street, yet has a fine rear garden. Though side by side with its neighbors, the houses are enriched with a variety of detail that maintains a discreet individuality while still blending into the larger whole. A few major buildings stand out, especially those of the nineteenth century; the mansions of the richest families and public buildings such as the churches, bank, and Atheneum claim our note, but not in confusion or competition. They provide focus and counterpoint for the district as a whole, and enrich it handsomely.

There was relatively little building in the late Victorian style; the old traditions continued, and the decline in Nantucket's fortunes in the latter part of the nineteenth century precluded the development that marks in the United States this period of industrial growth. By the end of the last century, the colonial revival reestablished the traditional patterns of design, and they persist today, aided by thoughtful historic district legislation.

It is not only buildings that create the urban landscape of historic Nantucket. It is with us in the streets and lanes themselves, sometimes winding and casual, sometimes straight, but all imbued with the thoughtfulness of time. Main Street, and a few others preserve the pleasures of cobblestone paving; warm to the eye, but if hard on the feet, they slow the hastening motorist to a proper pace. The intrusive overhead electric lines reveal the twentieth century's blindness to aesthetics; they are out of scale and not in harmony with the district and are crude reminders of the haste of our age. One is tempted to hazard that Nantucket will be with us longer than they, as their burial underground becomes yearly more urgent.

The physical isolation of the few historic island towns in the United States has served them well. Nantucket has perhaps most notably benefited from this geographical circumstance, and the sometimes cruel path of history. More period buildings are preserved here in a historic district than on any other American island. Many communities that were originally islands have become joined to the mainland by bridges, and the resultant development pressures have had great impact: Galveston in Texas, or Coronado in California, for example. Key West, though joined by a highway to the mainland of Florida, retains its historic character as a result of its remoteness. For every Nantucket enthusiast, there is one for the similar qualities of Martha's Vineyard . . . so close, and yet different in character and development from the subject of this book. At Edgartown and Oak Bluffs there are notable historic communities, but neither have had the benefit of federal recognition as National Landmarks, nor the benefit of intensive architectural history studies as this book so well represents. Mackinac Island in the Straits of Mackinac in Northern Michigan, has some of this distinctive feeling of separation that is such a significant feature of Nantucket. With a dominating eighteenth century fort, fine historic buildings, and a fascinating Victorian shopping area, Mackinac has a special character of its own, quite different from Nantucket, yet with a similarly persuasive emotional attraction to residents and visitors. Mackinac also has the good sense and fortune to ban all automobile traffic on the island . . . a blessing and a relief of major significance. Perhaps Nantucket will eventually face the need for some type of traffic limitation, as has Mackinac in a total way, or Bermuda in a careful and rational approach. Other islands, part of the continental United States, that one readily thinks of are small with scattered isolated buildings, and are not urban districts. Nonetheless, there are fine historic structures to be found in the Thousand Islands in New York, off the Maine coast, or in the State of Washington.

But to approximate Nantucket's exhilarating impact, one must search much farther afield. Perhaps to Bermuda, with an ancient and notable heritage of historic buildings ideally married to their beautiful environment, or to St. Thomas and St. Croix in the Virgin Islands where, however, there has been so much development, especially in Charlotte Amalie, that much of the delicate balance of architecture, history, and environment, which Nantucket and Bermuda have managed to preserve, has been destroyed. San Juan, though actually on an island, does not permit comparison, for although it is fortunate to have the best legislation for historic preservation to be found in the United States, it is the capitol of a large Commonwealth and a major commercial city.

The vitality of history is everywhere in Nantucket. It draws distinctions to life today, and provides a reminder of times past. Such survival is a fortunate accident of time and history; and its continuance lays grave responsibilities on us and suceeding generations. Historically its establishment and growth resulted from the long prosperity of a disciplined society. Its appearance was substantially set following its rebuilding after the 1846 fire, and a long period of depression prevented much later rebuilding and the destruction of old structures. Such is the combination that has created a great American historic district, and we are fortunate that it survived to be appreciated by our times. Many other areas have been lost by rapid growth and replacement of buildings, and by natural death and abandonment. Once gone, such a community can never be fully reborn; witness the contrived tastefulness of Williamsburg. Not so Nantucket; used, and loved through the years until this day.

Nantucket's depression and isolation have gone, and with easier accessibility and the growth of tourism, thousands come to enjoy the island. Fortunately we are at long last developing an awareness of our responsibility to preserve and use our cultural patrimony well. Thus the historic preservation movement, growing out of the antiquarian instincts that came early in the United States, and a love of our Colonial buildings from the late nineteenth century, has blossomed into a meaningful force in recent years. Nantucket has been especially fortunate to have had more than half a century of concern with the preservation of its historic past.

From the article "Ancient Buildings of Nantucket" in the 1906 Bulletin (Vol. 2, No. 5) of the Nantucket Historical Association, down to this thorough study by Clay Lancaster, there has been a series of studies, each growing more professional through the years. Through the Nantucket Historical Association, the precious fabric of Nantucket history and culture has been carefully collected, preserved, and presented to the public in its publications and museums. Later, off-island groups took an active interest in Nantucket's historic buildings, such as the Society for the Preservation of New England Antiquities from the 1920s and the Historic American Buildings Survey of the National Park Service in the 1930s. The extensive files of the SPNEA in Boston contain much documentation of Nantucket architecture, and the modest start made by HABS during the depression was later to blossom into the widescale documentary studies of the 1960s.

In 1955 Nantucket was the first town in Massachusetts to take advantage of state enabling legislation, and became an official historic district, with a Historic District Commission to oversee the designation, and prescribe regulations for its preservation. The *Nantucket Historic District Handbook*, their guidelines for construction and restoration are a model, setting goals for the traditional Nantucket look rather than prescribing cumbersome requirements. Although now, in 1972, we are well acquainted with such designations—from Maine to Hawaii—in 1955 it was a forward looking move of no little importance for the future of the island. In 1966 Nantucket was designated as a National Historic Landmark by the National Park Service. This, the most significant designation awarded privately owned sites and districts, recognizes the importance of Nantucket to the nation, and demonstrates the interest of the National Park Service in its history and preservation.

Of great potential import was the subsequent inclusion of the Nantucket Historic District on the National Register of Historic Places, by virtue of its Landmark status. This program, the heart of the Federal historic preservation apparatus, is the nation's official schedule of historic buildings, sites, and objects. Though much broader in scope than the highly selective Landmarks program, it is under the Register that a small measure of legal protection is afforded historic buildings and areas, and grants for preservation and restoration can be made. This National Park Service protection, though limited, is a start on the formal central government recognition and firm protection of historic areas that is common in Europe, but lacking in the United States, except for state and local legislation. The Register designation provides protection against harmful effects of federal undertakings, either direct projects, or federally financed or licensed projects. The Historic Preservation Act of 1966 is of vast, far-reaching significance, and it has already done much to help the preservation of the historic areas of the United States.

However, it has been the HABS, also a National Park Service program, that has represented the principal federal preservation involvement on Nantucket. The renewed work, starting in 1962, continued the earlier studies of the 1930s, and grew to become the most intensive study of an historic area ever undertaken by the Survey. Since 1965, this program has received the generous support of the Nantucket Historical Trust, and has resulted in the study of 124 buildings, two historic district surveys, and an urban planning history study, which are listed in an appendix to this book. These detailed records of Nantucket's architecture are deposited in the Division of Prints and Photographs of the Library of Congress, which maintains the survey archives now numbering over 16,000 historic structures throughout the United States. To bring the extensive documentation of Nantucket architecture to the public, in 1970 the Nantucket Historical Trust sponsored a major traveling exhibit, "The Historic Architecture and Urban Design of Nantucket." Organized by HABS for the Smithsonian Institution Traveling Exhibition Service, after its Nantucket opening, the exhibit started a nationwide circulation to museums and libraries.

These are but two of the projects that have been supported by the Nantucket Historical Trust since its formation in 1957. Though often unsung, it has steadfastly worked for the preservation and restoration of historic Nantucket, enhanced and protected the community's historic heritage, and aided in the contemporary development of the town in a manner compatible with its historic past. Also, it has encouraged the traditional crafts, especially weaving and embroidery, which have received wide acclaim. Most recently the Nantucket Institute has been incorporated to provide summer college level courses focusing on the unique architecture and environment of the island. Of especial interest to historic preservationists is a summer course, starting in 1972, for historic preservation and restoration training, being conducted in cooperation with the Institute by the University of Florida School of Architecture, with assistance from the National Trust for Historic Preservation, and other organizations.

Thus in these rapidly changing times, the protection and enhancement of Nantucket's unique historic heritage has gained a wide acceptance, and none too soon, as the accelerating destruction of our cultural patrimony in the United States will attest. During the decades since the HABS work started, some 25% of the recorded buildings have been lost or destructively altered nationally, and in several areas, such as Mobile, Alabama, the figure has reached over 50%.

With this concern for the future of Nantucket's historic heritage, and the growing threats to our national heritage, this book by Clay Lancaster is welcome and timely. Analytical and perceptive, Mr. Lancaster's deep love of Nantucket is obvious in his carefully prepared research and his detailed survey of historic Nantucket, street by street, period by period, and building type by building type. Indeed, it is a summation of the long interest in Nantucket's architecture, and provides for the first time a sympathetic yet comprehensive view of Nantucket's dwellings and their environment.

Hopefully this work will help to further public awareness of the unique treasure that is Nantucket, and protect this extraordinary place for future generations of Americans. Clay Lancaster deserves the hearty thanks of all of us who love Nantucket, Islanders and off-islanders alike, for his contributions.

James C. Massey

Acknowledgments

A study of this nature, dealing with a town that once had a population of 10,000 and covering its 800 existing century-old buildings, necessarily derives from many sources and involves many people. The sources are credited in notes and in the bibliography at the back of this book. The people, in most instances, are given recognition in the notes. Yet there are some who deserve special mention for their helpfulness to the author during work on this study.

The first group is too numerous to list here by name. It includes the owners and residents of the buildings visited. They were most agreeable and cooperative in imparting what information they had about their houses, and most kind in allowing the author free rein to inspect and often to photograph and measure the buildings. Their assistance is deeply appreciated.

The second category has to do with research, and it is headed by that most knowledgeable person on Nantucket house facts, Mrs. Marie M. Coffin. Mrs. Coffin has researched the Nantucket items in the Historic American Buildings Survey (in late years co-sponsored by the Nantucket Historical Trust), and she prepared the bibliography on things pertaining to the island that was published by the Nantucket Historical Trust in 1970. Her encouragement and many helpful suggestions during the preparation of the manuscript were succeeded by reading and making further valuable comments and corrections to the typescript. The result would have been only a fraction as valuable without the benefit of her guidance and great store of facts. For these the author is eternally in her debt.

He also is indebted to the directors and staffs of those institutions which have been actively collecting source materials, data, pictures, traditions, and memorabilia on Nantucket for many years. These include: The Nantucket Historical Association, in 1970 Mr. Edouard A. Stackpole, President, and Mrs. Elizabeth B. Worth, Chairman of the Historical Museum on Fair Street; the Atheneum (public library), Miss Barbara P. Andrews, Librarian, and Miss Janice Williams, Assistant Librarian; the Nantucket Historical Trust, Mr. John Welch, Executive Director; and the Nantucket field team of the Historic American Buildings Survey, headed by Mr. F. Blair Reeves, and assisted by Mrs. Constance Werner Ramirez, the latter also having been affiliated in research with the Nantucket Historical Trust.

The prints from old glass photographic negatives owned by the Nantucket Historical

Association, that figure as illustrations in this book, were made by Mr. Charles W. Folger of Nantucket, who also copied some of the nineteenth-century stereopticon views and printed some of the enlargements of photographs taken by the author. Most of the last were printed by Mr. Dick Williams of Modernage in New York City, who is due special recognition. The author is grateful to both Messrs. Folger and Williams for their personal efforts on this important aspect of the current volume.

Preface

Nantucket Town is an architectural miracle. Situated on an island many miles out to sea, without native trees sufficiently large for structural timbers, stone suitable for ashlar masonry, nor much use made of the clay pits in fashioning bricks, it nevertheless fostered and preserves one of the great, relatively unspoiled collections of late seventeenth- to mid-nineteenth-century buildings in the New World. In it are upward of eight hundred examples. Later Victorian buildings increase the number slightly, but the old community has mostly been spared the advent of modern constructions. A few bungalows are sprinkled along Easton Street and around the north perimeter of the town, and subsequent summer houses are even farther removed.

Founded on its present site overlooking the Great Harbor in 1720, the commercial nucleus of Nantucket is lower Main Street, which continues out over the water as Straight Wharf. The original wharf was built a few years after the establishment of the town. Main Street is paved with cobblestones practically out to the Civil War monument, and its brick sidewalks are buttressed by granite curbstones and connected by granite-slab crosswalks. The street is shaded by century-old elms.

The plan of Nantucket is no monotonous grid. True, sections were laid out on a rectangular scheme, but differences of orientation and successive changes have produced pleasant irregularities. House lots, too, often have odd shapes, accounting for later wings and additions jutting out at strange angles. Especially when adjoining a lane, an ell may bend with it in several directions. Yards usually are small but do not seem confined because of variations. Flowers, notably blue flat-top hydrangea and wild roses, bloom everywhere during the summer months, with rose vines climbing on trellises up the walls and over the roofs of dwellings.

A goodly number of houses do not front the streets, some having followed the early practice of facing south, and later ones having reverted to the archaic custom.

The majority of buildings are shingled and have a center chimney of brick. Clapboard and brick walls also exist, and sometimes façade and flanks display different treatment. Brick and stone frequently are used in combination for foundations.

In evidence everywhere are change and alteration, yet seldom are there unsightly incongruities in the results. The unifying element is simplicity: simplicity in materials and simplicity in forms. Nantucketers have had a penchant for moving and rebuilding houses, and a section of the Appendix (Part Three-N) is devoted to this subject. Yet for all the fluctuation that has gone into the makeup of the town, it gives the impression of having remained unchanged for generations.

Strangely enough, the house overhang, a feature of early New England architecture on the mainland, is totally absent in Nantucket; and the Cape Cod cottage, a prevalent domestic type for a century and a half from Maine to eastern Long Island, is represented by only one or two examples, and these are half-houses.

The Nantucket classifications include seventeenth-century "English houses," saltboxes or lean-tos, houses with chimneys on the roof ridge (the preponderance having a simple, roofed-over cubic shape with asymmetrically placed openings), and the later eighteenth-century and early nineteenth-century styles—primarily Federal and Greek Revival.

One notices the prevalence of roof walks with railings, cupolas, railing-type front fences, doorways with open sidelights and blind, shuttered fanlights, and, where high basements exist, lower walls usually lacking windows in front. Another Nantucket peculiarity is the transom over doors between rooms inside, said to be a device for detecting fires. The fear of conflagration in this wooden community also seems to have been the principal motivation for the roof walk, the busy seaman's wife having been more likely to use it for dumping a bucketful of sand or water down a burning chimney than for idly searching for a sail, as prevalently asserted.

Because of its uniqueness in both specimen types and the number of survivors, the larger part of Nantucket Town was proclaimed a Historic District by the Commonwealth of Massachusetts in 1955, subject to the preservation and alteration restrictions proper to such a designation. A wedge of tiny Siasconset, on the east arc of the island, was also so designated at the same time. The old buildings in the latter community have been investigated amply in Mr. Forman's book, *Early Nantucket and Its Whale Houses,* published in 1966. Although a number of interesting books dealing with various aspects of Nantucket proper have appeared, none has been as all-embracing as this one in regard to the physical makeup of the buildings. Special mention should be made of Mr. Duprey's *Old Houses on Nantucket* (1959), one of the handsomest regional studies available in the field of American architecture, a valuable record of a selection of some forty residences and notable for its interior photographs. Other sources are listed in the bibliography at the back of this book. At the annual town meeting in March of 1971, the voters passed an article to extend the Historic District to include all of Nantucket Island. Old houses on the circumference of the town, especially in the area south of and almost equal to the original Historic District, have thus acquired similar notice and protection.

Nantucket happily has escaped those two most offensive after-dark disfigurements of the American landscape and cityscape—traffic lights and electric commercial signs. It withstood the introduction of the motorcar until 1918; now, although its winter traffic simmers down to a respectable quantity, the vacation total becomes a menace. Telephone and utility wires, extant since the end of the nineteenth century, also abound, yet pleasant rumors presage their imminent burial. The matter of quaint facsimiles of ships' quarterboards, affixed even to private houses, is grossly overdone, and the town would improve considerably with their disappearance. However, the character of nineteenth-century Nantucket remains basically intact, and every effort should be made to insure that it endures.

The plan of this book is to throw light upon the town's old buildings from three viewpoints. Part One regards them chronologically, from the perspective of time, considering the first primitive beginnings and noting sequential advances—structural, technical, and those of accommodations and refinements. Part Two views the subject geographically and may be used as a tour guide. It begins with a look at the wharves, discusses Main Street as Nantucket's principal transverse road and individual buildings along the way, and in like manner takes up the other streets in alphabetical order. Incidentally, it is apropos to note here that three types of public ways are recognized in Nantucket Town. A short, dead-end spur is properly called a court. A narrow way, without sidewalks, usually only a block long, is a lane. The others, more important and with distinct roadways for vehicles and sidewalks for pedestrians, are streets. The nomenclature has altered, sometimes irrationally, in modern times, including the introduction of the term "avenue," where "lane" more aptly would apply. Included in the notes on each building are references to accounts and pictures elsewhere, should the reader be disposed to pursue the matter further. Part Three is composed of appendices or statistical listings having to do with the monuments themselves, as a means to relate various specimens to the others. In addition to the bibliography, there is a glossary of architectural terms to aid the layman unfamiliar with technical words and expressions used in the text. Supplementing the sections described are numerous illustrations, including maps, plans, drawings, prints, and photographs both old and new, presenting a sampling of the existing scene and a graphic record of the past.

Nantucket is a town belonging to the sea, a unique survivor of the days of sailing ships, of whalers and merchantmen, when its citizens took to the water out of necessity and won a fair share of romantic fame and wealth through their endeavors. Their search for the leviathan in far reaches of the oceanic world and their trading in exotic ports is recalled in history and fiction, and in mementoes in the whaling and historic museums on Broad Street; but the full life-size statement of their culture persists in the homes they built and lived in and the practical structures in which they conducted their affairs. These constitute picturesque Nantucket, the Little Gray Lady by the Sea.

Table of Contents

List of Illustrations

Part One :
The Architectural Styles

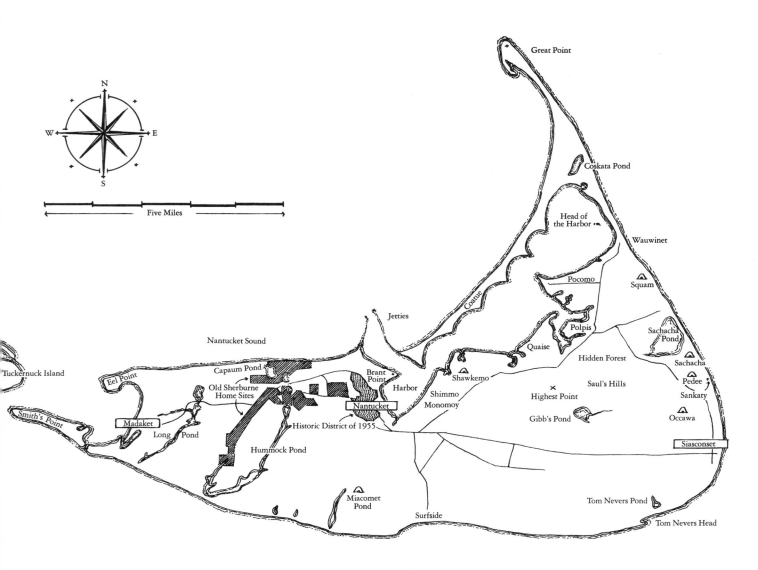

Fig. 1 Nantucket Island, Massachusetts, Showing Historic Sites and Geographic Features.

Chapter I

The Settling of Nantucket

Nantucket is the American Indian term for "Land Far Out To Sea." Situated in the Atlantic Ocean thirty miles south of Cape Cod, Nantucket Island forms a thirty-thousand-acre misshapen crescent with a great sheltered harbor within its cusps that was tremendously important in the development of the white civilization that came to the island during the middle of the seventeenth century. Nantucket measures about thirteen miles across at its greatest breadth, from east to west, and it varies from about two-and-a-half to six miles from north to south, excluding the narrow peninsula attached to the northeast tip which extends up to Great Point and dips back to embrace the harbor. A chain of low hills bisects the main body of the island, the highest point about ninety feet above sea level. The ridge was created in the Quartenary Period by a glacier and marks the extent of its progress. Although the knolls decline gradually to the west, they come to an abrupt bluff on the east coast, reaching from Squam Head to Siasconset. Outlying Tuckernuck and Muskeget islands to the west, stretches of the beach all around, and the peninsula beyond the head of the harbor are later geological adjuncts to Nantucket. The island had abundant vegetation, then lost it during periods of submersion and glaciation; but it has not been forested by stately specimens within the era of recorded history, and it did not have sizable trees until after the middle of the nineteenth century, these having been planted for their ornamental value within the town.

Whether Nantucket was seen or visited by the Norsemen in the tenth or eleventh century is irrelevant to its cultural history. It was inhabited by four civilizations prior to the arrival of the English: the first—going back nine thousand years—and second while Nantucket was still part of the mainland of North America, up until about five thousand years ago; the third and fourth coming to the island from southern New England, the last arriving about 100 A.D.[1] There were perhaps seven hundred inhabitants when the English first set foot on Nantucket. The Indians had six villages, four of them on the east highlands, of which one was on the west side of Squam Pond and the other three between Sachacha Pond and Siasconset; a fifth was on the

3

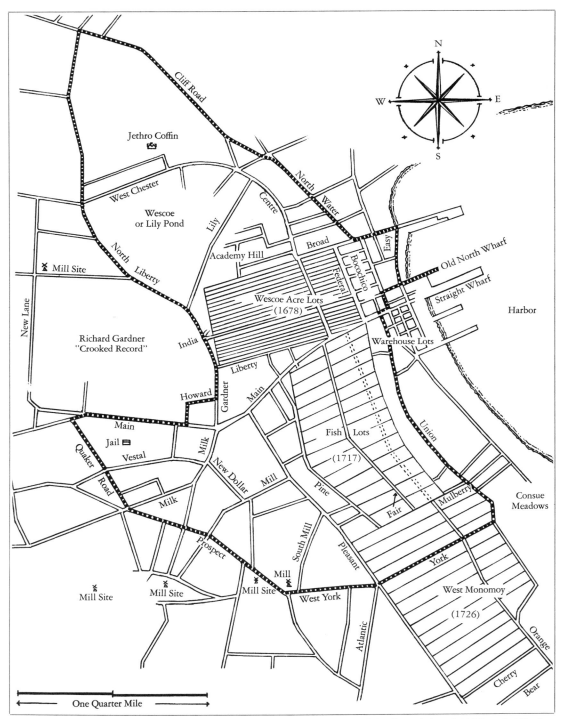

Fig. 2 Nantucket Town, Locating Early Lot-Layout Plans on the Harbor and Outline of the 1955 Historic District.

harbor at Shawkemo, and the last at the head of Miacomet Pond *(Fig. 1).*[2] The Indians lived in *Fig. 1*
wigwams having a framework of bent saplings. These did not differ from the shelters of their
race on the mainland, except that the absence of large animals and trees of adequate size on the
island ruled out the use of skins and bark as covering and limited it to thatch and mats.[3] Some,
at least, of the dwellings were dugouts, or partially underground. As elsewhere along the Atlantic
coast, such structures made little impression upon the English migrants. A notable exception was
temporary, on Cape Cod, where adaptation became a necessity for the Pilgrims to survive the
first winter. Their dugout wigwams, however, were provided with their own innovation—a
chimney fireplace. On Nantucket, the only type of Indian construction known to have been taken
over by the whites was the fishing stage or elevated lookout for spotting whales.

According to records, the first white people to view Nantucket belonged to the group
headed by Bartholemew Gosnold, who sailed from Falmouth for Virginia in the spring of 1602.
Their northerly course took them first to Cape Cod, whence, twelve leagues off, they came upon
the island. Through fear of mishap on the shoals, they passed Nantucket at a respectful distance
and continued to their destination. The journal of the voyage, by Gabriel Archer, was published
in 1625. Meanwhile, King James I created the Council for the Affairs of New England (1621),
which, in 1635, at the request of Charles I, conveyed to William, Earl of Stirling, certain "De-
pendencies on the Coast of Maine together with Long Island, and the adjacent Islands." The last
included Nantucket. Two years later the Earl of Stirling appointed James Forrett his agent in
New York for these territories, and, in 1641, the latter sold Nantucket for forty pounds to Thomas
Mayhew and Thomas Mayhew II of Watertown, Massachusetts. The Mayhews purchased other
islands and proceeded to promote religious missionary work among the Indians. Later they established schools. The Christianization of the aborigines made them tolerant of the English, and
they accepted the newcomers as neighbors.

The New England colonists sometimes were less charitable. In the middle of the seventeenth century, a bitter hostility arose against Baptists, Quakers, and other non-Church groups
for entertaining heretical views. Two Quaker men and one woman were hanged at Boston in
1650, and severe penalties were inflicted against anybody harboring or aiding a member of that
sect.[4] Consequently a small group of non-Puritans and separatist sympathizers, led by Tristram
Coffin of Salisbury, sought asylum off shore and applied to Thomas Mayhew for Nantucket.
Mayhew, then governor of Massachusetts, was residing on Martha's Vineyard, and he agreed to
sell the piece of land at the west end of the island that he had acquired through barter from the
Indians, plus the right to procure from the natives all but one tenth more, reserving that tithe
called Quaise for himself. The Salisbury group, besides Tristram Coffin, was composed of Thomas
Barnard, Peter Coffin (son of Tristram), Stephen Greenleaf, Christopher Hussey, Thomas Macy,
William Pike, and John and Richard Swain. Before the transaction was completed, each member
of the group had decided to take a partner, and the partners included Robert Barnard (brother of
Thomas), James Coffin (son of Tristram), Tristram Coffin II, Thomas Coleman, Thomas Look,
Robert Pike, John Smith, and Edward and Nathaniel Starbuck. These eighteen, together with
Governor Mayhew and his partner, who was his son, Thomas Mayhew II, became the First
Twenty Purchasers or original proprietors. For the most part, the surnames listed were to descend
to important figures in Nantucket history.[5]

In the autumn of 1659, Thomas Macy, his wife, and five children, Edward Starbuck,
James Coffin (aged 18), and Isaac Coleman (an orphan, aged 12) took ship to Nantucket. They
found the Indians kind and hospitable, and they spent the winter in a little hut at Madaket. In the
spring, Starbuck returned to the mainland and came back in the summer of 1660 with ten fami-

lies. Soon after, the Salisbury organization got together fourteen other families headed by crafts-men, each of whom was offered a half-share of ownership to settle on the island. At the first meeting of the proprietors on Nantucket, July 15, 1661, each man was allowed to select his home site on the basis of sixty square rods of land to a whole share. Tristram Coffin was given first choice and designated a location at the head of Cappamet Harbor (Capaum Pond). Edward Star-buck chose a spot near the north end of Hummock Pond, and Thomas Macy selected a place in the vicinity of Reed Pond.[6] The others took adjoining properties, projecting a series of lots curving southwesterly down to the cove end of Hummock Pond, and several assumed sites southeast of the location of Crooked Lane and West Chester Street, approaching the inland boundary of the

Fig. 1 1955 Historic District *(Fig. 1)*. However, the early settlement was entirely west and mostly south-west of the present Nantucket Town.[7] It was incorporated under the name Nantucket in 1671, the same year the island became part of New York Province. In 1673, Royal Governor Francis Love-lace renamed the settlement "Sherborne" (later more often rendered "Sherburne"), acting on the request of John and Richard Gardner to memorialize their ancestral village in England. The designation caused trouble after 1692, when Nantucket was shifted permanently to Massachu-setts, as there already was a community of this title in Massachusetts. The two rivals had to endure the inconvenience for more than a century, until the island town reverted to its original name in 1795.[8]

Quite aside from the escape from religious persecution on the New England mainland—the chief cause of immigration from England to the Massachusetts colony in the first place—there were practical considerations behind the Nantucket settlement. The Salisbury group, or First Twenty Purchasers, were organized under a proprietary, which was a common form of procedure in New England in the seventeenth century, whereby a group of individuals held in common a parcel of land to be developed for their mutual advantage. As each First Purchaser was a full shareowner, and the fourteen mechanics later taken in the proprietary were granted each a half-share, there were twenty-seven shares in all. We have seen that home sites were allotted in the summer of 1661. Because the land was poor, much of it covered with sand, peat swamps, and ponds, it had little value for farming, and to parcel out the island for working the soil would be for everybody to starve. The only industry that seemed practical was raising sheep. Thus, the moors beyond the home sites were designated sheep commons, with each proprietor allowed pasturage for a certain number of head, according to his share status. Accommodations for cows, horses, geese, and other animals were proportionate. The beasts were ear-clipped or otherwise identified and allowed to roam free. Ditches had to be dug to keep them off the land not yet pro-cured from the Indians and fences built to exclude them from the home sites.[9] The proprietary was a closed system that had medieval feudal overtones, discriminating against latecomers; and it led to insurrection of the half-share men in the 1670s.

Tristram Coffin, the leader in forming the proprietary in Salisbury, because of his own share, those of his three sons, and that of his son-in-law Stephen Greenleaf, held originally a quarter (later a bit less than a fifth) of the balance of power in the venture. Tristram's son, Peter Coffin, owned vast timberlands and a sawmill at Exeter, New Hampshire, and the new building boom on Nantucket meant a ready market for lumber. But beyond this family monopoly, the great resources for all of the settlers lay over the eighty-seven-mile shoreline. Their early suste-nance and later wealth were to be derived from the sea, through fishing, whaling, and—like all insular people so equipped—engaging in trade between distant ports. By far the most important was whaling, with which the name of Nantucket was to become inseparably linked.

When the first English arrived on Nantucket, the Indians were already experienced off-

Fig. 3 Windmill (1746) Built by Nathan Wilbur, Prospect at South Mill Street.

Fig. 4 North Shore Meeting House (*ca.* 1730), Now Called Old North Vestry, Behind First Congregational Church on Academy Hill.

shore whalers. After sighting the quarry from the fishing-stage or lookout, the braves gave chase by canoe. They made contact with a harpoon having a bone or stone head and attached to a bark rope. Pulling themselves close, they killed the mammal with arrows. Probably they attacked only the smaller varieties, such as blackfish. Indians ate the flesh and used the oil for cooking peas and maize. The whites observed and improved upon their methods, and moved forward to build a thriving industry. The whaling proficiency of the settlers cut into the Indians' larder and created hardship for them. Already they were deprived of their land, and because of the whites they were subjected to diseases against which they had no resistance. But primarily it was the introduction of rum that crazed and degraded the red man and led to his extinction. By the end of the 1700s, there were only a few Nantucket Indians left. The last, Dorcas Honorable, died at the age of seventy-nine in 1855, and afterward all that remained of the early race was the preponderance of place names throughout the island.[10]

The value of the whale to the white man had to do primarily with lighting—oil for lamps and tallow for candles. Minor by-products of the enterprise were whalebone for fashion, and ambergris, a base for perfume; one subject to varying demand and the other varying in availability. The first whaling venture was undertaken by the original purchasers. In 1668, a "scragg" whale entered the harbor and remained several days. It attracted the notice of the people, who devised a harpoon and were successful in subduing the creature. In the early 1670s, shore whaling was instituted and operated along the beach near Miacomet Pond. After a whale was captured, the carcass was towed ashore, the blubber cut off in chunks and subjected to the try-pots for removal of the oil. Other colonists on the North American mainland already were proficient in the endeavor, and in 1690 the Nantucketers engaged Ichabod Paddock of Cape Cod to instruct them in better techniques for killing whales and extracting oil. An occurrence in 1712 projected them into a greater orbit. In that year, Christopher Hussey was cruising near the shore in search of right whales when his ship was blown some distance from the land, and he encountered a school of sperm whales. He killed one and brought it to port. The event prompted the building of vessels of about thirty tons, and by 1715 six sloops were in operation for deep-sea whaling.[11] Nantucket ships gradually increased in number and range, until they roamed the seven seas in search of the leviathans. Try-works for pressing the oil and candle factories were built on the island, and it became the world's leading manufacturer of lighting fluid and tapers, steadily increasing its output up to the zenith year of 1842. The wealth and affluence that whaling provided are reflected in the homes of the shipowners and captains that are the chief attraction of Nantucket today.

A significant factor pertaining to Nantucket architecture was the removal from the settlement site. About 1717, the mouth of Cappamet Harbor was closed by shifting sands, as the result of several storms, and the isolated body of water became Capaum Pond. However, it already was an inadequate port because of its limited size. The great natural harbor of Nantucket Island lay around Brant Point to the east. It was the logical location for a community oriented toward the sea. Already, in 1678, an area bounded by the present Liberty Street on the south, Broad on the north, and extending westward from Federal Street to a little beyond Westminister had been divided into twenty narrow lots, one for each of as many proprietors, the other seven shares having been apportioned elsewhere *(Fig. 2)*. Each lot was two rods wide and eighty long, terminating *Fig. 2* on the shore now lying between Straight Wharf and Steamboat Wharf. Liberty, India, Federal, and Centre streets were included in the plan. The area described was called Wescoe Acre Lots. "Wescoe" in the Indian tongue means "White Stone," from a quartz block said still to exist under Straight Wharf.[12]

In 1716, Joseph Coffin was granted the right to build a "wharf at ye old landing forty feet wide, and it shall be his privilege so long as he keeps it in good repair."[13] Although it is not known precisely where this wharf was located, it must have reached out into the water from the Warehouse Lots, east of the proposed Wescoe Acre Lots. The wharf attracted attention to this vicinity, and in 1717 the land below Main was divided into house sites. The area extended down to Eagle Lane and Mulberry Street, and it included the area from Pine eastward to Quanaty Bank, the edge of the cliff between Orange and Union streets. Fair Street divided the two ranges of parcels which, significantly, numbered twenty-seven. These were the Fish Lots. They were built upon readily, and, in 1720, the official site of Sherburne was moved to the harbor. Confusion among the early grants may have had something to do with it, because in December 1722, each proprietor was made verbally to return his home tract for reapportioning. In that year, the last house was built in old Sherburne, the Elihu Coleman lean-to on Hummock Pond, the only one left in that vicinity. The others were disassembled and the parts reused in buildings going up in the new community. The white population at that time was about eight hundred.

In 1723, Richard Macy built the original Straight Wharf, thus justifying the move of the settlement and indicating the metamorphosis of Nantucket citizenry to a predominantly seafaring people. In 1726, two new residential districts were projected. The first was West Monomoy, south of Fish Lots and of about equal height, and likewise divided into two districts totaling twenty-seven parcels. Lots, however, were deeper, especially the inland range, extending west to Pleasant Street, and the other parcel east to Union (as Quanaty Bank levels off somewhat here), both fronting on Orange Street. Orange was elongated through the east range of the Fish Lots up to Main, and a series of transverse lanes was laid out through the lefthand Fish Lots, one for each parcel. These lot divisions afforded the first village character to the settlement, houses hereafter being built on them in alignments facing the street instead of southward as before. The second district was South Monomoy, which did not develop as planned but remained meadowland. Another small tract belongs to the group, the hilly, brook-traversed beach alongside Wescoe Acre Lots. It was leveled in 1744 and called Bocochico. Although a derivation from Spanish for "Little River" has been suggested, the name is more likely to have come from the Indian language meaning "near the harbor."[14]

Specialized structures proper to community life had begun to appear soon after the allotment of home sites. The most urgently needed was a grist mill. In 1665, the proprietary voted to build a horse mill. In the following spring the proposal was altered to make it a water mill, which was erected on the stream below Lily Pond, site of Chester Street, east of Centre. The water power apparently was inadequate for grinding corn, and the mill was converted to fulling cloth. A tide grist mill was established nearby in the 1670s, becoming the final enterprise undertaken by the proprietors.[15] The windmills of Nantucket came into existence between 1717 and 1746, one on New Lane (north side site of Brush Road) and four on Popsquatchett Hills. The round-top mill on New Lane was shown still standing on the Bache map of 1848. The last in the group, south of the town, built by Nathan Wilbur at what now is the northwest corner of Prospect and South Mill streets, is the only present survivor *(Fig. 3)*.

Fig. 3

The earliest Meeting House, Town House, and Jail may have been constructed reasonably close to one another. The Meeting House was built first, and it stood east of the north head of Hummock Pond on West Chester Street, which was the principal thoroughfare from old Sherburne to the harbor. The Meeting House was sponsored by the Society of Friends and constructed by Silvanus Hussey in 1711. It is believed to have been about thirty feet square, with an upper gallery; it seated two hundred persons. Waxed paper served for windowpanes until the sashes arrived from England in 1714. After its completion, official notices of public interest were posted upon its door. In 1716, a twenty-foot addition was attached to the east side. The acre of ground next to the Meeting House was used for burials up to 1760. The Friends, as a sect, increased rapidly on Nantucket, and in 1732 they erected a much larger building at the terminus of Main Street southwest of Quaker Road, where a cemetery still exists.[16] Perhaps six or seven years before this date, the Presbyterians had constructed a building at the south end of Capaum Pond called the North Shore Meeting House. It was this structure that was moved to Beacon Hill in 1765 and rebuilt, facing south, on the site of the First Congregational Church, later shifted to the rear when the larger edifice was conceived in 1834. Today known as Old North Vestry, it is the oldest existing building on Nantucket fashioned expressly for worship *(Fig. 4)*.

Fig. 4

The first Town House seems to have stood on the south side of West Chester Street, east of Crooked Lane. It was built by John Macy II in 1716, and it measured 24' × 34'. In 1789, it was moved to the southwest corner of Main and Milk streets, where it continued to function as a Town House. The building was described as having a second floor and a belfry, the latter probably added subsequent to the location change.[17] Less is known about the jail. A note appears among the town-meeting records of 1748 stating that "the old prison of Wesco" was sold to William Swain.[18] In 1768, there was a vote to repair the old jail and build a new one. At the end of the century a jail stood on High Street near Pine, probably the one mentioned in the records some thirty years earlier. The town built an adjacent 16' × 30' workhouse in 1770. The historic jail at 17 Vestal Street was erected there in 1805, and it is thought to have existed elsewhere for a quarter of a century before that *(Fig. 5)*. It is of unique construction for Nantucket, the walls

Fig. 5

composed of squared logs notched together at the corners, sheathed with iron straps inside and externally covered with shingles, the windows barred. Its outside staircase was destroyed by fire and its face charred in the summer of 1970, though the basic structure was sufficiently sound to warrant restoration. The house of detention built at Quaise in 1826 was moved and placed next to the east end of the jail in 1854, where it remained until demolition in 1954.

The settlement at the site of old Sherburne never attained a town character, in the sense of having houses and other buildings related to a street plan, but remained a group of isolated dwellings set on contiguous lots of various shapes. It had, however, a suggestion of a civic center in that church, Town House, and jail were built close to one another. A more uniform arrangement was introduced in the layout of Wescoe Acre Lots on the harbor in 1678, though the divisions were long and narrow and therefore accessible only from the short ends. The concept was furthered in the Fish Lots and West Monomoy of the second and third decades of the eighteenth century, wherein each land division was more compact and bounded by public ways. Good planning, fortified by the unlimited commercial vistas provided by an excellent protected harbor, favored the later community location; and whereas old Sherburne was doomed to disintegrate, the new Sherburne and later Nantucket was destined to increase and thrive. Our primary concern is with buildings in the historic town, and inasmuch as they were derived from what preceded them, we first must consider the archaic remains for the light they may shed.

Fig. 5 Old Jail (1805), 17 Vestal Street.

Notes

1   Bernard H. Stockley, "Archaeology and History, Partners in Preserving Nantucket's Heritage," *Historic Nantucket,* October 1964, pp. 13–19.

2   Emil Frederick Guba, *Nantucket Odyssey,* Waltham, Mass., 1951, p. 21.

3   Henry Chandlee Forman, *Early Nantucket and Its Whale Houses,* New York, 1966, pp. 6–16.

4   R. A. Douglas-Lithgow, *Nantucket, A History,* New York & London, 1914, pp. 115–116.

5   Alexander Starbuck, *The History of Nantucket,* Boston, 1924, pp. 18–21.

6   Guba, *op. cit.,* pp. 32–33.

7   Starbuck, *op. cit.,* fold-out diagram facing p. 56.

8   Harry B. Turner, *Nantucket Argument Settlers,* Nantucket, 1917, 1920, 1924, 1926, 1936, 1944, 1946, 1959 and 1966.

9   Henry Barnard Worth, *Nantucket Lands and Land Owners,* Nantucket Historical Association, Vol. II, Bulletin No. 4, 1904, pp. /183/–187.

10 Douglas-Lithgow, *op. cit.,* Chapter II, "Legends, Discovery and Amerind Place-Names," pp. 17–34; Chapter III, "The Aborigines," pp. 35–57.

11 Obed Macy, *The History of Nantucket,* Mansfield, 1880, pp. 30–36.

12 Guba, *op. cit.,* pp. 36–37.

13 Worth, *op. cit.,* p. 195.

14 Douglas-Lithgow, *op. cit.,* p. 27.

15 Worth, *op. cit.,* p. 191.

16 Robert J. Leach, "The First Two Quaker Meeting-Houses on Nantucket," *Proceedings of the Nantucket Historical Association,* 1950, pp. 24–33. Later Quaker meeting houses stood on the sites of 98 Main (1790), 76 Main (1829) and 9 Fair. Others still exist at 7 Fair and 29 Centre.

17 Starbuck, *op. cit.,* pp. 99–100; Worth, *Nantucket Lands,* Vol. II, Bulletin No. 5, pp. 234–235; Allen Coffin, "The Courts of Nantucket," *Proceedings of the Nantucket Historical Association,* 1907, p. 30.

18 Starbuck, *op. cit.,* p. 106.

Fig. 6 "Parliament House," The Nathaniel Starbuck Dwelling (*ca.* 1676), Re-erected (1820) and Enlarged at 10 Pine Street.

Chapter II

The Earliest Dwellings

The form of the initial shelters built by white people on Nantucket is unknown. These include the ones in which Thomas Mayhew II and his companions stayed while conducting missionary work among the Indians from the early 1640s to the late 1650s. It applies also to the temporary dwelling in which Thomas Macy and his family and friends (a total of ten persons) endured the winter of 1659 at Madaket. One assumes that they protected themselves from the elements much as the Pilgrims had during their first year on Cape Cod. A space was burrowed into an embankment, and over it was fashioned a rude vault of bent young tree trunks which was covered with moss and leaves and grasses, and then the hut was provided with some kind of fireplace. Their Indian helpers would have understood and promoted such a dwelling. Whatever it was, its primitive system was abandoned after the arrival of the fourteen mechanics sent from Salisbury a year or so later, and the rigid-framed "English house" became the rule. It was a medieval-type building, of the kind then still being constructed in rural parts of the British Isles, where the Renaissance style favored by the aristocracy had not yet filtered down to the common people. Transplanted to the Massachusetts colony, it was the accepted mode along the Merrimac River, whence the Nantucket settlers came.

Although no houses built by the First Purchasers have come down as such, the fact that they were dismantled and used in new constructions indicates that they were related to later houses still in existence. Many houses in Nantucket are claimed to have come from old Sherburne, though few have seventeenth-century characteristics, such as chamfered beams (see Appendices N and O, 2), and only two make any pretense at suggesting the identity of the original structure.[1] The more credible of the two was an outstanding dwelling in the community, both historically and in terms of size. The building was the residence of Nathaniel Starbuck, built about 1676 west of the north head of Hummock Pond.[2] Nathaniel's wife, Mary (Coffin), became a leader in the Society of Friends, and her home was used for the first regular Quaker meetings on Nantucket, beginning in 1704. The hall or great room is said to have held one hundred persons.[3] The as-

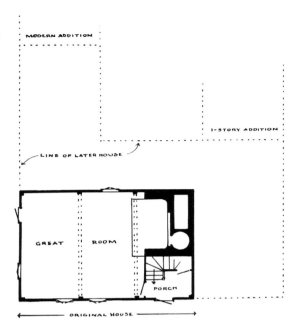

Fig. 7 Restored First-Floor Plan of Nathaniel Starbuck Dwelling on Hummock Pond.

semblies led to the house's being referred to as the "Parliament House," by which name its much-altered reincarnation still is known.

In 1820, the dwelling on Hummock Pond was acquired by John Folger, a Quaker carpenter, and re-erected on a high basement as the north section of the double house at 10 Pine Street.[4] It is fortunate that the new owner was a Friend and a builder, for, whether out of sympathy for the role of the house in the establishment of his sect on Nantucket or out of an ingrained conservativeness in house construction, he preserved the archaic features of the frame at this late date, when it was common practice to conceal the house skeleton behind lath and plaster. It was also in 1820 that the Classic mansion of John Barrett was built at 72 Main Street (Chapter Six). The considerably more primitive house at 10 Pine Street very probably kept the void pattern of the old dwelling, although the windows were changed from leaded casements to sashes *(Fig.*
Fig. 6   *6).* The transplanted house was enlarged, probably at first extended half again its width on the other side of the chimney, and later expanded about nine feet at the rear, with a two-story ell attached.

The original Starbuck house measured 20′ × 30′ in plan and was divided structurally into three bays of equal size. The porch and staircase with huge chimney behind occupied less than the first bay at the left end of the building. Twenty-two inches were taken from it and allotted to the great room, which, including the entirety of the other two bays, measured 19′ 2″
Fig. 7   deep by 21′ 6″ across *(Fig. 7).* The exposed posts are ten inches wide, and the lower edges of the beams are chamfered and terminate in lamb's-tongue cuts. The first beam in from the entry supported the hearth of the chamber on the second floor. The chimney was altered completely in rebuilding. We know from extant contemporary examples that the fireplace in the great room would have been much larger than the current one, and in the restored floor plan it comes out 9′ across and 4′ deep. It would have been provided with an oven in one of the back corners. The room itself has become obscured by later partition changes, as the north end of the house on Pine Street had to serve a much more complex family life in the nineteenth century than when it stood

alone overlooking Hummock Pond in the seventeenth. It is worth noting that a segment of a circular cool cellar (1820) is incorporated in the present foundations under the great room, and the round cellar beneath the south end of the other part of this double house is intact. Inside the garret, on the north gable, may be seen remains of the original rafters. The front one has been extended upward to accommodate the greater depth of the house, and a segment of the rear one is left dangling from its former apex. Rafters in the early houses were spaced about seven feet apart and connected by horizontal purlins to support the roof boards.

That the Starbuck house described was typical of early "English" dwellings on Nantucket is suggested by similarities in a second example of the period. Now located at 139 Main Street, the building formerly stood behind the residence to the west and, stripped of its chimney, was used as a carriage house. The land here was owned by Richard Gardner and was bounded by Main, New Lane, Franklin, North Liberty, Liberty, and Gardner Street, its irregular shape giving it the name of "Crooked Record" *(Fig. 2)*. The structure was built before 1688 for Richard Gardner or Richard Gardner II.[5] It presents a smaller and very much older appearance than the Starbuck house, because it sits low to the ground and its additions are one-storied; its fenestration has been converted to leaded casements, its door to a batten, and the chimney rebuilt with withes or vertical flanges *(Fig. 8)*. By actual measurement, the two houses were about equal. The porch of the Gardner house is slightly smaller, the stairs having all winder- or wedge-shaped steps and no straight flight. The hall or great room is within inches of the dimensions of that at 10 Pine, but the framing of 139 Main is composed of four bays, three of which determine the great room. It has, therefore, two equally-spaced summer beams running from front to back, supporting the smaller crosswise ceiling joists.[6] The quality of workmanship here is outstanding. Posts have a shaped bracket cap in the first story and a gunstock head in the second. The beam edges are chamfered, ending in lamb's-tongue cuttings. Fireplaces were carefully restored during 1927–28 and the house given appropriate furnishings, so that the ensemble takes one back to the seventeenth century.[7] An extension with shed roof on the east end and a lean-to added at the rear have produced an effect resembling that of houses built altogether in the following period. The appropriateness of casement windows in these later additions is questionable.

A fragment from the "English-house" era is the framing of the great room in 107 Main Street, incorporated in a large, full lean-to house built for Zaccheus Macy in the middle of the eighteenth century. A stairhall now cuts through the space of the former center chimney. Posts and chamfered beams enclose a room only 13′ 6″ × 15′ 6″ in area.[8] One suspects that this was about average for the early Nantucket home. For economic reasons, having to do with conserving materials and heat, early dwellings were small even on the mainland. Nantucketers had still more reason to be frugal, the island providing little fuel, no trees suitable for lumber, and no stone quarries, although there were glacial chunks to be found, some of granite, especially on the moraine or north slope of Saul's Hills. The settlers used such rocks for low foundations yet did not set their houses on full basements. Although elsewhere in New England stone was used for chimneys, the practice on Nantucket was to employ only brick. Clay beds, suitable for making bricks, exist here, but they were not worked until after the relocation of the town in 1720.[9] Throughout the colonies, window glass set in frames was imported from England. Delivery was an involved process that often caused considerable delay (as in the case of the first Quaker Meeting House). Glazed windows were kept to a minimum, and during the seventeenth century they remained hinged casements, the introduction of sash windows coinciding with the advent of the eighteenth century. Taking everything into consideration, the indications are that the early Nantucket house generally was a restricted shelter.

Fig. 2

Fig. 8

This is borne out by two seventeenth-century survivors at the east end of the island, the houses called "Auld Lang Syne" and "Shanunga," on the west side of Main Street and around the corner from Pump Square in Siasconset. They are the oldest dwellings in the village and have been tentatively dated 1675 and 1682. Certainly from the point of view of containing archaicisms, they seem to predate anything west of the harbor. The houses were investigated by the foremost authority on the medieval style in America, and to him we are indebted for their analysis.[10] "Auld Lang Syne" and "Shanunga" are oriented alike and follow a similar plan, originally rectangular and composed of a great room (approximately 12' × 14') and two chambers at the south end (each about 7' square). The chambers have a flat ceiling, and a ladder in the main room gave access to a cramped loft above for sleeping. The great room was open to the rafters, though spanned by several girders or tie-beams. The remarkable feature was the fireplace, located on the north wall in back of a screen partitioning off a narrow entry in the northeast corner. It was constructed without bricks, the earth floor of "Shununga," at least, serving as the hearth. The wall behind was plastered for a fireback, as was the first or chimney girt, to prevent scorching or burning. Smoke drifted up a wood chimney stack rising from the rear slope of the roof at the ridge. Contemporary Dutch houses of the Hudson Valley had fireplaces that were open at the sides, although with a masonry wall behind and a masonry chimney. The Jan Hasbrouck house (1705) at New Paltz had three, the one in the southwest room or kitchen remaining intact; another may be found in the Washington's Headquarters house at Newburg.[11] The dwellings at Siasconset were far simpler and built of scrub materials, perhaps including shipwreck salvage. Roof structures—wall plates and rafters—were made of tree trunks 5 to 6 inches in diameter, and they were covered with planks running from ridge to eaves, in place of shingles; perhaps the walls were of crude weatherboards, applied horizontally, as well. Both buildings have been enlarged and altered considerably, including, of course, the installation of brick fireplaces and chimneys.

The most revered house on Nantucket, and the one used most frequently as a symbol of the island and of the early architecture here, was in all probability very atypical of its period, and today it bears little resemblance to its pristine form. Before so-called restoration in the late 1920s, except for the loss of the northeast corner room that had burned and been removed, the house was primarily still in the early- to mid-eighteenth-century second phase of its development. The work at the time of the Depression precipitated it into a third and twentieth-century phase. The result came about through personal taste interfering with good intentions.

The building in question, of course, is the old house on Sunset Hill Lane, erected as a wedding present for Jethro and Mary (Gardner) Coffin in 1686, an auspicious marriage in Nantucket, inasmuch as it was one of several unions bringing together the leading families of the whole and half-share factions of the insurrection of the 1670s.[12] Furthermore, Jethro's father was Peter Coffin, owner of the lumber lands and sawmill at Exeter, New Hampshire, whence the materials for construction came. The house was meant to be special.

The Jethro Coffin house, technically, was a one-and-three-quarters-story building, because the eaves started at this level, but the upper rooms had full headroom with windows front and sides, and there was and is a garret on the third floor. Originally the roof was more steeply pitched than today, affording more space in the garret, and there were twin gables in the façade. Gables protruding crosswise from the roof were not unusual in seventeenth-century Massachusetts. They figured on the Old College at Harvard (1638–42) and Harvard Hall (1677), the first frame and second brick, at Cambridge; on the Scotch-Boardman house (1651) at Saugus; the Henry Bridgham house (1670) at Boston; and the John Turner (ca. 1670), Jonathan Corwin (1675),

Fig. 8 Richard Gardner II House (before 1686), 139 Main Street.

Benjamin Hooper (1682), and John Ward (1684) houses in Salem.[13] The construction dates range from thirty to two years prior to the building of the Nantucket example. The evidence for the façade gables first was noted officially by William Sumner Appleton, Corresponding Secretary of the Society for the Preservation of New England Antiquities. The Jethro Coffin house had been acquired by the Nantucket Historical Association in 1923, and two years later Mr. Appleton was asked to examine the building and make recommendations for its restoration. His report, dated December 28, 1925, to the President of the Association, William F. Macy, included the statement: "I strongly incline to the opinion that investigation will show that there were in this house what might be called front dormer windows, and that these constituted the main sources of light for the two chambers." On January 7, 1926, the letter was submitted to Winthrop Coffin, who had offered to finance the reconstruction. His reply to Macy, dated January 15, 1926, refers to the "dormers," to wit: "I suppose an investigation of the roof timbering would show conclusively whether or not such windows were there originally. Personally, I rather like the looks of the plain roof, but I am sure that Mr. Appleton would not advise putting the windows in unless the evidence of their early existence was absolute." Mr. Macy preferred the plainness of the roof too, responding to Coffin on the following day: "I recognize Mr. Appleton as an authority. . . . But unless he is insistent on this point, I personally should be inclined to leave the roof as it is, and I hope that he will waive that point."[14] The practicing architect chosen for the restoration of the Jethro Coffin house was Alfred E. Shurrocks, who worked closely with Appleton in devising the plans. His measured drawings show the rafter mortise holes of the two front "dormers" or gables, and the cut in the top side of the west upper front plate for the base of a casement window. As late as August 1927, Shurrocks' front and side elevations for the restoration included the gables.[15] But, as completed in 1929, the house was without them.

The Coffin house differs from the other three seventeenth-century examples in the harbor region not only in having remained *in situ* but in being a more commodious building, with rooms balanced to either side of a central chimney. The chimney is unusual. The figure in projecting bricks on its face has excited considerable speculation, its obvious resemblance to a horseshoe probably being far from the original intention. A nailed-up horseshoe open at the bottom stands for bad luck. In the realm of symbolism, it may rather stand for the happy coming together of the two families formerly at odds, relating to the wishbone. Or it simply may be a Jacobean chimney arch applied in provincial fashion. The brickwork in the head of the chimney above should flare outward with the other brick courses of this level but does not. The bricks, by the way, are typical of the period, averaging $10'' \times 4\frac{1}{4}'' \times 2\frac{1}{2}''$. In accordance with the common practice of the period, the building was oriented to face south. It measured $20' \times 39'$, and its walls rose $12'$ above a low rock foundation, inside which a crawl space was hollowed about $3'$ into the ground. The gables began to rise within $8''$ of the corners of the building and were about $16''$ apart at the

Fig. 9

center, their altitude about $10'$ as opposed to a height of $14'$ for the end gables *(Fig. 9)*. The valleys of the gables would have funneled rainwater directly over the entrance, which necessitated a shelter for the front door. No trace of such an excrescence remained on the house, but a Coffin descendant, who had lived there many years before, writing in 1881, recorded that there had been "an extensive wooden porch."[16] That it was "extensive" may have been relative to the smallness of the child who remembered it, or may have been childhood fancy or hearsay, but the existence of the shelter itself stands to reason. The walls and roof of the house probably were covered with shingles, although this would have been early for their use in such a remote setting. The employment of shingles had been introduced to America by the Dutch settlers on Long Island and adopted by the English in Connecticut by 1660. In the late 1670s it was known in Boston.[17] The early alternative was boards on roof and walls, as on the two Siasconset houses. Windows would have been leaded casements set in pegged plank frames, and the doors wood batten with strap hinges.

The inside porch was narrow and the stairs opposite the entrance were newel, as in the Gardner house. On the east was the hall and on the west the parlor, each a little greater than

Fig. 10

$14' \times 19'$ *(Fig. 10)*. Their fireplaces were back to back, that in the hall slightly larger than the other because of cooking, measuring $8'$ across and $3'$ deep, and having a recessed oven, $2'$ in diameter, in the southwest angle. The framing consists of eight posts—one at each corner of the two rooms—connected by horizontal sills and girts, with a large summer beam extending from the fireplace wall to the outer girts. This differs from the system used in the other houses considered, and it is more a Connecticut and Rhode Island than a Massachusetts practice, although the Fayerbanke house at Dedham (see Chapter Four, first paragraph) displays it. Floor joists run from front to back.[18] Whatever the outer facing may have been, the sustaining part of the wall was vertical boards fastened to sill and girts, with a filling of clay, for insulation, between these and the split laths for receiving the plaster inside. Though used in a different way, the clay filling reminds one of the wattle-and-daub in English half-timber construction. The two chambers on the second floor were equal in area to the hall and parlor. That on the west side of the chimney has a fireplace, and the other originally may have had one too. A narrow straight flight of steps leads up from the second-story landing toward the chimney and turns for access to the garret.

At some time during the first half of the eighteenth century, the Jethro Coffin house

Fig. 11

ceased to be the "English" type and was enlarged into a modish lean-to house *(Fig. 11)*. A one-

Fig. 9 Perspective Sketch of Jethro Coffin House (1686), Sunset Hill Lane, Restored to Original Form.

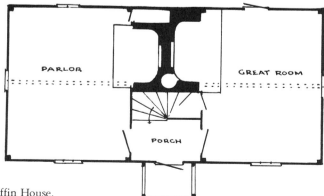

Fig. 10 Restored First-Floor Plan of Jethro Coffin House.

Fig. 11 Jethro Coffin House with Lean-To (second phase), Before Changes of 1920s.

story, 10½'-deep extension was added across the entire back to accommodate a kitchen, narrow milk room at the east end, and square borning room at the west. The new kitchen was given a fireplace comparable to that in the parlor, with an oven twice the diameter of the old one in the hall fireplace. The kitchen flue was run up the back of the original chimney. The walls of the new section were without clay fill, and the ceiling was supported on two summers but without joists. Also, about this time, the fireplaces in the principal rooms were made smaller by courses of brickwork.

The change in the outer appearance of the house was drastic. To avoid a broken surface, the long, north roof slope was given less pitch than it had had, and, for the front to correspond, it was brought down about 13°. In the process, the roof ridge was shifted from the front to the rear plane of the chimney. The alteration obviously would have disrupted the joinery pertaining to the two front gables, and, inasmuch as they would have been considered old-fashioned at this later date, they were removed. Sash windows, larger than casements, had become available, and a single opening on the flank could supply as much light as the old casements front and side. Cross-ventilation never has been a problem on sea-girt Nantucket. If the walls and roof were not shingled before, they were from this time onward. Thus the Jethro Coffin house had acquired its second definitive form. The restoration of the late 1920s included the superb engineering feat of re-building the chimney, but to replace the windows with an earlier type without replacing the architectural shape that went with them was to falsify the original structure, and the historic monument is left a hybrid tottering between two periods—actually constituting a third.

On the whole, early houses on Nantucket have not fared well. The change of community site made their location obsolete, and scarcity of materials subjected them to the status of lumber and brick yards, and window, door, and hardware stores. A rare instance of moving and reas-sembling an entire frame is the Starbuck-Coffin house at 10 Pine Street, though even it was obscured in a larger building. Most houses reputed to have come from old Sherburne are without distinct pre-1720 features to substantiate the claim. The single example of an "English house" remaining on its original site was the victim, long ago, of truncation and excrescence and, more recently, of a restoration fiasco that left it historically amorphous. To a lesser extent, the same is true for the house at 139 Main Street, though it was never such a unique specimen on Nantucket as that on Sunset Hill. It is impossible to draw any but tentative conclusions about the early architecture because of the insufficiency of examples. From what little we have to go on, it appears that the common form of early home was two-storied, having a porch with stairs in front of the chimney, a single room on each floor, and a garret above, covered by a gable roof. The Jethro Coffin house constituted a distinct departure. It would seem that its configuration was not liked sufficiently for Nantucketers to imitate it in their own dwellings during the seventeenth century, and it was not liked sufficiently for those who had control over its destiny to institute a true restoration in the 1920s.

Notes

1   The first, of course, is the Starbuck house, and the other is the Thomas Macy house. See Chapter 3 and 1 Tattle Court.

2   See "House-Lot Section, 1665–1680," Alexander Starbuck, *The History of Nantucket,* Boston, 1924, fold-out map facing p. 56.

3   Robert J. Leach, "The First Two Quaker Meeting-Houses on Nantucket," *Proceedings of the Nantucket Historical Association,* 1950, p. 24.

4   According to a statement made by John Folger to a grandson, Dr. Joseph Austin. Henry B. Worth, "Early Houses at Nantucket," *Proceedings of the Nantucket Historical Association,* 1904, p. 20.

5   Marie M. Coffin, *Historic American Buildings Survey,* Mass. 955.

6   Floor plan (with addition) in Henry Chandlee Forman, *Early Nantucket and Its Whale Houses,* New York, 1966, p. /224/.

7   Kenneth Duprey, *Old Houses on Nantucket,* New York, 1959, illustrations pp. 10–13.

8   Restored plan, Forman, *op. cit.,* p. 245.

9   Henry Barnard Worth, *Nantucket Lands and Land Owners,* Vol. II, Bulletin No. 5, Nantucket Historical Association, 1906 (reprinted 1928), p. 222.

10   Forman, *op. cit.,* Chapter 9, "The Two Oldest Known Buildings on Nantucket," pp. 111–/129/. Other books by Forman include, *The Architecture of the Old South, Early Manor and Plantation Houses of Maryland, Virginia Architecture in the Seventeenth Century,* and *Jamestown and St. Mary's: Buried Cities of Romance.*

11   Donald (Macdonald-) Millar, "A Quaint Dutch Survival," *The Architectural Record,* March, 1926, pp. 228–231.

12   Three daughters of James (son of Tristram) Coffin were married to sons of Richard Gardner—Mary to Richard, Ruth to Joseph, and Abigail to Nathaniel. The marriage of Mary Gardner to Jethro Coffin was unique as it meant a perpetuation of the Coffin name among the progeny. Alexander Starbuck, *The History of Nantucket,* Boston, 1924, Chapter 2, "The Revolt of the Half Shares Men," pp. 41–76, note especially footnote, p. 73.

13   Hugh Morrison, *Early American Architecture,* New York, 1952, pp. 83, 85–86, 55–56, 62–66.

14   Copies of the correspondence are in the archives of the Nantucket Historical Association.

15   The original drawings are in the archives of the Society for the Preservation of New England Antiquities, Boston, which also has numerous photos made during the restoration. Copies of the drawings are in the Nantucket Historical Association.

16   (Harriet B. Worron), *"Trustrum" and His Grandchildren,* Nantucket, 1881, pp. 55–58.

17   Morrison, *op. cit.,* p. 32.

18   Duprey, *op. cit.,* illustrations pp. 6–/9/.

Fig. 12 Caleb Gardner House (1733), 25 Hussey Street.

Chapter III

Lean-To Houses, Great and Small

Adding a lean-to to such early Nantucket houses as Coffin, Gardner, and others was a practice that came from the mainland, whence the original forms of the houses had come. The lean-to was a logical expedient for increasing accommodations, as it provided for several full-size rooms on the first floor and lesser chambers and storage space above. The new keeping room, or kitchen, left the hall free for purposes other than cooking, and rooms in the original part of the house were warmer in winter because of the insulation that the appendage furnished on the north side. It was inevitable that the lean-to would be adopted as an integral part of later houses, the fireplace at the rear included in the construction of the chimney, often recessed in its area rather than protruding into the room as it did where the lean-to was an addition. In spite of its containing more volume, the rear roof sloping down to a low wall made the house seem less pretentious, and thus it suited the New England Puritanical reserve; on Nantucket, it fitted in with the ideal of simplicity of the increasing Quaker population. As late as 1790, one Quaker of the older generation, Richard Macy, felt so strongly about the propriety of the lean-to house, that he remonstrated with his son, Job, over his intention to build a home with the new two-storied back, vowing never to set foot inside his door should it be executed. The house was built as planned at the west corner of Mill and New Dollar Street, and the father never visited it.[1] Another story is told of a house being erected near Stone Alley. The frame, brought from the mainland, was discovered to be two-storied all around, and the neighbors convened and petitioned the owner to cut down the back posts, to avoid inflicting change and extravagance upon the island. It is said that he complied.[2] Throughout New England, and especially in Massachusetts and Connecticut, the integral lean-to house with two-story front became the prevailing type from the end of the seventeenth century through the first half of the eighteenth century. A smaller, one-and-three-quarters-story version persevered into the early 1800s. In the revived interest in colonial architecture toward the end of the nineteenth century, this species came to be designated the "saltbox" house on the mainland.

Like the early "English" dwellings that preceded them, lean-to houses were oriented toward the south. More than any other type before or since, the lean-to house has a decided frontality, its sole two-storied wall being unmistakably the façade or face, and the long cat-slide roof covering the opposite extremity, the back, with distinct, asymmetrical left and right sides. The tall front caught the heat of the sun from the south, and the dipping roof directed the north wind over the housetop. A maritime people, the Nantucketers resorted to the use of the compass in such matters, sometimes with incredible accuracy. During the late 1800s, Professor Henry Mitchell undertook to determine the date of the Josiah Coffin house (60 Cliff Road) according to its precise orientation. Considering the slight variations that occur in the direction of the needle over the years, Professor Mitchell calculated that in 1723 the flanks of the building pointed toward magnetic north. Calling on the owner with his discovery, he was told that the residence had indeed been completed the year following his estimate.[3] Such directionism is proper to rural houses, and although most examples of this kind are located in town, a good percentage were not built on streets but awaited the coming of the streets to them. The ones that were sited on pre-existing streets were usually built on the upper side of those running east and west, thus facing south. Of the some forty two-and-a-half-story, integral lean-to houses in Nantucket, about two-thirds look southward, and of this number two-thirds also front the street (see Appendix B). Some of those not oriented have been moved to their present sites and were probably set correctly originally (Appendix N). Of the smaller one-and-three-quarters-story lean-to houses, slightly less than half face south, but, as pointed out above, the smaller examples mostly are later and therefore were built when residential orientation was on the decline.

The lean-to house appropriated certain traits of early buildings yet rejected others. The most medieval feature that was retained on some examples and for the longest time was the elaborated or articulated chimney stack, manifested as a projecting horseshoe on the front of the Jethro Coffin chimney and as three vertical withes on the questionable restoration of the Gardner house. There are twelve other flange chimneys in Nantucket, and all but one have three withes *Fig. 19* (see Appendix O, 1). The exception is the Josiah Coffin house *(Fig. 19)*. Its chimney has five withes, as on the Parson Joseph Capen house at Topsfield. The Capen house is an "English style" dwelling of 1683.[4] Its chimney—a restoration of 1913, presumably accurate—has identical articulation front and back, whereas the island chimney has an attached functioning stack from the lean-to fireplace. As the dating of the Nantucket houses with flange chimneys ranges from the end of the seventeenth century to the mid-1760s, it would appear that the use of chimney articulation was an arbitrary matter throughout the era of the lean-to house. Undoubtedly other examples had it, before their chimneys were demolished or rebuilt differently.

Of the innovations that came in with the lean-to house form, some made a considerable difference in the outward appearance of the house and others went unseen. The most apparent was the prevalent use of split shingles for wall and roof covering. The matter of shingle siding has been touched on as a change that began during the era of the "English house." If the Jethro Coffin house had board walls originally, there was certainly a switch to the new dress when the rear was added. Shingling was the normal revetment for the lean-to house. A fenestration change came early in the lifetime of the style. The first lean-to houses would have had leaded casement windows, whereas those built after 1700 used sashes with wood muntins. Pegged plank frames were retained, and in them the upper sash was fixed, the bottom capable of being raised open. The new fenestration adapted itself to the character of the lean-to house, providing the most and largest windows in front, fewer and narrower on the sides, and virtually only in the first story in back.[5] The normal pattern is for the main rooms to have two front windows of twelve-over-

Fig. 13 Matthew Myrick House, 14 Milk Street.

Fig. 14 Seth Coffin House (1740s), 53 Orange Street.

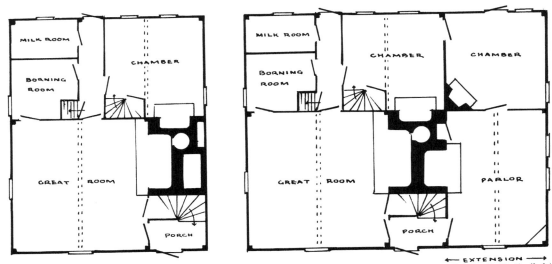

Fig. 15 Restored First-Floor Plan of Thomas Macy House, 1 Tattle Court (after 1717), as Originally Built *(left)* and with One-Story Extension at East End *(right).*

Fig. 16 Thomas Macy House.

twelve-paned sashes, and a single side window of nine-over-nine panes, the latter, or windows even smaller, used sparingly in the rooms to the rear. It is not unusual also to have smaller windows in the second story, either through fewer panes—as in the eight-over-twelve-paned sashes in the Josiah Coffin house (60 Cliff Road) and originally in the west half of the façade of the Caleb Gardner house (25 Hussey Street, *Fig. 12*)—or through the employment of smaller-sized panes above, as in the Macy houses at 9 Howard and 12 Liberty streets. Not at all apparent was the gradual abandonment of the practice of mud-filling the walls.[6]

    Exclusive of those later buildings that are less than two stories in height, lean-to houses generally fall, like their predecessors, into two categories; what we today call a half-house and a full, originally considered a house and a doubled house. A few examples are irregular and will be considered later. By far the greater number were built as half-houses, a third of which became full-houses through later additions. The obvious distinction between the two classes is width; but, as we shall see, there are narrow lean-tos that are not technically half-houses. The organic requirement of the half-house is that it provide for future expansion in fireplace facilities. The chimney rises above the roof ridge near the end closest to the front door. The outer half of the chimney was left hollow and incomplete, awaiting the character of the extension, whether one-storied (with shed roof) or two, sometimes with more than a single fireplace to the first floor, as at 1 Tattle Court. In some instances, the outer hollow space was made into a narrow closet serving the back room, apparently without any intention of expansion, as at 1 Bloom, 5 Ash, and 33 Orange Street. In each of these three examples, in recent times, the oven behind the great-room fireplace has been removed and the stairs altered in such manner as to allow the closet to become a passageway to the front door. The closet is an exception in itself. The significant feature of the half-house is the chimney position, which is aligned to the main entrance; so many houses of this species have had the back heightened to two stories that it is only this characteristic that betrays the original form, as at 5 Ash and 14 Milk Street *(Fig. 13)*. There are no detached two-and-a-half-storied half-houses later than saltboxes in Nantucket.[7]

    The size of the half-house is fairly constant, 24' or 25' across the front and 28' to 32' in depth. The framing of the front section is three-bayed, like that of "Parliament House" (10 Pine), except that there are no posts under the ends of the summer beam, which is supported on the front and back plates. The porch is narrow, and opposite the entrance are winder stairs, with a closet beneath, accessible either to the porch or great room. There is a huge fireplace with oven in the principal interior, which is square, often with a single window centered front and side, as at 1 Tattle Court, 9 Howard, and 53 Orange Street, the last having acquired a second façade window at some subsequent date *(Fig. 14)*. In the integral lean-to house (as opposed to the added lean-to), the first floor is level front and back, even though the ceiling of the lean-to usually is lower, causing a drop in the floor level upstairs. In some cases, a summer beam spans the back section; in others, the upper floor is carried on a series of joists set front to back. The three rooms in the lean-to of the half-house are, in order of magnitude, chamber, borning room, and milk room. The chamber has a fireplace recessed in the chimney area, its flue incorporated in the rectangular stack; there is a boxed-in secondary stair to the smaller sleeping rooms and storage spaces under the sloping roof. In the Thomas Macy house, 1 Tattle Court, one of the earliest houses erected on the Fish Lots (No. 19) laid out in 1717, a transverse corridor leading to a back door separates the three rooms *(Fig. 15)*. It seems odd that the ascending stairs do not open directly from this passage. A ladder-like stair, opposite, gives access to the cool cellar, a circular brick well 6' to 9' in diameter and 7' or 8' deep, for the storage of milk and vegetables, as it remains cool in summer and seldom reaches the freezing point in winter. The round cool cellar was to outlive

Fig. 12

Fig. 13

Fig. 14

Fig. 15

Fig. 17 Matthew Myrick House (*ca.* 1740s), Now at 6 Prospect Street.

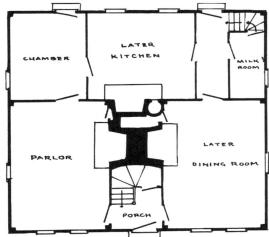

Fig. 18 First-Floor Plan of Matthew Myrick House, Restored to *ca.* 1800.

Fig. 19 Josiah Coffin House (*ca.* 1724), 60 Cliff Road.

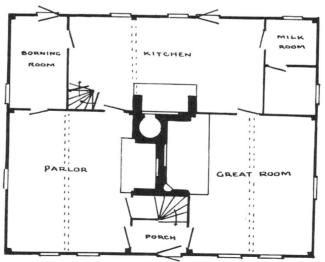

Fig. 20 Restored First-Floor Plan of Josiah Coffin House.

the lean-to house and persist for upwards of a century. It has been mentioned that there were two under the "Parliament House," dating from its rebuilding in 1820. The hall or great-room chamber, on the second floor of the Macy house, was of equal dimensions with its counterpart downstairs. The rooms behind were no larger than the borning room and, of course, had sloping ceilings. The main or front stairs continued to the garret, which was left unfinished.

Fig. 16   The side extension of the Thomas Macy house, added about two decades later, is of special interest, as it is covered by a shed roof that keys in exactly with the rear lean-to externally, in spite of the difference between the ceiling heights of the two rooms provided *(Fig. 16)*. The ceiling in the front section is level with that of the great room and the one behind corresponds with the ceiling height of the rear. Each of the two rooms on the main floor had a fireplace, that in back placed in a corner; and a corner cupboard was built into the outer angle of the larger room, the windows front and side being adjusted to center positions between it and the extremities of these walls. The room above is provided with more space than one would expect, its two façade windows staggered in accordance with the roof pitch.

As our name for it implies, the half-house was considered a residence that was to be completed on the other side of the chimney. The single-story extension at 1 Tattle Court was only a partial realization of the intention, the complete realization being the full-house. A saltbox that seems to have been first small and then enlarged is 6 Prospect Street. It was built before the mid-eighteenth century for Matthew Myrick on Milk Street near New Mill and moved to its present site about 1800. The windows on the west side of the façade are nine-over-nine paned, presumably denoting the early house, whereas those on the east side are twelve-over-twelve

Fig. 17   paned, indicating a later addition *(Fig. 17)*. There are two windows on either side of the center doorway in the first story and only a single window above each pair in the second, that over the entrance matching the westernmost set. The downstairs front windows are placed close together; in such an arrangement a plank, in place of plaster, was inserted between them inside. This is the mirror board, on which was hung a framed looking glass. The other "board," found in the lean-to and later house parlors, is the cradle board, a dado plank with grain running horizontally, about thirty inches high, set in the wall near the warmth of the fireplace as a buffer for the rocking infant's crib. Changes undoubtedly occurred inside the Myrick house at the time of relocation. The fireplaces in the principal rooms would have been rebuilt smaller. A little more space was allotted the porch or entry, and the stairs, rather than being all winders, begin with a straight flight of three risers, and then include five wedge-shaped steps fitted into a concave chimney wall

Fig. 18   *(Fig. 18)*. The great room to the west originally must have had an oven at the back of the fireplace, and there would have been three rooms in the lean-to behind. But with the additions and rebuilding, the center rear room became the kitchen, partially expanded into the new side of the house. The chamber is a fair-sized substitute for the small borning room, and the front room became a parlor. Its counterpart is the later dining room. A corridor leads from the latter to a back door, and across from the kitchen are a milk room and secondary stairway, the descending flight giving access to the circular cool cellar, the other going up to the chambers under the sloping roof.

A house with many parallels to 6 Prospect is 25 Pleasant Street, built after 1745 for Stephen Chase. The façade differs only in having a single window in the front wall of the parlor, in place of two. The staircase is further developed, as it eliminates winders in favor of three narrow, steep, straight flights, with square landings in the corners. The square newel post is chamfered at the top, and the railing is supported by plain upright banisters set diagonally on the closed stringer.[8] A door beneath the upper flight opens into a T-shaped closet, the stem of the

Fig. 21 Richard Gardner III House (1722–24), 32 West Chester Street.

figure lying between the fireplaces of the front rooms and even bending around the back corner of that on the west side. Each east room of these two houses has a plastered-over ceiling, and the rooms opposite have exposed ceiling joists parallel to front and back walls. The lean-to at 25 Pleasant Street apparently has been cut crosswise in half and the rear portion moved against the main rooms, creating a break in the north roof slope. The interior space thus became too narrow for use of the back fireplace, which has been sealed up.

The house on Prospect Street introduces us to the form of lean-to residence built originally as a full-house. A good example is the house at 60 Cliff Road, on the corner of North Liberty Street and facing neither road, built by Major Josiah Coffin (son of Jethro Coffin) for his son, Josiah Coffin II. The building has been mentioned several times before: first in connection with its precise orientation, which enabled Professor Henry Mitchell to ascertain its date of construction (1723–24); second, for having five withes to its chimney; and third, because of the smaller upper windows in the façade, all except the one over the door having twenty panes, as opposed to twenty-four below. Another remarkable feature is the front cornice overhang, supported on modillions *(Fig. 19)*. The blocks are omitted over the windows for lack of space, and although *Fig. 19*

Fig. 22 House Re-erected by Thomas and William Starbuck (*ca.* 1740), 15 Liberty Street.

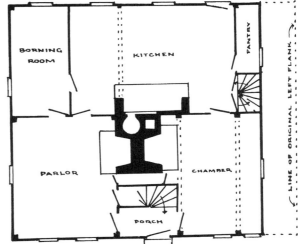

Fig. 23 First-Floor Plan of Starbuck House Restored as Re-erected about 1740.

very old they are probably not original. Only its crudity makes this classical element acceptable on the otherwise medieval building. The interior of the Josiah Coffin house has an organic simplicity akin to that of the Jethro Coffin dwelling *(Fig. 20)*. The porch and newel staircase are similar. *Fig. 20* The great room, on the east, has chamfered beams, the summer running from front to back, and although the room itself is not as deep the fireplace is wider. It has no oven but a shallow recessed warming shelf in the corresponding position. The parlor opposite, of equal dimensions (15'4" × 18'4"), has beams with beaded edges and a much smaller fireplace. Its smaller size compares to the older Coffin house, but in the Cliff Road residence both fireplaces have squared corners instead of being rounded at the back. The beading of the beam edges is a refinement introduced in the 1720s to replace the chamfer, and it is noteworthy that it was used here in the more formal room yet not in the other. Chamfered beams figure in both front rooms of the Elihu Coleman house, built a year earlier on Hummock Pond, whereas in the Richard Gardner III house, 32 West Chester Street, constructed months later, there is beading throughout. The kitchen at 60 Cliff Road originally occupied most of the rear lean-to, the borning room at the west end and milk room at the east being narrow and of about equal dimensions. The fireplace protrudes into the kitchen; its flue is in an appendage to the chimney, which suggests an addition, yet all other evidence is to the contrary. The oven is at the back of the fireplace. A steep staircase of winders is in the southwest corner. This sequence of features is to be found in the Elihu Coleman house, referred to above.[9] The Josiah Coffin house had been in the same family until the 1920s, when it was acquired by the present owner; therefore it had suffered little structural change. Shifted partitions were returned to their original positions. Fireplaces had been closed in but remained intact behind the new brickwork and thus could be restored accurately. A service ell, added at the northwest corner of the building, leaves the first story of the old house virtually undisturbed by modern conveniences. Furnished largely with seventeenth-century English antiques, the house takes a visitor back into the period when it was built.

The nearby, nearly contemporary Richard Gardner III house, at 32 West Chester Street, has a three-bayed façade, like the Elihu Coleman residence, though all windows have twelve-over-twelve-paned sashes *(Fig. 21)*. The plan is similar, except for the staircase, which has turned *Fig. 21* newel posts, heavy handrails, and round banisters on a closed stringer. Like the one in 25 Pleasant Street, it rises in three flights to the second floor.[10] The rear newel stairs adjoin the east end of the projecting kitchen fireplace. It has been mentioned earlier that the beams have beaded edges.

The two houses off North Liberty Street and the one on Hummock Pond that has been compared to both are fortunate—for early Nantucket examples—in not having been moved. Their standing *in situ* is largely responsible for their remaining so nearly unchanged. The reverse applies to the Starbuck brothers' house at 15 Liberty Street, given to their sister, Jemima (Mrs. Silvanus Allen), in 1743. It is a transplanted structure that had to be cut down when it was rebuilt on the present restricted lot. A strip of about three feet was deleted from the east end, leaving one pair of outermost windows practically at the new left-flank corner *(Fig. 22)*. The *Fig. 22* summer beam of the old great room is only a yard in; with posts set beneath its ends, the east side of the house is cantilevered from this arrangement. The fireplaces of the two principal rooms have been rebuilt smaller and with splayed sides, leaving space for a narrow cross passage between the chimney and front newel staircase *(Fig. 23)*. The parlor retains its identity, whereas the *Fig. 23* diminished great room became a chamber or dining room. The back stairs have been fitted into the half-outside bay. The down flight descends to a full basement with a cooking fireplace similar to that above. However, the entire chimney structure, including the articulated stack penetrating the roof, was one of the major parts to undergo renovation during the 1930s.[11]

Down the street, 5 Liberty, built for Barnabus Pinkham in 1748, is a transitional building

Fig. 24 and as such deserves our attention *(Fig. 24)*. Instead of the usual low head room under the lean-to roof in both stories, the first-floor rooms in back have the same ceiling height as those in front, making the upper floor level throughout. The roof came down only to within thirty-two inches of the second floor on the rear wall. Now two full stories in back, the north wall has a ledge indicating its original summit; in the garret, horizontal sheathing in both gables runs up as far as the old roof line, above which, at the rear, boards continue parallel to the roof slope. Many Nantucket houses that were originally saltboxes, in which the back has been heightened, display this same phenomenon in the garret, as at 5 Ash and 14 Milk Street. The late date and transitional tenden-

Fig. 25 cies of 5 Liberty Street show in the plan *(Fig. 25)*. The fore part of the house is similar to 25 Pleasant Street, built perhaps two years earlier. Both have a staircase of three straight flights without winders, and a closet under the stairs with an extension between the fireplaces to the front rooms. In the Pinkham house, there is an additional secret space farther back that becomes a vertical shaft over the kitchen oven, with certain bricks indented as toe-holes for climbing up inside the chimney. The rear wall of the staircase is slightly concave, as at 6 Prospect Street, and neither of these houses has an oven in the fireplaces of the front rooms. The east room is not a hall or great room but was used for dining. It opens behind into a side entry with service stairs which in turn give access to the kitchen. The pantry in back of the entry is entered only from the kitchen. This room has a fine, undisturbed cooking fireplace with a large recessed semicircular oven. To the east of the fireplace is the door to a straight flight of steps leading down to the basement, where practically the identical cooking arrangement found above is in the summer kitchen, as at 15 Liberty Street. At the northwest corner of the first floor is a square chamber, quadruple the size of the average borning room. It had a corner fireplace (currently enlarged) nearest the chimney. It is similar to that in the addition to 1 Tattle Court. Number 5 Liberty Street has a one-story extension on its east flank. It was probably the counting house of a later owner, Captain Paul West, before the construction of his detached office out back, at 5 Rose Lane.

Listed in Appendix B of this book are forty-two two-and-a-half-story lean-to houses, some half- and others full-houses, which follow the prescribed pattern. Also recorded are six examples that prove the saltbox capable of radically different arrangements. Of this number, one (9 Mill) has a kitchen ell that was probably an independent house moved here to be attached to a later building and somewhat altered. Another (10 North Liberty), also resited, was completely rebuilt inside during the middle of the nineteenth century. A third (6 North Liberty) is four-bayed and has a gambrel roof; it will be discussed in the next chapter. A fourth is 84 Main Street, the back of which has been made two full stories; a shed-roof extension has been added to the west flank

Fig. 26 *(Fig. 26)*. The house faces north. It was built during the mid-eighteenth century for John Barnard, and its lean-to, like that of the Pinkham house, retains full head-height downstairs and a three-quarter eaves-height above. The plan is unorthodox. In the first place, the chimney is in the wrong position for a lean-to. Instead of being located behind the door and stairway, it is between

Fig. 27 the parlor and back chamber *(Fig. 27)*. The front door opens into a stairhall over nine feet broad, with a straight flight ascending transversely against the parlor wall. The kitchen, originally quite small, is behind, and its pantry must have been at the back, in the area now occupied by an entry and back stairs. The one-story extension enlarged the kitchen and provided for a pantry, as well as a large closet or small office at the front, off the stairhall, currently an open recess. The final plan resembles that of the typical Nantucket house, the subject of Chapter Five. Related to 84 Main in the placing of the chimney is 3 Beaver Lane, which faces south and has the entry and winder stairs on the west side of the chimney, in back of the parlor. It had the kitchen at the rear

Fig. 24 Barnabas Pinkham House (1748), 5 Liberty Street.

Fig. 25 Restored First-Floor Plan of Barnabas Pinkham House with Extension on East End.

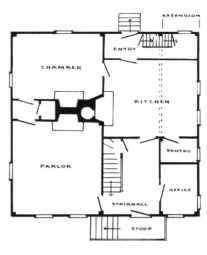

Fig. 26 (left) John Barnard House, 84 Main Street.
Fig. 27 (right) Restored First-Floor Plan of John Barnard House Including Later Extension on West End.

and a chamber in the southeast corner. Each of the three downstairs rooms has a fireplace, anticipating the following example.

Fig. 28   The remaining lean-to oddity is 114 Orange Street (now the Spouter Pottery Shop—*Fig. 28*). It was built for Christopher Baxter in 1756 or perhaps moved from some other place.[12] Its two-story wall faces south but has no front door. Unlike 84 Main and 3 Beaver, the chimney is in the right position for the great room, which, however, has two windows in the west wall yet

Fig. 29   only one in the south *(Fig. 29)*. In place of the expected porch and newel stairs is a chamber with a corner fireplace. The stairway is off an entry in the lean-to at the back, with a milk room and minuscule borning room lying between the passage and right-flank wall. The northeast corner of the house provides another chamber. This unusual scheme also bears certain affinities to the forthcoming typical Nantucket house. A wing was added to the east side.

The one-and-three-quarters-story lean-to is a smaller version of the normal two-and-a-half-story saltbox, the front wall not so tall and normally without upper windows, the plan similar though with only a single staircase. It seems that the earlier examples, such as 86 Centre (1740s) and 10 Martin's Lane (1750s), have winder stairs in front of the chimney, whereas the later have a straight flight at the back. The smaller building has the same frontality and distinct right and left sides, which distinguish it from the symmetrically-sided story-and-a-half Cape Cod cottage that figures very little on Nantucket.[13] As mentioned earlier, there is little regard for orientation in the diminutive lean-to, as it belongs to the second half of the eighteenth century. It may cover as much area as the taller variety and thus have a similar first-floor arrangement, but the upstairs rooms are restricted to the front, and even these have sloping ceilings that come down to within a few feet of the floor. Fireplaces, usually limited to the first story, are smaller, proper to their period.[14] The kitchen in the lean-to assumes the complete role of a keeping room, so that the

Fig. 28 Christopher Baxter House (1756), Rear View, 114 Orange Street.

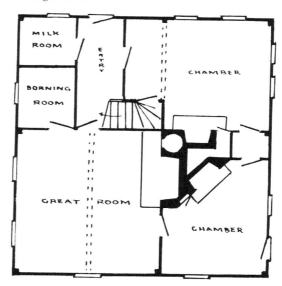

Fig. 29 Restored First-Floor Plan of Christopher Baxter House.

Fig. 30 Edward Allen House (1763), 21 Prospect Street.

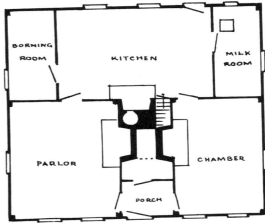

Fig. 31 Restored First-Floor Plan of Edward Allen House.

equivalent of the hall (great room) becomes the principal (and only full-sized) chamber, balancing the parlor in the full-house.

A representative specimen of the type is the Edward Allen house, 21 Prospect Street, built in 1763. Henry Worth informs us that Allen was a carpenter who constructed several houses on this street (formerly known as Copper), perhaps including the kindred building at 17 Prospect.[15] There were others along here that have been demolished. The Allen house has a five-bayed façade *(Fig. 30)*. Its windows are twenty-four-paned but not strictly symmetrical in their placing. The front plane of the chimney is at the roof ridge, and the lean-to roof angles slightly with the upper pitch. One misses the stairway upon entering, a closet taking its place, with a narrow recess between the fireplace backs *(Fig. 31)*. The front rooms have each a nine-over-nine or six-over-nine-paned window in the side wall. The kitchen occupies the center and greater part of the lean-to, and it was flanked by the small borning and milk rooms, the latter mostly intact and having a trap door to the circular cool cellar under the southwest corner of the house. The borning-room partition has been removed. Next to the hearth, the stairs to the second floor are narrow and steep and go up partly over the chamber fireplace. There is a single bedroom at each end of the upper space. A later ell was attached at the southwest corner.

One notes in the Appendix (C, 2) that although the greater number of small lean-to houses are five-bayed, there are four- and three-bayed examples as well. Number 2 Copper Lane has an enclosed entrance pent, and the house is listed as four-bayed because of the number of openings in the façade, but the form is that of a five-bayed house. There are four other smaller lean-tos that are four-bayed and six altogether that are three-bayed.

The smallest lean-to house on Nantucket is 9 Eagle Lane, on the corner of Pine Street *(Fig. 32)*. It measures a mere seventeen feet across the front, and the spanning girt and plate are supported by only a single post at each outer corner. Old deeds refer to the division among the heirs of the James Williams house on this property, and the portion sold by Anna to Zebulon Whippy in 1811 may have become physically a separate building fashioned from the west end.[16] The house has no cellar of any kind, which seems to confirm its having been moved here. If so, the relocation took place before 1833, since a house existed on this corner at that time, according to the William Coffin map. Eagle Lane was then known as Jefferson, and the shift in street names is reflected in contemporary land records. Although the breadth of the structure is that of an average room, it has a three-bayed façade, and the front door opens into a porch, forty-four inches wide, in which winder stairs begin on the diagonal. The door thus cannot open more than three-quarters of a right angle, and originally it may have opened out *(Fig. 33)*. A slender door gives access to a closet under and behind the steps. The parlor is 12′ 8″ × 11′ 4″; the kitchen fireplace causes an obtuse angle alongside the fireplace. A five-foot projection on the west end of the building provides for a small pantry and most of the chamber on the first floor, and it gives headroom where it was most needed to one of the three chambers on the second. Number 9 Eagle Lane is an unusual little domicile and may be compared to one other of about equal size, though not a saltbox, eight blocks south at 7 Cherry Street, thought to have been built about the time of the American Revolution.[17] The Cherry Street house is and seems always to have been one-and-three-quarter-storied, back as well as front. It has lost its front stairs and has a later flight farther to the rear. Fireplace changes also are in evidence, but that the original form basically was that of the Eagle Lane house shows in the basement masonry. There is a summer kitchen below ground level, its cooking fireplace complete with oven, despite the fact that the only access to the room was a ladder-like stairs through a trap door in the floor of the upper kitchen. Perhaps 9 Eagle Lane also had such an arrangement.

Fig. 30

Fig. 31

Fig. 32

Fig. 33

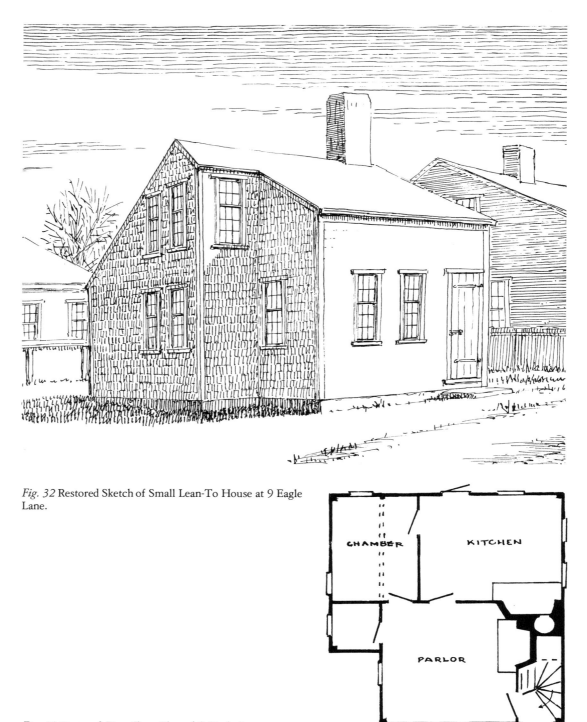

Fig. 32 Restored Sketch of Small Lean-To House at 9 Eagle Lane.

Fig. 33 Restored First-Floor Plan of 9 Eagle Lane.

Fig. 34 Restored Bird's-Eye View of Jonathan Swain II House (1829), 9 Beaver Lane.
Fig. 35 Restored First-Floor Plan of Jonathan Swain II House.

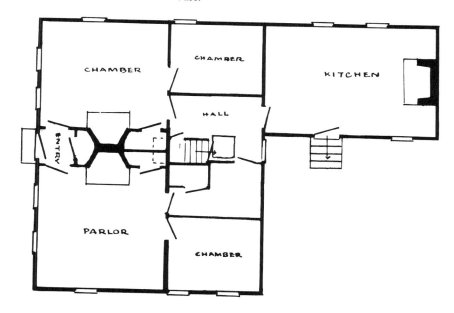

Fig. 34
The final phase of the story-and-three-quarters lean-to in Nantucket is exemplified in 9 Beaver Lane *(Fig. 34).* It was built in 1829 for Captain Jonathan Swain II. Having a five-bayed façade, like 21 Prospect, though the windows are narrower (nine-over-nine paned), the fore-part of the plan is similar and normal; but the two principal rooms have closets back-to-back beyond their fireplaces, the stairway rises from a rear hall instead of a kitchen, and a small chamber is in each north corner *(Fig. 35).* The kitchen is in a rear ell, with cooking fireplace at the far end.

Fig. 35
Plastered walls and ceiling masking construction timbers, and chairrailing and plain Federal mantels and trim distinguish the interior from its predecessors.

The lean-to house on Nantucket is characterized by its high front and low back. It is a one-chimney building, and, whether half or whole in size, that chimney is aligned to the front door. The normal lean-to has a two-story façade and was built as a half-house, with fireplace provision for later expansion, either for a one-story addition with shed roof or completion of the two-storied full-house. Although the earliest integral lean-to houses may have had casement windows and weatherboarded walls, all known to us have sash windows and shingled walls. However, the lean-to has been the victim of changes, many in location and enlargement, and all in alteration and remodeling. Included were a few sports—houses that depart from the accepted norm in one way or another—but these only prove the saltbox capable of diversity. Some full-size lean-tos of the mid-eighteenth century were given full basements. The later lean-to was less than two stories in height and made provision for the main bedroom downstairs. Toward the close of its career, this species forewent the distinctive all-purpose room centered at the back, with fireplace keyed into the great chimney, in favor of the nineteenth-century scheme of installing the kitchen in a rear extension. It was the dissolution of the form. The appeal of the lean-to lies in the synthesis of its construction and restraint of decoration, proportions determined by function, honest use of materials, and, perhaps above all, the manifested recognition of the basic requirements of human shelter and forthright solution of these problems. Although the peak of the era of this type has passed the two-and-a-half-century timestone, many examples still make attractive, convenient, and comfortable homes today.

Notes

1   Henry Barnard Worth, *Nantucket Lands and Land Owners,* Vol. II, Bulletin No. 5, Nantucket Historical Association, 1906 (reissued 1928), p. 232.

2   Everett U. Crosby, *Ninety Five Per Cent Perfect,* Nantucket, 1953, p. 30.

3   Henry Barnard Worth, "Early Houses on Nantucket," *Proceedings of the Nantucket Historical Association,* 1904, p. 21.

4   Donald (Macdonald-) Millar, "A Seventeenth Century New England House," *Architectural Record,* Vol. XXXVIII, No. 3, September 1915, pp. 349–361.

5   However, the Elihu Coleman house (on Hummock Pond) has a single, shallow window at floor level upstairs over the back door, and old photographs (discovered after restoration) of 1 Tattle Court show several under the north eaves here.

6   Alfred M. P. Amey informed the author that his former home at 10 Gardner Street, said to have been moved to its present location in 1771, has walls filled with crushed clam shells.

7   Number 31 Fair Street was built as a two-storied half-house *addition* to a lean-to half-house but does not stand independently. See Chapter Six. 46 Centre and perhaps 11 Hussey were built as half-houses, two-storied at back as well as front, but enlarged, the last made into a full-house.

8   Kenneth Duprey, *Old Houses on Nantucket,* New York, 1959, illus. p. 67.

9   A photograph of the Coleman-house kitchen is in Henry Chandlee Forman, *Early Nantucket and Its Whale Houses,* New York, 1966, p. /249/.

10   Duprey, *op. cit.,* pp. /30/-31.

11   The author is indebted to Mrs. Alan Newhouse for lending him for perusal the alteration drawings by Alfred E. Shurrocks.

12   Worth, *Nantucket Lands,* p. 250.

13   See discussion of the type in the later part of Chapter Six.

14   Exceptions having upstairs fireplaces are 5 Spring (with two), and 10 Martin's Lane and 59 Union (each with one).

15   Worth, *Nantucket Lands,* p. 250.

16   Deed Book 15, pp. 285–287; Deed Book 22, p. 9; Deed Book 30, pp. 448–449; Nantucket County records.

17   According to Everett Backus, courtesy of Mrs. Lawrence Ellis.

Fig. 36 View of the Fire in Main Street, Nantucket, May 10, 1836. Lithograph after a Painting by E. F. Starbuck, Moore's Litho., Boston.

Chapter IV

Gambrel-Roof Buildings

The double-pitched curb or gambrel roof never attained widespread popularity in America, though its use along the Atlantic coast covered a wide range and long span of time. It is of English origin: the Great Hall of Henry VIII's Hampton Court Palace was built with a gambrel roof in 1530–32. Essex farmhouses of the seventeenth century had the same roof form.[1] Perhaps its origin lay in economy: cutting down the height of the steep medieval roof in this manner saved materials. Economy played a role in its employment in the New World, too. As taxes were levied in proportion to the number of stories of a dwelling, by bending the roof pitch and bringing the cornice level down, one still had practically as much upstairs room as if the vertical wall continued up another story, but the assessment was less, on a technicality. Gambrel roofs appeared from Maine to Maryland during the seventeenth century, examples being located at Newport, Rhode Island; Windsor, Connecticut; Dedham, Haverhill, Cambridge, Medford, and Plymouth, Massachusetts; York, Maine; and in Anne Arundel, Prince Georges, and Saint Marys counties, Maryland.[2] It is of interest that the oldest frame house in this country, that of Jonathan Fayerbanke, built at Dedham about 1637, was given a gambrel-roofed addition on the east end in 1641, as a separate dwelling for the eldest son, John, and his bride. Another wing with similar covering was added to the west flank in 1654, completing a most picturesque composition.

A special example from the seventeenth century is the Peter Tufts house built at Medford in 1675. The town of Medford was one of the principal brickmaking centers in Massachusetts, and the Tufts house is the earliest known brick residence in New England, though preceded by the Indian College (1654–56) and the start of Harvard Hall (1674–77) at Cambridge, the latter having a gambrel roof. The house at Medford is two-storied and has a central transverse stairhall with two rooms on either side. Fireplaces are on the outer walls, and the flues are brought together to a single chimney stack on each gable. Walls are eighteen inches thick and have a projecting stringer at the first and belt courses at second-floor level.[3] The roof is steep and truncated at the top, substantiating the theory that the gambrel originated in the saving of materials.

Fig. 37 George Gardner House (1748), 8 Pine Street.

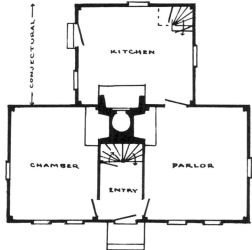

Fig. 38 Restored First-Floor Plan of George Gardner House.

Fig. 39 View of India Street, Looking West, with Silas Paddock House (1767) on left.

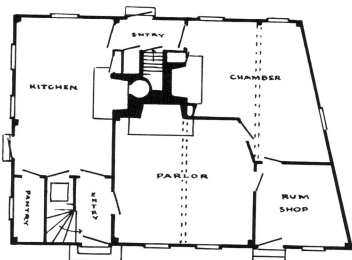

Fig. 40 Restored First-Floor Plan of Silas Paddock House.

Fig. 41 Grindell Gardner House (1772), 30 Hussey Street.

Nantucket retains a better share of gambrel-roof houses than other communities of similar age. It has eight, built during the half-century from 1748 to 1798. It seems likely that at one time the town had a larger percentage of gambrels, because in the E. F. Starbuck watercolor-lithograph, *View of the Fire in Main Street, Nantucket, May 10, 1836,* three appear in the fore-
Fig. 36 ground among a total of nine or ten buildings depicted *(Fig. 36).* The fire broke out near the kitchen of the Washington House, about opposite Federal. It spread eastward from the hotel to the Francis F. Hussey shop and dwelling, then to the William C. Swain hardware store on the corner of Union Street and behind to the Cowan tailor shop.[4] The Starbuck view was made from the second-story window in the southwest corner of the Rotch Market. It shows the bases of the hotel portico beneath the billowing smoke, and Main Street receding westward in the distance. The gambrel-roofed building in the left foreground was at the corner of Washington Street. The two of the same style at the right stood between South Water and the continuation of Union Street, separated by Coal Lane. The T. A. Gardner store faced the small recessed square, the north side of Main Street from here to Centre not having been set back to its present line until after the Great Fire, ten years later. The gambrels represented are commercial buildings, and we shall refer to this matter later. All the surviving buildings with curb roofs in Nantucket are dwellings.

The earliest of the group is the George Gardner house, 8 Pine Street, ascribed to 1748. It is small, the front block measuring only $15' \times 28'$; the façade has a center doorway with a
Fig. 37 transom flanked by pairs of narrow nine-over-nine-paned windows *(Fig. 37).* The original center

Fig. 42 Silas Jones House (*right*—1770s), 5 Orange Street.

chimney was much larger than the present one, and there was a single window in both first and second stories at each end, the upper ones slightly smaller. The porch or entry is fairly deep; there are winder stairs at the rear, the north set descending to the circular cool cellar *(Fig. 38)*.   *Fig. 38*
The former chimney area behind has been gutted. It obviously provided fireplaces for the two main rooms and probably for a kitchen in an attached ell as well. The plan, therefore, would have been T-shaped. The present rear wing is much later and obscures what was there originally. The bedrooms on the upper floor are small and lighted only at the ends.

In the winter of 1971 it was discovered that 37 Orange Street, built for John Jackson in the mid-1750s, originally had a gambrel roof. Plans were made to restore it.

A period of one to two decades intervened before the next extant Nantucket gambrels were built. That of Silas Paddock, 18 India Street, is an asymmetrical, compact mass, with a trapezoidal extension covered by a shed roof on the west end *(Fig. 39)*. The excrescence served   *Fig. 39*
as a rum shop and originally had an entrance on the street. Front windows have twelve-over-twelve-paned sashes. The main door with transom opens into a vestibule with winder stairs on the east side, the parlor opposite, and kitchen to the rear *(Fig. 40)*. Rooms are clustered around   *Fig. 40*
the single chimney, which has no relationship to the stairway, as it would have had in the normal lean-to plan. The arrangement comes closest to that of 84 Main Street and bears an affinity to the typical Nantucket or "Quaker" house plan (Chapter Five). A chamber in the southwest corner originally was quite small, but it was enlarged through an addition on the left flank exactly as was the kitchen in 84 Main. A beam spanning the ceiling from front to back denotes

Fig. 43 Rotch Market (1775), Foot of Main Street at South Water, as it Appeared before Great Fire of 1846.

the early outer wall position. A wedge shape has been taken from the corner of the parlor to benefit the back room. The narrow passage connecting the chamber and kitchen across the rear adjoins several tiny closets and a steep, restricted, ascending stairs, only fifty-four inches deep including the square upper landing. The kitchen, in the southeast angle, once had an oven practically under the back stairway, and an outside door in the right flank wall. A trap door to the round cool cellar is under the front stairs, and between here and the side of the building is a pantry with a narrow window. Three bedrooms are on the second floor of the main part of the house, and there is one more in the newer wing attached at the back.

Constructed also in the mid-1760s and similar to the Paddock house is that of Christopher Swain at 7 Farmer Street. The plan is inverted and simplified, and there is no side extension. The original façade windows had twelve-over-twelve-paned sashes, but these have been replaced (incorrectly) by nine-over-nines, as in the side walls.[5] The house was renovated in the 1930s by Everett U. Crosby, who had a passage winding back to the kitchen chopped through the chimney, as was done in the house at 33 Orange Street.

The Grindell Gardner dwelling, 30 Hussey Street, was built in 1772 and is a half-gambrel; that is, it has an odd roof shape, double-pitched in front and like a lean-to at the back *(Fig. 41)*. The indifference of the design to symmetry is expressed further in the four-bayed façade, in which there are two windows to the south of the doorway and a single one to the north. The windows originally had nine-over-six-paned sashes. The present "Dutch" dormers were added about the turn of the century.

Fig. 41

The oldest house in Nantucket with exposed brick ends is 5 Orange Street. It has been assigned to various dates ranging from before the American Revolution to the last decade of the eighteenth century. To place it within a couple of years preceding or succeeding the war would probably not be far off. The two-and-a-half-story house originally had a clapboarded front and rear wall, with flanks constructed of small hard-burned bricks (measuring $2'' \times 7'' \times 3\frac{1}{2}''$), laid in common bond *(Fig. 42)*.[6] The only openings in them were a single window in each third-story gable, the one in the north end with twelve-over-twelve-paned sashes, and that in the south with fifteen-over-fifteen. Twin chimneys rise above, inside the gambrel angle. The shape and proportions of these flanks are practically identical to those of the Thomas Hancock house (1737–40) that stood on Beacon Street, Boston.[7] The Hancock residence, however, had side windows in the first and second stories, and quoins at the extremities, which coincidentally strike a response with the later fenestration and front masonry wall of the Orange Street example. Indigenous to both are the projecting belt courses at second and third-floor levels.

Fig. 42

Although built about four decades later, the plan of the Nantucket gambrel is more primitive or provincial than the Boston Georgian.[8] Alike in having a center transverse stairhall with two rooms right and left, the Nantucket house has the hall divided with the staircase in the front half. The four fireplaces were flanked by presses or had paneling filling in the spaces to the sides of the chimneybreasts. The two rear rooms on the first floor and two on the south side of the second retain these original features. There is no subsidiary cross-passage in the Nantucket dwelling, as there was in the Boston, though perhaps there was a service stair in the back section of the transverse hall. The kitchen was in the northwest corner of the basement, under the dining room. The house was remodeled in the early 1830s, affecting the fore part of the first story and north upper chambers. Windows were cut in the end walls and presses removed, leaving exposed chimneybreasts. Wide doorways were opened between the front and rear parlors, and the sitting and dining rooms. Trim around doors, windows, and fireplaces was replaced by woodwork typically Federal in style. Oddly enough, the staircase, too, was replaced; the replacement was set a couple of feet forward. The steps were made narrower and the cutout consoles, banisters, and railing were changed to contemporary patterns. At the base of the handrail is a volute curving over the projection of the first riser.[9] The clapboard front undoubtedly was replaced by the present brick wall at the same time, as the building was indicated as brick on the William Coffin map of 1833, which hardly would have been the case with masonry sides alone. The bricks are larger than those of the flanks and laid in all-stretcher courses. These are exactly like the walls of the old Town House, 2 Union Street, built as two stores about 1830; brownstone sills and lintels also occur in both buildings. The new house façade is on a plane slightly in advance of the old wooden front, and the floorboards in the front rooms have been pieced out accordingly. At the north corner, where the street slopes downhill, exposing more of the basement, granite slabs serve as revetments and footings for the brickwork. Perhaps the sidewalk today dips more than originally intended. The doorway, with transom and sidelights, and the six-paned sash windows look contemporary with those of The Block (1831), farther south on the same side of the street (Chapter Six).

The masonry of one other building in Nantucket relates to that of the north and south walls of 5 Orange Street. The bricks are identical in size and kind, they are laid in the same pattern of common bond, and there are belt courses at second- and third-floor levels. The building is the Rotch Market, at the lower end of Main Street, and the characteristics are displayed on the south and west sides, and somewhat on the north, the east end having been stuccoed. In November 1774, William Rotch made an agreement with a committee appointed by the Proprietors to erect a building to be occupied jointly as a public market and his own commercial enterprises. At that time, it was determined to be 18' × 40' in plan. The town was to have the use of the first floor and half of the second; the balance of the building was to be Rotch's. In return for the cost of construction, Rotch was to receive the parcel of land for the site, measuring 30' × 95'. During May of the following year, another small strip of land was offered in exchange for an increase in the size of the building.[10] The Rotch Market at present measures 28'6" × 42'6"; it is three stories tall. However, the full top story is known to have been added after the building was gutted during the Great Fire of 1846. Rotch's own business was allotted half of the second story and whatever space was in the garret. For his investment to have been worthwhile, the third floor garret would have to have been fairly ample and provided with fenestration. With this in mind, let us consider the west wall. If one eliminates the later door and window in the first story and overlooks the incongruous pilasters and entablature applied to the brickwork, the arrangement of two pairs of large windows in balance surmounted by a smaller pair placed closer together at the third level suggests a gambrel roof. One can refer to a similar disposition of openings in the portion of the gable shown on the left edge of the Starbuck fire

Fig. 36 scene, and the second building from the right margin shows a dormer piercing the roof *(Fig. 36)*. These were neighboring buildings to the Rotch Market—were, in fact, depicted from the market itself—and their similarity adds further weight to the gambrel-roof outline suggested by the

Fig. 43 early void pattern in the west wall *(Fig. 43)*.[11]

After the fire, the south center doorway was enlarged into the gaping entrance framed in brownstone that most disfigures the main façade. The window frames were replaced and sashes changed from nine to six panes. As stated above, the walls were extended upward another story. The west garret windows of this period have been bricked up. One room was set aside for customs from the 1780s until 1916, and during about half of this period the building was owned by insurance companies.[12] In 1860, it was purchased by a group of shipmasters, and since then the first story has been the headquarters of the Pacific Club.

There are two gambrel-roofed houses on Union Street. The earlier is 32 Union Street, built about 1780 for William Coffin. It is a two-and-a-half-story frame house with a center chimney. The rooms are grouped around this shaft in much the same way as in the Paddock house, though on a larger scale. The unit corresponding to the pantry on India Street here is a good-sized room, though without a fireplace. This space at one time became a penny-candy shop, and appropriate changes were made to the front wall. The present windows are the result of remodeling in the early 1940s. The inside staircase was also modernized at that time.[13] The original façade was four-bayed and therefore not in formal balance, yet the house does not suffer for want of good proportions. Behind it is a little stable or barn, partially covered by a curb roof, that has been converted into a dwelling. Not far off to the north, on Coffin Street, is a compact, symmetrical old gambrel-roof barn; which has also been made into a residence. Others of the

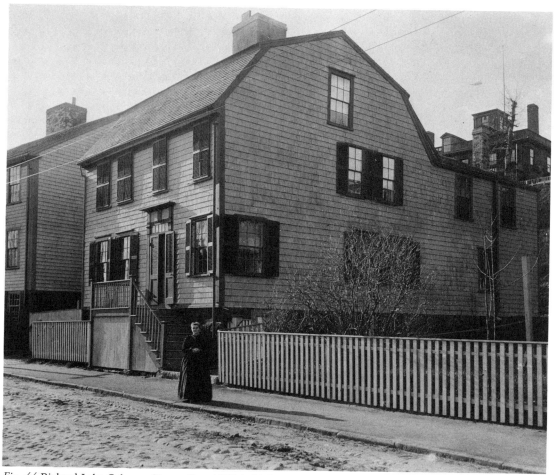

Fig. 44 Richard Lake Coleman House (late 1790s), 21 Union Street.

same kind are on the south side of Madaket Road beyond the Quaker cemetery, on the west side of Lily Street, on Cliff Road beyond the Sea Cliff Inn, and on the west side of Orange Street, south corner of Cherry.

Number 21 Union Street was constructed in the late 1790s by Richard Lake Coleman, a housewright. Like its neighbor, the Coffin house, the façade is four-bayed, only here we have the typical Nantucket house, the room alongside the staircase being only a closet (Chapter Five). The house itself is quite large *(Fig. 44)*.

At the opposite end of town is another contemporary four-bayed gambrel, at 6 North Liberty Street. It was built for Seth Ray. The impression it gives is entirely different from that of the others: it rises tall and narrow, the curb roof steep and covering only the fore part of the building, becoming a low-pitched lean-to at the back *(Fig. 45)*. The chimney was big and square and penetrated the roof back of the ridge. The chimney has been rebuilt and the interior area around it changed considerably, but it is apparent that the room arrangement of the first story was something like an inversion of the Paddock plan on India Street, without the rum shop but

Fig. 44

Fig. 45

Fig. 45 Seth Ray House (*ca.* 1798), 6 North Liberty Street.

substituting an 8′ × 12′ pent on the right flank, the long sill across the back indicating that it was part of the original building.

The building that should be Nantucket's most important gambrel—the Rotch Market—has had this appealing feature obliterated by an addition at the top. Its gable once faced the lower square of Main Street, which was adorned by three others of the same kind, shown in the Starbuck scene of the burning of the Washington House in 1836. Around the corner of the next block to the left stood the gambrel house with brick ends on Orange Street, newly given its brick front; and another was on Orange at Plumb Lane. Two frame houses with curb roofs were located south of the flaming structures, on Union Street. There were two others west of these on Farmer and Pine streets. Another was north of Main near Centre on India, and one near the other end of India on Hussey. Yet another was on a line with the last two and about an equal distance away on North Liberty Street. Six (mostly converted) barns, added to the eight existing residences, one altered house, one market, and three defunct commercial examples, give us a not-inconsequential representation of the gambrel roof in Nantucket.

Notes

1   Martin Shaw Briggs, *Homes of the Pilgrim Fathers in England and America, 1620–1685,* New York, 1932, p. 8l.

2   Tabulated in Hugh Morrison, *Early American Architecture,* New York, 1952, note, pp. 37–38. See also Henry Chandlee Forman, *The Architecture of the Old South,* Cambridge (Mass.), 1948, p. 151.

3   *Carpentry and Building,* Vol. VI, No. 8, 1884, pp. /145/–146.

4   *Nantucket Inquirer,* 11 May 1836, p. 2.

5   Henry Barnard Worth, *Some of the Old Houses of Nantucket,* with photographs taken in 1905 by Fred W. Palmer, album given to the Nantucket Historical Association, 1946, p. 30.

6   It is not unique for early American houses to have masonry ends and frame front and rear. Tuckahoe (after 1690), Goochland County, Virginia, and the Usher-Royall house (completed 1733–37) at Medford, Massachusetts, are well-known examples. Architects' Emergency Committee, *Great Georgian Houses in America,* New York, 1933–37 (Dover reprint, 1970), Vol. II, pp. 68–76; Fiske Kimball, *Domestic Architecture of the American Colonies and of the Early Republic,* New York, 1927, fig. 19 (p. 39) and fig. 61 (p. 89).

7   Kimball, *op. cit.,* fig. 58 (p. 85).

8   *Ibid.,* fig. 40 (p. /66/).

9   Kenneth Duprey, *Old Houses on Nantucket,* New York, 1959, pp. 152–156.

10   Henry Barnard Worth, *Nantucket Lands and Land Owners,* Vol. 2, Bulletin No. 5, Nantucket Historical Association, 1906 (reprint 1928), pp. 236–238.

11   Since writing the foregoing, I have found the following statement regarding the Rotch Market: "In its reconstruction in 1846 the old gambrel roof of two slopes was changed to its present form." *Nantucket Journal,* April 9, 1891.

12   *Ibid.,* p. 238.

13   Information courtesy Mrs. Marjorie Mills Burns.

Chapter V

The Typical Nantucket House

The imprint of the Quaker principle of simplicity upon Nantucket architecture is as apparent as the Zen tenet of eliminating the non-essential is upon Japanese. During the early years of the eighteenth century, when members of the Society of Friends were beginning to infiltrate the island and make converts among the older inhabitants, they readily adopted the lean-to house of Puritan starkness for their homes. But little by little they developed their own brand of dwelling, which, because of their numbers and because Nantucket was their chief stronghold in New England, became the prevailing successor to the saltbox and regionally the most characteristic type. It most appropriately may be designated the typical Nantucket house. Out of approximately 800 residences predating the Civil War in the town, about 175 are manifestations of the typical Nantucket house, this being about two-and-a-half times the number of lean-to houses and about one fifth of the total count (see Appendix D).

Quakerism has no creed, but it is motivated by a profound faith in the Inner Light. This Inner Light is a reflection in the human heart of God, the Infinite Light, and it is the illumination that prompts one to see the intrinsic qualities in things and to act justly. It eschews the superficialities, the vanities, the falsities, and the adornments—the worldly diversions—including all forms of entertainment, music and dancing, art for art's sake, gambling and, of course, the vices. The Quaker ideals were high thinking, plain living, fair dealing, honest work, simple dress, and sober and humble deportment. These are apparent in the Quaker house, which is unostentatious yet adequate, which substitutes craftsmanship for ornamentation, basic comforts for luxuries, and which is un-prettied yet appealing. The Quaker mode of reflection created a sort of functionalism that took into consideration the fundamental requirements of a house: a central masonry chimney shaft providing heat and cooking facilities, a structural framework properly covered for a controlled environment, and fenestration admitting sufficient light and ventilation. It was a

---

Fig. 46 (left) Doorway of 9 Quince Street Before Removal of Clapboards.

Fig. 47 Job Macy House (1790), 11 Mill Street.

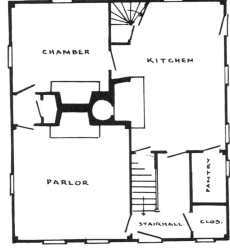

Fig. 48 Restored First-Floor Plan of Job Macy House.

departure from the Puritan lean-to, being not so limited by an archaic plan, much more open because of the absence of the long cat-slide roof in back, and more fluid in room arrangement and circulation. Yet the philosophy of the Friends was not as sophisticated as that of Japanese Zen, and it ignored aesthetics. There was no high regard for the natural color and texture of materials: both interior woodwork and outer walls were generally painted.[1] There was no awareness of a developed joinery that fostered slender structural members for a light and airy effect, and there was no sensitivity about living with cooking and eating utensils always in view; but these unrealized shortcomings made for the quaint and homey atmosphere that was the Quaker dwelling.

The typical Nantucket house follows a pattern as standard as that of the lean-to house, and its individual variations compare favorably. The length of its duration is about equal to that of the lean-to even though, as the immediate successor to the saltbox, its life span was interrupted by two wars that temporarily crippled Nantucket—the American Revolution and War of 1812, both of which the island as a whole tried to avoid because of the Quakers' aversion to fighting. The chief outer distinction between the typical Nantucket house and the lean-to is the heightening of the back wall to two full stories. This trait was inevitable with the establishment of the village, when orientation was abandoned as houses were aligned to city streets. The typical Nantucket house was achieved only after and because of the equalization of the opposite faces of the form. It is a two-and-a-half-storied compact mass with single chimney rising from the crosswise ridge. Early versions had horizontal dimensions similar to those of the half–lean-to house. The typical Nantucket house shows an indifference to symmetry both in elevation and plan. The façade is four-bayed, with two windows on one side, both upstairs and down having twelve-over-twelve-paned sashes (in some instances the upper only eight-over-twelve paned); on the other side are the doorway with transom and narrower nine-over-nine-paned windows (or six-over-nine above).

The front door opens into an entry, or what we now call a hall, featuring the staircase ascending transversely and ending in winders at the top. The most distinctive element of the plan is the three- to five-foot strip between the stairhall and outer wall of the building, divided into a front closet and pantry or buttery behind, each with a window. A door in the wall opposite opens into the parlor, which measures about fourteen feet square. The fireplace is nearly centered on the back wall, and a constricted space with closet adjoining the chimney leads to the chamber at the rear. This room is a little smaller than the parlor (from about ten to twelve feet square), and its fireplace is back-to-back with that in the front room. The kitchen, occupying the fourth corner of the house, is usually about equal to the chamber in width and is greater in depth than the parlor. Its fireplace is at the side, the oven recessed in the chimney between the other two rooms. Usually there are back stairs. The pantry (mentioned earlier) and the space under the main stairs are accessible from the kitchen. The circular cool cellar is reached by trap door and ladder or steps beneath one of the stairways. The arrangement of rooms is virtually repeated on the second floor. The garret, reached by a continuation of the back stairs, sometimes had a finished chamber. A ladder-like stairs ascended to the roof hatch, and in many cases there was a roof walk astride the ridge, encircled by a railing.

The arrangement described bears affinities to two houses discussed and illustrated with plans. The first is 84 Main, the "sport" lean-to (Chapter Three), and the second is 18 India, with gambrel roof (Chapter Four). The first predates any typical Nantucket house and the second belongs to the initial decade of its appearance, so they may be considered contributors to the realization of the basic layout. The interior treatment of the typical Nantucket house is related to earlier houses in that construction members are left exposed and simplicity reigns. In the parlor, the cradle-board is next to the hearth and the mirror-board between the windows. The baseboard is often painted black, and the band continues around the room even across doors and casings, as a mop-splash zone; it also may encompass the fireplace as a mask for smoke stains. A Nantucket characteristic that comes to the fore in the typical house is the use of transoms over interior doors, which, as we have mentioned, is thought to be a device for quickly spotting fires, a constant hazard in the predominantly wooden-house town. Only the main staircase becomes a little pretentious. It is far more easily ascended than the wedge-shape steps of earlier times. In the Quaker house, one finds a handrail connected to shaped newel-posts, with plain square banisters set on a closed stringer.[2]

The typical Nantucket house probably came into existence during the 1760s. A prior date has been claimed for 4 Trader's Lane, but this seems a bit early. The houses at 81 Main and 10 Gardner Street are ascribed to the 1760s, the latter purchased for removal to its present site in 1771. The present form may not be what it was originally. Number 5 Mill is thought to have been constructed just before or after the American Revolution. The period during which the typical Nantucket house flourished was the last decade of the eighteenth century and the first of the nineteenth, with a resumption after recovery from the War of 1812, and a gradual decline down to the hegemony of the Greek Revival style in the mid-1830s. A characteristic late-eighteenth-century Quaker house is 11 Mill Street. However, all Quakers did not endorse it: this is the Job Macy residence, referred to at the beginning of Chapter Three as the one whose builder was admonished by his father for not following the lean-to scheme. It was erected in 1790 and has a slightly lower second-story ceiling than most, the upper windows resorting to eight-over-twelve- and six-over-nine-paned sashes *(Fig. 47)*. The plan is normal for a "typical" Quaker house of simple rectangular shape *(Fig. 48)*. A contemporary inversion of the floor plan is at 1 Vestal Street, built for Hezekiah Swain and his brother, but better known for having been later the home of William Mitchell and birthplace of his daughter, Maria, Nantucket's distinguished astronomer *(Fig. 49)*. The Vestal Street building has twelve-over-twelve- and nine-over-nine-paned sashes in the upper windows as well as in the lower. The front staircase is on the closet- rather than on the parlor-side of the hall, and the oven (later removed) was alongside the kitchen fireplace.[3] Both houses acquired service wings behind in the nineteenth century, and the Maria Mitchell homestead suffers from alterations to the original block inflicted at the time and because of the addition.

As one walks around Nantucket, one sees a wide assortment of variations. Number 6 Chester has the single window next to the door well removed from the corner because it lights the stairhall, the front closet having a window at the side. Number 30 Union Street has a window crowded next to the door at first-story level, and only three windows in the upper tier. Number 14 Union has no window next to the door but four above. At 16 Union, the upper corner window is omitted. Number 3 Mulberry has no window over the door. Number 4 Pine has no window between the corner and door and none above on axis, this space left blank, thus presenting a three-bayed façade. The same may be said for 37 Pine and 4 Liberty, both later alterations. The placing of the openings may be normal, though the character of them unusual, as at 41 India Street, which has small nine-over-six-paned sashes in the second story, and twelve-over-twelve-paned sashes in the first. Number 8 Pleasant Street has narrow four-over-four-paned sashes, relating it to four houses on West Chester Street (Numbers 3, 8, 11, and 21), which have similar windows in combination with others of six-paned sashes. The most unique of the group adhering to the traditional form is 16 Pleasant, which has brick first-story walls on both flanks and shingles elsewhere. The most atypical "typical" house is the gambrel lean-to at 6 North Liberty Street, whose roof shape allows for nothing like a standard second story, providing space only over the front rooms, yet practically as much in a similar location on the third (Chapter Four, *Fig. 45*).

Fig. 47
Fig. 48

Fig. 49

Fig. 45

Fig. 49 Hezekiah Swain House (*ca.* 1790), 1 Vestal Street. Later the Home of Maria Mitchell.

Attention should be called to broad versions of the typical Nantucket house, in which the single window beyond the door is brought in from the corner of the building and the area properly a closet is enlarged into a legitimate room (office or chamber). Examples include 15 Union (opened up to the stairhall in modern times), 27 and 33 India, and 24 North Water. Number 32 Union Street, the gambrel-roofed house of William Coffin (Chapter Four), may be looked upon as among the widest of the kind.

A subcategory of the "typical Nantucket" style was manifested briefly at the end of the eighteenth and beginning of the nineteenth century. It is characterized by a one-story extension on the flank opposite the entrance side of the house. The extension protrudes about eight feet, beginning level with the rear of the building and coming forward to about two-thirds of the house

Fig. 50 Captain Reuben R. Bunker House (*ca.* 1806, remodeled *ca.* 1820), Academy Hill.

depth; it is covered by a shed roof. In this variation, the stairhall runs back as far as the parlor, and the kitchen is wider. A newel stairway is at the rear, between the kitchen and chamber, and the fireplace to the chamber is in the space adjoining the stairs, facing the outside wall. This would be a narrow room, like the bedroom overhead, were it not for expansion into the side outshoot. Closets are provided at the front of the extension. Examples include 26 Milk, 148 Main, and 3 Pleasant Street, the last built for Reuben Dow in 1804, its extension later raised to two full stories with gable. Principal- and second-floor plans of the first (26 Milk), in which Isaiah Folger lived during the middle of the nineteenth century, are reproduced in Mr. Duprey's book.[4] One notes that in these turn-of-the-century houses, the oven no longer is at the back of the kitchen fireplace but at the side, where it is to remain for as long as ovens endure. All three

Fig. 51 Captain Seth Pinkham House, 42 Fair Street.

examples cited have subsequent service ells to the rear which provide modern kitchen facilities.

One other innovation appears in the *circa* 1800 houses that has not been encountered before. It has to do with the roof construction. Instead of rafters placed six or seven feet apart, with purlins spanning each bay supporting wide boards running from ridge to lower eaves, they have rafters set considerably closer together with horizontal planks superimposed to take the shingles. The changeover was not consistent on Nantucket, as the new roof of the Peter Folger II house (51 Centre), constructed perhaps as late as 1815, made use of the archaic purlin system (Chapter Six).

Early in the nineteenth century Quaker restrictions against elaboration relaxed, especially when building activities resumed after the War of 1812, and the typical Nantucket house under-

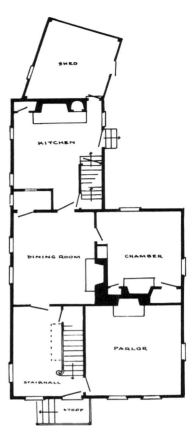

Fig. 52 (left) Captain Seth Pinkham House (1827–28), 40 Fair Street.
Fig. 53 (right) Restored First-Floor Plan of Pinkham House, 40 Fair Street.

went changes proper to the period and entered upon the final stage of its career. The doorway acquired some sort of enframement more refined than the old plank frame. It varied from a wide molding surmounted by a cornice hood, as at 5 New Mill Street, to pilasters and modified entablature, as at 20 Union. A particularly handsome doorway is at 9 Quince Street, with pilasters and shuttered fan and sidelights *(Fig. 46)*. In some cases, a wider doorway such as this displaced both the old door and adjoining single window, as at 43 and 45 India Street, the four upper windows remaining intact. The same scheme occurs at 11 Academy Lane, only the wide doorway is a later insertion, Greek Revival in style. The Greek Revival entrance alteration is easily discernible because of its heaviness, the supports to either side being thick and flat, as at 18 and 25 Orange, 7 Summer, 65 North Centre, 15 North Water, and 29 India. The same sort of pilasters have been attenuated and affixed at the corners of the house at 74 Orange Street. Entrance porches invariably are later. Number 25 India not only has an altered Greek doorway but an added distyle Doric portico as well. Parenthetically, instead of acquiring an elaborated doorway, some façades lost the one they had by its being moved to the side and replaced by a window, as at 23 India and 4 Step Lane. A fenestration change, consisting of a shaped lintel to the plank frame, appeared before the turn of the century, as at 5 New Mill and at 3 Pleasant. After the War of 1812, a more radical window innovation was made possible by the availability of larger panes of glass. The old twelve-paned sashes of 7″ × 9″ glass were superseded by six-paned sashes of 9½″ × 13″ panes. The sashes themselves remained about the same size. In some instances, the front of the house alone received the larger-paned windows, as at 9 Quince Street, where they are in the façade and south half of the side, though there are twelve-paned sash windows elsewhere. The counterpart of this new look is the clapboarded front wall, which figured at 9 Quince until the fall of 1970, when, unfortunately, the horizontal boards were stripped off and replaced by shingles. Still clapboarded are the façades of 6 Pleasant and 36 Liberty Street, both with six-paned sashes. Number 27 India, while retaining the older multi-paned windows and shingles, has the front wall dressed up with quoins at the extremities. The Captain Reuben R. Bunker house on Academy Hill (Church Lane), built about 1806, was modernized about 1820 with both clapboarding and quoins on the façade. The house was extended one bay and a small graceful portico was appended to the entrance *(Fig. 50)*. The renovation just missed attaining strict symmetry because of the irregular spacing of the openings. A more exact balance in a façade was achieved by the small addition to the south end of 11 Pleasant Street.

Fig. 50

There are four major interior changes in the later typical Nantucket house. The first is the use of thicker walls, which mask the corner posts and beams and provide insulation in the bargain. The second is the opening up of the front stairhall to include the area of the former closet and pantry. An example is 33 Milk Street.[5] Older houses were remodeled to attain such spaciousness, as was 29 India, for John H. Shaw in the early 1830s, when the new staircase was made to curve around an open well. Also apparent in the nineteenth-century renovation of this house is the little classic pediment at the front of the east projection or ell. This introduces the third of the later innovations: the rear service wing. The former kitchen became the new dining room in the main block of the house, and the oven disappears from the chimney. To bring older houses up to date, many—in fact most—acquired later kitchen extensions, and the old oven was bricked up or ripped out, as in the Maria Mitchell house. The new "typical" house no longer was a compact mass but a complex composition. The fourth characteristic of later versions was the raising of the building off the ground and the expansion of the early, restricted, round cool cellar into a full rectangular basement, sometimes containing a summer kitchen with fireplace, as at 47 Fair Street and 10 Gardner.[6]

Number 40 Fair Street is a good example of the last stage of the typical Nantucket house. It was built in 1827–28 for Captain Seth Pinkham, who resided in the smaller house next door (42 Fair), the first floor of which followed the plan of a "typical house," though the building is only one-and-three-quarters-storied *(Fig. 51)*. The account of the construction of 40 Fair Street has been published.[7] The walls are shingled, and it originally had a roof walk. Front rooms have six-paned sashes, whereas elsewhere in the house, nine- and twelve-paned frames are used *(Fig. 52)*. The stairhall occupies the northeast quadrant of the main pavilion *(Fig. 53)*. Its staircase begins with a protruding first step, over which the handrail spirals around a shaped newel post, capped by a small brass dome signifying that the house is clear of debt. There is an open stringer, and the straight flight rises in a large well to a square landing, with a second short flight of three steps branching off to the left and replacing earlier winders at the top. The larger quadrant to the south of the stairhall is the parlor. With the framing concealed, more attention is paid to decoration. The fireplace is centered on the east wall and has a pilastered mantel. Chairrailing, continuous with window sills, encircles the room. Doors are six-paneled, and transoms have disappeared in favor of glass set in the two small top panels. Although these elements have been covered with modern flat paint, an unspoiled mantel in the chamber over the parlor is marbleized and indicates that the same treatment existed below. The more common alternative was feather-

Fig. 51

Fig. 52
Fig. 53

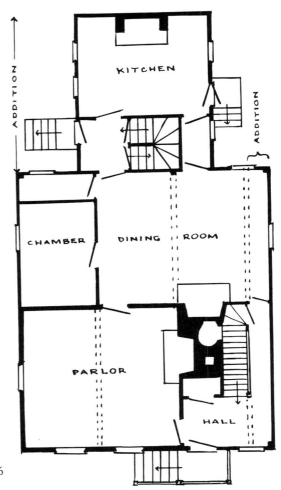

Fig. 55 (far right) William Brock House (1760), 46 Centre Street. Enlarged and Altered.

graining, an artificial wood grain often painted in a reddish-violet hue on a gray background. A square of the original multicolor spatter has been preserved on the hall floor, as a sample of what was used throughout the main part of the house. The remainder of the first story is occupied by the dining room and a bedroom. The dining-room fireplace has been closed up.

In accordance with the period, the kitchen and service stairs are located in the rear appendage. A door near the outside corner of the dining room opens to the butler's pantry with serving window at the back. Direct access to the kitchen is between the serving room and the enclosed stairs to the basement. A door to the ascending flight is around the corner to the right. The cooking fireplace is at the far end, and probably the oven was to the side, this part having been altered. The wing is a full two stories tall. A low, trapezoid cleaning shed is behind, its angle with the house determined by the irregular lot line on the north side. The baser work connected with food preparation has become well separated from the specialized eating area. Nantucketers had a special name for the kitchen ell in the nineteenth century. It was called the "porch," a word causing confusion because of its earlier connotation of stair-entry and, of course, because

of its later and present designation for a small portico or veranda. Its application to the service wing probably derived from the Latin *portus,* "storage space," and its use indicates the ideal in local education of a basic foundation in the ancient Roman and Greek languages.[8]

A building that fits into a class by itself is 46 Centre Street. Its form, fenestration, and entrance arrangement (except for the later Greek Revival enframement) all seem to belong to the typical Nantucket house type. The feature that takes exception is the position of the chimney, which rises through the roof ridge directly behind the door *(Fig. 55).* The parlor fireplace, therefore, is in the side and not the back wall *(Fig. 54).* As built for William Brock in 1760, the house was a plain rectangle, and it was about two-and-a-half feet shorter on the left or north side. Its plan was that of a saltbox half-house, though the building was full two stories in back as well as in front. Early in the nineteenth century, the house was lengthened another bay beyond the entrance, the winder stairway was removed in the entry and mostly replaced by a closet in the first story, a straight flight of steps was run alongside the chimney stack (perhaps in the area of a former closet), and the narrow new section became a corridor back to the former kitchen, now widened into the new dining room. The fireplace here was diminished and bricked off from the oven, which became a cubbyhole accessible from below the stairs. A kitchen ell was added at the rear, including an enclosed back stairway. The borning room and pantry remained unchanged (the present fenestration came later) as a small chamber and closet. Walls of the original great room in front, the subsequent parlor, were furred out to conceal the corner posts, with splayed window recesses. The trim is Federal in period. The framing of the north-side enlargement was patterned after the old. In the garret, purlins were notched into the original end rafters and spanned the thirty inches to the later north flank structural work, the new roof planks placed parallel to their predecessors. By comparison to a regular "typical" plan, such as that of 11 Mill Street *(Fig. 48),* one sees the shortcoming of the heating arrangement in the older layout, the chamber being without a fireplace. The Brock dwelling was built at the time of the inception of the characteristic Nantucket house type, but it did not catch up with it until several decades later, and then only partially. It has been converted into a shop, but, except for the removal of the front staircase, few changes have been inflicted upon the early house, though complex additions have been made at the back.

The four-bayed, two-and-a-half-storied house, with rooms grouped informally around the chimney stack and provided with diverse closets and lesser spaces for storage, is largely responsible for the charm and picturesqueness of Nantucket Town. It is a residence that reflects the nature of the people who lived here over a period of about three quarters of a century, beginning around 1760, and it abounds in all sections of the old community. Plainness was its key word, and during the early years of its regime, differences between one example and another remained slight. But during the latter half of the period, the influx of the Federal style lent a variety of architectural embellishments in the matter of doorway, wall, and window treatment. However, because of its limitations in aesthetic and spatial considerations, the typical Nantucket house was not open for development into a house thoroughly agreeable to mid-nineteenth-century taste and hence came to an abrupt end. The American architectural modes of the later eighteenth and early nineteenth century were more fully expressed outside the realm of the Quaker domicile, and we shall look into their range and diversity in the following chapter.

Fig. 55
Fig. 54

Fig. 48

Notes

1. As shown in Phebe Folger's *ca.* 1797 watercolor view, made from the north window of her brother's house at 8 Pleasant Street, in which the predominant color of houses shown is red. Katherine Seeler, "Phebe Folger's Watercolors," *Historic Nantucket,* October 1966, pp. 15–16 incl. illus.

2. Kenneth Duprey, *Old Houses on Nantucket,* New York, 1959, illustrations pp. 79, 94, 216 (measured drawings).

3. *Ibid.,* pp. 90–101. Historic American Buildings Survey, Mass. 901, sheet 2 (first-floor plan).

4. *Ibid.,* p. 217.

5. H. A. B. S., Mass. 854, sheet 2 (first-floor plan).

6. Duprey, *op. cit.,* p. 89. The early date claimed for this building hardly accords with this feature, which was perhaps a later innovation.

7. Florence Bennett Anderson, *Through the Hawse-Hole,* New York, 1932, pp. 192–196.

8. Derivation suggested by Prof. George C. Wood of Nantucket.

Fig. 56 29–31 Fair Street.

Chapter VI

Late Colonial and Federal Types

Each of the three species of building considered in the preceding chapters was a province unto itself. The mainstream of architectural evolution was channeled through less distinctive types, which grew out of medieval antecedents and laid the foundations for the subsequent classical revival, elements of which were incorporated in later members of the group considered in this chapter to an even greater extent than in later examples of the typical Nantucket house. The period concerned is slightly longer than that of the "typical" house, inasmuch as examples brought in as background for the developed Quaker house belong properly to the subject of this chapter; therefore, we shall begin this study a little earlier in time than the previous chapter.

The great stabilizing factor in the Quaker house was a sort of self-satisfied viewpoint, which necessarily remained ingrown. By contrast, the builders of the residue of contemporary building on Nantucket swung to extremes. On the one hand, they remained ultraconservative, departing only in one characteristic from the basic form of the lean-to house, but on the other they became aware of architectural progress elsewhere and benefitted by it.

It was during the period from shortly before 1750 up to 1830 that Nantucket took whole-heartedly to the sea. Though its geography was unaltered, intercourse meant its citizens no longer remained insular. They set out to sea for their livelihood, fame, and adventure, and in the process they inevitably brought back foreign wares, curios, and especially ideas to broaden their own way of life. The incentive was the whale. In the early days, these mammals could be seen from shore, but exploitation had lessened their numbers and set them on guard, and they had to be sought ever farther afield. Their capture became imperative to the economic stability of the island. In the 1720s, wharfs were built and Nantucket had a whaling fleet of twenty-five vessels. The population was one thousand people, yet it could not sufficiently man the boats that the owners wished to outfit, and recruits had to be sought from ports on Cape Cod and Long Island. It was found that Boston merchants were shipping Nantucket oil to England and making a nice profit, and Nantucketers, to secure this revenue for themselves, encompassed this trade in

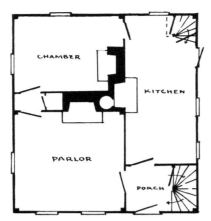

Fig. 57 Restored First-Floor Plan of 2 Cliff Road.

1745. Their ships returned laden with needed items such as hardware, hemp, sailcloth, and other goods, obtained at a fraction of their cost through roundabout channels. Thenceforth trade was an established practice on Nantucket.[1] Twenty years later, the population had increased to upward of three thousand, and the fleet to over one hundred ships. In 1772, the first candle factory was started and a new lucrative industry was launched for Nantucket. By 1775, the town numbered more than four thousand five hundred souls, and of vessels there were one hundred and fifty.[2] Affluence had been on the increase, though it was not without periodic setbacks. The numerous wars in which Great Britain was involved during the third quarter of the eighteenth century inflicted repercussions on Nantucket interests at sea. In 1755–56, six island vessels went unaccounted for and six more were captured and burned by the French, their crews taken into captivity.[3] French and Spanish privateers continued to be troublesome throughout the next two decades. It was a preview of the really terrible times ahead.

The American Revolution overspread Nantucket like a pall. Trade and communication with the outside world were reduced to a trickle. Vessels arriving home were necessarily laid up, as there was too much risk of life and property to venture out again. Moreover, the Provincial Congress of Massachusetts and later the Continental Congress restricted such voyages. Some people resorted to surreptitious trade in swift, light vessels designed to outrun a pursuer, but this often proved disastrous since they carried such a press of sail that they were frequently swamped and their crews drowned.[4] Because the majority of the islanders were members of the Society of Friends, they were opposed to war and thus took no active part in the conflict; but this did not keep its consequences from their shores. On May 23, 1775, over one hundred provincial troops landed at the wharf and marched into town with drums beating and flags flying. They professed to be after flour that was supposed to have been shipped to Nantucket for the British, but when they left they took some fifty whale boats with them.[5] During the fall of 1778, word was received on Nantucket that British men-of-war were on Martha's Vineyard plundering the people and destroying property, and that they intended to visit Nantucket next. Many Nantucketers hurriedly loaded their goods onto wagons and transported them out of town. It proved unnecessary, however, as the English were diverted. In the following year, the island was not so fortunate. Early in April, seven vessels of refugee loyalists from Newport landed with the intent of pillaging rebels. They took goods from the stores of William Rotch and Thomas Jenkins. Several times during the following months they returned to commit further annoyances. In August, English privateers captured a brig and a sloop.[6] During the course of the war, one

Fig. 58 Captain Nathaniel Davis Gorham House (1824), 2 Gorham's Court.

Fig. 59 Joshua Coffin House (rebuilt 1756, with later alterations), 52 Centre Street.

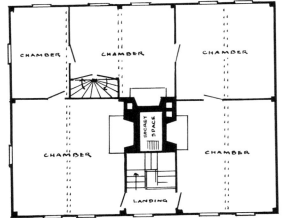

Fig. 60 Restored Second-Floor Plan of Joshua Coffin House.

hundred and thirty-four Nantucket ships were thus taken, and fifteen more disappeared at sea, leaving only twenty-three survivors. Sixteen hundred citizens, amounting to one-third of the population, perished as a result of the conflict. Lack of supplies and the freezing of the harbor in the winter of 1779–80 added to the misery. Many people felt that the situation was hopeless for the island and emigrated to the Hudson River Valley, Maine, Nova Scotia, and even across the Atlantic to Dunkirk, France, and Milford Haven, England.[7]

However, a new energy infused the town upon cessation of hostilities, and little by little recovery was effected. The discovery of whales in the Pacific in 1781 opened up new fields for conquest. By 1785, the population of Nantucket was about equal to what it had been before the Revolution. Prosperity increased for a quarter of a century, but then it was curtailed by the next clash with England: the War of 1812. Pacific whaling was impeded by Peruvian privateers, who preyed on American vessels under the pretext of being British allies. The United States government dispatched a force to protect its commercial ventures and was somewhat successful, but Nantucket ships had greater dangers to face in the Atlantic. The harbor was besieged by British armed vessels, and in August of 1814 the town agreed to a neutrality pact with the English. Privation and an ice-bound harbor during the winters of 1815–16 and 1816–17 inflicted hardships reminiscent of those of the Revolution. The war eventually ended, and recovery proved to be not so tedious as before, nor had the loss of human life been so great. By 1820, the population soared to upward of seven thousand. Ships engaged in whaling numbered more than sixty and trading vessels more than seventy-five.[8] An era of prosperity not to be interrupted by world conflict was in progress. The architecture of the late colonial and early Federal period reflects the metamorphosis from simple hominess to comparative ostentatiousness.

The period begins with the expiration of the taller lean-to house. Number 29 Fair Street was built as a two-and-a-half-story saltbox half-house in the mid-eighteenth century. It faces the street—east—and the chimney is at the north end, beyond which is Hiller's Lane. Perhaps the existence of the public way at that time prevented the normal expansion and realization of a full-house on the chimney end. In any event, an addition was built on the south flank, and it was similar to the older building in plan and size; but it was made fully two-storied in back. Probably at the same time, the rear of 29 Fair was heightened and the roof rebuilt. This left the second-floor level lower in back and, externally, the old chimney stranded in front of the new roof ridge *(Fig. 56)*. The resulting building was made to serve as a single residence, with rooms   *Fig. 56* on both sides in the newer construction accessible to the staircase, which, by the way, is of early newel form and may have been taken out of 29 Fair Street. Although the main chamber on the second floor of 31 has beaded edges to the beams (as throughout number 29), the frame of the principal downstairs room is crude and not tooled at all, and lath marks on the underside of the joists indicate all was hidden by a plastered ceiling. This, then, was a parlor in the latest late-eighteenth-century vogue of the mainland. The corresponding room in the older unit became the dining room, and the fireplace in the former lean-to was used for cooking.

Considered independently, the newer unit—31 Fair Street—is a rarity on the island, having been built two-storied in back yet retaining the lean-to half-house plan. Another example noted (Chapter Five) is the original form of 46 Centre Street, to which may be added, perhaps, the first stage of 11 Hussey. Usually, houses of this size of the second half of the eighteenth and early nineteenth century have a very different arrangement, involving the shifting of the chimney along the ridge away from alignment with the front door. A characteristic example is 2 Cliff Road, on the west corner of Chester Street. The late eighteenth-century house has been altered and enlarged, but its original form can be ascertained through examination of the structural system. It is about equal in size to either 29 or 31 Fair Street, or any similar saltbox. One enters a small hall or porch, with a newel stair to the right side, whose two flights lead up to the second floor and down to the basement. The rest of the main story is portioned into a parlor, kitchen, and chamber; the fireplaces for these rooms cluster at the center of the house *(Fig. 57)*. There probably was a back stair at the northwest corner of the kitchen, with a narrow passage across to the bedroom over the downstairs chamber, which is isolated from the front stairway. Disregarding the difference in stairhalls, the disposition of rooms favors that of the sport lean-to, 84 Main Street, before the one-story extension was added on the west side *(Fig. 26)*. It is also not unlike the grouping of rooms in the typical Nantucket house, like 11 Mill Street, exclusive of the closet-pantry unit *(Fig. 47)*. There are about sixty-five Nantucket houses belonging to this category, one of the last built being 2 Gorham's Court, dated 1824 (*Fig. 58*—see Appendix E).

Fig. 57

Fig. 26

Fig. 47
Fig. 58

Although the lean-to half-house plan came to a dead end with the discontinuation of the low back roof slope, the same cannot be said for the full-house. As it seems natural that the early center-chimney house should have proceeded from the two-story, single-room-deep "English house" to the lean-to that was two rooms deep downstairs, so the next logical step was for it to become two rooms deep on the second floor as well. The half–lean-to house had been enlarged into the full-house; now it was the turn of the lean-to full-house to take the next forward step.

One of the earliest of the kind is 52 Centre Street, of which the southeast section is said to have been brought from old Sherburne, rebuilt, and enlarged for Joshua Coffin in 1756 *(Fig. 59)*.[9] If so, it was a fairly new house when moved, as the beams on both sides of the porch or entry are beaded and therefore belong to the second quarter of the eighteenth century. The plan is almost an inversion of 5 Liberty Street *(Fig. 25)*, the staircase ascending conversely, the chamber (though without angle fireplace) in the opposite rear corner, and the parlor and dining room switched about.[10] The Coffin house has a more fully developed secret space inside the chimney, becoming a small room in the second story, reached from below or by steep ladder-like stairs through a trap door in the garret floor.[11] An elliptical oven is at the side of the kitchen fireplace, rather than at the back, and both are recessed in the chimney area. The ceilings front and back are of equal height in both first and second stories. The notable feature is the fireplace at the rear of the chimney on the second floor, which, of course, never occurs in a lean-to *(Fig. 60)*. An ell has been attached to the southwest corner of the Joshua Coffin house, and all of the exterior details are Federal-period replacements.

Fig. 59

Fig. 25

Fig. 60

The noblest of the symmetrical-sided houses retaining the basic lean-to plan in Nantucket is 51 Centre Street, which, although next in number to the example just discussed, is located three blocks north. It was erected on the site of the old William Geyer house (1684) by the builder Jethro Hussey, for Peter Folger II, about 1765. The building is three stories high and initially was known as the "flat-roofed house." The roof indeed was nearly flat, and it still exists as the garret floor. Originally it was a deck of wide boards that were tarred on the top surface, covered with paper and a thin coating of cement. The deck was enframed by a railing supported by posts denoting each bay of the building, and it was reached through a trap door behind the chimney. The railing post holes are still discernible, and the trap door is intact. The present pitched roof, although added about 1815, displays archaic features. The end-gable overhangs stem from the pre-existing cornices *(Fig. 61)*. Structurally, instead of following the contemporary practice of closely-spaced rafters supporting roofing planks running crosswise, the roof has huge rafters set about seven feet apart and joined by purlins, on which are fastened planks parallel to the rakings. This is a seventeenth-century system, and it bespeaks the fallacy of dating

Fig. 61

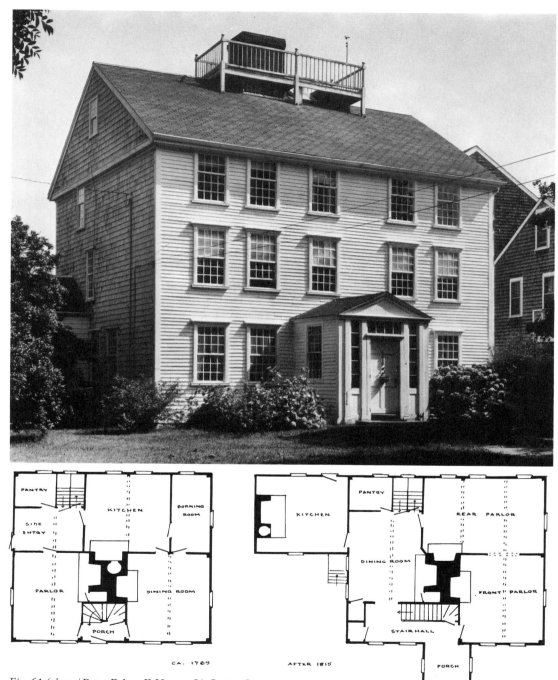

Fig. 61 (above) Peter Folger II House, 51 Centre Street.

Fig. 62 (below) Restored First-Floor Plan of Peter Folger II House as Built (1765, *left*) and as Remodeled and Enlarged (1815, *right*).

Fig. 63 Captain Edward Cary House (1790s), 117 Main Street.

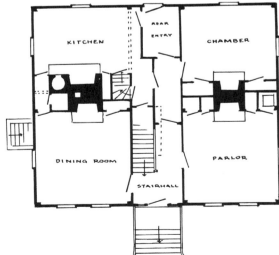

Fig. 64 Restored First-Floor Plan of Captain Edward Cary House.

structures in Nantucket purely on the grounds of style or manner. With the addition of the steep roof, the chimney was heightened and a roof walk built to encompass it, reminiscent of the former, more ample deck.

Despite the late date of its original construction, the plan of the Peter Folger II house was not as advanced as the two houses last considered (52 Centre and 5 Liberty). The staircase was a shallow newel type and the chamber in the back corner a narrow borning room *(Fig. 62)*. However, it seems initially to have had a side entry between parlor and kitchen and a back stair of straight flights opening from the entry. There are three fireplaces on the second as well as the first floor. In addition to the new roof, in the 1815 remodeling the house's constricted porch was expanded by a new eight-foot-square projecting pent in front. Retaining the same stairwell, a straight flight of steps was substituted for the lower winders by extending a stairhall sidewise across what formerly was the fore part of the parlor, reserving the space beyond the front windows for closets. The back of the parlor was opened up to the earlier side entry, another window was inserted on the north wall, and a kitchen wing attached to the right flank. The old parlor thus became the later dining room. The original kitchen and borning room were joined, and a wide doorway was made of the two former doors to these rooms from the front room. The old dining room now became the front parlor, and the enlarged room behind henceforth was a big rear parlor.

There are about thirty center-chimney houses in the old island town, and they date from throughout the last half of the eighteenth century and into the early years of the nineteenth, thus almost up to the time when the Folger house was renovated (Appendix F). The so-called 1800 House (4 Mill), which is an example of the kind, dates from the beginning of the nineteenth century. For such a plan to have been followed so late on Nantucket indicates how retarded architecture was here, since on the mainland it had been virtually abandoned shortly after the American Revolution.

The center chimney limited the floor plan, because rooms depended upon it for fireplaces, and except where a couple of lean-tos managed to get a corner fireplace in the rear chamber (5 Liberty and 1 Tattle Court), only three rooms to each story could be accommodated. The fireplaces in the two main rooms were placed off center. However, greater awareness of symmetry was being felt in American architecture as a result of models of English Renaissance style, fermenting there since Inigo Jones designed the Queen's House at Greenwich (1618) and the Banqueting House at Whitehall Palace (1619–21). The formality was taken up and given far-reaching fame not only through the work of such professional architects as Sir Christopher Wren, Colen Campbell, and James Gibbs, but also by a host of amateur gentlemen-architects who delighted in designing their own country seats, and by those who produced builder's handbooks, including Gibbs, Batty Langley, William Halfpenny, Abraham Swan, and Robert Morris.[12] These books were known and used in America, and Langley's *Builder's Jewel* and Swan's *British Architect* were reprinted in this country.[13] The big solid chimney of the Jethro and Josiah Coffin houses was cleft for closets and secret places in the later Barnabus Pinkham and Joshua Coffin houses, and the chimney was mounted by a stairway in the small Edward Allen lean-to at 21 Prospect Street (Chapter Three). The next step was for the chimney shaft to become two, which is what happened in the typical Georgian house in America, as in the Governor's Palace (1706–20) and Wythe house (1755) in Williamsburg; Carter's Grove (1750-53) on the James River, Virginia; Miles Brewton house (*ca.* 1765), Charleston, South Carolina; Matthias Hammond house (1773–74), Annapolis, Maryland; Joshua Wentworth house (1770), Portsmouth, New Hampshire; John Vassall (Longfellow) house (1759), Cambridge, Massachusetts; and the

Fig. 62

Fig. 65 Residence Remodeled and Enlarged for Thomas Macy (*ca.* 1830), 99 Main Street.

Federal-style Grosse Mount (1804), Burlington, Vermont.[14] In Nantucket, there are about the same number of twin-chimney as single-chimney two-storied houses (Appendices F and G). The dates for the double-chimney type are generally later, from about 1770 until the general advent of the Greek Revival style in the early 1830s.

The dual-chimney house is usually longer by a few feet than the single-chimney building, and it has a transverse stairhall (with back stairs) and four squarish rooms on both first- and second-floor levels, each with a centered fireplace and each with two outside walls for ample light and ventilation. With the introduction of this type, the dark medieval house, culminating in the lean-to variety, had truly become a thing of the past. Now the entrance door had not only a transom above but sidelights flanking it. The staircase was easy of ascent, being totally without winders. Most important, circulation took its most important leap forward. One no longer had to walk around the central chimney and pass through rooms to get from one to another; one now could enter each room directly by means of the middle hallway.

All but one of the some thirty twin-chimney, two-storied houses in Nantucket have gable roofs. The exception is 117 Main Street, built for Captain Edward Cary or his son, Robert, during

Fig. 66 Matthew Crosby House (*ca.* 1828), 90 Main Street.

Fig. 63

the 1790s *(Fig. 63).* It is crowned by a hip roof, called "Dutch cap" on the island and "Italian roof" in Virginia, the latter recognizing its south-Europe Renaissance source as concerns British architecture. The five-bayed, two-storied house is raised on a brick basement. The door and sidelights are enframed by simple, flat pilasters with subtle entasis and supporting impost-block entablature and thin cornice. The twenty-four-paned windows in front have slight cornice hoods, while on the flanks they have normal plank frames with lintels projecting a bit at each side. The building measures approximately 40′ × 35′, the shorter dimension, from front to back, being about equal to the width of the Folger house façade (51 Centre). In the Cary house, the staircase faces the entrance, and the wall space beneath the straight flight is paneled in late eighteenth-century fashion, as are the fireplace walls in the four rooms. The parlor, on the east side in front, had two sets of balanced doors flanking the chimneypiece, the outermost originally opening into a closet with trap door to the wine cellar *(Fig. 64).* The dining room, on the west side, has a single narrow door to the left of each space alongside the fireplace, that on the west side opening into the passage that presumably originally had a service window through to the kitchen. A chamber is in the northeast corner of the first story, reached through a middle hall

Fig. 64

Fig. 67 Reuben Russell House (*ca.* 1830), 45 Centre Street.

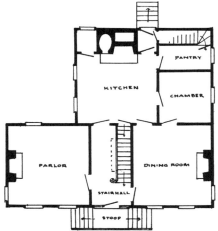

Fig. 68 Restored First-Floor Plan of Reuben Russell House.

that connected with a back entry. The kitchen, occupying the fourth quadrant, has an irregular shape. It is narrower than the other rooms, because of the large size of the fireplace and former oven, with a wood closet and service stairs on the inner side; beyond these is a passageway to the closet under the main staircase and cellar stairs under the service stairs. A summer kitchen was in the basement. Four chambers are on the second floor, and a stair leads up to the garret, where the slaves were quartered.[15] A two-storied ell subsequently was built on the rear west end of the house, and dormer windows were added to the west and back planes of the hip roof.

The Thomas Coffin house (7 Milk), built a decade later, is a similar house except for the gabled roof, and it has six-paned sashes, probably a later change. The interior staircase is a more developed type, having an open stringer and a railing making a spiral over the newel post on the protruding curved end of the first step.[16] The house currently is a natural history education center. The nearby and similar Joseph Starbuck house (4 New Dollar), of 1809, likewise has six panes in each sash. Its doorway is Greek Revival of the 1840s.

The handsomest façade of its kind in Nantucket is that of 99 Main Street, the result of enlargement *(Fig. 65)*. The original dwelling, built about 1770 by Valentine Swain, was a typical Nantucket house, two-and-a-half-storied with a four-bayed façade. This is clearly indicated by the framing seen in both the garret and basement. An original beam placed transversely under the inside (west) wall of the parlor measures thirty-five feet in length. The plan was an inversion of that of 11 Milk Street. This early house is depicted second from the left in the Phebe Folger watercolor of 1797, painted from the north window of her brother's house at 8 Pleasant Street.[17] The building is shown with a single chimney and small walk on the ridge of the roof, which has gable ends. The façade is portrayed with three windows in the second story and four, with center door, in the first. (Phebe's having represented 7 Summer Street with three upper windows instead of four, which seem always to have been there, leads one to assume that the young girl took poetic license in rendering architecture.) In customary fashion, a decade or two later, a kitchen wing was constructed at the rear.

Fig. 65

The house was purchased by Thomas Macy and enlarged to its present form in 1830.[18] The east side was left practically undisturbed, whereas all but the last couple of feet of the west side was relegated to a central stairhall (necessitating a shift of two beams under the first floor), and a fourteen-foot extension was added beyond. A chimney was built matching the old one. The new work made possible two new rooms about sixteen feet square on each of two floors, their fireplaces back to back, and the house now displayed perfect symmetry. However, the architectural dress of the residence seems rather elaborate for its sponsor to have been a Quaker. The walls are clapboarded, and centered in the five-bayed façade is a doorway with elliptical fanlight and sidelights, though the fan is blind since the ceiling height of the early house was not sufficient for it to be open. Because of its fine design, the doorway has become a symbol for Nantucket architecture and indeed appears on other buildings here, some of them modern reproductions, but it is not unique to the island.[19] A more typical Nantucket feature is the railing fence—in place of a picket or spike fence—which enframes the stoop and embraces small benches to either side, descends the steps, and extends in both directions at the edge of the sidewalk *(Frontispiece)*. In a strong gale or hurricane, such a railing can be helpful to pedestrians making their way home. The fenestration has six-paned sashes; only the window over the doorway has narrow sidelights as well, a rarity here. All windows, including those in the doorway, had outside shutters. The house has a deep cornice on narrow, long modillions across the front, surmounted by a parapet with balustrade insets aligned to the windows, another element that was to become popular. A roof deck extends nearly the length of the ridge, and its railing matches the front fence.

Fig. 69 John Wendell Barrett House (1820), 72 Main Street.

Paneled fireplace walls in the east half of the house are of the early period, though beams have been concealed by a lowered plaster ceiling. The décor and the flooring in the stairhall and west parlor belong to the 1830 remodeling. The staircase has an open stringer and square banisters supporting a railing that encircles a spiral carved newel post at the base. Despite their having been realized piecemeal, all parts of the house are in perfect harmony.

The residence of Matthew Crosby at 90 Main Street, believed to have been built about 1828, contains the same elements of plan and façade but misses the subtle niceties of the Macy *Fig. 66* house *(Fig. 66).* It is perched on a high basement, without greenery between building and street; its stoop has wedge-shaped steps on each side, its railing isolated. The height of the first-story

Fig. 70 Jared Coffin House (*Moors' End*—1829–34), 19 Pleasant Street.

ceilings would permit a glazed lunette over the doorway, but it is blind. The space between the two ranges of windows is somewhat greater than on the façade across the street, and the shutters of the paired windows slightly overlap, missing the finer proportions of number 99. Two nearby houses have modern adaptations of the Macy and Crosby doorways. One is 89 Main, originally a lean-to type of the 1740s, enlarged in 1875, and remodeled to resemble an old house in 1926. The other is 92 Main, a Greek Revival design of about 1838, in which the fan has been inserted inappropriately in the heavy pilastered door enframement.

Trends in Nantucket architecture seldom followed a logical sequence, but appeared, then disappeared, sporadically came back or else did not, and sometimes were manifested initially in a

Fig. 71 Frederick Mitchell House (1834), 69 Main Street.

highly developed form. A radical new house plan that was to become prevalent here during the second quarter of the nineteenth century had been introduced just prior to the American Revolution in the gambrel-roof house with brick end walls at 5 Orange Street (Chapter Four). We have referred to the placing of the chimneys against the outside walls, which leaves the middle part of the house—up to then occupied by the chimney—free for circulation. As mentioned in connection with the Orange Street house, this arrangement in America goes back to the seventeenth century. Its rationality in a structure with brick ends is sound, but it permitted certain advantages in a frame house as well, which was the reason for its recall. Three end-chimneys are to be found in the Reuben Russell house, 45 Centre Street, dating from about 1830. The two-storied house is L-shaped, with a five-bayed façade. The front doorway has glazed sidelights and a blind fan not

Fig. 67   unlike that of the Macy frontispiece, and it has windows of six-paned sashes *(Fig. 67).* In the transverse hall, the staircase railing makes a loop over the newel post on the projected end of the first step. A square parlor is on the north side and dining room on the south *(Fig. 68)*. The kitchen is in the extension behind, with doors opening into the stairhall and dining room. In spite of the advanced elegance shown in the front suite, the back of the house is strangely old-fashioned. The direct accessibility of the kitchen to dining room is one point. Another is that the room fitted into the angle between the kitchen and dining room is a chamber, its square shape alone distinguishing it from the traditional borning room, though it relates to the bedroom in the later lean-to house, as at 5 Liberty Street. The narrow area at the end of the wing is a pantry with back stairs to the full second story. The house has a high basement, and although one might expect a summer kitchen at the back the only working fireplace on the lower level was in the chimney serving the dining room.

Fig. 68

An amplification of the plan is embodied in 72 Main Street, constructed earlier, in 1820, for John Wendell Barrett; the builder is believed to have been John Coleman. The main block of the house is two rooms deep, with a pair of chimneys on each end wall. The façade is somewhat austere: a high basement without openings, the clapboard wall above framed in attenuated flanged pilasters, the cornice supported from the capitals by only a narrow intervening architrave but topped by a thoroughly Federal device, a parapet with balustrade insets aligned to the windows, as on the Macy house *(Fig. 69)*. Two external elements belong to the early Greek Revival style: the elevated portico with coupled Ionic columns and attic treatment over the cornice, and the pilastered belvedere set on the hip roof (the finest and largest in Nantucket). It is an ample house, with a sense of great airiness inside. Its decor is in the late Federal manner, the door and window trim with running moldings at sides and top meeting at corner blocks embellished with carved rosettes. The parlor windows are capped by low pediments, the fireplaces flanked by colonnettes supporting paneled friezes which in turn hold a projecting mantel shelf. Chandeliers are hung from foliated centerpieces in the ceiling.[20] The Barrett house is a transitional essay, and its conservativism set the pace for the Main Street residences of Nantucket merchant princes for the balance of the affluent period, later examples of which will be discussed in the following chapter.

Fig. 69

The next important step in the development of Nantucket architecture was the substitution of brick for wood construction. During the years from 1829 to 1834, Jared Coffin's house was built at what now is 19 Pleasant Street. Being on the edge of town, it appropriately was given the name "Moors' End." The entire façade is of common-bond brickwork, beginning at sidewalk level and including the high basement (windowless, as in the Barrett house) and the stoop, with its steps of brownstone. The front doorway has working sidelights but a blind fan that is semicircular and rises almost to the sill of the second-story window *(Fig. 70)*. Brick parapets connect the twin chimneys at each end. The house has a center transverse stairhall and two rooms to each side, though the north suite has been thrown into a single interior with double chimneybreasts. The house has been greatly remodeled, the last time, in 1925, by Fiske Kimball, who made an attempt at restoring some of the older features.[21] A brick service wing skirts Mill Street at an angle with the main part of the house. The gross brick wall enclosing the yard to the south of the house dates from the 1890s. It embraces a garden house at the Angora Street corner and continues as a pleasanter latticework clairvoyée to the barn or stable, the 1890s renovation of which Kimball described as being "glorified into a Venetian church."

Fig. 70

The last of the more ample Nantucket houses of strict Federal style is 69 Main Street, built for Frederick Mitchell in 1834 *(Fig. 71)*. Although almost a decade and a half later than the Barrett house, it has none of the new Greek idiom. The basement is of unbroken granite, and the Flemish-bond brick wall above is relieved only by the front door with fan and sidelights and the

Fig. 71

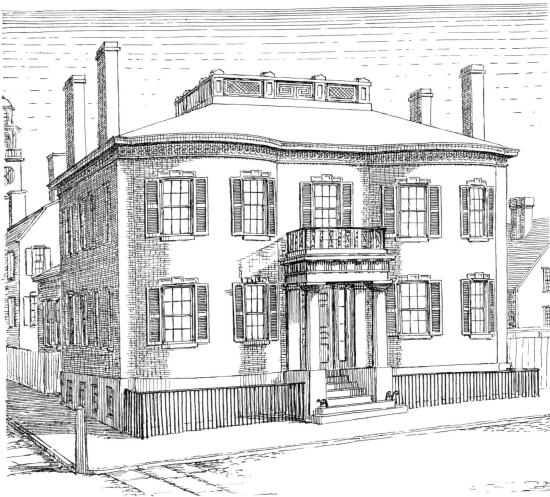

Fig. 72 Restored Sketch of Philip H. Folger House (*ca.* 1831), 58–60 Main Street.

two tiers of windows. The façade's only concession to the latest trend is the recession of the arched doorway. The balustraded parapet over the main cornice is Renaissance. Like Moors' End, the house has parapets spanning the double chimneys and an octagonal cupola set on the roof ridge. The Mitchell house has been given little notice in publications, because it is only recently that the house has been restored, the work completed in 1964.

Although built three years earlier, the Philip H. Folger residence is more advanced, stylistically, than the Frederick Mitchell house; following Moors' End, it is the second brick domestic essay in Nantucket. Designated 58–60 Main Street, at the west corner of Orange, the formal building on a granite basement has convex projections to the façade, like certain contemporary row houses on Louisburg Square in Boston.[22] The curved sections of the 1831 Nantucket house flank the distyle portico of brownstone, with Greek Doric columns set on antepodia embracing the entrance steps. An iron fence was once attached to the front of the podium. The façade wall

Fig. 73 "The Block," Folger Duplex Row House (*ca.* 1831), 15, 17, 19, 21, and 23 Orange Street.

Fig. 74 Restored First-Floor Plan of 40 Pine Street.

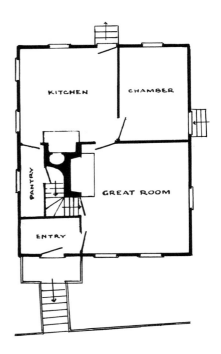

Fig. 72
is crowned by a whorled relief design and cornice, originally surmounted by a visible hip roof capped by an architectonic railing, and with chimneys much taller than at present *(Fig. 72)*. The central stairhall remains little changed. To the west was the double parlor, bowed at front and rear, with two chimneybreasts on the outer wall. Although now commercial space, with floor lowered to street level, the room's elaborate cornice, with grape design, and beautifully modeled floral centerpieces, all still intact, give some impression of its former magnificence. Opposite were two distinct rooms, one used for dining, now also desecrated for business purposes. The front of the building is disfigured by display windows, and even the lower fenestration on the east side has been changed, the first-story openings cut down to the granite, and the former basement windows blocked up. The house awaits sensitive restoration.

Fig. 73
Another distinctive architectural project commissioned by Philip H. Folger and erected simultaneously with his own home is "The Block," Nantucket's only row of town houses, inclusive of the odd numbers from 15 to 23 Orange Street *(Fig. 73)*. The clapboard group was built as a speculative venture, and it consists of five dwellings, which have alternately inverted floorplans, so that two doorways come together—at least in two pairs—and therefore constitute duplexes. Each is three-bayed and has a high brick basement accommodating kitchen (in the rear) and front dining room; two parlors are on the main floor and bedrooms on the second, with additional chambers in the garret, lighted by dormer windows. New extensions have been affixed at the back for kitchens on the principal level and utility rooms below. The basements are no longer being used as originally intended.

The greatest changes in the metamorphosis of architecture from one era to the next occur in the more ambitious projects, in public buildings and the homes of the wealthy. Conversely, secondary structures (barns and sheds) and smaller dwellings remain more conservative. Yet these simpler buildings constitute an integral part of the total scene. The earliest Nantucket

Fig. 75 Southeast Corner Pine and Lyon Streets (38 Pine with 40 seen beyond).

homes were all modest structures, and we have seen that they remained medieval in character at a time when the civilization from which they derived had become Renaissance and Baroque in the upper strata. A century later (late eighteenth and early nineteenth), while the Federal style was being impressed upon the new residences of the merchant princes on Main Street, there was hardly a trace of it on the cottages being built on the lanes and back streets of the town. Like the smaller two-storied houses of this period, exemplified by 2 Cliff Road, the innovations in less-than-two-storied houses were prompted by practical considerations, not by style, and have to do mostly with room arrangement.

It seems odd that the Cape Cod cottage, so prevalent throughout the New England mainland and Long Island and even on Martha's Vineyard, going back reputedly to the seventeenth century,[23] barely figures on Nantucket. The Cape Cod cottage is a story-and-a-half house with a ridge chimney, and, like the lean-to house, it is to be found in two sizes, the half-house and the full-house. The first-floor plan resembles that of the lean-to. The chief difference between them occurs upstairs, the rooms being centered between the two equal roof slopes in the Cape Cod, rather than across the front, as in the saltbox. A rare genuine "Cape" in Nantucket is 40 Pine Street, a half-house. The chimney is aligned to the front door. One comes into a "porch," or entry, that leads into the great room on the right. The enclosed stairway (now altered) was originally wrapped around the chimney, ascending from the great room, in a manner characteristic of the small Cape house *(Fig. 74).*[24] Across the back are a bedroom and kitchen, the cooking fire- *Fig. 74* place sharing the chimney with that of the great room; there is a narrow pantry between the stairs and outer wall. The high full basement is not normal to a house of this species, which should sit close to the ground and have a round cool cellar, like a lean-to; it indicates a late version. Window sashes have been changed front and sides, and an ell was added on the rear. A second example of a small Cape was 5 Cliff Road *(Fig. 123),* a victim of modern alterations. A few Nan-

Fig. 76 Captain Alexander Bunker House (*ca.* 1820), 8 Academy Lane.

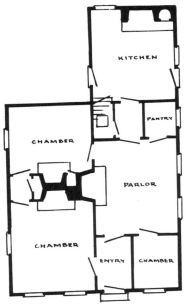

Fig. 77 First-Floor Plan of Bunker House.

tucket houses of the period are of similar size and have a ridge chimney. Superficially, therefore, they seem to belong to the same category, but their layout bears no relation to that of the Cape. Examples are 6 and 7 Eagle Lane, 2, 3, and 5 Farmer, 2 Flora, and 38 Pine Street, the last next door to the authentic specimen *(Fig. 75)*. Number 38 Pine Street is one of the deepest (from front to back) of the lot. The minuscule Nantucket dwelling is most often a one-and-three-quarters-story building. Of the close to one hundred of the kind here, only a fraction are five-bayed (such as 6 Atlantic and 60 Pleasant), about one-fourth are four-bayed, and the great majority are three-bayed (Appendix H, 2a).

Fig. 75

Representative of the four-bayed group is 8 Academy Lane. By coincidence, it is identical in horizontal measurements to the two-and-a-half-storied house at 2 Cliff Road. The Academy Lane residence was built about 1820 for Captain Alexander Bunker, and, being a later manifestation of the type, its façade shows some refinement. The front is clapboarded instead of shingled; the doorway is pilastered and has modillions in the entablature, the same motif being repeated under the main cornice *(Fig. 76)*. The entrance hall runs between a large and small chamber and leads into the parlor, which is centered on the left or west side of the plan *(Fig. 77)*. Another and medium-sized chamber is in the southeast corner. There is a connector behind the parlor between a pantry and hatch under the stairs to the cool cellar. Unlike 2 Cliff Road, the Bunker house has always had a one-story kitchen at the back; from here one ascends to the rooms under the sloping roof. Because they are small and short of head room, these are not the major chambers, which are downstairs. Mantels are pilastered, and door and window trim inside is composed of simple, shaped moldings. The introduction of these embellishments, outside as well as in, paved the way for the more general ornamentation of a house of this size in the Greek Revival period that followed (Chapter Seven).

Fig. 76
Fig. 77

Although architectural interest in early Nantucket primarily turns to domestic work, there are, nevertheless, a few other buildings that date from the opening years of the nineteenth century which deserve attention. The first is only partially extant: the Masonic Lodge Hall at 63 Main Street, adjacent to the Pacific National Bank. The building was two-storied and five-bayed, the façade organized by tall Roman Ionic pilasters distinguishing the center bay and stationed at the outer corners.[25] This Renaissance device had been employed earlier on Georgian-manner buildings in America, going back to the late seventeenth century, as on the Foster-Hutchinson house in Boston (*ca.* 1688), a three-storied residence that also had Ionic shafts separating the middle bay and buttressing the ends. Better known is the same scheme on the existing two-storied John Vassall (Longfellow) house (1759) in Cambridge, Massachusetts.[26] Like it, the structure in Nantucket, built by the Masons in 1802, is of frame construction, clapboarded between the pilasters. Usually arched or otherwise more developed fenestration would appear in the lower wall, but here it is above, the second floor being the principal story and that used for lodge meetings. The upper windows are enframed by miniature pilasters and archivolts, each with a keystone. The building was crowned by an entablature and hipped roof, and an "Image on top of the Hall."[27] During the anti-Masonic feeling of the 1830s the building was conveyed to the trustees of the Coffin School, to avoid its confiscation; the first floor was let to tenants and partly used for classes. The lower façade was remodeled for shops, divided by a new entablature set on insignificant piers displacing the lower shafts of the original pilasters *(Fig. 78)*.[28] In 1872, the two westernmost bays were wrecked to make room for a dwelling, since razed. Perhaps to compensate for the distortion, a pilaster, presumably taken from the right flank corner, was inserted in the space between the eastern windows. The abbreviated structure has survived and lately (1970) was refurbished for banking facilities extended from its neighbor.

Fig. 78

Fig. 79

The religious building in Nantucket that attracts the most attention—because of the hourly tolling of its bell, if for no other reason—is the Second Congregational Church at 11 Orange Street, built by Elisha Ramsdell in 1809. Its first tower was erected in 1815; it was replaced by another, by Perez Jenkins, in 1830 *(Fig. 79)*. In the interim, the congregation had become Unitarian. The three-bayed, three-storied clapboarded façade, with blind-fan doorway, rises higher than the auditorium itself, a characteristic of Asher Benjamin's meeting house at West Boston, drawings of which were published by him when it was built in 1806.[29] The Boston edifice has a square tower as the fifth story, whereas the Unitarian Church in Nantucket narrows to a square clock tower for the fourth level, which is surmounted by an arched octagonal bell pavilion, and in turn by an eight-sided lantern, bonnet, and weathervane. The lantern or cupola was used for the town fire watch. The auditorium behind originally had a balcony and was lighted by two tiers of windows. However, in 1844, the building was altered by Frederick Brown Coleman, whose work included the addition of the curved stairs in the vestibule, the opening up of the auditorium by elimination of the balcony, substitution of tall windows on the sides, installation of the apsidal

Fig. 80

posterior for the pulpit, and covering the room with a shallow elliptical dome *(Fig. 80)*. The painted architectural decorations were by Carl Wendte. The building is referred to as South Tower, distinguishing it from the First Congregational Church at 62 Centre Street, which is designated North Tower.

The handsomest and most sophisticated of early nineteenth-century buildings in Nantucket, built of brick laid in Flemish bond on granite foundations, is the Pacific National Bank

Fig. 81

on the corner of Centre at 51 Main Street *(Fig. 81)*. It was built in 1818 as a successor to the early building on the east side of Federal Street between Main and Cambridge. The two-storied bank facing lower Main, or Market Square, is a three-bayed symmetrical block crowned by a hip roof. The windows are recessed, those below in applied arches, those above in rectangular panels. The spaces around the windows were originally stuccoed or at least painted a near-white in contrast to the red brickwork. The upper windows themselves have a segmental-arch head. The entrance door has a fanlight and is sheltered by a semicircular portico with Roman Ionic columns, its steps of brownstone fanning forward with a wrought-iron railing at the outer edge. The façade is held together, visually, by horizontal belts of brownstone at windowsill level on both the first and second stories. Originally following an L-shaped plan, with the base of the figure on Liberty Street, the building later acquired a three-bayed addition on Main Street, the new part stepped back a few inches from the plane of the old. Still later—after 1895—a second addition, of two bays, was attached at the west end, the details copying exactly those of the oldest unit, a slight variation having been introduced in the intermediary section. The bank is the oldest commercial building in Nantucket to have seen continuous service fulfilling its original intention.

The period from the mid-eighteenth to a little beyond the first quarter of the nineteenth century was that in which Nantucket grew from a sparse settlement of medieval lean-to houses into a thriving town of some architectural merit. Houses passed from an indrawn stage focused on the central chimney to an outgoing phase preoccupied with the outside wall. This is evident not only in the treatment of doors and windows, but in the adoption of other elements as well, such as pilasters and parapets with balustrade. Even the chimney sometimes left its center position and took its stand, in duplication, against the outer wall, thrusting fireplaces to the perimeter of the house, where one sat in front of the fire and gazed through adjoining windows outward. A home was no longer merely an enclosed volume but a façade to the passing world. The Quaker

Fig. 78 View Looking West on Main Street with Masonic Lodge Hall (1802) on Right Beyond Brick Flank of Pacific National Bank.

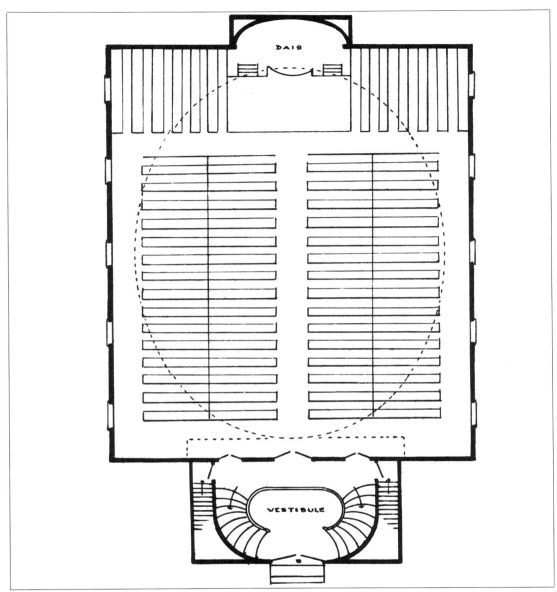

DAIS

VESTIBULE

Fig. 79 (left) Second Congregational Church (now Unitarian-Universalist) (1809 with additions), 11 Orange Street.
Fig. 80 (above) Principal-Floor Plan of Second Congregational Church After 1844 Remodeling.

self-sufficiency in humility had given way to moderate pride. One consideration in home building now was a desire to provoke admiration. Such worldliness came about through an increase in wealth. For the few, the new opulence set new standards and sought new trends in architecture that were to culminate in the middle of the nineteenth century. The authority for proper forms was the cult of international classicism, which took a special twist in America, becoming the Greek Revival style, the principal interest of the ensuing chapter.

Fig. 81 Pacific National Bank (1818), 61 Main Street.

Notes

1   Alexander Starbuck, *The History of Nantucket,* Boston, 1924, pp. 357–358.

2   Harry B. Turner, *Nantucket Argument Settlers,* Nantucket, 1917, 1920, 1924, 1926, 1936, 1944, 1946, 1959, and 1966.

3   Starbuck, *op. cit.,* p. 364.

4   Obed Macy, *The History of Nantucket,* Boston, 1835, p. 86.

5   William F. Macy, *The Story of Old Nantucket,* Boston, 1928, p. 188.

6   Starbuck, *op. cit.,* pp. 209–218.

7   George Allen Fowlkes, *A Mirror of Nantucket,* Nantucket, 1959, p. 42.

8   Starbuck, *op. cit.,* p. 319.

9   Knowlton Miner, *Old Houses of New England,* New York, 1929, pp. 235–238. The present owner, Mrs. Louis S. Edgarton, says that when the front of the house was shingled, an upright seam was found in the horizontal siding a few feet north of the main door; it was interpreted by the workmen as a former corner of the building.

10   Historic American Buildings Survey, Mass. 920, sheet 3 (first-floor plan).

11   Kenneth Duprey, *Old Houses on Nantucket,* New York, 1959, illus. p. 58.

12   Hugh Morrison, *Early American Architecture,* New York, 1952, pp. 272–291.

13   Batty Langley, *The Builder's Jewel,* originally London, 1741, American edition Boston, 1800; Abraham Swan, *The British Architect,* originally London, 1745, American edition Philadelphia, 1775 (the first book on architecture published in America).

14   Thomas Tileston Waterman, *The Mansions of Virginia, 1706–1776,* Chapel Hill, 1945, pp. 38–61, 214–220, 183–192; Architects' Emergency Committee, *Great Georgian Houses of America,* New York, 1933–37 (Dover 1970), Vol. I, pp. 34–38, 154–160; Vol. II, pp. 235–240; Donald (Macdonald-) Millar, *Some Colonial and Georgian Houses,* New York, 1916–30, Vol. II, plates 52–62; *Great Georgian Houses,* Vol. I, pp. 246–247.

15   According to a statement prepared by Eliza Mitchell (1809–96) *ca.* 1881. Courtesy Mr. and Mrs. Howard Olsen.

16   Duprey, *op. cit.,* illus. p. 158.

17   Katherine Seeler, "Phebe Folger's Watercolors," *Historic Nantucket,* October 1966, pp. 13–18, illus. p. 16. The original is in a sketch book in the collection of Philip Hofer.

18   M. M. Coffin, article, *Inquirer and Mirror,* October 7, 1965, p. 4.

19   A similar example is in a two-storied house at Edgartown, Martha's Vineyard, and another in a small house near Truro, Cape Cod. Alfred Easton Poor, *Colonial Architecture of Cape Cod, Nantucket and Martha's Vineyard,* New York, 1932 (Dover 1970), plates 95, 14.

20   Duprey, *op. cit.,* pp. /186/–/188/.

21   Fiske Kimball, "Moors' End, Nantucket, Massachusetts," *The Architectural Record,* September 1927, pp. 191–200.

22   Marjorie Drake Ross, *The Book of Boston,* New York, 1960–64, Vol. II, "The Federal Period, 1775 to 1838," pp. 120–121, 162–169.

23   The Jabez Wilder house at South Hingham, Massachusetts, is said to date from 1690. Morrison, *op. cit.,* p. 68. A Martha's Vineyard example, at West Tisbury, is pictured in Poor, *op. cit.,* plate 13.

24   A most informative article on this subject is Ernest Allen Connally, "The Cape Cod House: an Introductory Study," *Journal of the Society of Architectural Historians,* May 1960, pp. 47–56.

25   In his "Notes on Nantucket," August 1, 1807, the Rev. James Freeman describes the "Free Masons Hall" as "an elegant building with Ionick pilasters in front." (From Collections of the Massachusetts Historical Society, 2nd Series, Vol. III) Everett U. Crosby, *Nantucket In Print,* Nantucket, 1946, p. 127.

26   Fiske Kimball, *Domestic Architecture of the American Colonies and of the Early Republic,* New York, 1927, fig. 35 (p. 62), fig. 68 (p. 96).

27   On November 4, 1805, the lodge "Voted that the Image on top of the Hall be painted & where the water Issues through be putted." Alexander Starbuck, *A Century of Free Masonry,* Nantucket Historical Association, Vol. III, Bulletin No. 1, 1903, p. 24.

28   A photograph of the Masonic Lodge Hall predating 1872 is reproduced in the booklet, *Union Lodge, F. & A. M., Nantucket, Massachusetts,* published by the Inquirer and Mirror Press, Nantucket, 1941, facing p. 24.

29   Asher Benjamin, *The American Builder's Companion,* Boston, 1806, plate LVII.

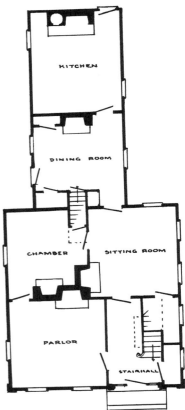

Fig. 82 (left) Façade of 12 Academy Lane.

Fig. 83 (above) Restored First-Floor Plan of 12 Academy Lane.

Chapter VII
The Classic and Greek Revival

A new era of affluence came to Nantucket with recovery from the War of 1812, which, as stated earlier, was not so prolonged as its recovery from the American Revolution. The second repulsion of the British bolstered national pride, and it sought expression in the creation of a new environment that showed an expanded cultural awareness and a demand for a more refined way of life. The archaic mode of centering family life in the kitchen was replaced among all but the most humble by a more active concern with the decorum of the parlor. The hearth-consciousness proper to the mainland Puritan was never so strong in the breast of the Nantucketer, whose vista ranged the seas and the continents beyond, and whose homes already contained mementoes of many foreign cultures. The then current international vogue for the Classic in general and the more strictly American focus upon the Greek Revival in particular were welcomed by the islanders and interpreted according to their understanding of them. Peace reigned and prosperity steadily increased for upward of three decades, or until the summer of 1846 when, on July 13th, the worst fire in Nantucket's history beset the town and devoured one seventh of the total area, including the waterfront north of present South Wharf and practically all of the commercial district. Close upon this catastrophe came another, more widespread in its effects, which the people of Nantucket could neither combat nor repair. It was the introduction of kerosene and gas for lighting, which dealt the whale-oil industry its death blow. The apprehension and unrest that followed resulted in a minor exodus, accelerated by the vision of unlimited wealth for the taking in the Gold Rush to California of 1849. But between the second war with England and the afflictions of the late 1840s, the classic trend—already seeded—germinated and flowered and endowed us with the most sophisticated manifestations of Nantucket architecture.

It is only natural that Americans would have become enamored of the English classic style of Sir John Soane, Robert and James Adam, William Pain, and James Paine: it was in their racial and cultural background. But remembrance of British tyranny and the unpleasant consequences of liberation sparked the desire for an alternative. Thomas Jefferson found inspiration in France from two sources. The first was in Roman antiquities, such as the best-preserved classic temple in Europe, the so-called Maison Carrée at Nîmes, which Jefferson used as a model in designing the Virginia Capitol (1785) at Richmond, in collaboration with Charles-Louis Clérisseau. The second was in buildings recently erected in Paris which he was able to examine during his tenure as ambassador to France (1784–89). Rousseau's Hôtel de Salm (1782), with terraces to the Seine, prompted a complete renovation of Jefferson's own home, Monticello, near Charlottesville. But the French taste was a bit too Gallic for the average American's Anglo-Saxon temperament. Curiously enough—or perhaps appropriately—the stimulus that received the most positive response and set the style for architecture in the United States for at least a third of a century prior to the Civil War came from England. It was four volumes of measured drawings of Greek temples by James Stuart and Nicholas Revett, entitled *The Antiquities of Athens,* published at London between 1762 and 1816 with a supplement in 1830. The great appeal of these monuments was that they symbolized the free city-states of ancient Greece rather than the pomposity of imperialist Rome, and soon (during the 1820s) the Greek War of Independence from the Turks struck a further strong chord of sympathy over here. Also, the architectural forms of Greece were simpler than those of Rome and made easier models for provincial artisans to follow.

The early imported British builder's guides had fallen into disfavor and had been supplanted by handbooks prepared and issued in the United States. The most popular author was Asher Benjamin, who conducted an architectural school at Boston and worked throughout New England, where a number of late eighteenth- and early nineteenth-century houses and churches are either by him or after his designs.[1] Benjamin first published *The Country Builder's Assistant* at Greenfield, Massachusetts, in 1797. For it, he borrowed designs for the orders from William Chambers' *A Treatise on Civil Architecture* (London, 1759), and structural details from Peter Nicholson's *The Carpenter's New Guide* (London, 1792). The second Benjamin book was *The American Builder's Companion,* Boston, 1806, and his most beautiful was *The Practical House Carpenter,* Boston, 1830. He produced seven books on architecture, which went into forty-five editions down to 1856 or 1857, some twelve years after his decease. American contemporaries of Asher Benjamin include: Owen Biddle (1 book, 8 editions or printings, 1805–58), Robert Griffith Hatfield (1 book, 6 or more printings, 1844–95), John Haviland (1 book, 2 editions, also an enlarged edition of Biddle, 1818–33), and Chester Hills (1 book, 4 printings, 1835–47).

The early builder's guides showed elements stylistically akin to the late Georgian, orders being greatly altered from ancient Roman archetypes for adaptation to wood construction and a light, decorative effect, quite unrelated to the stone construction of the originals. A change became apparent after the War of 1812, and its roots go back to the end of the eighteenth century. Benjamin Henry Latrobe, an Englishman born of an American mother, had come to the United States and built the first edifice in the New World in the Greek style. It was the Bank of Pennsylvania, designed in 1798 and completed in 1801. Like Jefferson's earlier Richmond Capitol, it was a temple-form building, but using the Greek rather than the Roman Ionic order and having porticos at both ends. The first Greek details appearing in an American handbook were in John Haviland's *The Builder's Assistant,* published in three volumes, from 1818 to 1821, at Philadelphia (the city of Latrobe's bank). The next manifestation was by the conservative Asher Benjamin, in the sixth enlarged edition of his second book, *The American Builder's Companion,* Boston, 1827. One notes that thirty years had elapsed since his first publication. The majority of the architectural books devoted primarily or exclusively to the Greek Revival were printed during the 1830s. Besides Haviland and Benjamin, the principal authors were Minard Lafever,

William Brown, William H. Ranlett, and Edward Shaw. Lafever's were the most influential. Altogether, his five titles went into fourteen editions between his first, in 1829, and last, published posthumously in 1856. The best known are *The Modern Builder's Guide* (New York, 1833) and *The Beauties of Modern Architecture* (New York, 1835). The use of the word "modern" in both is indicative of Lafever's conviction that antique forms were only to be used as inspiration for contemporary designs, not to be slavishly copied. The principle had been apparent in Latrobe's Bank of Pennsylvania, and it became the keynote of the Greek Revival in general.

As these instances suggest, there was more to the Greek Revival than an employment of Hellenic motifs, and, inasmuch as it became the national style during the middle decades of the nineteenth century, it merits a few words of analysis. Although classic designers like Thomas Jefferson, Charles Bulfinch, and Dr. William Thornton exploited Roman models for a grandeur of effect, crystallizing in the colossal-order portico, in many parts of the country there was little or no realization of this until after the introduction of the Greek. It was true for Nantucket, at least insofar as existing buildings are concerned. The first Atheneum, built as the Universalist Church in 1825, had a giant portico of four Ionic columns. The Washington House, on Main facing Federal Street, also had a huge tetrastyle portico. But the hotel burned in 1836 and the old library ten years later. The only Federal porticoes remaining are quite small, the semicircular Ionic on the Pacific National Bank, the arched Tuscan on the house on Academy Hill, and two transitional residences on Main Street and one on Orange (Appendix P). By contrast, the Greek Revival period has left us five two-storied porticoes: on the Methodist Church, the new Atheneum, and the Coffin School—the last two recessed—and on the residences at 94 and 96 Main Street. Thirty other Greek houses have one-story porticoes. Even in the smaller Greek porches, there is a sense of bigness and monumentality not found earlier, because of an adherence to the original antique (stone) proportions. Colossal pilasters, attached to the façade, may substitute for a free-standing portico, as on the Baptist Church and nearby house at 1 Pleasant Street; and, in one rare case, the motif becomes more pronounced in the form of square engaged piers or antae—on 14 Orange Street. The same characteristic applies to doorways, which have thick pilasters and full entablature, as at 78 Main Street where the doorway is of brownstone, like the later example on the south side of the Rotch Market, though hardly comparable to it in effect. The impressiveness of frontispieces on Greek buildings is accentuated by their being elevated on high basements and reached by a substantial flight of steps. The elevated basement generally became useful for the kitchen and, in two notable examples (96 Main and 1 Pleasant), for the dining room as well. The porchless entrance was deeply recessed for the shelter it afforded, but it is also illustrative of the Greek Revival ideal of spaciousness, of bringing a pocket of outside space into the volume of the building. The principle is more apparent inside, in soaring staircases around open wells and in wide doorways between parlors, allowing the flexibility of two rooms that become one. The fenestration down to floor level and the iron balcony outside in the double parlor at 1 Pleasant and the domed second-story ballroom at 94 Main are further indications of space-consciousness.

A great amount of design fluency in the Greek Revival period was achieved through new practice methods and technical advances. By the second quarter of the nineteenth century, there was considerable specialization in the building trade. The professional architect had come to the fore as the unqualified controller of the design. Unlike the earlier situation, when the builder was responsible for the structure and the carpenter or carver for its fittings, all elements were now planned by the architect. The unity achieved in earlier buildings was due to set modes of working and did not allow for creativity. The advantage of the new method was that it could

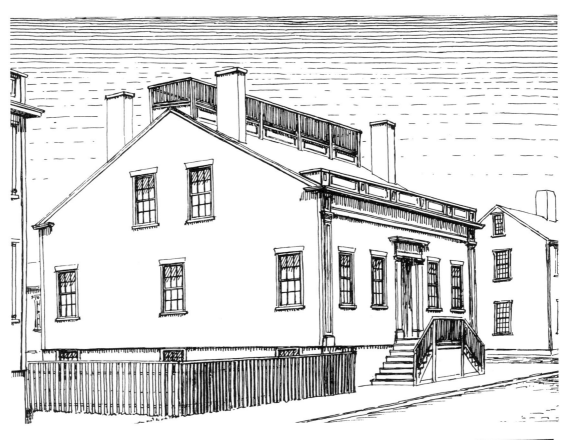

Fig. 84 Restored Sketch of Edward Hammond House (*ca.* 1830), 39 Orange Street.

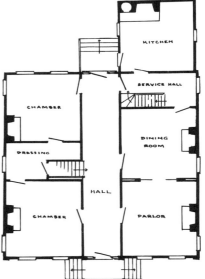

Fig. 85 Restored First-Floor Plan of Edward Hammond House.

achieve rather radical departures while retaining unity. In the Greek era, we find a considerable variety of types. The supervisory responsibility given the architect prompted him to engage in inventiveness as a matter of pride. He took advantage of the various skilled workers now at his command: wood carvers for elaborate column capitals and cartouches, marble carvers for mantels, plaster workers for centerpieces and cornices, iron forgers and casters for fences and outside trim, and the new steam-powered machinery which ran off plain moldings at an unprecedented rate. Mass-production in itself contributed to the bigness of design proper to the Greek Revival style. On lesser structures, it tended toward standardization and sameness, and we have to look to the more ambitious projects for the aesthetic rewards of which the system was capable.

The dichotomy between the greater and lesser buildings of the second quarter of the nineteenth century with regard to their inclusion of or indifference toward the new principles leaves us without tangible means of identifying all examples as belonging to the period. Details furnish such a measure. The obvious hallmark of the Greek Revival is the doorway framed by broad, flat pilasters with bases and capitals and an equally heavy entablature spanning the void between them. A characteristic molding is a sort of flat splay, rounded under at the outer edge, that appears as echinus in the capital, as crown molding in the cornice, in interior door and window frames, and, in reduced scale, encircling the panels in doors. The six-panel door of two small divisions at the top and four taller (set two-over-two) below is Federal. The distinctive Greek door presents two tall upright panels side by side. More often it has two or three short panels at the bottom and an equal number of taller panels above (9 Pleasant). The old pegged-plank window frame became obsolete and was replaced by a Federal type with narrow half-round sides and a flat lintel with splayed extremities (like a broad wedge shape—20 Union). The later Federal and Greek version has a convex member at the top as well as sides, the lintel included, oftentimes, surmounting it (72 Main, 78 Orange). Other Greek types have flat exterior frames with a deeper architrave capped by a horizontal or low sloping cornice (96 Main), or with a stepped member outlined by a raised fillet making angular helices (1 Pleasant Street, and the Baptist Church on Summer). Inside the house, door and window casings became heavier, frequently with shaped moldings and corner blocks. Fireplaces were accented by a pilaster-entablature treatment, like what framed the front door. Staircases (unless enclosed by walls) invariably had open stringers and banisters, and a plain square newel or one of complex round vase or baluster form.

To clarify these generalized distinctions, let us compare two specific houses, one Federal and the other Greek Revival, which are close to one another in size as well as location. The older, the Alexander Bunker house at 8 Academy Lane, was illustrated in the foregoing chapter *(Figs. 76–77);* the later is two doors away, 12 Academy Lane *(Figs. 82–83).* Both houses are one-and-three-quarters-storied and have gables at the sides. Both have a kitchen ell at the rear. The main block of the later house is about two feet wider than its neighbor. Its façade has only two, rather than three, windows, though the doorway is flanked by sidelights and is recessed between pilasters. The clapboard front also has pilasters stationed at each outer corner and sustaining a plain architrave and cornice. As in 8 Academy Lane, the first-floor accommodations are contained in three rooms around a center chimney. Number 12 has a staircase in the front hall in addition. The railing makes a volute at the base and encircles an open well. There is a shallow closet at the foot and another behind, partly under the steps. A back stairs ascends from the first room in the ell. This is the dining room and may originally have been the kitchen, if the back room is a later addition. It now serves as a bedroom and bath, so the cooking fireplace in the second room is conjectural. There are three chambers on the second floor. The interior woodwork is transitional in character.

Figs. 76–77,
Figs. 82–83

The symmetrical house with end gables, so prevalent during the Greek period on the mainland, materialized in the island town with Nantucket peculiarities. A representative early example is 39 Orange Street, built about 1830 for Edward Hammond. The story-and-three-quarters residence has been considerably altered, but its original form has remained mostly constant *(Fig. 84)*. From inside the basement, the first-story framing shows that there had been four chimneys against the outer walls. These served as many rooms, two on either side of a transverse hall, with a half-space between those to the south and another at the rear to the north *(Fig. 85)*. The last was a service stairhall, behind the dining room and parlor and connecting with a kitchen in the rear ell.[2] The other small space was a dressing room between two bedrooms. The principal staircase was incorporated here, between walls, its handrail mounted on a ramp adjoining the front chamber, so that virtually only the carved newel post at the base was displayed. Despite the liberties taken with the inner space, the shell of the house proper adhered to a strict bilateral symmetry. In the façade, the center doorway is flanked by a pair of windows right and left. Each end wall had three windows in the main story and two above. At some later period the original chimneys were ripped out, including the foundations. The two rooms to the north were joined into a single living room with a fireplace in the southwest corner, and the rear chamber was extended into the area of the hall for a large dining room, its fireplace centered on the north wall

Fig. 84

Fig. 85

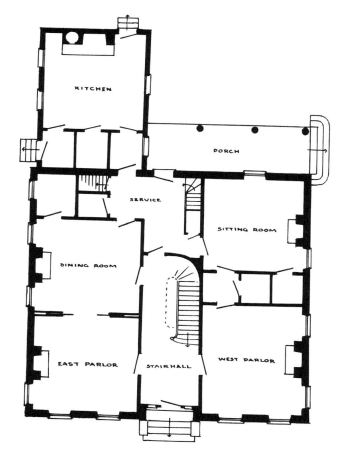

in the new chimney.[3] The old kitchen was exchanged for an addition spanning the rear of the house. New windows at both levels were cut into the side walls, and Dutch and gabled dormers were set upon the roof, replacing a modest parapet over the cornice, though without disturbing the roof walk atop the ridge.

The house with center hall and four end chimneys appeared most often as a full two-storied building during the Greek Revival era, as at 10 Hussey, and 72 and 98 Main Street. These are of frame construction. The type also was executed in brick. Numbers 75 and 78 Main, across the street from one another, were constructed by James Field (master builder) and Christopher Capen (head mason) for Henry and Charles G. Coffin in 1831–33, and they may be considered transitional Federal Classic to Greek Revival in style *(Fig. 86)*. The half-round engaged-columned doorway and baluster insets in the parapet of 75 belong to the earlier period, whereas the heavy pilastered doorway in brownstone of 78 is decidedly Greek. However, the high basement and recessed entrance of the former are Greek, whereas the terrace with its spike fence of the latter is Federal. Other external features can be either. Number 75 has a cupola. The houses are the same size except that the rear ell of 75 is two-storied. In the transverse hall of each is a long flight of steps that curves at the top around an open well *(Fig. 87)*. The floor plans are reversed, so that corresponding rooms occur on the east or west side. With plenty of space for bedrooms

Fig. 86

Fig. 87

Fig. 88 Starbuck Houses ("Three Bricks"—1836–38), 93, 95, and 97 Main Street.

upstairs, the first story provides east and west parlors in front, and a dining room and sitting room behind, with closets between the rooms on the west side and service stairs and rooms behind the two on the east, the kitchen adjoining. The interior fittings are Federal, the wood trim around doors and windows having running moldings and corner blocks, and the black marble mantels in the main rooms having colonnettes, frieze panels, and imposts.[4] Wood mantels in the bedrooms are somewhat heavier and therefore more Greek. The Quaker background of the Coffins, as Quaker restraint was understood in the early 1830s, has had a restraining influence upon the two houses.

Matching houses for brothers recur farther along Main Street in the three externally identical residences of William, Matthew, and George Starbuck, numbers 93, 95, and 97, known *Fig. 88* as "East Brick," "Middle Brick," and "West Brick" *(Fig. 88)*. They were begun three years after the Coffin houses were finished, and the same mason worked on them, though another builder, James Childs, was brought from the mainland. Of the two just considered, the trio resemble more closely the Henry Coffin house, having windowless, high granite basements and parapets with baluster insets above the cornice in front, stepped brick parapets on the gable ends, and a cupola

Fig. 89 Jared Coffin House (1845), 29 Broad Street.

on the roof, elements not found on the Charles G. Coffin house. In addition, the Starbuck residences have distyle porticoes, the Greek Ionic columns set on antepodia, or projecting blocks, between which rise the front steps. The portico is without pilaster supports against the wall but has a pretty decorative crowning device. The early iron fence (intact only in front of 97) is Gothic in design: the posts are clustered colonnettes with pinnacle caps. Interiors of the Starbuck houses are on the order of those of the Coffin houses, but they are not alike. For instance, there are black marble mantels in the principal rooms of "East Brick," whereas in "West Brick" the corresponding chimneypieces are of wood.[5]

The greatest house of this type is that of Jared Coffin, 29 Broad Street, erected in 1845 full three-stories high *(Fig. 89)*. Except for its extra height, it bears a remarkable affinity to the Starbuck designs, having a plain granite basement front, windows above with stone lintels, a distyle Ionic portico, and a parapet above the cornice. It even has a similar cupola, although it is at the apex of a hip roof. Monotony is avoided in the three tiers of windows by giving triple lights to those on an axis with the frontispiece. Granite posts and iron railings on the stone retaining wall of the encircling terrace show off the building to advantage. Jared Coffin had the mansion

Fig. 89

Fig. 90 24 Hussey Street.

built because his former home, Moors' End, was too far from the center of town to please his wife, but Nantucket proved too provincial for her after all, and the family moved to Boston. The house was untenanted when the disastrous fire of July 13, 1846, raged through the town up to its corner. The building was saved because it was all masonry, including the roof slates from Wales. The residence was sold to the Nantucket Steamboat Company, which turned it into a hotel called The Ocean House, and it has remained a hostelry down to the present day.

     The radical new look of the Federal period had been the innovation of chimneys at the outer sides of houses. It appeared quite frequently. An even more drastic change in the external appearance was introduced at the end of the Federal period but did not leave its imprint very much until the Greek Revival. This involved a reorientation of the house form, whereby the gable was turned about to face the street. We have seen the phenomenon in Nantucket earlier
Fig. 36 in gambrel-roof commercial buildings on Main Street *(Fig. 36)*, but the new manifestation was in residences. The roof pitch becomes lower than before and raking cornices have an unprecedented overhang; as often as not, the gable is developed into a triangular pediment, which in itself explains the lower pitch of the roof. It occurs first on two-storied houses, as 22 and 24
Fig. 90 Hussey Street *(Fig. 90)*. The three-bayed façades are inverted and show variations in trim. The doorways are off center and have sidelights enclosed by pilasters and entablature. There are tall, narrow pilasters at the corners of the buildings as well, and these connect with encompassing entablatures. The shafts of 24 Hussey have square pierced blocks at the summit substituting for capitals. The windows are framed in moldings like inside woodwork with corner blocks. Here the crowning pediment had a low arched window divided into three parts. The pediment of 22
Fig. 91 Hussey displays a superb leaded window, triangular outside and embracing a wheel motif *(Fig. 91)*. Its doorway has attenuated fluted pilasters with entasis to either side. This doorway, the window

Fig. 91 22 Hussey Street.

Fig. 92 32–34 Pine Street at Turn of Century.

Fig. 92

Fig. 93

Fig. 94

trim of both houses, and the corner shafts and lunettes in the pediments are all Federal motifs. From a count of five front-gable designs of the late Federal period, amounting to a mere fraction of the total number of two-storied houses built, the proportion of this type rose to one third of the number of two-storied houses constructed during the Greek Revival era (Appendices H, 1 and I, 1). The full architectural dress is vital to the attractiveness of the building, as one can see by comparing the original façade of 32 Pine Street in an old photograph with its stripped condition today *(Fig. 92)*. There are no smaller gable-front houses in the Federal period, whereas in the Greek, about half of the story-and-three-quarters cottages built have their roof ends to the street (Appendices H, 2 and I, 2).

An appealing and localized type of Nantucket Greek cottage is clapboarded on all sides and raised on a high brick basement. There are substantial pilasters with paneled shafts at the corners, sustaining full entablatures that span the flanks of the building. Three upper windows occupy this level within the front gable area. Raking cornices drop too low to allow for full-size rectangular outer windows, which are therefore given quarter-round heads. The resulting shutter pattern is unusual but acceptable in its logic. The best preserved façade is 72 Centre Street *(Fig. 93)*. The railings framing the stoop dip down both sides of the front stairs and curve outward to square posts. A spike fence completes the paling and relates the house to sidewalk and street. There are many houses like this in Nantucket (one of them next door, 70 Centre Street), and there were others. Considering its present condition, it is difficult to believe that the business house at 10 Federal Street, across from the post office, was once one of them *(Fig. 94)*.

Fig. 93 Façade of 72 Centre Street.

Fig. 94 Southwest Corner Federal and India Streets (10 Federal Street).

Variations of the façade may have a slightly higher roof pitch and corbel-arched or triangular-headed second-story windows (6 Winter and originally 5 North Water—see Chapter Eight), or two in place of three upper windows (38 and 49 Cliff Road).

The off-center doorway seems a bit incongruous in the façade of a house using a style as formal as the Greek Revival. A happy solution to the problem was to make the front openings all windows and put the main entrance somewhere on the side. Number 123 Main Street, built for George Wendell Macy in 1840, has a gabled street face about equal to that of the type of house just discussed, and, like the two Cliff Road dwellings, having two-over-three windows.

Fig. 95   A cupola crowns the roof *(Fig. 95)*. The principal doorway is sheltered by a single-column portico at the front of a one-story projection on the east side. A second projection, farther back, shelters a service door, over which a pointed gable embraces a delightful "Gothic" window. The plan provides several surprises. One enters a crosswise stairhall with steps that curve around an

Fig. 96   open well *(Fig. 96)*. The front quarter of the house is a parlor, which is half again as large as the average in Nantucket, having three windows on the long side. It is divided by a steamboat-gothic arch one third of the way from the west end, and a closet protrudes awkwardly in the north corner. The room never had a fireplace and was presumably heated by a stove set up in winter, if at all. On the west side, there are two chambers behind, one with fireplace. The dining room is beyond the stairhall. It originally had a fireplace although not at present. A twenty-four-foot square ell at the rear is more than half occupied by a tremendous kitchen, and the balance is divided

Fig. 95 George Wendell Macy House (1840), 123 Main Street.

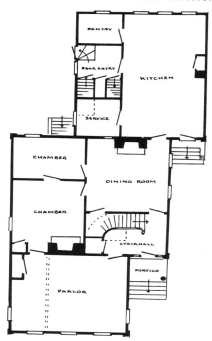

Fig. 96 Restored First-Floor Plan of George Wendell Macy House.

Fig. 97 Levi Starbuck House (1838), 14 Orange Street.

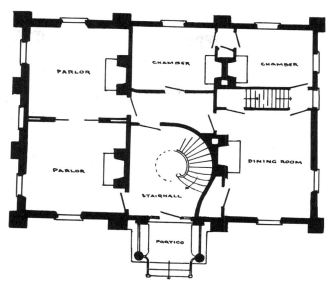

Fig. 98 Restored First-Floor Plan of Levi Starbuck House.

into a serving room (with serving window alongside the dining-room chimney), entry with stairs to cellar and second floor, and a pantry. A three-quarters story covers the entire house. At the front, over the parlor, an upstairs sitting room has a vaulted ceiling springing from short columns in the four corners of the room, and a colonnetted mantel on the west wall. It contains no fire-place but has provision for a stove flue behind the partition connecting to the chimney on the north side, an arrangement not without potential hazard. The rooms immediately behind make use of arch and vault forms.

A similar house, without the rear section, is 17 Pleasant Street.

An obsolete idea rejuvenated in the Greek period was the orientation of the front of the house southward, so that the gable or pedimented end was on the street side. Two-story examples are 31 and 53 Centre Street, the latter with distyle Ionic portico and capital volutes turned toward the entrance walk, as at 123 Main. The most distinguished of the group is 14 Orange Street, constructed in 1838 by William M. Andrews, a builder, and sold to Levi Starbuck. The house has many special features, some of them sacrificing convenience for architectural effect, which one attributes to Andrews' working to please himself rather than a client. The strictly rectangular building follows a rigid scheme imposed by an even spacing of square piers or antae dividing south, west, and north sides each into three bays *(Fig. 97).* The effect is massive, and it reminds one of a design by Minard Lafever that was published in the year in which the Orange Street house was built. The Lafever scheme for a formal country villa was shown in perspective on plate 3 in *The Modern Practice of Staircase and Hand-rail Construction.* It has a two-storied center pavilion with a three-bayed pedimented front upheld by four massive square supports. The door is on the side, opening onto one of the matching flanking colonnades with rounded ends and embracing curved rooms. Four chimneys rise over the roof of the principal block. The plans, however, are not analogous. The architect in Nantucket has fitted a small two-columned Ionic portico with side benches and railings between the centermost piers on the south side. As on the Starbuck houses on Main Street, the portico has a parapet, but unlike the others it possesses pilasters against the wall. Number 14 Orange is an all-wood house, whose boards are affixed flush, rather than overlapping like clapboards, and therefore resemble ashlar masonry or stucco

Fig. 97

Fig. 99 William H. Crosby House (1837), 1 Pleasant Street.

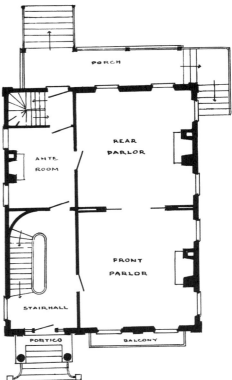

Fig. 100 Restored First-Floor Plan of William H. Crosby House.

Fig. 101 William Hadwen House (mid-1840s), 96 Main Street.

surfacing. Simple details are placed strategically, such as the Greek key or meander at the top and bottom of the anta panels and in the upper window heads. One absolutely unique feature is the blind windows centered on the street side, which, instead of the usual closed outside shutters, have glazed sashes behind which are paneled inside shutters. They back up to a partition between the parlors downstairs and chambers above. Despite the regulative limitations imposed from without, the plan of the house shows remarkable variety *(Fig. 98)*. The entrance hall is dominated by a circular open-newel staircase bounded by a curved wall. To the west are the twin parlors, each with chimneybreast against the inside wall, and joined or separated by sliding doors. Although the mantels are plain, baseboards are exceedingly high and cornices quite elaborate, composed of double acanthus and grape borders, and the walls are decorated with large

Fig. 98

Fig. 102 George W. Wright House (*ca.* 1845), 94 Main Street, Portico Detail.

panel stencils.[6] The largest single room in the house is the dining room, which is reached through a passageway behind the stairhall. The curve at the front of the staircase provides space for a china closet off the dining room. The kitchen being in the basement, service was performed through the secondary stairs at the east end of the house. Two chambers, one perhaps an office, completed the accommodations of the first story on the north side. There were additional bedrooms on the second floor, and, because of the full entablature encircling the house, considerable space was provided on the third floor, lighted by wide, arched windows in the pediments. The east flank, away from the street, was not meant to be viewed and has piers only at the corners, with windows placed where convenient to the rooms. A single-storied kitchen wing later was attached here.

Originally a house of equally severe rectangular mass and made three-bayed at the front by colossal-order pilasters is 1 Pleasant Street. It was built in 1837 by Henry Macy for William H. Crosby. The walls are clapboarded between the pilasters, and the façade is crowned by a pediment. A square belvedere is astride the roof. The entrance is in the first bay, sheltered by a portico with two channeled Doric columns set on granite antepodia, with steps of the same material between, and iron railings connecting to a pair of granite posts, an iron fence once continuing along the sidewalk, as at the Jared Coffin house on Broad Street *(Fig. 99)*. First-story windows at front, north side, and rear are floor length with three six-paned sashes, as in some

Fig. 99

Fig. 103 Methodist Church (1822–24, portico 1840), 2 Centre Street.

Fig. 100

of Thomas Jefferson's best houses, such as Monticello and Farmington near Charlottesville. An iron balcony initially spanned the pair facing the street. The fenestration imparts a light and airy effect to the double parlors, which occupy more than half the first floor *(Fig. 100)*. The windows are equipped with folding inside shutters, in three tiers, and there are great sliding doors between the rooms. Chimneybreasts on the outside wall are adorned with gray marble mantels in Gothic style, with Tudor arches over the fireplaces and spandrel panels. The principal staircase rose around an open oblong well from the basement, where, without precedent in Nantucket except for the Block on Orange Street, the dining room as well as the kitchen was situated. A service stairway was at the southwest corner of the building. Four bedrooms and dressing rooms were on the second floor and a chamber and attic space on the third. The top story is made possible by a fairly steep roof, which distorts the shape of the front pediment. An extension on the south side, elongated into a wing at the back, dating from the turn of the century, adds space for extra rooms but nullifies the impact of the former simple shape.

Two nearby residences stand for the culmination of the Greek Revival style on Nantucket, as they alone are endowed with colossal-order porticoes. Both were built by Frederick Brown Coleman for William Hadwen during the mid-1840s, 96 Main Street for Hadwen himself and 94 Main for a niece, Hadwen's adopted daughter. The sponsor of the projects came from Newport, Rhode Island, which may account in part for the elegance of the houses. Number 94 is similar to the Captain Augustus Littlefield residence at 76 Pelham Street, built in 1838–40.[7] That the plans were by a Newport architect (as has been claimed) seems unlikely, as Coleman was perfectly capable of devising them. Both buildings are clapboarded and their walls articulated by tall pilasters. That on the corner has a five-bayed façade with centered tetrastyle Ionic portico

Fig. 101

(Fig. 101). It embodies a middle-stairhall plan. The twin parlors on the west side have mantels identical to those in 1 Pleasant Street, and the dining room and kitchen were in the basement.

Though smaller, 94 Main Street is the more interesting building. It manifests a prostyle temple form with Corinthian columns whose campaniform capitals are embellished with acanthus and anthemion ornaments, a more elaborate version of the order of the Tower of the Winds at Athens, made familiar to the West through Stuart and Revett's *Antiquities,* the original having

Fig. 102

only grasses attached to the upper flare *(Fig. 102)*. The entablature of the Nantucket house exhibits both dentils and modillions. Square-piered flankers, becoming service rooms behind, give further distinction to the external architectural design. The main block is equal in size to 1 Pleasant Street and the original floor plan was similar, only the rear room was used for dining, as the kitchen alone was in the basement. The chimneybreasts were against inside walls, that in the parlor being still in place, although stripped of fireplace and flues; the mantel, like those in 1 Pleasant and 96 Main, was affixed to the new outside chimney in the ballroom above. This second-story domed interior with adjoining domed stairhall constitutes the handsomest suite in Nantucket. The domes are ornamented with upright panels set with plaster rosettes, the stairhall walls with recessed niches containing classic sculptures; entablatures in both are sustained by Corinthian pilasters styled after the order of the Olympieion at Athens, and the overdoors decorated with carved anthemions and scrolls in the manner of Minard Lafever.[8] The ballroom floor was constructed with a system that deflects vibrations to avoid possible damage to the parlor ceiling below. Extensive alterations were made to the house in 1927: the entire first floor was rebuilt with new joists, the inappropriate paneling and fireplace were installed on the west wall in the parlor, its former mantel was moved upstairs, and the rear half of the

---

Fig. 104 First Baptist Church (1840), 1 Summer Street.

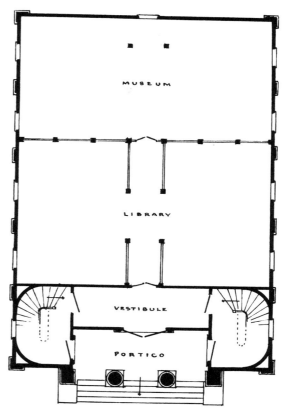

Fig. 105 (left) The Atheneum (1847), 1 India Street.

Fig. 106 (right) Restored First-Floor Plan of Atheneum.

house was changed radically. The first-story façade trim and the external chimney stack, which cuts so awkwardly through the cornice on the west side of the house, were part of the unfortunate renovation. However, it is said that the building was in a very dilapidated condition and barely escaped being razed.

The two Hadwen houses were connected by a granite retaining wall supporting a pedestal fence, similar in kind to that at the Atheneum, also built by Coleman, a couple of years later. A small section remains intact at the east end of 94 Main. The balustrade around 96 Main is in the Neo-Classic manner made popular by the World's Columbian Exposition at Chicago in 1892–93. An old photograph (probably by J. Freeman), predating 1876, mounted on a map of Nantucket displayed at the Philadelphia Centennial and now owned by the Nantucket Historical Association, shows the original paling.

Frederick Brown Coleman changed the appearance of Nantucket more than any other individual. If he did not, like Augustus, find Rome a city of brick and leave it one of marble, at least Coleman left Nantucket with a number of impressive wooden porticoes. In addition to those on the Hadwen houses, he is thought to have added the hexastyle, plain-shafted Ionic portico to the earlier Methodist Church at the head of Centre Street *(Fig. 103).* That was in 1840, and in the same year he designed and built the First Baptist Church on Summer Street *(Fig. 104).* A portico was planned for it but was deleted because of the cost. The building instead was given a façade with four pilasters supporting an entablature, a pediment much too steep

Fig. 103

Fig. 104

for a classic building, and a tower of four superimposed diminishing cubes finished with an octagonal steeple and weathervane.

Coleman's masterpiece is the Atheneum on lower India or Pearl Street, built to replace its predecessor destroyed in the Great Fire of 1846. Coleman here served as full-fledged architect; Charles Wood was the builder or contractor for the building. The original Atheneum was the former Universalist Church of 1825, perhaps having the first colossal-order portico on the island. Its successor has the same rectangular shape but is more powerful in design, the walls articulated by giant pilasters rising to the encircling entablature, the spaces between filled with flush boards—as at 14 Orange Street—and having, on the flanks, two tiers of windows capped

Fig. 105 by hoods *(Fig. 105).* The façade has an impressive monumentality. It is windowless, like an ancient Aegean temple, with pilasters at the outer corners, the entire south front covered by a pediment. Fluted piers project forward, embracing a recessed portico with a pair of fluted Ionic columns *in antis,* and this architectural unit also is pedimented. The great portal itself is framed by pilasters and capped with a pediment. The front yard is enclosed by a low railed fence with pedestal posts on brick foundations. One approaches the building via a brick walk on axis, and steps ascend between the plinths of the columns. A lateral hall extended across the building back of the portico and connected twin stairhalls in the front corners, which were accessible also from the

Fig. 106 portico *(Fig. 106).* The stairs wound up into vestibules to the lecture hall with coved ceiling occupying most of the second story. The first story housed the library and museum.[9] The area was conceived with considerable flexibility, the weight of the upper floor being supported on alignments of square piers, with screen walls between that could be removed if the occasion demanded. The arrangement suggests a corridor down the center, with a row of supports dividing the front from the rear half. The building was heated by iron stoves in winter. The interior was changed considerably when it became a public library in 1900. The east staircase was removed and another installed in the northeast corner of the building. A part of the basement was refurbished for a children's reading room in 1963, and in 1966 a one-story wing was added, providing a fireproof vault for rare materials.[10] The adjoining lot was landscaped into a small formal garden.

The great impetus for Greek Revival buildings in downtown Nantucket was the necessity of rebuilding after the 1846 fire, at which time the Greek happened to be the style in vogue. One lesson learned from the harrowing experience was the advisability of constructing in masonry, so the north side of Main from Cod Lane to Centre and part of the south side east of Orange Street became the sites for two-storied brick commercial buildings. The block west of Federal presents the greatest variety, the first shop on the corner retaining its piered first story, and both it and its neighbor having pilastered second stories. Numbers 43–45 Main constitute a seven-bayed façade, of which five are crowned by a pediment. Numbers 47, 51, 55, and 57 Main Street present a fourteen-bayed façade, of which the centermost six are pedimented. The west end of this building, on Centre Street, is as positive in design and handsome as the front. It is nine-bayed and pedimented, the tympanum broken by a false stepped parapet. An entablature spans seven voids, and the second-story windows are set in shallow panels. To a large extent, the cornices of these buildings are also of brick.

Just north on Centre Street is a handsome frame block constituting a seven-part composition. Built for George Harris and Benjamin F. Riddell, its sections alternate from one to two stories, with a seven-bayed focus on Sherburne Hall, the headquarters of the Independent Order

Fig. 107 Sherburne Hall (after 1846), 7–21 Centre Street.

of Odd Fellows *(Fig. 107)*. The building is pilastered and pedimented and flanked by smaller, double-storied, three-bayed pavilions, each one shop away. Railings over the cornice of the low sections give unity to the group, which includes the odd numbers from 7 to 21 Centre Street.

Fig. 107

More severe forms are the warehouses and factories belonging to this period. The warehouse of Thomas Macy on Straight Wharf and the Richard Mitchell & Sons Candle Factory at 11 Broad are similar two-and-a-half-storied, five-bayed brick structures with pedimented front gables. The former has window and door sills and lintels of granite, and iron rings for solid shutters *(Fig. 108)*. It was renovated in 1944 as an art gallery. The old candle factory was converted into the whaling museum in 1929, at which time the Federal-manner doorway, suitable to the building in neither period nor character, was installed.

Fig. 108

A later Greek Revival edifice in Nantucket deserving mention is the Coffin School. In 1827, Admiral Sir Isaac Coffin of the British navy endowed the Lancastrian School for the benefit of all Tristram Coffin descendants. Classes were held on Fair Street until the new building at 4 Winter Street was completed in 1852. Having a recessed portico, it bears a resemblance to the Atheneum, but it achieves neither the logic nor the refinement of the earlier building *(Fig. 109)*. Except for the pair of wood Doric columns *in antis,* all of the vertical structure is of masonry. The basement is of limestone in front and granite on the sides; the walls above and even the members of the entablature and pediment are of brick. The great axial doorway is false, the real entrances being the small doors to left and right of the porch. In the south vestibule, stairs ascend to the upper part of the building, but the main part of the school was a single large room, with a two-storied section at the rear. An extension at the west end was added in 1918.[11] An open belfry straddles the roof ridge. The cast-iron fence at the front of the lot is an unusual feature, its bold and simple design (halberd or harpoon motif?) in perfect accord with the architecture.

Fig. 109

The Classic and Greek Revival came to Nantucket at the peak of its opulence and cultural awareness and contributed some of the island's most impressive and interesting monuments. No former era of equal duration showed such diversity of types. There was a perseverance of early smaller forms in a new dress and also a wide range of innovations, such as pedimented fronts of all sizes and an elegance made possible by affixing temple porticoes to building façades. There were also new achievements in interior planning derived from shifting former centrally located chimneys to outside walls, installing soaring staircases around open wells, arranging rooms in suites with wide doorways between, and sometimes resorting to coved-ceiling and domed rooms. A good many elegant public buildings constructed during the period gave an urbanity to the Little Gray Lady by the Sea. Most of the brick buildings of the town were erected under the aegis of the Greek Revival. Variety in fence types, some iron and finely modeled, some wood and substantial, supplemented the recently paved cobblestone streets and elm-planted sidewalks, and these combined with the architecture to create an attractive community environment.

Fig. 108 Thomas Macy Warehouse (1847), Straight Wharf.

Fig. 109 Coffin School (1852), 4 Winter Street.

Notes

1   His churches include examples in Windsor, Vermont, and Northampton, Massachusetts, and the Charles Street Meetinghouse and West Church in Boston, which was compared in the preceding chapter to the Unitarian Church in Nantucket. Vermont builder Lavins Fillmore borrowed a Benjamin design for his First Congregational Church in Bennington, 1800.

2   The north and west sides of the service ell are shown in an old photograph of Plumb Lane in the collection of the Nantucket Historical Association.

3   Views of the house made in the early 1870s and about 1880, the first a stereopticon by J. Freeman from the tower of the Unitarian church, and the second looking north on Orange Street from the bend, show a single chimney at the peak of the south gable, probably serving an early furnace.

4   Kenneth Duprey, *Old Houses on Nantucket,* New York, 1959, pp. /189/–193.

5   *Ibid.,* pp. 194–201.

6   *Ibid.,* pp. /202/–205.

7   Antoinette F. Downing and Vincent J. Scully, Jr., *The Architectural Heritage of Newport, Rhode Island,* Cambridge, Mass., 1952, p. 110, pl. 150.

8   Duprey, *op. cit.,* pp. 207–/210/.

9   Sarah F. Barnard, "The Nantucket Atheneum," *The Inquirer and Mirror,* April 21, 1900, p. 4.

10   *The Nantucket Atheneum,* leaflet prepared by the library in 1970 as a memorial to Philip Swain McConnell.

11   *The Vocational School on Nantucket Island,* Massachusetts, a leaflet prepared about 1955 for fund-raising purposes.

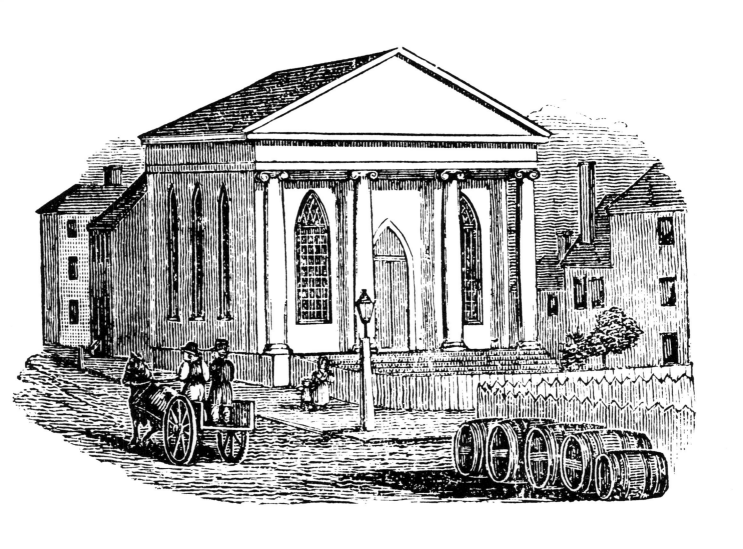

Fig. 110 Universalist Church (1825), Northeast Corner India and Federal Streets. Became the Atheneum in 1834.

134   THE ARCHITECTURE OF HISTORIC NANTUCKET

Chapter VIII

Gothic Revival and Romantic Touches

The most drastic stylistic change in American architecture—and in Nantucket—was the introduction of the Gothic Revival. The Gothic itself was no stranger to the New World, since the earliest buildings along the Atlantic seaboard were executed in this manner. The Jethro Coffin and Richard Gardner houses are examples. The later Gothic Revival, however, bore only a superficial resemblance, in its steep roofs, lozenge-paned windows, and its aspect of quaintness, which was altogether self-conscious and not natural as before.

The Gothic Revival came to the United States from England, as had the Greek Revival, though Americans made the Greek their national style while reserving the Gothic for religious and romantic interludes. The Gothic had been developed in the Middle Ages primarily for churches, monasteries, and great cathedrals, and it always was regarded as the Christian style. In England it had never been abandoned for church building, and classical architects such as Sir Christopher Wren and Sir John Vanbrugh, who looked upon the style as "barbarian," were nonetheless persuaded to accept commissions for houses of worship in this manner. Early in the nineteenth century, to combat lawlessness and vice and encourage a return to religion, the British government passed the Church Building Act. Out of 214 new buildings erected, 177 were imitations of the medieval mode.[1] Its sober aspect was balanced by a romantic, literary side. To be sure, this aspect sometimes was somber too, in the verses of the Graveyard Poets for example, but the Gothic served especially well as a setting for the romances or novels of the eighteenth and nineteenth centuries, and each of the chief literary figures of the age built himself a suitable castle. Thus, Horace Walpole, author of *The Castle of Otranto,* built Strawberry Hill (1753–78), for which Thomas Gray—famous for his poem, "Elegy Written in a Country Churchyard"—acted as archaeology adviser. William Beckford, who wrote the extravaganza *Vathek,* had Sir James Wyatt design and construct his Fonthill Abbey (1796–1807), one of the outstanding follies of all time. The best-known writer of the period, Sir Walter Scott, commissioned William Atkinson to build Abbotsford in 1812, which stimulated and inspired his composing of the Waverly novels that found an eager reading public in America. Other books that promoted the Gothic Revival were not literary but illustrative, for example the works of Augustus Welby Pugin, a draftsman in the office of John Nash, who set him to collecting architectonic details for use in his own compositions. Pugin's main publication was *Specimens of Gothic Architecture* (London, 1825), and the author-artist-architect himself built over sixty-five churches throughout the United Kingdom and was responsible for much of the visible body of Westminster Palace or the Houses of Parliament (1840–60) in London.

The first Gothic Revival design in America was conceived by Benjamin Henry Latrobe in 1799, when he was working on the first Greek Revival edifice in Philadelphia. The romantic example was Sedgeley, William Crammond's country villa built in what is now Fairmount Park. The next important Gothic Revival house in the United States was Glenellen (1832), the Robert Gilmore villa outside Baltimore, designed by Ithiel Town and Alexander Jackson Davis of New York, whose firm was to create many such picturesque residences in the Hudson River Valley during the next few decades.[2] Davis furnished designs to illustrate the important books on horticulture and rural establishments by Andrew Jackson Downing of Newburgh, New York. Davis' plans were published independently as elegant portfolios, entitled *Rural Residences* (New York, 1837); but the Downing books, *A Treatise on the Theory and Practice of Landscape Gardening* (New York, 1841), with its chapter on "Landscape or Rural Architecture," and his *Cottage Residences* (New York, 1842) and *The Architecture of Country Houses* (New York, 1850) sparked a whole new trend of country living in a suitable setting, and through them the Davis designs were given widespread circulation and were much imitated.

Latrobe conceived Gothic plans for the Baltimore Cathedral in 1804, but the building was executed in a different style. His Philadelphia Bank (1807–8) at Fourth and Chestnut streets had a plain façade pierced by a tall recessed Tudor portal and superstructure with a rose window between buttresses capped by obelisks and narrow lancet windows to either side.[3] It was demolished about 1832. Another early Gothic building in Philadelphia was William Strickland's Masonic Hall (1809–11) at Chestnut and Eighth streets.[4] The first American town house in the style also stood on Chestnut Street. It was built by John Dorsey in 1810. After these came a whole host of churches, beginning in the east-coast cities in such notable structures as Richard Upjohn's Trinity Church (1839–46) on Broadway facing Wall Street, and James Renwick's Grace Church (1843–46) on Broadway at Tenth Street, New York, and Minard Lafever's Church of the Holy Trinity (1844–47) at Clinton Street and Montague, Brooklyn, and filtering inland from there.

These Gothic Revival essays are quite different from earlier "Gothic" church features in America, which correspond to the survivals of the medieval style in England into the Renaissance period. They constitute a poorly understood deviation from the main stream of Georgian design that may be called Rococo Gothic, a concession dictated by the purpose of the building. One example in the United States was the second Trinity Church (1789—the predecessor to Upjohn's) in New York City. The medieval "Christian" elements were pointed windows, a semicircular entrance porch supported by attenuated colonnettes, and rows of obelisk-pinnacles incorporated in the balustrade over the main cornice and at the base of the spire.[5] The first imprint of it on *Fig. 110* Nantucket appeared in the pointed windows of the Universalist Church at India and Federal streets, built in 1825, nine years later becoming the first Atheneum *(Fig. 110).* The pointed windows seem incongruous with the classic columns and pediment. By contrast, the later Gothic Revival, which reached its peak during the late 1830s and 1840s, was an entity unto itself, with social status derived from the cultural background that had preceded it. It utilized Gothic motifs with a full appreciation of their forms, historically and aesthetically.

Fig. 111 First Congregational Church (1834, 1840), 62 Centre Street.

The Gothic, in either of its phases, made but little impression upon Nantucket architecture. The edifice showing the greatest use of it is the First Congregational Church on Beacon Hill (62 Centre Street), constructed by a "Mr. Waldron" of Boston in 1834.[6] The clapboard rectangular building originally had three tall pointed windows in each flank. Its entrance, in a square tower at the east end, has a tracery fanlight over the main door, with a soaring window above, the tower capped by a smaller cube and an octagonal spire. About 1840, the auditorium was *Fig. 111* enlarged one bay and the spire was removed (it was replaced in 1968—*Fig. 111*). Like the old Atheneum or Universalist Church, the First Congregational Church combines Gothic and Classic elements, though the latter are not so much in evidence. Pilasters at all of its vertical corners supplant medieval buttresses and therefore seem not as inappropriate as a freestanding portico. The reverse-curve fanlight over the doorway is an obvious Federal device that has been Gothicized. The fenestration on the flanks has sashes, like any other early nineteenth-century building, distinguished from the usual square or semicircular top only in that here it is pointed. The front windows are different: although they have sashes, or shutters, the vertical spaces are divided by mullions branching into tracery at the summit. These—one functioning window in the tower and two blind windows in the main body of the building—most probably date from the 1840 remodeling, and they constitute the one element that is Gothic Revival and not just Gothic manner.

The only church constructions in Nantucket to succeed the building on Beacon Hill

Fig. 112 E. F. Easton House (*ca.* 1850), 4 North Water Street.

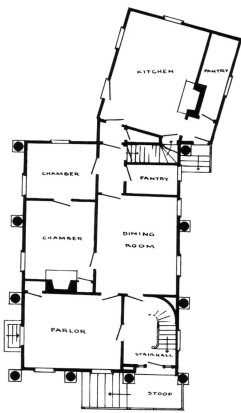

Fig. 113 Restored First-Floor Plan of E. F. Easton House.

within a sixty-year period were the addition of the portico to the Methodist Church, at the south end of Centre Street, the erection of the Baptist Church on Summer Street (both in 1840), and two Quaker projects (Appendix L). The Baptists and Society of Friends would not be well disposed toward the medieval Catholic style, and the Gothic Revival was hardly adaptable to a portico design. Whatever other imprint there is of the pointed mode on the island is in the residences. But there is not very much, for three reasons: first, since the bottom of the economy had fallen out just before mid-century, when the Gothic Revival was beginning to come to the fore, there was little building of any kind; second, the style was best suited to churches and country houses, but as we already have seen little impression was made upon religious architecture, and no rural villas were built on Nantucket at all; and third, Nantucket basically was too conservative, architecturally, to venture so far afield during this period. At best, Gothic motifs figure as a hybrid admixture in the Greek Revival style, admittedly a provincialism of which Nantucket was entirely capable.

The most interesting house in this regard is 4 North Water Street, built in the area overrun by the Great Fire of 1846. It originally was the home of E. F. Easton, though better known as the residence of a later owner, Obed M. Joy. The building consists of two sections: a rectangular main block, surrounded by a peristyle of twelve-sided wooden piers on tall square brick plinths supporting an entablature, with a steep pediment or gable front and back; attached at an angle at the rear, there is a low kitchen ell *(Fig. 112)*. The peristyle, high basement, entablature, and *Fig. 112* pediment are Greek Revival, whereas the piers without capitals, the steep roof pitch, and especially the twin peaked windows with diamond-paned sashes in the façade gable are Gothic. The bay window on the south side and the dormers on the north are romantic details, but they are later *Fig. 113* additions. The plan is close to the normal Nantucket house of the 1850s *(Fig. 113).* It has an entrance hall with a staircase that curves at the top, a parlor without fireplace to one side, a dining room in back of the stairhall with adjoining chambers, and the kitchen farther back; parallels are found in the George Wendell Macy house at 123 Main Street (Chapter Seven). The rear kitchen wing of the Macy house projecting on the east side displays a triangular-headed dormer window not unlike those in the Easton-Joy pediment.

Nearby 9 North Water, a Greek Revival house, has an arched triangular window in the pediment in place of a lunette. Number 3 Whaler's Lane has a double window with blind pointed *Fig. 114* arches over the portico *(Fig. 114).* Number 4 Darling Street has a pair of windows in the pediment with blind arches. Number 6 Winter Street has three corbel-arched windows in the front gable; *Fig. 115* the same windows were once to be found in the house at 5 North Water *(Fig. 115).* Other motifs in the late-medieval idiom are to be found throughout the town (Appendix J).

In closing the list of references to Gothic, it might be recalled that the cast-iron fence in front of The Three Bricks on Main Street has posts of clustered colonnettes, as in a cathedral nave, with pinnacle finials, as on tower buttresses, and quatrefoil motifs in the upright pickets. This is intact only in front of 97 Main Street; the pickets are crudely copied in wood two doors south.

Fig. 114 3 Whaler's Lane.

Although the architecture of the post-Civil War period is beyond the scope of this study, attention may be called to a few notable buildings of the Reconstruction era. Number 13 North Water is a "Victorian Gothic" house with elaborate bargeboards on its steeply-pitched gables. The pierced designs are not inspired by anything from the Middle Ages but belong to a species proper to the time of the Philadelphia Centennial and after; they are associated with the English designer and author of the principal contemporary book on the Gothic Revival, Charles Eastlake.[7] The pattern source is floral, though greatly simplified. Its character is flat, linear, and decorative.

Many of the post-war houses fall into the bracketed category, that is, they have deep horizontal cornices supported on curvilinear attached brackets. Number 30 Centre Street is of the type and has a low-pitched roof. Number 73 Main, the H-plan residence of Mrs. Eliza Barney, built in 1871, is another. It has a more steeply-pitched roof that is hipped and truncated, with a cupola on top and railing around the deck *(Fig. 116)*. Eastlake motifs appear in the caps of the *Fig. 116* wall corner shafts, and the front fence is noteworthy for its elaborateness and correlation with the architecture. The place was restored in the 1960s. The next degree of roof pitch brings us to the mansard, which was popularized by the building of the Nouveau Louvre in Paris during the late 1850s. The bonnet-like superstructure provides a full story of additional rooms, making it desirable for guest houses of the period when Nantucket's chief source of revenue had shifted from whales to summer visitors. The two inns at 19 and 21 Broad Street have mansards and are bracketed, the latter constructed by builder Charles Robinson in 1872.[8]

Wherever forms depart radically from the relatively restrained bracketed and French

Fig. 115 5 North Water Street.

Fig. 116 Eliza Barney House (1871), 73 Main Street.

Second Empire (mansard) types and are a combination of all sorts of extraneous motifs, the style is "Queen Anne." The term came from England and refers back to the practice at the beginning of the eighteenth century—during the reign of the daughter of James II—of mixing Gothic and Renaissance elements in the most eclectic fashion. The foremost protagonist of the later "Queen Anne" in Britain was Norman Shaw, who worked during the 1870s and '80s. His counterparts in America performed during the 1880s and '90s. Nantucket examples are 34 Easton Street and the Sea Cliff Inn on Cliff Road.

A typical private house proper to the New England coast at the end of the nineteenth century is 37 Easton. It has shingle walls and compact massing in the manner of Henry Hobson Richardson of Boston, architect of Trinity Church. It also has a gambrel roof, in itself an early Nantucket feature but here manipulated quite differently. Perhaps this prompted the recent replacement of windows with small-paned sashes, which are very much out of character with the style of the building.

Finally, the 1877 architectural tour of colonial New England made by architects Charles Follen McKim, William Rutherford Mead, and Stanford White bore fruit in the Colonial Revival, which persisted up to and after World War I. It was most vital around the turn of the century, and a characteristic example in Nantucket is the William Barnes house at 30 Orange Street, a rebuilding of shifted segments of the Victorian hotel on the site known as Sherburne House. A few other specimens of the last four decades of the nineteenth century are listed in Appendix K.

The Romantic styles—including the Gothic Revival—hardly became an integral part of traditional Nantucket architecture, occurring, as they did, after the great and vital days of the whaling industry. They embellish the town through contrast with its earlier buildings, and they symbolize its later, less serious role as host to off-island vacationists. They are the icing on the cake, a thin upper frosting that seems sugary by comparison to the substantial loaf beneath. By virtue of their superficialities, the Romantic modes throw the early types into a perspective of functional reality and cause us to appreciate the older buildings more. Thus, indirectly, the later essays are a considerable asset to the architecture of the town, and, as such, it is important that they be preserved and continue to be used for contemporary needs. Besides this, they are indispensable to retaining the full-round architectural heritage of Nantucket.

Notes

1   Kenneth Clark, *The Gothic Revival,* London, 1929, Chapter V.

2   Roger Hale Newton, *Town and Davis, Architects,* New York, 1942, pp. 215–216.

3   Theo B. White, ed., *Philadelphia Architecture in the Nineteenth Century,* Philadelphia, 1953, plate 9.

4   *Ibid.,* plate 11.

5   Theodore Bolton, "Gothic Revival Architecture in America: The History of a Style," Part I, *American Collector,* April 1948, illus. 2, p. 6.

6   The church records identify him only as "Mr. Waldron, Boston." In all likelihood he was Samuel Waldron, listed in the 1825 Boston City Directory as "Surveyor of Lumber," and in the 1834 directory as "housewright, 20 Vine St." His name continues to appear in the latter capacity through 1846–47. Information courtesy Mrs. Theresa Cederholm, Fine Arts Department, Boston Public Library, letter of July 23, 1971.

7   Charles L. Eastlake, *A History of the Gothic Revival,* London, 1872.

8   Information courtesy present owner, George Burgess II.

Part Two

Description of Streets and Notes on Historic Buildings

Fig. 117 Nantucket Waterfront from End of Old North Wharf.

The Wharves of Nantucket

Acquaintance with Nantucket Town begins with the waterfront, the part first glimpsed when arriving by boat, the only proper mode of reaching Nantucket. As one rounds the lighthouse on Brant Point, wharves swing into view which interlace the water like lanes of an otherwise invisible village. They are, in fact, extensions of the web of streets and alleys of the old community itself, the traffic link between the land and the sea. As we have seen, the settlement on the harbor developed because of the construction of the wharves, and they are its eastern boundary, geographically as well as historically.

The earliest record of a wharf at Nantucket was of the one built in 1716 by Joseph Coffin (Chapter One), but its location is unknown. The oldest of which any trace has been found is that constructed in 1723 by Richard Macy, some of its piles having been excavated at the head of Straight Wharf in 1930. The Macy construction was the original Straight Wharf, but the recently rebuilt namesake bears little resemblance to it. We shall return to this subject later.

Just below Straight Wharf is Old South Wharf, built between 1760 and 1762, when the whaling industry was on the increase. After its decline, South Wharf was converted into a business wharf. Henry Lang, who owned it during the second decade of the present century, turned it over to the government for the duration of World War I; afterward, it reverted to commerce and was known as the Island Service Wharf.[1] The low shacks at the west end of the north range and the tall grain elevator at the east extremity of the south row date from the early twentieth century. Otherwise, the buildings here are modern.

Beyond South Wharf, and the only one still standing in this direction, is Commercial Wharf, constructed from 1800 to 1820 by Zenas Coffin and Sons. It was unique in having solid foundations, rough granite blocks brought from Connecticut. Located nearby were three large buildings: a sail-loft on the north side; the Crosby and Sons Candle Manufactory on the south side (the building was formerly the Quaker Church and brought from the southwest corner of Main and Pleasant streets); and a little farther west the Charles G. and Henry Coffin Warehouse, a brick building one door north of the intersection of Washington and Coffin streets. All that remains of the three buildings is the main body of the last (21 Washington), which has been considerably altered to serve as the American Legion headquarters. Some of the materials of the other two went into the folly on Squam Head, itself recently razed.[2] Commercial Wharf has been devoted mostly to fishing endeavors, though the steamboat docked here during the second quarter of the nineteenth century, before it was provided with its own landing.

There was one more pier farther south, on a level with present Fayette Street. It was called Peleg's Wharf, after Peleg Macy, and it was mostly a distribution center for coal and lumber. Some decades ago a few stones marked its site, but they are not to be seen today.

On the other side of Straight Wharf is North Wharf, which retains more old shacks than any other and was the only one included in the 1955 Historic District. Although not without recent changes, such as the covered porches on the outer side, the first half-dozen or so structures in from Easy Street go back at least a century. At that time, the wharf was partly owned by Barzillai R. Burdett and was known as Burdett's Wharf. It frames a part of what was and is Nantucket's prettiest cove, though changed by time (Fig. 117). A good percentage of the former water space between North and Straight Wharf has been filled in and made solid ground.

The uppermost pier, built expressly for the packets, was known during the first three-quarters of the nineteenth century as New North Wharf. Even in the whaling days this was a regular point of debarkation. From 1881 to 1917, the Nantucket Railroad had its terminus at the base of the wharf and ran branch lines to Surfside and Siasconset. By the last quarter of the nineteenth century, the ship company had acquired the wharf and the name was changed to Steamboat Wharf. It was rebuilt in 1915, and is now owned by the Woods Hole, Martha's Vineyard and Nantucket Steamship Authority, which has its main office at the port on the Cape.

From the point of view of historical significance and central location, the most important of the group is Straight Wharf, named for its position on an axis with Main Street. Here was the bustling waterfront center for whaling and trading vessels in the era of Nantucket's greatest prosperity, and here later tied up excursion boats, beginning with the period of the tourist industry in the 1870s. Still Dock, a former waterway behind the buildings on the north side, was filled in before the drawing of the 1834 map of Nantucket. There are two historic buildings in this row. The first is the Thomas Macy Warehouse, built in 1846. It is a two-and-a-half-storied structure of brick with a five-bayed pedimented façade (Fig. 108). Sills and lintels are of granite, and embedded in the wall alongside the windows are iron rings for solid shutters. The building was renovated in 1944 and became the Kenneth Taylor Gallery for art.[3] Adjacent on the east side is the Benjamin Gardner Store, built about 1849. The frame building also is two-and-a-half-storied, though its gables are at the ends. Early in the twentieth century a carriage business was conducted here. Like its neighbor, it now serves a cultural purpose, being the Straight Wharf Theatre devoted to stage productions.[4]

Other buildings here are relatively or entirely new, the whole area having been replanned and rebuilt in the mid 1960s. Included in the layout were a supermarket parking lot, camouflaged, as well as can be, by shrubs and trees in a garden scheme, and a plaza focused on a bandstand for weekend summer concerts. The latter has raised shop terraces surrounding it, employing a superficial and decorative arrangement of piles. However, the wharf had gotten so dilapidated that it was threatened with total annihilation, and it was far better for Nantucket to retain a modern version of its principal pier than none at all. Straight Wharf connects with Main Street at the pre-Revolutionary brick building, Rotch Market.

Notes

1   Much of the information recorded herein is taken from the prize-winning essay by Catherine Jones, "Wharves of Nantucket," published in the *Proceedings of the Nantucket Historical Association,* July 1931, pp. 23–28.
2   Clay Lancaster, *Architectural Follies in America,* Rutland, Vermont, 1960, pp. 152–154.
3   Marie M. Coffin, *Historic American Buildings Survey,* #914.
4   *Ibid.,* #913.

Main Street

Laid out by the Proprietors about 1697, although not mentioned in the records until after the town seat was established on the harbor and Straight Wharf built in 1723, Main Street was designated by this name when Isaac Coffin listed the streets in 1799. Soon after, it was called State Street, but the name shifted back to Main and is so lettered on the Survey Map of 1833.[1] Main Street is five-eighths of a mile long and cuts across Nantucket longitudinally, separating the north and south halves of the town. House numbers begin at the east end for streets running crosswise; for streets running up and down the numbers begin at Main. Odd numbers are generally on the pedestrian's righthand side and the even ones on his left, as one progresses numerically.

Main begins at the head of Straight Wharf, and the first broad stretch of three blocks is referred to as Lower Main or Market Square. Rotch Market is at the east end and the Pacific National Bank at the west. This area was and is the commercial nucleus of the town. Before the Great Fire of 1846, perimeter buildings housed a dozen groceries, sixteen dry-goods stores, five hardware stores, two auction houses, five boot and shoe shops, four clock and jewelry stores, three ships' outfitters, two variety stores, five grain dealers, eight barbers, a cordage store, a stationery shop, an oil and candle shop, a hat shop, and an apothecary. As is true today, in season, farm wagons sold produce at the curb. After the Great Fire (which began in an overheated stovepipe in William H. Geary's hat shop, on the south side west of Union, and spread and gutted the Rotch Market and destroyed every intervening building facing Main up to Orange and Center—and a good deal besides), the north side of the street was set back twenty feet to its present line.[2] Buildings between Cod Lane and Centre Street were rebuilt in the Greek Revival style of brick and brownstone, with cornices (and some pediments) of the same materials. Two buildings on the south side followed their example. Over Congdon's Pharmacy (47 Main) was Pantheon Hall, where social dances were held. Music was provided by the Handy family performing in the orchestra gallery, which projected from the upper wall and was reached by a ladder.[3]

The horse fountain in the middle of the east end of the square was presented to the town by William Hadwen Starbuck and first was placed temporarily at the head of Orange Street in 1885. It was cast in iron by Henry F. Jenks of Pawtucket, Rhode Island. At the other end, white marble blocks in the paving in front of the Folger building (58–60 Main) and on the east corner of Centre mark the southwest limits of the spread of the Great Fire. The obelisk at the curb alongside the Pacific National Bank denotes the north point of a meridian laid out in 1840, the south point of which is a similar stone located in front of the Friends' School on Fair Street.

Rotch Market is a unique pre-Revolution Georgian brick building, originally two-storied plus a curb roof *(Fig. 43);* the full third story, the south brownstone doorway, and other changes date from after the Great Fire. Other and more complete survivors are the Pacific National Bank (1818) and Philip Folger house (1831) at the opposite end of the Square, both of Federal style, the latter converted into shops *(Figs. 81, 72).* The little clapboard building behind the bank is three fifths of the old Masonic Lodge Hall (1802), the west section having been demolished to accommodate a later house on that site *(Fig. 78).* On the rise diagonally across the street (site of 74–76 Main) stood the Friends' Meeting House built in 1829, later becoming the Atlantic Straw Works (a hat factory) and then Atlantic Hall, before its removal in 1883 to Brant Point to become a pavilion of the Nantucket Hotel, and thence back to South Water Street to become part of Dreamland Theatre.

Main Street proceeds southwest for a quarter of a mile, and along this stretch are to be found some of the finest residences of Nantucket. Most were built or remodeled between 1820 and the early 1840s and exhibit the classic taste of those decades. Number 69 Main Street, although constructed fourteen years after 72 Main, is no more advanced stylistically, its arched doorway a retarded feature (Figs. 71, 69). It contains (as restored) a leaded fanlight, whereas several houses in these blocks are endowed with the more characteristically Nantucket blind fan, a half-ellipse over the door with louvres radiating from a carved gilded eagle, and opaque wall behind. The prototype example is 99 Main, having a well-proportioned five-bayed façade, with a window of three lights above the doorway and a parapet-balustrade superimposed over the cornice (Fig. 65). Another unique Nantucket characteristic is the absence of front windows in high basements, as at 69, 72, 75, 77, 78, and 93, 95, and 97 Main Street.

Wood fences here are of the railing (rather than picket) type, the exception being the lattice spike fence in front of 78 Main, which, after being missing for many years, was retrieved from the garret and replaced on its granite retaining wall. The prevalent material for sidewalks is brick, but slabs of bluestone are used instead before 73, 77, 86, 93, 95, 97, and 98 Main. Granite curbstones are consistent, as well as granite crosswalks. Main Street was paved with cobblestones brought from Gloucester, beginning in 1831, and before 1852 the cobbles reached beyond Pleasant. From this point a surface of yellow vitrified brick was continued in 1903. Elm trees along the way were planted by Charles G. and Henry Coffin (builders of 75 and 78 Main) about mid-century. In 1854 gas lights were installed at least in the business district.[4]

The post-Civil War Nantucket residence that incites the greatest interest is 73 Main Street (Fig. 116). The elaborate H-plan wood house was built for Mrs. Eliza Barney in 1871. Its cutout ornaments, crowning railing and belvedere, and pedestal fence were restored in the 1960s.

The stronghold of Greek Revival residences is several blocks beyond, centered around the junction of Main and Pleasant streets. Facing the junction are the "Three Bricks" (93, 95, and 97), built in the mid-1830s by Joseph Starbuck for his three sons (Fig. 88). Except for the distyle Ionic porticoes, their design is mostly Federal, differing little from that of the Henry Coffin house (75) built fifteen years earlier (Fig. 86). The same is true for the interiors, with colonnetted fireplaces. The iron fence with Gothic motifs in front of "West Brick" (97) is intact, but the uprights have been replaced with crude wood substitutes at "East Brick," and a complete late-nineteenth-century fence of insignificant pattern has been installed at "Middle Brick."

The full impact of the Greek Revival style is realized across the way in the houses built by Frederick Brown Coleman for William Hadwen, 96 Main for himself and 94 Main for an adopted niece (Figs. 101 and 102). Both houses have colossal-order porticoes, the second from the corner following the temple form, its Corinthian capitals of unique design, ornamented with acanthus and anthemion motifs. Across the Pleasant Street intersection, the somewhat earlier Benjamin Coffin house, clapboarded like the Hadwen houses, has a high basement, giant pilasters at the corners, and, instead of a projecting portico, a recessed portal sheltering the front steps. On this site, from 1792 to 1834, stood the Friends' Meeting House, brought from Quaker Road and afterward taken to the head of Commercial Wharf to serve as the Crosby and Sons Candle Manufactory.

In 1833, the town sponsored three fire cisterns on Main Street, the first of which was dug in front of the Quaker Church at the corner of Pleasant Street. The other two were on the lower square, one in front of the Pacific National Bank and the other west of Rotch Market. At the junction of Main, Milk, and Gardner is the Civil War Soldiers and Sailors' Monument, erected in 1874. The foundation of the obelisk mounted on a pedestal is the millstone from the old Round Top Mill, which stood on the east side of New Lane at Brush Road. On the southwest corner of Main and Milk streets was the old Town House of 1716, moved here from West Chester Street in 1783 and used for fifty years, until its brick successor on Union was ready for occupancy. On the second floor of the transplanted civic building was a school room, and in the turret hung the island's largest bell, which served as a fire signal. In front stood a flagstaff, known as the Liberty Pole, and alongside was a wooden oil lamppost.[5] The building was taken down in 1865. Across the street, the little shingle shop with flush-board and corbel-gable front was built a decade later and first was Coffin's Grocery, then Whittemore Gardner's Grocery Store.

Beyond the monument, the last quarter-mile of Main Street is oriented directly west. A few houses here are Greek Revival (110, 112, 113, 114, 123, and 124), the most interesting of which is 123 Main, with the entrance portico at the side having a single Ionic column, and a projecting wing behind with a pretty "Gothic" window gable (Fig. 95). A late eighteenth-century house, 117 Main is a prevalent New England type, though unusual for the island in having a hip roof (Figs. 63 and 64). The typical Nantucket house is exemplified in ten buildings, numbers 109, 118, 120, 122, 126, 127, 129, 145, 148, and 154, though 126 and 145 have been altered. The most

Fig. 118 Old House that Stood East of 153 Main Street, Moved to Quarter Mile Hill.

picturesque dwelling is 139 Main Street, moved several hundred feet to its present location *(Fig. 8)*. It was built before 1688 for Richard Gardner, Senior or Junior, and has been added to and remodeled. The elder Gardner was the original owner of all the land north of the upper stretch of Main Street known as "Crooked Record" *(Fig. 2)*. Number 153 is an early eighteenth-century lean-to house, though the long back roof slope has been obscured by a modern wing on the east flank. A slightly later lean-to house that stood on the town side *(Fig. 118)* was transported to a rise of ground behind the Main Street alignment. Called Quarter Mile Hill, it is reached by a narrow lane between numbers 123 and 125. Several small, one-and-three-quarters-story early nineteenth-century houses complete the series up to Caton Circle, whence Main Street continues only a short distance before it veers to the right and becomes New Lane. A more direct branch at the circle becomes Madaket Road and skirts the old Quaker burying ground.

Notes

1   The William Coffin *Map of the Town of Nantucket . . . ,* dated 1833, was published by Clapp of Nantucket in 1834, and the data on the original drawing seem to have been updated to the year of printing or later.

2   Edouard A. Stackpole, "The 'Great Fire' of 1846," *Proceedings of the Nantucket Historical Association,* 1946, pp. 35–45.

3   Annie W. Bodfish, "A Few Facts Relating to Main Street," *Ibid.,* 1917, pp. 36–38; 1918, pp. 32–33; 1919, pp. 25–27; 1920, pp. 57–61.

4   H. Errol Coffin, "Nantucket Street Lighting," *Historical Nantucket,* October 1967, pp. 17–19.

5   Allen Coffin, "The Courts of Nantucket — The Law and the Lawyers from an Early Period," *Proceedings of the Nantucket Historical Association,* 1907, p. 30.

1   ROTCH MARKET (Pacific Club), built 1775 for William Rotch, 1st floor and half of 2nd reserved for use of town (Rotch's offices occupied other half of 2nd and garret) in exchange for grant of public land on which sited. Originally 2½-story common-bond brick, end chimneys, molded-brick stringer on south, west, and north sides at 1st-floor level, belt courses 2nd and 3rd-floor levels (only partially left on north side), 5-bayed façade facing south. Building gutted during 1846 Fire. Afterward heightened to 3½ stories, windows not aligned. Brownstone frame around enlarged south door, sills and sides of windows are Greek Revival period replacements. Original windows probably had 9/9-paned sashes, building crowned with gambrel roof (see Chapter Four). Later gable windows bricked up, door and window cut in west wall, and pilastered 1st-story treatment added. From 1780s to 1916, one room used for customs. Building owned by insurance companies from 1804 to 1860, when group of shipmasters purchased it for club house. (H. B. Worth, *Nantucket Lands*, pp. 236–238; E. A. Stackpole, *Rambling*, pp. 10–11; *Guidebook*, p. 31; G. A. Fowlkes, *Mirror of Nantucket*, pp. 53–54; E. U. Crosby, *Ninety Five Per Cent*, photo p. 67; A. E. Poor, *Colonial Architecture*, pl. 53; *H. A. B. S.* #836)

14, 16   Built after 1846 Fire, double shop. 2-story flush boards, 6-bayed façade crowned by pediment. Much altered. (E. U. Crosby, *Ninety Five Per Cent*, illus. p. 145; *H. A. B. S.* #951)

17   Built after 1846 Fire. 2½-story shingle, 4-bayed façade with gable, 6/6-paned windows, shop below. (E. U. Crosby, *Ninety Five Per Cent*, illus. p. 143)

19, 21   Built after 1846 Fire, originally 2 separate buildings. Number 21 was occupied by newspaper, *The Mirror*, until merged with *Inquirer* in 1865. 2-story shingle, each had 3-bayed façade, 6/6-paned windows, shop fronts below. Buildings combined and given jerkin-headed roof. Number 21 deeper than adjacent building, early gable line may be seen at rear. *(Historic Nantucket*, Oct. 1955, p. 12; E. A. Stackpole, *Rambling*, pp. 13–14)

23   Built after 1846 Fire, Greek Revival style. 2-story brick, 3-bayed façade, piers at corners and brick entablature, 6/6-paned windows above modern shop front. Slate roof on entire block to Federal. (E. U. Crosby, *Ninety Five Per Cent*, illus. p. 142)

25   Built after 1846 Fire, Greek Revival style. 2-story brick, 3-bayed façade, 6/6-paned windows over shop front. (E. U. Crosby, *Ninety Five Per Cent*, illus. p. 142; for entire row here to 57 Main, *H. A. B. S.* #952)

27, 29   Built after 1846 Fire, double shop, Greek Revival style. 2-story brick, 6-bayed façade, piers at outer corners and brick entablature, 6/6-paned windows over shop fronts. (E. U. Crosby, *Ninety Five Per Cent*, illus. p. 142)

31   (For corner unit see 3 Federal Street below)

33, 35   Built after 1846 Fire, double shop, Greek Revival style. 2-story brownstone front, brick side, 2-tiered pilastered façade, 6-bayed. Corner store retains 1st-story piers although missing on 35, 6/6-paned windows above. (E. U. Crosby, *Ninety Five Per Cent*, illus. p. 141)

37   Built after 1846 Fire, Greek Revival style. 2-story brick, 3-bayed façade, 6/6-paned windows over altered shop front. (E. U. Crosby, *Ninety Five Per Cent*, illus. p. 141)

43, 45   Built after 1846 Fire, 2 shops and entrance to upper hall, Greek Revival style. 2-story brick, 7-bayed façade of which 5 are covered by pediment, brownstone cornice, recessed windows (with later 2/2-paned sashes) over stores. (E. U. Crosby, *Ninety Five Per Cent*, illus. p. 141)

47, 51, 55, 57   Built after 1846 Fire, 4 shops and 2 entrances to upper hall, Greek Revival style. 2-story brick, 14-bayed façade of which 6 centermost are pedimented with brownstone cornice, 6/6-paned windows over stores. West end on Centre Street 9-bayed and pedimented, windows in vertical recesses, 1st-story entablature spans 7 bays, 2 shop fronts. (E. U. Crosby, *Ninety Five Percent*, illus. p. 140; T. F. Hamlin, *Greek Revival*, pl. XXXIX)

54, 56   Built after 1846 Fire, 2 shops flanking entrance to upper hall, Greek Revival style. 2-story brick with gable west end, 7-bayed façade with brick cornice, 6/6-paned windows 2nd story. (E. U. Crosby, *Ninety Five Per Cent*, illus. p. 136; *H. A. B. S.* #950)

58, 60   Built 1831 as residence for Philip H. Folger, late Federal style. 2-story brick, hip roof, end chimneys, 5-bayed façade with outer convex surfaces, crowned by whorled frieze, recessed center doorway with sidelights sheltered by distyle Greek Doric portico of brownstone on granite stoop, 6/6-paned windows. Roof entirely rebuilt and chimneys shortened. First story of convex sections converted into shop fronts and floor lowered to street level. *(H. A. B. S. #949, 3 data pages)*

61   PACIFIC NATIONAL BANK, built 1818, Federal style. 2-story Flemish-bond brick on granite foundations, hip roof, brownstone trim, such as horizontal stringers at 1st- and 2nd-story window-sill level, front and side stoop and steps, wood semicircular front portico with Roman Ionic columns, fanlight over door, iron railings to flaring steps, half-round blind arches enframe 1st-story windows, recessed panels above to segmented-arch windows. Late 19th century bracketed cornice. Early 20th-century front iron railing. Original flank of building on Main Street was 2-bayed, soon 3 bays added, last 2 extended after 1895. Interior remodeled 1912, 1925, 1954. (M. M. Coffin, *H. A. B. S.* #938; G. A. Fowlkes, *Mirror of Nantucket*, pp. 60–62; *Guidebook*, p. 11; bank owns 1870 photo; N. H. A. Museum has late 19th century view taken from tower of Unitarian Church; similar view in H. S. Wyer, *Nantucket, Picturesque*, plate /10/; another in J. F. Murphy, *Fifty Glimpses*, p. 29; E. A. Stackpole, *Rambling*, p. 15, Hathaway painting of Main Street before 1846 Fire—at Atheneum—reproduced p. /8/; E. U. Crosby, *Ninety Five Per Cent*, photo p. 68)

63   MASONIC LODGE HALL, built 1802, Federal style. Originally 2-story clapboard, hip roof, 5-bayed façade with colossal-order Roman Ionic pilasters flanking center bay and at outer corners, full entablature, arched windows 2nd story enframed by small pilasters supporting archivolts and keystones. During 1830s, 1st story remodeled into Greek Revival store front with short pilasters and entablature replacing lower part of original tall pilasters. West 2 bays demolished 1872; former pilaster top at west end inserted between 2 upper windows in from east end. (*Union Lodge, F. & A. M., Nantucket, Mass.*, Nantucket, 1941, photo of building before 1872 mutilation facing p. 24; M. M. Coffin, *H. A. B. S.* #899; E. A. Stackpole, *Rambling*, p. 36; G. A. Fowlkes, *Mirror of Nantucket*, pp. 68–70)

69   Built 1834 for Frederick Mitchell, late Federal style. 2½-story Flemish-bond brick on granite basement (no windows in front), end chimneys connected by parapets, were lower parapets, square cupola on slate roof, 5-bayed façade, recessed arched center doorway with sidelights and leaded fan, 6/6-paned windows, parapet over cornice with balustrade insets aligned to windows. Restored in 1963–64. (M. M. Coffin, *H. A. B. S.* #936; *Historic Nantucket*, April 1964, pp. 5–8; E. A. Stackpole, *Rambling*, p. 37)

72   Built 1820 for John Wendell Barrett, builder believed to have been John Coleman, transitional Federal-Greek Revival style. 2½-story clapboard on high Flemish-bond brick basement (no windows in front), hip roof crowned with elaborate pilastered belvedere, 4 chimneys at ends, 5-bayed façade with flanged pilasters at corners, center doorway with transom and sidelights, portico with coupled Greek Ionic columns, articulated attic treatment, granite stoop with steps both sides, iron railing, 6/6-paned windows. Parapet over cornice with balustrade insets aligned to windows. Dormers modern. Sidewalk paved with bluestone, granite rainwater channels at each end of house. (M. M. Coffin, *H. A. B. S.* #915; G. A. Fowlkes, *Mirror of Nantucket*, pp. 72–73; K. Duprey, *Old Houses*, pp. /186/-/188/; E. A. Stackpole, *Rambling*, pp. 36–37; Worth-Palmer, Photos, 1905 photo shows house without dormers, p. 14: *Inquirer & Mirror*, Nov. 24, 1965, p. 5; E. U. Crosby, *Ninety Five Per Cent*, photo of entrance p. 69; T. F. Hamlin, *Greek Revival*, pl. XL; A. E. Poor, *Colonial Architecture*, pls. 49, 88)

75   Built 1832–33 for Henry Coffin, James Field head carpenter, Christopher Capen head mason, similar plan to 78 Main, inverted, more elaborate exterior, late Federal style. 2½-story unbonded brick on granite basement (no windows in front), 4 end chimneys connected by parapets, cupola, 5-bayed façade, recessed center doorway with sidelights enframed by engaged Tuscan columns and entablature, 6/6 paned windows. Parapet over cornice with balustrade insets aligned to windows. Sidewalk paved with bluestone. High brick wall on Liberty Street at rear of lot. (G. A. Fowlkes, *Mirror of Nantucket*, pp. 77–78, 80; K. Duprey, *Old Houses*, pp. /189/-193; M. M. Coffin, *H. A. B. S.* #811; E. A. Stackpole, *Rambling*, pp. 37, 38; E. U. Crosby, *Ninety Five Per Cent*, photo p. 69; A. E. Poor, *Colonial Architecture*, pl. 43)

77   Built 1836 for John H. Shaw, Greek Revival style. Former Francis Macy house (1790s) on site moved to become rear wing and may be seen from Walnut Lane. 2½-story clapboard on high brick (now stuccoed) basement (no windows in front), 4 end chimneys, parapets, roof walk, 5-bayed portico on granite

podium, 6/6-paned windows. Probably had parapet-balustrade over front cornice. Modern enclosed porch on east flank. Sidewalk paved with bluestone. (H. B. Worth, *Nantucket Lands*, p. 280; G. A. Fowlkes, *Mirror of Nantucket*, p. 114; M. M. Coffin, *H. A. B. S.* #931; E. A. Stackpole, *Rambling*, p. 38; E. U. Crosby, *Ninety Five Per Cent*, photo p. 70)

78   Built 1831–33 for Charles G. Coffin, James Field head carpenter, Christopher Capen head mason, simplified Greek Revival style. 2½-story unbonded brick on granite foundations (no windows in front), horizontal parapets between 4 end chimneys, had parapets also front and rear of chimneys, slate roof, roof walk, 5-bayed façade, center recessed doorway with sidelights enframed by brownstone pilasters and entablature, 6/6-paned windows. Terraced front yard with lattice spike fence on granite retaining wall. Original fence reset after being stored in garret for many years. (G. A. Fowlkes, *Mirror of Nantucket*, pp. 76–79; E. A. Stackpole, *Rambling*, p. 37; E. U. Crosby, *Ninety Five Per Cent*, photo p. 70)

81   Built 1760s, typical Nantucket house. 2½-story clapboard front, shingle sides, ridge chimney, 4-bayed façade, door with transom, later 6/6-paned windows (some 12/12-paned windows on east side). (E. A. Stackpole, *Rambling; pp. 38–39; G. A. Fowlkes, *Mirror of Nantucket, pp. 45–46)*

82   Built early 19th century, Federal style. 2-story clapboard front, shingle sides, on high brick basement, single chimney at each end, 5-bayed façade, center doorway with transom and sidelights, wood stoop with double steps, 12/12-paned windows. Southwest wing added *ca.* 1890, also roof walk on early house. (W. Phillip Graves; A. E. Poor, *Colonial Architecture*, pl. 29)

84   Built mid-18th century for John Barnard, transitional lean-to house. Rear heightened probably late 18th century. 2½-story shingle on brick basement, ridge chimney, 3-bayed façade, wood stoop, 12/12-paned windows. Narrow extension with shed roof on west flank perhaps added when rear raised to 2 full stories. (W. B. Worth, *Nantucket Lands*, p. 273; E. A. Stackpole, *Rambling*, p. 40; G. A. Fowlkes, *Mirror of Nantucket*, p. 114)

85   East section built *ca.* 1725 for Jabez Bunker, west side added after 1795 for Prince Gardner, 2½-story shingle, 2 ridge chimneys, 5-bayed façade, pilastered Greek Revival doorway with sidelights, 6/6-paned windows. (E. A. Stackpole, *Rambling*, p. 41; N. H. A. leaflet, *Main Street;* E. U. Crosby, *Ninety Five Per Cent*, p 71)

86   Built or remodeled in 1830s for Ann Coffin Crosby, early Revival-Eclectic style. 2½-story clapboard on high brick basement, end chimneys, cupola on roof, 3-bayed façade with ribbed shafts at corners, crowned by pediment pierced by pointed "Gothic" window, Greek Revival doorway, wood stoop. Sidewalk paved with bluestone. (N. H. A. leaflet, *Main Street*)

87   Built 1830s for Charles Clark, typical Nantucket house. 2½-story clapboard front, shingle sides, ridge chimney, 4-bayed façade, pilastered doorway, 6/6-paned windows. (E. A. Stackpole, *Rambling*, p. 41; E. U. Crosby, *Ninety Five Per Cent*, photo p. 71)

88   Built early 1830s for Job Coleman, Federal style. 2½-story clapboard, high brick basement, 4 end chimneys, 5-bayed asymmetrical façade, doorway in middle opening with transom and sidelights, wood stoop with double stairs, 6/6-paned windows. (N. H. A. leaflet, *Main Street*)

89   Original (east) section built 1740s, lean-to house. Purchased from heirs of Sylvanus Macy 1834 by Jared Coffin. Enlarged to 2 full stories 1875. Remodeled 1926, including new doorway. (M. M. Coffin, *H. A. B. S.* #921; E. A. Stackpole, *Rambling*, pp. 41, 43; G. A. Fowlkes, *Mirror of Nantucket*, pp. 114–115)

90   Built *ca.* 1828 for Matthew Crosby, Federal style. 2½-story clapboard, 2 ridge chimneys, 5-bayed façade, center doorway with leaded sidelights, blind fan with carved eagle, wood stoop with winder steps both sides, 6/6-paned windows. Parapet over front cornice with balustrade insets, aligned to windows. Later addition west end. (G. A. Fowlkes, *Mirror of Nantucket*, pp. 66–67; E. A. Stackpole, *Rambling*, p. 43; E. U. Crosby, *Ninety Five Per Cent*, photo p. 71)

91   Rebuilt early 1820s for Henry Swift, modified typical Nantucket house. 2½-story shingle, ridge chimney, 4-bayed façade, later pilastered Greek Revival doorway with sidelights, 6/6-paned windows. (G. A. Fowlkes, *Mirror of Nantucket*, pp. 64–66; E. A. Stackpole, *Rambling*, p. 43; E. U. Crosby, *Ninety Five Per Cent*, photo p. 72; M. M. Coffin, *H. A. B. S.* #167)

92   Built *ca.* 1838 for William C. Swain, Greek Revival style. 2½-story clapboard on high brick basement, end chimneys, 4-bayed façade, had 6/6-paned windows (now 6/9-paned 1st story). Doorway

with sidelights and blind fan is inappropriate replacement. (E. A. Stackpole, *Rambling*, p. 43; E. U. Crosby, *Ninety Five Per Cent*, photo p. 71)

93, 95, 97   Built 1836–38 William ("East Brick"), Matthew ("Middle Brick") and George ("West Brick") Starbuck, sons of and sponsored by Joseph Starbuck; James Childs master builder and Christopher Capen head mason, transitional Federal-Greek Revival style. 2½-story unbonded brick on granite basement (no windows in front), stepped parapets connecting 4 end chimneys, square cupola on slate roof, 5-bayed façade recessed center doorway with sidelights, distyle Greek Ionic portico with parapet, granite steps, 6/6-paned windows. Parapet over front cornice with balustrade insets aligned to windows. Iron fence on stone retaining wall, 97 complete with Gothic-naturalistic forms. Sidewalk paved with bluestone. The 3 houses are identical outside, similar inside. (W. Gardner, *Three Bricks and Three Brothers*; G. A. Fowlkes, *Mirror of Nantucket*, pp. 83–86; K. Duprey, *Old Houses*, pp. 194–201; E. A. Stackpole, *Rambling*, pp. 43–44; M. M. Coffin, *H. A. B. S.* #941; E. U. Crosby, *Ninety Five Per Cent*, photo p. 73; A. E. Poor, *Colonial Architecture*, pl. 43; R. Pratt, *Golden Treasury*, pp. 134–/137/)

94   Built *ca.* 1845 by Frederick Brown Coleman for William Hadwen as home for niece, Mary G. Swain (Mrs. George W. Wright), Greek Revival style. 2½-story clapboard on brick basement, prostyle temple form with colossal Corinthian portico of 4 columns, unique capitals (somewhat like those of Tower of the Winds, Athens) with acanthus and anthemion ornaments, had chimneys near ridge, perhaps masked by square cupola on roof, 6/6-paned windows. Square-piered galleries on flanks. House elevated on terrace, granite retaining wall still in place though missing wood fence, except at east end of lot (gates). 1st-story pedimented hoods over doorway and windows, and external chimney on west side date from 1927, at which time the house was extensively renovated. Has elaborately carved original trim inside, domed stairhall and ballroom 2nd story, latter with specially contrived spring system to floor. (M. M. Coffin, *H. A. B. S.* #905; G. A. Fowlkes, *Mirror of Nantucket*, pp. 92–95; K. Duprey, *Old Houses*, pp. 206–/210/; E. A. Stackpole, *Rambling*, p. 44; *Guidebook*, p. /22/; E. U. Crosby, *Ninety Five Per Cent*, photo p. 72)

96   Built 1844 by Frederick Brown Coleman for William Hadwen, who occupied this house, Greek Revival style. 2½-story clapboard on brick basement, hip roof with square cupola on summit, end chimneys, 5-bayed façade with colossal pilasters and pedimented tetrastyle Ionic portico, center recessed pilastered doorway with sidelights, 6/6-paned windows. House elevated on terrace with granite retaining wall continuous with that in front of 94 Main, originally had railing-type fence (between plain pedestals) similar to that at Atheneum. Hadwen's Newport origin is reflected in the style of both 94 and 96 Main. (G. A. Fowlkes, *Mirror of Nantucket*, pp. 92–95; E. A. Stackpole, *Rambling*, p. 44; M. M. Coffin, *H. A. B. S.* #929; A. Starbuck, *History,* photo of 1880s shows house with Eclectic fence, p. 631; Nantucket Literary Union map and photo display at Philadelphia Centenial includes view of Main and Pleasant showing original fence in front of 94 and 96 Main–N. H. A. Museum; E. U. Crosby, *Ninety Five Per Cent*, photo p. 74; T. F. Hamlin, *Greek Revival*, pl. XLI)

98   Built 1834 for Benjamin F. Coffin, Greek Revival style. 2½-story clapboard on brick basement, stepped parapets mask base of 4 end chimneys and gables, 5-bayed façade with pilasters at corners, recessed center doorway with sidelight enframed by pilasters and entablature, granite steps, 6/6-paned windows, parapet over front cornice. Sidewalk paved with bluestone. Site of Friends' Meeting House from 1792 until land acquired by Coffin. (G. A. Fowlkes, *Mirror of Nantucket*, p. 115; E. A. Stackpole, *Rambling,* p. 46; E. U. Crosby, *Ninety Five Per Cent,* photo p. 75)

99   Original 1770 residence of Valentine Swain was typical Nantucket house, later given wing at rear, enlarged to present form for Thomas Macy *ca.* 1830, Federal style. 2½-story clapboard, 2 ridge chimneys, roof walk, 5-bayed façade, center doorway with sidelights and blind fan with carved eagle at radial point, triple-light window above, 6/6-paned windows. Parapet over front cornice with balustrade insets aligned to windows. (M. M. Coffin, *H. A. B. S.* #944; *Inquirer & Mirror*, Oct. 7, 1965; E. A. Stackpole, *Rambling*, pp. 44, 46; G. A. Fowlkes, *Mirror of Nantucket*, pp. 66–68; E. U. Crosby, *Ninety Five Per Cent*, photo p. 75; A. E. Poor, *Colonial Architecture*, pls. 37, 92)

100   Built shortly after 1800, an older house incorporated into it at the rear. Remodeled *ca.* 1840 for William Hadwen before he moved to 96 Main. 2½-story clapboard front, shingle sides, had 2 ridge chimneys (west only remaining), formerly had roof walk, 5-bayed façade, pilastered Greek Revival center doorway with sidelights, 6/6-paned windows. Railing-type front fence, sidewalk paved with

bluestone. (G. A. Fowlkes, *Mirror of Nantucket*, pp. 57–58; E. A. Stackpole, *Rambling*, p. 46; J. F. Murphy, *Fifty Glimpses, ca.* 1895 photo p. 25; E. U. Crosby, *Ninety Five Per Cent*, photo p. 76)

102 Built late 18th century for James Bunker, was typical Nantucket house. 2½-story clapboard front, shingle sides, ridge chimney, now 3-bayed façade, 12/12-paned windows, later pilastered Greek Revival doorway with sidelights. Sidewalk paved with bluestone. (E. A. Stackpole, *Rambling*, p. 47; K. Duprey, *Old Houses*, p. 84; E. U. Crosby, *Ninety Five Per Cent*, photo p. 76)

105 Tradition holds that east section brought from old Sherburne and west section added for Christopher Starbuck *ca.* 1757, faces south, side aligned to Gardner Street, lean-to house. 2½-story shingle, articulated ridge chimney, 3-bayed façade, center door with transom, 12/12-paned windows. Restored 1920s, sashes given wide muntins. (M. M. Coffin, *H. A. B. S.* #939; K. Duprey, *Old Houses*, pp. 19–/23/; H. B. Worth, *Nantucket Lands*, 1881 photo facing p. 225; G. A. Fowlkes, *Mirror of Nantucket*, pp. 37–39, 115–116; E. A. Stackpole, *Rambling*, p. 47; *Proceedings*, 1950, p. 24; *Inquirer & Mirror*, Oct. 14, 1965, p. 3; E. U. Crosby, *Ninety Five Per Cent*, photo p. 77; A. E. Poor, *Colonial Architecture*, pl. 19)

107 West section built late 17th century at old Sherburne, moved to site and expanded *ca.* 1748 for Zaccheus Macy, making it a lean-to house. 2½-story shingle, ridge chimney (altered), 5-bayed façade, center door (though door itself late 19th century), 12/12-paned windows 1st story, 8/12-paned windows 2nd story. Center chimney removed and replaced by stairhall before 1880. (H. C. Forman, *Early Nantucket*, pp. 228, 245; M. M. Coffin, *H. A. B. S.* #934; H. B. Worth, *Nantucket Lands*, 1881 photo facing p. 255; E. A. Stackpole, *Rambling*, p. 48)

109 Built *ca.* 1830 for Capt. Reuben Joy II, typical Nantucket house. 2½-story shingle, ridge chimney, 4-bayed façade, 6/6-paned windows. (E. A. Stackpole, *Rambling*, p. 79; E. U. Crosby, *Ninety Five Per Cent*, photo p. 79)

110 Built *ca.* 1840, Greek Revival style. 1¾-story clapboard on high brick basement, end chimneys, 4-bayed façade, pilasters at corners supporting encircling entablature, pediment toward street, 6/6-paned windows, entrance on east side. Had square cupola on roof. Later Palladian window in pediment. (Photo looking up Main Street from Monument *ca.* 1880 owned by Franklin Folger Webster)

111 Built 1746 for Ebenezer Gardner, given to daughter Margaret (Mrs. Nathan Daggett), lean-to house. *Ca.* 1800, rear taken off and 2-story house from old Sherburne moved and joined to back at right angles, the addition having its own center chimney. 2½-story shingle, 5-bayed façade, center doorway with sidelights. 12/12-paned windows modern. (M. M. Coffin, *H. A. B. S.* #922; E. A. Stackpole, *Rambling*, pp. 49, 77, 79)

112 Built *ca.* 1836, Greek Revival style. 2½-story shingle on brick basement, end chimneys, shafts at corners, 3-bayed gabled façade, doorway stripped, 6/6-paned windows. Later 1-story projecting bay window. (Newspaper dated 1836 found folded up under garret floor; Franklin Folger Webster)

113 Built 1834 for Capt. David Paddack, Greek Revival Style. 2½-story clapboard on high brick basement. 4 end chimneys, roof walk, 5-bayed façade, pilastered center doorway with sidelights, wood stoop with stairs both sides, 6/6-paned windows. No basement windows in front. (E. A. Stackpole, *Rambling*, p. 77)

114 Contemporary with 112 Main. Probably 1¾-story shingle (later raised to 2 full stories) on brick basement, end chimneys, shafts at corners, 3-bayed gabled façade, pilastered Greek Revival doorway, 6/6-paned windows. Later 2-story projecting bay window.

117 Built 1790s for Capt. Edward Cary or son Robert, hip-roof house. 2½-story shingle, 2 large square chimneys on side slopes of hip roof, 5-bayed façade, center doorway early Federal style with transom and sidelights, 12/12-paned windows. Later dormer west slope of roof. (M. M. Coffin, *H. A. B. S.* #855; G. A. Fowlkes, *Mirror of Nantucket*, pp. 56–57; E. A. Stackpole, *Rambling*, p. 76, illus. p. /80/; H. B. Worth, *Nantucket Lands*, p. 266, 1881 photo facing p. 271; E. U. Crosby, *Ninety Five Per Cent*, photo p. 80)

118 Built 1805 for Capt. Thomas Barnard, typical Nantucket house. 2½-story shingle, ridge chimney, 4-bayed façade, 12/12-paned windows. (E. A. Stackpole, *Rambling*, p. 76)

119 2½-story shingle, ridge chimney, 3-bayed façade, pilastered Greek Revival doorway with sidelights, 6/6-paned windows.

120 Typical Nantucket house. 2½-story shingle, ridge chimney, 4-bayed façade, door with transom,

12/12-paned windows.

121   Similar to 119 Main. 2-storied extension at northwest corner. (E. U. Crosby, *Ninety Five Per Cent*, photo p. 80)

122   Early 19th century typical Nantucket house. 2½-story shingle on brick basement, ridge chimney, 4-bayed façade, pilastered doorway with transom, 12/12-paned windows.

123   Built 1840 for George Wendell Macy, Greek Revival style. 1¾-story shingle on brick basement, ridge chimney and cupola on roof, 3-bayed façade with gable at front, pilasters at corners supporting entablature on flanks, Ionic column to entrance portico on east flank, also wing farther back with "Gothic" pointed dormer gable. House similar to 17 Pleasant Street. (E. A. Stackpole, *Rambling*, p. 75)

124   Built *ca.* 1840, Greek Revival style. 2½-story shingle on brick basement, end chimneys, 3-bayed façade, pilastered doorway with sidelights, 6/6-paned windows.

126   Originally typical Nantucket house. 2½-story shingle on brick basement, ridge chimney, now 3-bayed façade, pilastered doorway with transom (modern), wood stoop, 6/6-paned windows. Reputed to have been moved from old Sherburne.

127   Typical Nantucket house. 2½-story shingle, ridge chimney, 4-bayed façade, pilastered doorway (modern), 6/6-paned windows. (N. H. A. *Photo Albums*, Book 3, p. /7/)

128   2½-story clapboard on high brick basement, ridge chimney, 3-bayed façade, pilastered Greek Revival doorway, wood stoop, 6/6-paned windows.

129   Typical Nantucket house. 2½-story shingle on brick basement, ridge chimney, 4-bayed façade, pilastered doorway, 6/6-paned windows.

134   Federal period house. 2½-story shingle, ridge chimney, 3-bayed façade, pilastered doorway, late 2/1-paned windows.

138   1¾-story shingle on high brick basement, ridge chimney, 3-bayed façade, pilastered Greek Revival doorway, 6/6-paned windows. Modern additions include front Dutch dormer.

139   Built before 1688 for Richard Gardner or Richard Gardner II, "English house" type. 2½-story shingle, articulated ridge chimney (restored), arched head to front door, leaded casement windows (replaced). Original house consisted of porch with newel stairs, single great room, chamber above. East extension with shed roof and rear lean-to added early 18th century by Joseph or Caleb Gardner. Building was serving as carriage house to George C. Gardner residence about 500 feet northwest of present site. Moved and restored 1927–28 by A. E. Shurrocks for Gladys Wood. (M. M. Coffin, *H. A. B. S.* #955; K. Duprey, *Old Houses*, pp. 10–13; H. C. Forman, *Early Nantucket*, pp. 225, 227, illus, pp. /223/, 226; H. B. Worth, *Nantucket Lands*, pp. 227–230; G. A. Fowlkes, *Mirror of Nantucket*, pp. 31–32; 116; E. A. Stackpole, *Rambling*, p. 75; *Guidebook*, p. 14; *Inquirer & Mirror*, Sept. 23, 1965, p. 3; E. U. Crosby, *Ninety Five Per Cent*, photo p. 81)

140   Built early 19th century. 1½-story shingle, ridge chimney, 3-bayed façade, 12/12-paned windows and other details modern, including box dormer in front. (N. H. A. *Photo Albums*, Book 3, p. /8/)

141   Built 1832, Federal style. 1¾-story clapboard, 4 end chimneys, 5-bayed façade, center doorway with sidelights, 6/6-paned windows. Later had colonnaded porch encompassing it (part made into enclosed porch at northeast corner), more recent entrance porch. (Gladys Wood)

144   Built early 19th century. 1¾-story shingle, ridge chimney (new), 3-bayed façade, pilastered doorway with transom, 12/12-paned windows (modern). (N. H. A. *Photo Albums*, Book 3, p. /8/)

145   Built after 1760 for Charles Gardner, originally typical Nantucket house. 2½-story clapboard, ridge chimney, now 3-bayed façade, later Greek Revival doorway with sidelights, 6/6-paned windows. (H. B. Worth, *Nantucket Lands*, p. 265; N. H. A. *Photo Albums*, Book 3, p. /9/)

148   Typical Nantucket house. 2½-story clapboard front, shingle sides, rock foundations, ridge chimney, 4-bayed façade, 6/6-paned windows, modern doorway with sidelights.

150   1¾-story clapboard, ridge chimney, Greek Revival doorway, later bay window and other changes.

151   (see QUARTER MILE HILL)

Fig. 119 South Front of 10 Ash Street.

152	Built early 19th century. 1¾-story clapboard front, shingle sides, on brick foundations, ridge chimney, 3-bayed façade, Federal doorway with frame and corner blocks (part of cornice missing), 6/6-paned windows. (N. H. A. *Photo Albums*, Book 3, p. /9/)
153	Built soon after 1723 for Barnabas Gardner, lean-to house. 2½-story shingle, ridge chimney, 5-bayed façade, 12/12-paned windows. Later pilastered doorway, 2-story rear wing east end. (K. Duprey, *Old Houses*, pp. 36–41; M. M. Coffin, *H. A. B. S.* #925; E. A. Stackpole, *Rambling*, pp. 74–75; H. B. Worth, *Nantucket Lands*, p. 265, 1881 photo facing p. 263; E. U. Crosby, *Ninety Five Per Cent*, photo p. 81)
154	Originally typical Nantucket house. 2½-story shingle, had ridge chimney, 4-bayed façade, 12/12-paned windows. Restored: house had been altered to have 2 end chimneys, 2/2-paned windows. (N. H. A. *Photo Albums*, Book 3, p. /9/)
156	2½-story shingle, ridge chimney, 3-bayed façade, restored 12/12-paned windows, modern doorway and shed-roof addition on west flank. (N. H. A. *Photo Albums*, Book 3, p. /10/)
158	1¾-story shingle, 2 ridge chimneys, 5-bayed façade, pilastered Greek Revival doorway with sidelights, 6/6-paned windows. Later dormers.
160	1¾-story shingle, ridge chimney (new), had 3-bayed façade, pilastered doorway, later bay window.
162	1¾-story shingle, ridge chimney (new), 4-bayed façade, pilastered doorway, 6/6-paned windows.

Academy Hill and Academy Lane (Avenue)

The area takes its name from the Academy, which was located a few yards north of the present high school. The eminence was originally called Beacon Hill and was thus known when Old North Vestry was moved to the site of the First Congregational Church in 1765 (see 62 Centre). The land for the Academy—south of the church lot—was sold by George Clark in 1800 to Shubael Coffin, Rowland Gelston, Jonathan Myricks II, Joshua Coffin, committee for the owners and proprietors of the institution.[1] The Academy was a private school. It was replaced in 1856 by the first Nantucket High School, which was public. This building stood until 1929, when it, in turn, was superseded by the present edifice.[2] Although one residence (3 Academy) and the old Meeting House predate the Academy by several decades (it lasted only a little more than fifty years and has been gone for upwards of a century), the designation "Academy," has persevered, even overshadowing the more venerable title, Beacon Hill.

Described by Isaac Coffin in his 1799 survey as running "in a zig-zag course, west, north and west,"[3] Academy Lane branches off Centre above Gay, and one offshoot extends northward to connect with Church Lane, while the other passes Westminster to come to a dead end. Stylistic differences between the Federal and Greek Revival are expressed in the two houses of similar size, numbers 8 and 12 *(Figs. 76–77, 82–83)*. Since the last quarter of the nineteenth century, the street has been called "Academy Avenue," sounding a bit pretentious for its physical characteristics. The house on Church Lane, with its unique arched portico, aesthetically rewards the visitor who goes out of his way to see it *(Fig. 50)*. Old North Vestry may be visited en route *(Fig. 4)*.

Notes

1 Henry Barnard Worth, *Nantucket Lands and Land Owners*, Nantucket Historical Association, Vol. II, Bulletin No. 5, 1906 (reissued 1928), p. 241.
2 Edouard A. Stackpole, *Rambling Through the Streets and Lanes of Nantucket*, New Bedford, Mass., 1969, p. 26.
3 Worth, *op. cit.*, p. /240/.

Historic Buildings

Academy Hill (Church Lane)

X	Built *ca.* 1806 for Capt. Reuben R. Bunker, originally a typical Nantucket house. *Ca.* 1820 remodeled in Federal style. 2½-story clapboard front, shingle sides, ridge chimney, roof walk, 5-bayed façade (1 bay added west end), 12/12-paned windows, quoins at corners, doorway sheltered by arched portico with pair of slender colonnettes and beautifully detailed entablature, fanlight over door modern. (M. M. Coffin, *H. A. B. S.* #916; K. Duprey, *Old Houses*, pp. 127–/133/; G. A. Fowlkes,

Mirror of Nantucket, pp. 104–105; E. A. Stackpole, *Rambling,* pp. 23, 25; E. U. Crosby, *Ninety Five Per Cent,* photo p. 43; R. Pratt, *Golden Treasury,* photo p. /137/)

Academy Lane (Avenue)

3   Built 1760 for Gideon Worth, center-chimney house. 2½-story shingle, ridge chimney, 4-bayed façade, enclosed pent sheltering entrance, window over and that to west 9/9-paned, others 12/12-paned. New wing west end. (K. Duprey, *Old Houses,* pp. 143–146; E. A. Stackpole, *Rambling,* p. 25; E. U. Crosby, *Ninety Five Per Cent,* photo p. 43)

4   Typical Nantucket house. 2½-story shingle on high brick basement, ridge chimney, 4-bayed façade, 6/6-paned windows.

6   Federal period. 1¾-story clapboard front, shingle sides, ridge chimney, 4-bayed façade, 6/6-paned windows, modern pilastered doorway with sidelights on west side. Extension on south end. Originally was similar to 8 Academy, inverted plan.

8   Built *ca.* 1820 for Capt. Alexander Bunker, Federal style. 1¾-story clapboard front, shingle sides, ridge chimney, 4-bayed façade, pilastered doorway with transom, modillions under cornices of doorway and façade, 6/6 paned windows. (E. A. Stackpole, *Rambling,* p. 25)

10   Late Federal. 2-storied clapboard front, shingle sides, end chimney, 4-bayed façade, enframed doorway with sidelights, 6/6-paned windows.

11   Originally typical Nantucket house. 2½-story clapboard, ridge chimney, roof walk, had 4-bayed façade, now pilastered Greek Revival doorway spans 2 bays, 6/6-paned windows. (N. H. A. *Photo Albums,* Book 1, p. /1/)

12   Greek Revival. 1¾-story clapboard front, shingle sides, ridge chimney, pilasters at corners, entablature across 3-bayed façade, pilastered doorway with sidelights, 6/6-paned windows.

Angora Street

Angora Street is an alley connecting Pleasant Street with North Mill Lane and skirting the south boundary of Moors' End. The name is of modern origin, derived—through confusion—from that of an earlier street farther south called Angola. Angola Street branched westward from the junction of Pleasant and South Mill, and it was named after the Portuguese West African country because of the colored people living in this area since the late eighteenth century. The former name for Angora was Gardner's Lane,[1] which on the 1833–34 Coffin map was shown to turn and intersect with Mill Street between numbers 4 (The 1800 House) and 8.

Note

1   Edouard A. Stackpole, *Rambling Through the Streets and Lanes of Nantucket,* New Bedford, Mass., 1969, p. 66.

Ash Lane and Ash Street

Both listed in the Coffin Survey of 1799, Ash Lane and Ash Street run from Centre to North Water, in the direction of and between Broad and Step Lane. Three ancient houses of note are here: the Levi Joy house, on the corner at 43 Centre, built about 1765 and having withes on the sides of the chimney, which is unique in Nantucket; the slightly earlier half-house lean-to at 5 Ash Street, remodeled after the Great Fire of 1846, when most of its neighbors were being built; and the contemporary 10 Ash Street, originally similar to number 5 but enlarged to a full-house, and then remodeled in the early nineteenth century. The last two houses face south, and, despite its address, the enlarged example actually fronts Ash Lane *(Fig. 119).*

Historic Buildings

Ash Lane

6   2½-story shingle on brick foundations, ridge chimney, 3-bayed façade, 6/6-paned windows. Renovated.

Ash Street

1   Built after 1846 Fire, Greek Revival style. 1¾-story shingle on brick basement, chimneys (modern) on roof slope, pilasters at corners supporting front entablature, 5-bayed façade, center doorway with sidelights sheltered by distyle Tuscan portico, 6/6-paned windows.

2   Built after 1846 Fire, Greek Revival period. 1¾-story clapboard front, shingle sides, ridge chimney, 3-bayed façade with gable, 6/6-paned windows, entrance on east side.

4   Built after 1846 Fire, Greek Revival period. 2½-story shingle on concrete-block foundations, ridge chimney, 3-bayed façade with gable, 6/6-paned windows, entrance on west side having modern enclosed porch.

5   Built 2nd quarter 18th century, originally lean-to half-house, facing south. Rear raised to 2 full stories, probably late 18th century and wing attached at rear. 2½-story shingle front, clapboard west side, brick basement, ridge chimney (rebuilt), 3-bayed façade. Doorway moved to west side Greek Revival period (at which time it was clapboarded), 6/6-paned windows. Later enclosed porch here on right flank.

8   Built after 1846 Fire, Greek Revival style. 2½-story shingle on brick basement, 4 end chimneys, 5-bayed façade, center pilastered doorway with sidelights, stoop with double stairs, 6/6-paned windows.

10   Original east section reputedly brought from old Sherburne, 2nd quarter 18th century lean-to half-house, faces south (Ash Lane). Enlarged to full-house. 2½-story shingle, rear on high brick basement, ridge chimney, 5-bayed façade with center doorway, 12/12-paned windows except 9/9-paned over entrance. During early 19th century made into duplex for Alex (east) and George (west side) Folger, woodwork in east parlor dates from period after they sold house in 1811. (J. F. Murphy, 65 *Views*, photo of rear around turn of century, pl. /18/; information Dr. Byron Lingeman)

Atlantic Avenue

Atlantic Avenue originates at the intersection of Pleasant and York streets, runs southwardly past the termination of South Prospect, William Lane, Sparks Avenue, and Vesper Lane, and continues past the grammar and high schools toward Surfside. On the William Coffin map of 1833–34, Atlantic is labeled New Guinea Street, probably due to the dark-skinned people who made their homes here.

Historic Buildings

3   Similar to 39 Pleasant, later 2/2-paned windows. (N. H. A. *Photo Albums,* Book 1, p. /1/)

5   1¾-story shingle, ridge chimney, 4-bayed façade, extension northwest end. 1971 restoration includes new 12/12-paned windows.

6   1¾-story shingle, ridge chimney (new), 5-bayed façade, later door and 2/2-paned windows.

8   1¾-story shingle, had ridge chimney, 4-bayed façade, later 4/4-paned windows, extension north flank.

9   1¾-story shingle, ridge chimney, 3-bayed façade, later porch, 2/2-paned windows and front dormer.

53   Lean-to house. 1¾-story shingle, ridge chimney replaced, 5-bayed façade, later 4/4-paned windows, enclosed front porch, house moved here early 20th century from east side Atlantic several lots north. (Mrs. Josephine Devine; N. H. A. *Photo Albums,* Book 6, p. /10/)

Back Street

Back Street was in existence at the time of the Isaac Coffin Survey of 1799. It runs from Pleasant to Orange Street, between New and William. The houses on it are small, less than two-storied.

Historic Buildings

8	Built 1840 for Abraham Ewer. 1¾-story shingle, ridge chimney, pilastered Greek Revival doorway, 6/6-paned windows. (Mrs. Gerta Kerr Mason)
9	1¾-story shingle, had ridge chimney, 3-bayed façade, 6/6-paned windows, extension on front and another on northeast corner.
11	1¾-story shingle, ridge chimney, 3-bayed façade, pilastered Greek Revival doorway, 6/6-paned windows.
16	1¾-story shingle, ridge chimney, gabled 3-bayed façade, pilastered Greek Revival doorway, later 2/2-paned windows.

Bear Street

Bear Street is the third street south of Back and of equal length. It, too, is accounted for in the 1799 survey. It contains only a single old house, but one that is noteworthy, an expertly restored early saltbox.

Historic Building

3	Built 1720s and moved to site in 1756 for Tristram Bunker, lean-to house. 2½-story shingle, ridge chimney, 2-bayed façade, batten door, 12/12-paned windows. (M. M. Coffin, *H. A. B. S.* #900)

Beaver Lane

Also referred to as Beaver Street since the 1830s, Beaver Lane is short and connects Orange and Union streets two blocks above their junction. The name and demarcation go back to the eighteenth century, the name perhaps derived from the first American whaler in the Pacific, built for Captain Paul Worth in 1791.

Historic Buildings

1	1¾-story shingle, ridge chimney (new), 3-bayed façade, pilastered doorway, 6/6 paned windows.
2	Greek Revival style. 1¾-story shingle, chimney on side, 3-bayed gabled façade with pilasters at corners, pilastered doorway with sidelight, 6/6-paned windows, upper outer windows with ¼-round heads.
3	Lean-to house. 2½-story shingle, ridge chimney (new), had 3-bayed façade, later 6/6-paned windows, shed-roof extension east end, main entrance on west side. Unusual plan with winder stairs west side of chimney, fireplaces to both front rooms. (N. H. A. *Photo Albums,* Book 6, p. /12/)
5	2½-story shingle, ridge chimney, 3-bayed façade, pilastered Greek Revival doorway that had sidelights, 6/6-paned windows.
6	1¾-story shingle, ridge chimney (replaced), 3-bayed façade, Federal pilastered doorway, later bay window and porch, lean-to added to rear and later box dormer.
7	Built 1839. 2½-story shingle, ridge chimney, 3-bayed façade, pilastered doorway, 6/6-paned windows. Its barn now converted to residence, 8 Beaver, across street. (Thomas Coffin)
9	Built 1829 for Capt. Jonathan Swain II, lean-to house. 1¾-story shingle, ridge chimney, 5-bayed façade, doorway with transom, 9/9-paned windows. Kitchen ell integral with house. (Deed Book 30, pp. 105–106)

Blackberry Lane

Blackberry Lane is a driveway that extends southward from West Chester Street between Gull Island Lane and Wescoe Place.

Historic Building

1   Built between 1834 and 1848. 2-story shingle on brick basement, chimney each end, 5-bayed façade facing east, center doorway, 6/6-paned windows. Later wing south flank.

Bloom Lane

Bloom Lane connects Main and Vestal and is between Milk Street and Quaker Road.

Historic Buildings

1   Built mid-18th century, lean-to half-house. 2½-story shingle, ridge chimney, 3-bayed façade, later 6/6-paned windows, modern door with transom, roof walk (modern). (*Guidebook,* p. /17/)

4   Built late 1830s for William E. Macy, Greek Revival style. 1¾-story clapboard front, shingle sides, brick basement, had end chimneys, 5-bayed façade with pilasters at corners, full entablature across front, pilastered doorway with sidelights, wood stoop with stairs both sides, 6/6-paned windows. Inside window frames of front rooms broader than window openings to include recesses for folding shutters. (E. A. Stackpole, *Rambling,* p. 74)

Broad Street

Broad Street was the north boundary of the east range of Wescoe Acre Lots, laid out in 1678. In 1799, Isaac Coffin described Broad as extending from Centre Street "east to New North Wharf."[1] The advent of mechanized ships, during the last quarter of the nineteenth century, instigated the renaming of the pier to Steamboat Wharf, and it was rebuilt in 1915. The brick Whaling Museum, on the north side of Broad between South Beach and North Water, was built in 1847 as a candle factory. The façade of the new (1970) historical museum attached was modeled after that of the Coffin School on Winter Street. The Nantucket Town and County Building opposite was built in 1964. The Great Fire of 1846 devastated everything on Broad Street with the exception of the brick Jared Coffin house, on the corner of Centre *(Fig. 89).* To its east is the site of an early Quaker Meeting House, replaced in 1838 by Trinity Church, the first Episcopal house of worship on the island.[2] A modern annex to the hotel replaces it. A small Greek Revival doctors' office and larger residence beyond are succeeded by two bracketed mansard-roof houses of the 1870s *(Fig. 120).* The old cobblestones still exist under the asphalt paving.

Notes
1   Henry Barnard Worth, *Nantucket Lands and Land Owners,* Nantucket Historical Association, Vol. II, Bulletin No. 5, 1906 (reissued 1928), p. 243.

2   Edouard A. Stackpole, *Rambling Through the Streets and Lanes of Nantucket,* New Bedford, Mass., 1969, p. 20.

Historic Buildings

11   RICHARD MITCHELL & SONS CANDLE FACTORY, built 1847, Greek Revival style. 2½-story brick, 5-bayed façade with pediment, brick cornices, slate roof. In 1929 converted into the Whaling Museum, given a Federal-manner doorway with sidelights and blind fan inappropriate to a mid-19th-century building. In 1969–71, large wing added on west end for historical museum. (M. M. Coffin, *H. A. B. S.* #907; G. A. Fowlkes, *Mirror of Nantucket,* p. 125; *Guidebook,* p. 28; *Proceedings,* 1930, photo frontispiece; *Historic Nantucket,* July 1955, p. 14; E. U. Crosby, *Ninety Five Per Cent,* photo p. 44)

17   Built after 1846 Fire, Greek Revival style. 1¾-story clapboard front, shingle sides, high brick basement, ridge and side chimneys, pilasters at corners supporting entablature on flanks, 4-bayed façade with gable, 3 windows above, 6/6-paned windows, entrance on porch east side.

18   Built after 1846 Fire, Greek Revival style. 1¾-story clapboard front, shingle sides, high brick base-

Fig. 120 View of Broad Street in 1880s.

ment, ridge chimney, pilasters at corners supporting entablature on flanks, 3-bayed gabled façade, 6/6-paned windows, outer windows 2nd story ¼-round heads, pilastered doorway on east side.

20   Built after 1846 Fire, Greek Revival style. 1¾-story clapboard on high brick basement, ridge chimney, pilasters at corners, 3-bayed gabled façade, 6/6-paned windows, pilastered doorway with sidelights east side.

22   Built after 1846 Fire. 2½-story clapboard front, shingle sides, brick basement, ridge chimney, 3-bayed façade, pilastered Greek Revival doorway with sidelights, 6/6-paned windows. Modern roof deck and other alterations.

23   Built after 1846 Fire, Greek Revival style. 2½-story clapboard on high brick basement, ridge chimneys, pilasters at corners supporting entablature, 3-bayed façade with pediment, 6/6-paned windows, enframements with "Greek ears," entrance on west side.

24   Built after 1846 Fire, Greek Revival style. 2½-story clapboard front, shingle sides, on high brick basement, pilasters at corners supporting entablature, 4-bayed pedimented façade, 6/6-paned windows, enframements with "Greek ears," pilastered doorway with sidelights on west side.

25   Built after 1846 Fire, Greek Revival style. 1-story office, flush-board front, shingle sides, 3-bayed pilastered façade with pediment, center doorway, later windows.

29   Built 1845 for Jared Coffin, Greek Revival style. 3-story brick on granite basement (no windows in front), end chimneys, slate hip roof capped by square cupola, 5-bayed façade, brick entablature, parapet over cornice with balustrade insets aligned to windows, center doorway with sidelights sheltered by distyle Ionic portico with parapet, 6/6-paned windows, triple-light windows over portico. Granite posts and iron railing enclosing front yard. Coffins moved to Boston early in 1846 (before fire). House purchased by Nantucket Steamboat Co. for hotel 1847, called Ocean House. Sold to Eben W. Allen 1857 and brick annex built. Resold to Messrs. Howe & Elmer, Boston, 1872 and encircling porch added. Acquired by Nantucket Historical Trust in 1961 and restored. Present hotel called Jared Coffin House. (H. B. Worth, *Nantucket Lands,* p. 241; *Historic Nantucket,* April 1962, pp. 40–55; M. M. Coffin, *H. A. B. S.* #918; G. A. Fowlkes, *Mirror of Nantucket,* p. 118; E. A. Stackpole, *Rambling,* p. 20, 1874 photo p. 17; *Guidebook,* p. 26; vignette lower left corner J. J. Stoner, *View,* 1881; J. F. Murphy, *Fifty Glimpses, ca.* 1895 photo p. 23; E. U. Crosby, *Ninety Five Per Cent,* illus. p. 45)

Cambridge Street

Cambridge is one block north of Main and runs from South Water to Federal. It is shown on the 1834 Coffin map. with Madison Street between it and Main. Madison was eliminated by the setback of the north side of Main following the Great Fire of 1846.

Historic Building

1   Built after 1846 Fire. 1-story brick, end chimneys (new), 5-bayed façade with brick cornice, center door. Later 2/2-paned windows. Shop covered by shed roof extended north side to face India Street. (N. H. A. *Photo Albums,* Book 1, p. /3/)

Centre Street

Centre Street was part of the Wescoe Acre Lots layout of 1678 and therefore is one of the oldest streets in Nantucket *(Fig. 2).* It begins on the north side of Main at the west end of Market Square *(Fig. 121).* Here, to the left, are two Federal-period buildings, the Pacific National Bank (1818) and Methodist Church (1822–23), the latter with an added, colossal Greek Revival portico (1840–*Figs. 81, 103).* All of the structures on the east side between Main and Broad were destroyed by the Great Fire of 1846, and those existing postdate the catastrophe. The first is the flank of the row of brick commercial houses on Main (47–57). The next building centers on Sherburne Hall, headquarters of the Independent Order of Odd Fellows. It is composed of a symmetrical group of three taller,

Fig. 121 View of Centre Street from Tower of Unitarian Church.

pedimented, pilastered pavilions connected by low wings (5–21—*Fig. 109*). Although designed in the masculine Greek Revival manner, the block is referred to as "Petticoat Row" because of the former preponderance of women shopkeepers here. Under Centre Street, at the intersection of India, is one of the five fire cisterns dug in 1803. The shop on the southwest corner originally was an attractive residence *(Fig. 122)*. Across the street is the former Friends' Meeting House (29), built in 1850, now annex to a guest house. On the same side in the next block stands a second-growth willow tree. The original shoot was brought from Napoleon's grave on St. Helena by Henry Flaskett Clapp and planted with two others nearby in 1842. The parent tree was cut down in 1918, and the present offshoot comes from the truncated root.[1] Buildings between Quince and Gay have been altered from their role as residences *(Figs. 54–55)*. Facing the lower stretch of Centre, at 29 Broad, is the Jared Coffin house, built in 1845 and a survivor of the Fire. Nantucket's only three-story brick residence, it has spent most of its existence as a hostelry.

Centre Street veers to the left as it passes Broad and continues northward. A notable house here is number 52, the southeast section of which is claimed to have been brought from old Sherburne and enlarged for Joshua Coffin in 1756 *(Fig. 59)*. A secret room is enveloped by the great chimney *(Fig. 60)*. A second notable example in Federal style is the Reuben Russell house (45) on the east side *(Figs. 67–68)*. The earlier house of Peter Folger II is set back from the street farther along (51). Built about 1765, the three-storied frame is pretentious according to local pre-Revolutionary standards *(Figs. 61–62)*. Across the street, the First Congregational Church on old Beacon Hill, later Academy Hill, was built in 1834 and enlarged about 1840, and it is partly Rococo-Gothic and partly Gothic Revival *(Fig. 111)*. It replaces Old North Vestry *(ca.* 1730), the oldest existing house of worship in Nantucket, which stood on the site after 1765 and was shifted to the rear to make way for its more impressive successor *(Fig. 4)*. On the same side of the street, at the bend in Centre, are two identical Greek Revival houses (70 and 72) of considerable character *(Fig. 93)*. The quarter-round-headed windows in their gables constitute an interesting solution to the problem of fenestration in a restricted shape. Just beyond is a duplex (74 and 76), the two halves of which were built half a century apart. Passing Chester Street, Centre angles to the right and is called North Centre up to where it meets Cliff Road. Number 86 in this stretch is a smaller lean-to house, much altered, that was built to face south rather than the street.

Note
1 "Napoleon Willow," *Historic Nantucket,* April 1961, pp. 48–49.

2   METHODIST CHURCH, built 1822–23 with hip roof, Greek Revival portico added and appropriate changes made to early building 1840, Frederick Brown Coleman believed to have been architect for alterations. 2-story flush-board façade, clapboard sides, on brick basement, colossal pilasters at corners, full entablature front and sides, prostyle 6-columned Ionic portico, supports with plain shafts, pediment facing Centre Street, 3 doorways on portico, 12/12-paned windows. (G. A. Fowlkes, *Mirror of Nantucket*, pp. 88–90; M. M. Coffin, *H. A. B. S.* #1007; E. A. Stackpole, *Rambling*, p. 16; *Inquirer & Mirror*, Sept. 16, 1965, p. 3; E. U. Crosby, *Ninety Five Per Cent*, photo p. 46)

5, 7, 9, 11,   Built after 1846 Fire for George Harris and Benjamin F. Riddell, Greek Revival style. 7-part architec-
17, 19, 21   tural composition centered on SHERBURNE HALL (11), I. O. O. F. (Odd Fellows) occupying upper floor. 2-story flush-board, 7-bayed façade with pilasters over piers supporting pediment, 9/9-paned windows 2nd story, entablature spanning shop fronts below. Each wing of 3 parts is made up of a 2-story, 3-bayed pavilion with vertical shafts and pediment (7 and 19), connected and flanked by 1-story sections, all serving commercial purposes. Roof of 21 has been lowered to correspond with adjoining building on north. Because shops here were conducted by women (considered radical in the mid-19th century), the group came to be known as "Petticoat Row." (M. M. Coffin, *H. A. B. S.* #908; E. U. Crosby, *Ninety Five Per Cent*, line drawing pp. 152–153)

20   Built after 1846 Fire, Greek Revival style. 2½-story shingle street front, clapboard south side, brick basement, end chimney, 4-bayed façade with pediment, pilasters at corners supporting entablature along each flank, 6/6-paned windows, pilastered doorway with sidelights south side. Modern shop front on Centre Street.

23, 25   Built after 1846 Fire, double shop. 1½-story clapboard gable end with Greek Revival window frames (on India Street). Store front on Centre. Trapezoid plan because of angle of street intersection.

24   Built after 1846 Fire. 2½-story clapboard front, shingle sides, 6-bayed façade, 6/6-paned windows, modern shop fronts, much altered.

28   Built after 1846 Fire, Greek Revival style. Plan of building is parallelogram. 2½-story, originally clapboard walls, chimneys at sides, pilasters at corners supporting entablature, pediment in front with fan window, 4-bayed façade, pilastered doorway with transom, 6/6-paned windows. Had parapet over cornice on flank. Shop front now fills space north of doorway. (*ca.* 1860 photo in collection N. H. A.)

29   Built 1850 as meeting house for body of Friends which left the orthodox church in Nantucket, simplified Greek Revival style. 2½-story clapboard on brick foundations, gable toward street, shafts at corners. Later became a Baptist church, later still a dining hall for adjoining Bayberry Inn. (E. A. Stackpole, *Rambling*, p. 18; H. Turner, *Nantucket Argument Settlers*)

31   Built after 1846 Fire, Greek Revival style. 2½-story clapboard on brick basement, end chimneys, pilasters at corners supporting encircling entablature, 4-bayed façade crowned by pediment, 6/6-paned windows, entrance south side.

33   Built after 1846 Fire, Greek Revival style. 2½-story shingle, brick basement, ridge chimney, pilasters at corners, gable at front, 4 windows 1st story, 3 above, 6/6-paned windows, pilastered doorway with sidelights on south side. House is parallelogram in plan.

34   Moved here from east side Howard Street after 1900. Greek Revival style. 2½-story shingle on high brick basement, ridge chimney, 3-bayed façade with pedimented gable, pilastered doorway with sidelights, wood stoop, 6/6-paned windows. (N. H. A. *Photo Albums*, Book 2, p. /11/)

36   Built after 1846 Fire, Greek Revival style. 1¾-story clapboard on high brick basement, ridge chimney, 3-bayed gabled façade with pilasters at corners, entablature along each side, deeply recessed doorway. 12/12-paned windows modern (should be 6/6-paned).

37   Was typical Nantucket house, altered. 2½-story shingle on brick basement, ridge chimney, 4-bayed façade, 6/6-paned windows, doorway changed to window. Now extension of Jared Coffin House.

38   Built after 1846 Fire, Greek Revival style. 2½-story clapboard on high brick basement, chimneys at side, pedimented façade with pilasters at corners, 2 windows with ¼ round heads in tympanum, deeply recessed doorway, 6/6-paned windows, façade was 3-bayed. Shops now lower floors.

43   Built *ca.* 1765 for Levi Joy. 2½-story shingle, ridge chimney with flanges on sides, 5-bayed façade, later pilastered Greek Revival doorway, 6/6-paned windows. (H. B. Worth, *Nantucket Lands*, p. 241;

E. U. Crosby, *Ninety Five Per Cent,* photo p. 47)

45   Built *ca.* 1830 probably for Reuben Russell, who sold house in 1847, Federal style. 2-story clapboard on high brick basement, L-plan, end chimneys, 5-bayed façade, pilastered doorway with sidelights and blind fan, stoop with double stairs, 6/6-paned windows. Roof walk modern (Mrs. Henry W. Fee II)

46   Built 1760 for William Brock, 3-bayed house, later enlarged into typical Nantucket house. 2½-story shingle on brick basement, ridge chimney, 4-bayed façade, 12/12-paned windows 1st story and 8/12-paned windows above. Converted into shop. (Mr. & Mrs. Harry A. Howard II; N. H. A. *Photo Albums,* Book 1, p. /4/)

47   Built early 19th century, typical Nantucket house. 2½-story shingle on brick basement, ridge chimney, pilastered Greek Revival doorway with transom, 6/6-paned windows. (G. A. Fowlkes *Mirror of Nantucket,* pp. 43–44; E. U. Crosby, *Ninety Five Per Cent*, photo p. 47)

48   2½-storied, had clapboard front, shingle sides, 2 ridge chimneys (north remains), 5-bayed façade, center Greek Revival pilastered doorway with sidelights, 6/6-paned windows. Modern front on south half, box dormer over north. (N. H. A. *Photo Albums,* Book 1, p. /4/)

49   Built early 19th century, typical Nantucket house. 2½-story shingle on brick basement, ridge chimney, 4-bayed façade, later pilastered doorway with sidelights, 6/6-paned windows.

51   Built by Jethro Hussey *ca.* 1765 for Peter Folger II on site of William Geyer house (1684); was known as "flat-roofed house," encircled by railing, present roof added by Uriah Folger before 1815. 3½-story clapboard front, shingle sides, ridge chimney, roof walk, gable overhang, 5-bayed façade with center doorway behind enclosed entrance porch, 12/12-paned windows 1st and 2nd stories, 8/12-paned windows in 3rd. (M. M. Coffin, *H. A. B. S.* #924; E. A. Stackpole, *Rambling,* p. 22; G. A. Fowlkes, *Mirror of Nantucket,* p. 108; *Inquirer & Mirror,* Oct. 21, 1965, p. 5; E. U. Crosby, *Ninety Five Per Cent,* photo p. 48; A. E. Poor, *Colonial Architecture,* pl. 52)

52   Southeast section said to have been brought from old Sherburne, rebuilt here and enlarged 1756 for Joshua Coffin. 2½-story shingle, ridge chimney, formerly had roof walk and "Gothic" tracery parapet over front cornice, 5-bayed façade, early 19th century. (Federal) center pilastered doorway with sidelights, 6/6-paned windows, rear ell and woodshed. House has secret space (1st-3rd floors) within chimney. (M. M. Coffin, *H. A. B. S.* #1004; K. Duprey, *Old Houses,* pp. 57–58; E. A. Stackpole, *Rambling,* p. 21; K. Mixer, *Old Houses of New England,* pp. 235–238; N. H. A. *Photo Albums,* Book 1, p. /5/; A. E. Poor, *Colonial Architecture,* pls. 34, 91)

53   Built *ca.* 1840, Greek Revival style. 2½-story clapboard on brick basement, end chimneys, square cupola astride roof, 4-bayed façade with corner pilasters and pediment, 6/6-paned windows, doorway on south side sheltered by distyle Ionic portico, voluted capitals set facing street.

54   Built 1821, Federal style. 2-story shingle on brick basement, hip roof, 2 ridge chimneys, 3-bayed façade, pilastered doorway with transom and sidelights, new brick steps, 6/6-paned windows. (E. A. Stackpole, *Rambling,* p. 21)

55   Built late 18th century or early 19th century. 2½-story shingle, ridge chimney, 5-bayed façade, center door with transom, restored 12/12-paned windows. At end of 19th century had clapboard front, shingle sides, 6/6-paned windows (except over door). Modern roof walk. (N. H. A. *Photo Albums,* Book 1, p /7/)

56   Built 1842 for Harrison Gray Otis Dunham, Greek Revival style. 2½-story shingle on brick basement, 4 end chimneys, 5-bayed façade, center doorway with sidelights sheltered by distyle Ionic portico, 6/6-paned windows. Late dormers. (E. A. Stackpole, *Rambling,* p. 21)

57   1¾-story shingle, ridge chimney, pilastered Greek Revival doorway, 6/6 paned windows, modern box dormer on front. (N. H. A. *Photo Albums,* Book 1, p. /8/)

59   Similar to 57 Centre Street, had parapet at turn of century. Modern front porch. (N. H. A. *Photo Albums,* Book 1, p. /8/)

60   Typical Nantucket house, moved from adjoining lot to south. 2½-story shingle, ridge chimney, roof walk, 4-bayed façade, pilastered Greek Revival doorway, 6/6-paned windows. House encompassed by modern porch. (N. H. A. *Photo Albums,* Book 1, p. /9/)

61   Built early 19th century. Original house 2½-story shingle on high brick basement, ridge chimney, 3-bayed façade, pilastered doorway with sidelights. 2-bayed north section added. Dormers, roof walk,

and front porch modern. (N. H. A. *Photo Albums*, Book 6, p. /9/)

62   FIRST CONGREGATIONAL CHURCH, known as North Church, built 1834 to replace Old North Vestry, by "Mr. Waldron, Boston" (Samuel Waldron, housewright), transitional Rococo Gothic and Gothic Revival. Clapboard on brick foundations, square tower on east front surmounted by double stepped belfry and octagonal steeple, colossal pilasters at corners of tower and auditorium supporting entablatures, pointed fanlight with tracery mullions over main doorway. Perpendicular fenestration in front. Originally 3 tall pointed windows on each flank, enlarged 1 bay *ca.* 1840, about which time steeple removed and 4 pinnacles erected at corners. Present steeple built and set in place by helicopter 1968. Architectural (*trompe l'oeil*) painting of interior by E. H. Whitaker, Boston, 1852. Remodeled 1868, 1948. (E. A. Stackpole, *Rambling*, pp. 21–22; G. A. Fowlkes, *Mirror of Nantucket*, pp. 86–88; *Historical Nantucket*, January 1969, pp. 14–/21/; M. M. Coffin, *H. A. B. S.* #902; E. U. Crosby, *Ninety Five Per Cent*, photo p. 49; letter, Mrs. Theresa Cederholm, Fine Arts Dept., Boston Public Library, July 23, 1971)

62   (behind First Congregational Church) Originally NORTH SHORE MEETING HOUSE (Presbyterian) now called OLD NORTH VESTRY. Built *ca.* 1725 at south end of Capaum Pond (2 miles west), moved to Beacon Hill in 1765 and re-erected on site of present First Congregational Church, removed to current location in 1834. The oldest existing building on Nantucket built for worship, it is a plain shingled form with 2 doors in south gabled end, 3 high windows on west flank; presumably had same on east, and 3 below on each side; would have had upper gallery at rear and along sides. Exposed framing inside. Additions on all four sides, including later church on east. (H. B. Worth, *Nantucket Lands*, pp. 235–236; R. A. Douglas-Lithgow, *Nantucket*, pp. 86–87; H. C. Forman, *Early Nantucket*, p. 239; M. M. Coffin, *H. A. B. S.* #903; E. A. Stackpole, *Rambling*, pp. 21–22; G. A. Fowlkes, *Mirror of Nantucket*, p. 119; R. J. Leach, *Proceedings*, 1950, p. 27; Worth-Palmer, *Photos*, 1905 photo, p. 124)

64   2½-story shingle on rock basement, ridge chimney, South section is original house. Window panes all sizes. Inscribed: "Edna Frances Hayward House 1790 Given First Congregational Church 1950."

65   (North) Typical Nantucket house, built 1821. 2½-story shingle on high brick basement, ridge chimney, 4-bayed façade, later pilastered Greek Revival doorway, stoop with double stairs, 2/2- and 6/6-paned windows.

66   Built 1806 for Capt. Archelus Hammond. 2½-story shingle, 2 ridge chimneys, 5-bayed façade, pilastered doorway, 6/6-paned windows. (A. E. Poor, *Colonial Architecture*, pl. 28)

67   (North) Small lean-to house. 1¾-story shingle, ridge chimney, 4-bayed façade, 6/6-paned windows, new doorway. (N. H. A. *Photo Albums*, Book 1, p. /11/)

68   Typical Nantucket house. 2½-story shingle on brick basement, ridge chimney, roof walk, 4-bayed façade, door with transom, 6/6-paned windows.

70, 72   Mid-19th-century twin houses, Greek Revival style. 1¾-story clapboard on high brick basement, chimney at sides (modern), pilasters at corners supporting entablature along flanks, 3-bayed façade with gable, pilastered doorway with sidelights, stoop with curving railings down front steps, 6/6-paned windows, outer upper windows have ¼-round heads.

74, 76   Duplex: 76 inscribed "1785," 74 inscribed "1835." 2½-story shingle, each has ridge chimney, 3-bayed façade, pilastered Greek Revival doorway, 6/6-paned windows (4/4-paned windows over doors). At turn of century 76 had roof walk (was not there in 1874). (N. H. A. *Photo Albums*, Book 1, p. /8/)

78   Typical Nantucket house. 2½-story shingle, ridge chimney, 4-bayed façade, later pilastered Greek Revival doorway, 6/6-paned windows. Modern dormers.

86   (North) East section mid-18th-century lean-to house facing south. 1¾-story on rock foundations, ridge chimney, originally 3-bayed façade (half-house) with shed-roof extension west flank. Modern extension on front, restored 12/12-paned windows. (K. Duprey, *Old Houses*, pp. 49–52; H. B. Worth, *Nantucket Lands*, p. 270; J. Freeman stereopticon view looking north from steeple First Congregational Church, *ca.* 1874)

Fig. 122 28 Centre Street, at Intersection of India, About 1860.

Charter Street

One block long, connecting Fair and Pine streets, between School and Hiller's Lane, Charter Street was opened in 1747 through the middle of Fish Lot Number 22. It was made one rod (16½′) wide. The land on the north side was owned by Damaris Coffin, who, in 1760, sold the lot at the west end to her son Micajah.[1] His house, on the corner (14 Pine), although altered, is still standing.

Note

1 Henry Barnard Worth, *Nantucket Lands and Land Owners*, Nantucket Historical Association, Vol. II, Bulletin No. 5, 1906 (reissued 1928), p. 247.

Historic Buildings

3   2½-story shingle, ridge chimney, original house (east section) 3-bayed, west (1 bay) added. Later Greek Revival pilastered doorway, much later 2/2-paned windows.

8   1¾-story shingle, ridge chimney, 3-bayed façade, door with transom, 2/2-paned windows (later).

Cherry Street

Cherry Street was called Cherry Lane in the Isaac Coffin survey of 1799. It connects Orange and Pleasant Street and lies between William and Bear.

Historic Buildings

3   1¾-story shingle, ridge chimney (replaced), 3-bayed façade, later door frame and 2/2-paned windows.

7   1¾-story shingle, ridge chimney (replaced), 3-bayed façade, later door and 1/1-paned windows.

8   1¾-story shingle, ridge chimney, 4-bayed façade, pilastered doorway, 6/6-paned windows, rear lean-to added.

10   1¾-story shingle, ridge chimney, 4-bayed façade, 6/6-paned windows, lean-to added.

Chester Street

A single block between Centre and North Water has retained the name of Chester Street, which originally designated the main thoroughfare from Capaum to the Great Harbor, the longest stretch of which today is called West Chester (see below). The two come together where Centre becomes North Centre, and the eastward continuation of Chester Street proper, beyond the intersection of North Water and Cliff Road, is called Easton Street.

Historic Buildings

1   Early 19th century 2½-story shingle on stone basement, 2 ridge chimneys, 5-bayed façade, 12/12-paned windows, later Greek Revival doorway, stoop with twin stairs.

2   Late 18th- or early 19th-century typical Nantucket house. 2½-story shingle on stone and brick foundations, ridge chimney, 4-bayed façade, doorway with transom, 12/12- and 9/9-paned windows. (N. H. A. *Photo Albums*, Book 1, p. /11/; E. U. Crosby, *Ninety Five Per Cent*, photo p. 50)

5   Similar to 2 Cliff Road. 2½-story shingle, ridge chimney, 3-bayed façade, 12/12-paned windows, later doorway.

6   Slightly modified late 18th century typical Nantucket house. 2½-story shingle on high rock basement, ridge chimney, 4-bayed façade, doorway with transom, later 6/6-paned windows. Closet is in northeast corner beyond window next to front door lighting stairhall. Rear wing is early 2-story dwelling with 9/9-paned windows 1st story, 6/6-paned windows 2nd story. (N. H. A. *Photo Albums*, Book 1, p. /12/)

Chestnut Street

The street extending the single block from Centre to Federal, and lying between Broad and India, was laid out in 1719 in the Wescoe Acre Lots district and called Chestnut Street.[1] By this title it was listed in the Isaac Coffin Survey of 1799. All early buildings on Chestnut were destroyed in the Great Fire of 1846.

Note
1   Henry Barnard Worth, *Nantucket Lands and Land Owners,* Nantucket Historical Association, Vol. II, Bulletin No. 5, 1906 (reissued 1926), p. 248.

Historic Buildings

1   Built after 1846 Fire. 2½-story shingle, end chimneys (that on west side new), gable toward street, 3-bayed façade, 6/6-paned windows, distyle Greek Doric portico. Much renovated.

2   Built after 1846 Fire, Greek Revival style. 2½-story shingle on brick basement, end chimneys, 5-bayed façade, recessed center doorway, 6/6-paned windows. Box dormer new.

3   Built after 1846 Fire, Greek Revival. 1¾-story shingle on brick basement, ridge chimney, front gable, 4 windows 1st story, 3 above, 6/6-paned, entrance east side.

5   Built after 1846 Fire, Greek Revival style. 2½-story clapboard on brick basement, chimneys on roof slope, pilasters at corners supporting encircling entablature, fan in pediment on west side, 5-bayed façade, 6/6-paned windows. House plan is parallelogram because of lot shape. Shop front west end. Dormers modern.

Cliff Road

Isaac Coffin described this road in 1799 as beginning at Chester Street, passing by a number of houses no longer in existence, "and so to Western Shearpen."[1] The western shearing pen was at Maxcy's Pond, midway between Capaum and the upper end of Hummock Pond. The road was called North Street up through the first third of the twentieth century, after which its geographic location suggested its present designation of Cliff Road. At its beginning are a number of dwellings built in the 1700s, including three mid-century lean-tos (12 and 20 Cliff Road and 86 North Centre) and seven later ridge-chimney types (2, 3, 5, 6, 9, 16, and 17), the upper three being typical Nantucket houses. Number 5, before additions, was an engaging little cottage (*Fig. 123*). Residences beyond belong to the early- to mid-nineteenth century, the majority being Greek Revival in style. At the west corner of North Liberty Street stands the Josiah Coffin lean-to of 1723–24, one of the best preserved, best restored, and most distinguished of early Nantucket houses (*Figs. 19–20*).

Note
1   Henry Barnard Worth, *Nantucket Lands and Land Owners*, Nantucket Historical Association, Vol. II, Bulletin No. 5, 1906 (reissued 1928), p. 269.

Historic Buildings

2   Late 18th-century type. 2½-story clapboard front, shingle sides, ridge chimney, 3-bayed façade, later pilastered Greek Revival doorway with sidelights, 6/6-paned windows. Additions north side and rear.

3   Built mid- to late-18th century, center-chimney type. 2½-story shingle, ridge chimney, 5-bayed façade, later 6/6-paned windows, center door sheltered by enclosed entrance pent.

5   1¾-story shingle, ridge chimney, originally 3-bayed façade (south section) with 2-bay extension having shed roof on north end, had 12/12-paned windows. Roof extended over entire building and windows changed to 6/6-paned sashes. (old photo Miller R. Hutchison II Collection, N. H. A.)

6   Built 1795 for Isaiah Folger. Originally 2½-story shingle, ridge chimney, 2- or 3-bayed façade, extension north side with shed roof. Extensively altered and enlarged mid-19th century and given center hallway and end chimneys. Present doorway and fenestration modern. (Mr. & Mrs. Paul V. Hoadley)

9   Originally typical Nantucket house. 2½-story shingle, very high brick basement, ridge chimney,

	roof walk, had 4-bayed façade. Modern portico and stoop, doorway with sidelights, dormers, bay window and 2/2-paned windows.
10	Greek Revival style. 2-story shingle, hip roof with end chimneys, 5-bayed façade, pilastered doorway with sidelights, 6/6-paned windows. Later porch and dormers.
12	Built 2nd quarter 18th century, lean-to half-house. Early addition north side. 2½-story shingle on rock foundations, ridge chimney, 3-bayed façade, 6/6-paned windows (later), rear heightened. New porch, front dormer, enclosed porch south side. (N. H. A. *Photo Albums,* Book 1, p. /13/)
16	Typical Nantucket house. 2½-story shingle on brick basement, ridge chimney, 4-bayed façade, 12/12-paned windows, later pilastered Greek Revival doorway, stoop with double steps, new dormers.
17	Was typical Nantucket house. 2½-story shingle, ridge chimney, 4-bayed façade. Pilastered Greek Revival doorway shifted to north bay of front, later 2/2 paned windows (formerly had 12/12 and 6/6.)
18	1¾-story clapboard front, shingle sides, ridge chimney, roof walk, 4-bayed façade, Federal framed doorway with sidelights, 6/6-paned windows, front porch with parapet.
20	Mid-18th century lean-to house, faces south. 2½-story shingle, ridge chimney, 3-bayed façade, later 6/6-paned windows. Extended west side for larger stairhall. Additions at rear.
21	Built early 19th century. 2-story shingle, end chimneys, 5-bayed façade, center door, late 2/2-paned windows.
22	1¾-story shingle on brick basement, ridge chimney, 3-bayed façade, 6/6-paned windows. New box dormer.
24	Early 19th century typical Nantucket house. 2½-story shingle on high brick basement, ridge chimney, 4-bayed façade, doorway with transom, high stoop with stairs both sides, 6/6-paned windows.
28	Greek Revival period. 1¾-story shingle, chimney on roof slope, shafts at corners, entablature along flanks, 3-bayed façade with gable, 6/6-paned windows. New porch, side dormers.
29	Greek Revival style. 1¾-story shingle, had end chimneys, pilasters at corners supporting entablature across front, 5-bayed façade, center pilastered doorway with sidelights, 6/6-paned windows. Modern Dutch dormers and wing on north side.
30	1¾-story shingle, ridge chimney. Bay window added and other changes.
36	Greek Revival style. 1¾-story shingle, ridge chimney (replaced), shafts at corners, 3-bayed façade, pilastered doorway, 6/6-paned windows. Late front dormer.
38	Greek Revival style. 1¾-story shingle, ridge chimney (rebuilt), pilasters at corners, entablature along flanks, 3-bayed façade with 2 windows in gable, pilastered doorway, 6/6-paned windows. Later wing north side and dormers.
41	Originally similar to 38 Cliff Road. Added to and altered. Owned by painter Eastman Johnson. (James Hunt Barker)
44	Originally 1¾-story shingle, ridge chimney, 3-bayed façade with front gable, Greek Revival pilastered doorway, 6/6-paned windows. Extended south end.
46	2½-story shingle, ridge chimney, presently 6-bayed façade, parts of Greek Revival doorway, added to and altered.
49	Greek Revival style. 1¾-story shingle, ridge chimney, shafts at corners, 3-bayed façade with gable, pilastered doorway with sidelights, 6/6-paned windows (2 in second story). (N. H. A. *Photo Albums,* Book 1, p. /13/)
51	1¾-story shingle, ridge chimney, 3-bayed façade, Greek Revival doorway, modern 12/12-paned windows, box dormer.
60	Built 1723–24 for Maj. Josiah Coffin for son of same name, faces south, lean-to house. 2½-story shingle, reduplicated articulation of ridge chimney, front cornice with modillions (omitted over windows, lacking space), 5-bayed façade, center batten door with transom, 12/12-paned windows 1st story, 8/12-paned windows 2nd story except 4/6 over door. (H. C. Forman, *Early Nantucket,* pp. /252/–/253/; M. M. Coffin, *H. A. B. S.* #911; H. B. Worth, *Nantucket Lands,* 1881 photo facing p. 237; G. A. Fowlkes, *Mirror of Nantucket,* pp. 35–37; *Proceedings,* 1904, p. 21; E. U. Crosby, *Ninety Five Per Cent,* photo p. 50; A. E. Poor, *Colonial Architecture,* pl. 63–labeled "Nantucket, North Street"; R. Pratt, *Golden Treasury,* pp. 138–139)

Fig. 123 5 Cliff Road Before Alterations.

Coffin Street

Coffin Street connects Washington and Union streets, originating at the head of Commercial Wharf, constructed at the beginning of the nineteenth century by Zenas Coffin and Sons, whence the street derives its name. It is not to be confused with the former Coffin Court, now Gay Street. Only the west section of Coffin Street figures on the 1834 map and here is called "Crocker's C." ("Court").

Coon Lane

Coon Lane, one block above Beaver, is of later origin. It was not given recognition either in the Isaac Coffin Survey of 1799 or on the William Coffin map of 1833–34, but first appears on the Bache map of 1848, a clue to the dating of its houses.

Historic Buildings

2   1¾-story shingle, ridge chimney, 4-bayed façade, Federal pilastered doorway, 6/6-paned windows. (N. H. A. *Photo Albums,* Book 6, p. /3/)

3   Greek Revival style. 1¾-story shingle, chimney at side, pilasters at corners, 3-bayed gabled façade, pilastered doorway with sidelights, 6/6-paned windows, outer upper windows had ¼-round heads until changed 1971.

| 5 | 2½-story shingle, ridge chimney, 3-bayed façade, pilastered doorway, 6/6-paned windows. (N. H. A. *Photo Albums,* Book 1, p. /16/) |
| 7 | 1½-story shingle, ridge chimney (replaced), 3-bayed façade, pilastered doorway, later 2/2-paned windows, box dormer. |

Copper Lane

This little elbow of a court, running eastward from Quaker Road (originally Grave Street) and bending back to Milk, was called Silver Street in the Isaac Coffin Survey of 1799. By the middle of the nineteenth century, it shared this name with the street at the south end of Fair, connecting Pleasant and Orange. About the turn of the century, the original Silver Street began to be called Copper Lane, which avoids confusion with its later namesake but launched a new one through the similarity to Copper Street, the old name for Prospect Street, sometimes rendered Cooper Street, as on the Walling map of 1858.

Historic Building

| 2 | Built late 18th century, perhaps by Edward Allen, housewright, lean-to house. 1¾-story shingle, ridge chimney, 4-bayed façade, enclosed entrance pent, 12/12-paned windows. (E. U. Crosby, *Ninety Five Per Cent,* photo p. 51; N. H. A. *Photo Albums,* Book 1, p. /16/) |

Cottage Court

A spur off the west side of Orange Street, between Warren and York, Cottage Court came into existence in the mid-1830s with the building of the three similar cottages facing east, north, and south.

Historic Buildings

1	(north side) 1¾-story shingle, stone foundations, ridge chimney, 3-bayed façade, pilastered doorway, late 2/2-paned windows.
2	(south side) 1¾-story shingle, ridge chimney (new), pilastered doorway, later bay window.
3	(west end) 1¾-story shingle, later front gable and ridge chimney, 3-bayed façade, door and windows altered, and rear additions.

Darling Street

Darling Street looks much the same today as it did when the latest of its houses (at either end on the south side) were built a century and a quarter ago. Isaac Coffin described it in 1799 as beginning at the "South-east corner of James Cartwright house," which is still standing at the north corner facing Fair Street (33).[1] The farthest house in this range originally fronted Darling (11), but now its entrance is on the flank toward Pine. The street was given the surname of John Darling, who came from Boston and married a Folger.[2]

Notes

1 Henry Barnard Worth, *Nantucket Lands and Land Owners,* Nantucket Historical Association, Vol. II, Bulletin No. 5, 1906 (reissued 1928), p. 251.
2 Edouard A. Stackpole, *Rambling Through the Streets and Lanes of Nantucket,* New Bedford, Mass., 1969, p. 53.

Historic Buildings

| 3 | Typical Nantucket house. 2½-story shingle, ridge chimney, 4-bayed façade, pilastered doorway with |

	transom, 6/6-paned windows. Modern brick stoop. Had roof walk. (N. H. A. *Photo Albums,* Book 1, p. /18/)
4	Greek Revival style. 2½-story clapboard on high brick basement, chimneys at sides, pilasters at corners supporting entablature, 3-bayed pedimented façade, pair of windows in tympanum with blind pointed arches, pilastered doorway with sidelights, wood stoop, 6/6-paned windows, triple window over doorway.
6	Built early 19th century, 2½-story shingle, 2 ridge chimneys, 5-bayed façade, center doorway with transom and sidelights, 6/6-paned windows. Had roof walk. (N. H. A. *Photo Albums,* Book 1, p. /18/; E. U. Crosby, *Ninety Five Per Cent,* photo p. 52)
8	Built mid-18th century for Capt. James H. Barnard. 2½-story shingle, ridge chimney, 3-bayed façade, 12/12-paned windows, later pilastered doorway. (E. A. Stackpole, *Rambling,* p. 53; E. U. Crosby, *Ninety Five Per Cent,* photo p. 52)
9	Built 1810–20. 2½-story shingle on high brick basement, had end chimneys, roof walk, 5-bayed façade, later Greek Revival pilastered doorway with sidelights, wood stoop with steps both sides, 6/6-paned windows. (E. A. Stackpole, *Rambling,* p. 53; N. H. A. *Photo Albums,* Book 1, p. /18/)
10	Late 18th-century type center-chimney house, faces south. 2½-story shingle, ridge chimney, 5-bayed façade (but no window over center door), 12/12-paned windows, extension east side.
11	Early 19th-century typical Nantucket house. 2½-story shingle, ridge chimney, 4-bayed façade on Darling Street but entrance changed to Pine Street side, 6/6-paned windows, modern porch on west end. Became home of Capt. Henry Plaskett. (E. A. Stackpole, *Rambling,* p. 53; N. H. A. *Photo Albums,* Book 1, p. /16/)
12, 14	Similar houses, Greek Revival period. 1¾-story clapboard (14 has shingle sides), ridge chimney, 3-bayed façade with pilasters at corners, doorway with sidelights, 6/6-paned windows.

Dover Street

Located one block north of and parallel to York Street, Dover Street proper is only the short section between Orange and Union, the longer stretch, extending from Orange to Pleasant, now being called West Dover (see below). The street is in the area of the West Monomoy subdivision laid out in 1726, although it was not included in the original plan. The name Dover already existed at the time of the Isaac Coffin survey (1799).

Historic Buildings

2	1¾-story shingle, ridge chimney (new), 3-bayed façade, pilastered doorway, 2/1-paned windows.
4	1¾-story shingle, ridge chimney, 3-bayed façade, 6/6-paned windows, door moved to west side.
5	1¾-story shingle, ridge chimney (new), 3-bayed façade, pilastered doorway, 2/1-paned windows.
8	1¾-story shingle, brick foundations, ridge chimney, 3-bayed façade, pilastered doorway, 6/6-paned windows.

Eagle Lane

Fair Street, which divided the east and west Fish Lots ranges, was left a dead end by the West Monomoy subdivision, planned in 1726. Orange Street was cut through the east range of the Fish Lots, and the west range was subdivided by crosswise streets to Pine, of which the southernmost is Eagle Lane. It is listed in the Isaac Coffin 1799 survey. On the 1834 and 1858 maps of Nantucket, this street is labeled "Jefferson Lane," which name now applies to the next street north. One suspects that some other way was the original Eagle Lane. The tiny house on the corner of Pine is a noteworthy lean-to *(Figs. 32–33).* All six houses listed below are indicated as being in existence on the William Coffin 1833–34 map.

3   1¾-story shingle, high brick basement, ridge chimney, 3-bayed façade, pilastered doorway, late 19th-century 2/2-paned windows.

4   1¾-story shingle, ridge chimney, 3-bayed façade, pilastered doorway with transom, late 2/2-paned windows. (N. H. A. *Photo Albums,* Book 1, p. /19/)

5   1¾-story shingle, ridge chimney, 3-bayed façade, later 2/2-paned windows.

7   1½-story shingle, ridge chimney, 3-bayed façade, later 1/1-paned windows, box dormer in front.

8   1½-story shingle, ridge chimney, 3-bayed façade, later 2/2-paned windows. (N. H. A. *Photo Albums,* Book 1, p. /19/)

9   Small lean-to house. 1¾-story shingle, ridge chimney, 3-bayed façade, originally had 6/9-paned windows, extension on northwest corner is integral part of construction. Perhaps moved to present site.

Easton Street

The continuation of Chester Street beyond Cliff Road and North Water Street is called Easton after the family holding property in this vicinity. Easton Street runs to Brant Point, site of the foremost lighthouse on the Great Harbor. Formerly there was a marine railway southwest of the light (1834 and 1858 maps), and later (from about 1883 to 1905) the Nantucket Hotel was north of it. Early twentieth-century bungalows line the south side of Easton between Water and Beach, where stood the block-long ropewalk that disappeared during the 1850s.

Fair Street

The two alignments of shares laid out below Main Street in 1717 and known as the Fish Lots were separated and reached by Fair Street *(Fig. 2).* The street extends south by southeast a quarter of a mile, with a slight angle at about its halfway point. Fair ends abruptly in front of 60, the site of which is over the line in the later West Monomoy subdivision (1726). Near the upper end of Fair Street, on the west side, stands the old Friends' school (1838), later having become the Friends' Meeting House, after the original meeting house—just south of it—was moved to the Cape in 1863. The remaining building was shifted to new foundations early in the present century when the historical museum was appended. At the curb in front is the south meridian obelisk, the north counterpart of which may be seen alongside the Pacific National Bank (see Main Street). Across the way is an old lean-to house (10) with rear heightened. Farther south is Saint Paul's Episcopal Church, built in 1901 in a belated Richardsonian Romanesque manner (though with pointed arches) of pink Quincy granite and brownstone trim. Opposite (between Mooer's and Mott lanes) stood the Levi Starbuck house *(ca.* 1800), moved during the 1830s to become the imposing domicile on the west side of Surfside Road.[1] Just south is the Ship's Inn, originally the Captain Obed Starbuck residence built in 1831, a three-storied house with hip roof. Next door is the late eighteenth-century house of Thomas Coffin II, remodeled in the mid-nineteenth *(Fig. 124).* Another present-day inn, The Woodbox, adjoining Hiller's Lane, is a double house of which the north section (29) was built as a half lean-to and the south part added with a full two-storied back, after which the older section was enlarged to match *(Fig. 56).* Two houses consecutively tenanted by Captain Seth Pinkham and his family are in the next block on the east side *(Figs. 51–53).* They show a similar plan executed as a story-and-three-quarters (42) and as a full two-storied building (40). Across the street in Tattle Court stands the Thomas Macy lean-to built about the time Fair Street was opened *(Figs. 15–16, 125).* At the south terminus of Fair are several houses with attractive doorways. Number 58 has a pilastered frontispiece with blind fan over the door and triglyphs in the entablature. Numbers 59 and 61 have engaged columns to their doorways, and the second also has triglyphs. The house at the end has a pilastered frontispiece with sidelights, and a whorled design in the fascia beneath the entablature.

Note
1 Marie M. Coffin, *Historic American Buildings Survey,* Mass. #943.

Fig. 124 13 and 15 Fair Street at Turn of Century.

Historic Buildings

5   Built 1820 for Capt. Frederick Chase. 2½-story shingle, 2 ridge chimneys, 5-bayed façade, center doorway sheltered by Greek Revival distyle Doric portico, 6/6-paned windows. Later dormers, addition at rear. (E. A. Stackpole, *Rambling,* p. 91; A. E. Poor, *Colonial Architecture,* portico pl. 90)

7   FRIENDS' SCHOOL, built 1838 by James Weeks. 2-storied clapboard (front and left flank) and shingle on brick foundations, hip roof, 12/12-paned windows. John Boadle was 1st teacher here in "Monthly Meeting School," later assisted by Hepsibeth Hussey. When adjoining Meeting House was removed in 1863, part of the 2nd floor in the school was taken out for conversion to a meeting hall. The building was shifted a short way to new foundations when the Nantucket Historical Association's concrete headquarters was built adjoining the northwest corner in 1904. (E. A. Stackpole, *Rambling,* p. 91; G. A. Fowlkes, *Mirror of Nantucket,* pp. 110–111; *Proceedings,* 1903, p. 17; *H. A. B. S.* #966)

8   Typical Nantucket house of relatively late date. 2½-story shingle on high brick basement, ridge chimney, 4-bayed façade, doorway with transom, wood stoop with steps both sides, 6/6-paned windows.

9   1850s' type Greek Revival house on site of old Friends' Meeting House removed to Cape in 1863. 2-storied clapboard on brick foundations, no basement windows in front, 3-bayed pedimented façade with pilasters at corners, doorway with sidelights sheltered by distyle square-piered portico with parapet over cornice, high wood stoop, 6/6-paned windows. Converted into apartments.

10   Claimed built early 18th century at old Sherburne, originally a lean-to house, rear now heightened to 2 stories. 2½-story shingle on high brick basement, ridge chimney, 3-bayed façade, wood stoop.

Late 2/2-paned windows. (H. B. Worth, *Transcript of Books,* p. 157)

13   Built 1831 for Capt. Obed Starbuck. 3-storied clapboard front, shingle sides, brick basement. Look-out platform (modern) atop hip roof, twin chimneys. 5-bayed façade, center doorway pilastered with transom and sidelights, wood stoop with steps both sides, 12/12-paned windows 1st and 2nd stories, 8/8-paned windows 3rd story. Modern box dormer in front. (E. A. Stackpole, *Rambling,* p. 90; E. U. Crosby, *Ninety Five Per Cent,* photo p. 53—labeled "15 Fair St.")

14   2½-story shingle on high brick basement, ridge chimney, 5-bayed façade, center doorway has Greek Revival trim, wood stoop, 6/6-paned windows. Now St. Paul's parish house.

15   Built late 18th century for Thomas Coffin II, remodeled mid-19th century. 2½-story clapboard, 2 ridge chimneys, 5-bayed façade, shafts with vertical grooves at corners, center doorway Greek Revival with pilasters and sidelights, wood stoop with steps both sides, 6/6-paned windows. (H. B. Worth, *Nantucket Lands,* p. 276; E. A. Stackpole, *Rambling,* p. 90; N. H. A. *Photo Albums,* Book 2, p. /1/)

17   Built early 1800s for Jonathan Macy. 2½-story clapboard front, shingle sides, end chimneys. 4-bayed on Fair Street. Remodeled in Greek Revival style after 1855 for Capt. Alden Adams, including new portico on south side with pilasters and 2 square piers. (E. A. Stackpole, *Rambling,* p. 90)

22   Late 18th-century type. 2½-story shingle, ridge chimney, 5-bayed façade, pilastered center door with transom, wood stoop, 6/6-paned windows. (N. H. A. *Photo Albums,* Book 2, p. /1/)

24   North section built before Revolution, considerably changed and enlarged. 2-storied shingle, later end chimneys, 6-bayed façade, 6/6-paned windows. Extension rear of south side follows angles of lane.

25   Built *ca.* 1800 for Gershorn Drew. 2½-story clapboard front, shingle sides, ridge chimney, 3-bayed façade, later Greek Revival doorway with sidelights, 6/6-paned windows. (T. Bunker, *Research,* #3163)

27   Built mid-1830s, Greek Revival style. 2½-story shingle, ridge chimney, 3-bayed façade, pilastered doorway, 6/6-paned windows.

29, 31   Attached houses, 29 built middle of 18th century as lean-to half-house, 31 added as full 2-storied (half-house) and rear of 29 taken up to match. Each 2½-story shingle, ridge chimney, 3-bayed façade with 12/12-paned windows. (H. B. Worth, *Nantucket Lands,* p. 253, 1881 photo facing p. 279; E. A. Stackpole, *Rambling,* p. 89; H. C. Forman, *Early Nantucket,* plan of 29 p. /94/; A. E. Poor, *Colonial Architecture,* pl. 22; E. U. Crosby, *Ninety Five Per Cent,* photo p. 53)

30   Typical Nantucket house, early 19th century. 2½-story clapboard front, shingle sides, ridge chimney, 4-bayed façade, pilastered doorway, 6/6-paned windows.

33   Built or assembled late 18th century for James Cartwright. 2½-story shingle, 2 ridge chimneys. Original section 3 south bays, 2 on north end added. 12/12-paned windows, except 9/9-over center door. (H. B. Worth, *Nantucket Lands,* p. 251)

34   Built 3rd quarter 18th century. 2½-story shingle, ridge chimney (new), 4-bayed façade, restored 12/12-paned windows 1st story, 8/12- and 6/9-paned 2nd story. (N. H. A. *Photo Albums,* Book 2, p. /2/)

36   Built 2nd quarter 19th century. 2½-story clapboard front, shingle sides, ridge chimney, 3-bayed façade, pilastered Greek Revival doorway with sidelights, 6/6-paned windows.

37   2½-story clapboard front, shingle sides, high brick basement, ridge chimney, 3-bayed façade, pilastered Greek Revival doorway with sidelights, stoop, 6/6-paned windows. Had roof walk, "Gothic" tracery parapet over front cornice. (N. H. A. *Photo Albums,* Book 2, p. /3/)

38   2½-story shingle, ridge chimney, 3-bayed façade, Federal pilastered doorway with transom, 8/12-paned windows 2nd story, later 6/6-paned windows 1st story. At turn of century had 6/6-paned windows both stories.

39   Built before 1832 for Henry Chase, Greek Revival style. 1¾-story shingle on high brick basement, ridge chimney, 3-bayed façade with pilasters at corners supporting entablature, pilastered doorway with sidelights, 6/6-paned windows. (Mrs. Byron Mooney)

40   Built 1827–28 for Capt. Seth Pinkham, typical Nantucket house. 2½-story shingle on brick basement, ridge chimney, roof walk, 4-bayed façade, door with transom, 6/6-paned windows. (F. B.

Anderson, *Through the Hawse-Hole,* pp. 172–176; E. A. Stackpole, *Rambling,* pp. 88–89; Mr. & Mrs. Howard M. Jelleme)

41   2½-story shingle, ridge chimney (replaced), 3-bayed façade, 6/6-paned windows.

42   Built early 19th century for Capt. Seth Pinkham, who lived here while building 40 Fair. 1¾-story shingle, ridge chimney, 4-bayed façade, doorway with transom, had 12/12- and 9/9-paned windows. Modern box dormer. (N. H. A. *Photo Albums,* Book 2, p. /4/)

43   Built late 18th century for Jethro Pinkham, typical Nantucket house. Added to and altered. 2½-story shingle, ridge chimney. Became double house, 5-bayed façade, 12/12-paned windows, extension with shed roof south end. (N. H. A. *Photo Albums,* Book 2, p. /3/; E. A. Stackpole, *Rambling,* p. 88)

46, 48   Double House. 2½-story shingle on stone foundations, each with ridge chimney, 3-bayed façade, extension north end, had 12/12- and 9/9-paned windows. (N. H. A. *Photo Albums,* Book 2, p. /5/)

47   Was typical Nantucket house. 2½-story shingle, high brick basement, ridge chimney, had 4-bayed façade, fenestration changes include 2/2-paned windows. Presently (1971) undergoing restoration. (N. H. A. *Photo Albums,* Book 2, p. /4/)

49   Typical Nantucket house. 2½-story shingle on high brick basement, ridge chimney, 4-bayed façade, late 2/2-paned windows, doorway altered.

50   2½-story shingle, 2 ridge chimneys, 5-bayed façade, center doorway with pilasters and sidelights, 6/6-paned windows.

54   Typical Nantucket house, altered. 2½-story shingle, ridge chimney (new), 3-bayed façade, 6/6-paned windows (4/4-paned window over door), later protruding bay window.

57   2½-story shingle, ridge chimney, 3-bayed façade, pilastered Federal doorway with transom, 6/6-paned windows, extension south end.

58   2½-story clapboard, ridge chimney, 3-bayed façade, doorway transitional Federal to Greek Revival, pilasters, blind fan, triglyphs in entablature, 6/6-paned windows. (E. U. Crosby, *Ninety Five Per Cent,* photo of doorway p. 54)

59   2½-story shingle, ridge chimney (new), 3-bayed façade, ½-round engaged-column Federal doorway with inner molding and corner blocks, 6/6-paned windows.

60   2½-story clapboard front, shingle sides, ridge chimney, 3-bayed façade, pilastered doorway with sidelights and unusual fascia relief, 6/6-paned windows. (N. H. A. *Photo Albums,* Book 2, p. /7/; E. U. Crosby, *Ninety Five Per Cent,* photo of doorway p. 55)

61   Similar to 59 Fair, doorway has triglyphs, later bay window.

Farmer Street

The lane situated south of Darling and north of Twin Street was described by Isaac Coffin in 1799 as: "Farmer street. North-east corner house of Jethro Pinkham on Fair street, west by Christopher Swain's house to Pine street."[1] Both houses mentioned are still standing. The Pinkham residence at 43 Fair is a late eighteenth-century typical Nantucket house. The Swain dwelling is that with a gambrel roof at 7 Farmer, its front windows "restored" incorrectly.

Note
1   Henry Barnard Worth, *Nantucket Lands and Land Owners*, Nantucket Historical Association, Vol. II, Bulletin No 5, 1906 (reissued 1928), p. 254.

Historic Buildings
1   2½-story shingle, ridge chimney, 3-bayed façade, pilastered Greek Revival doorway, 6/6-paned windows.

2   1½-story shingle, ridge chimney, 3-bayed façade. Late 19th-century bracketed doorway and 2/2-paned windows.

3   1½-story shingle, ridge chimney, 3-bayed façade, 6/6-paned windows. Modern box dormer in front.

4   2½-story shingle, ridge chimney, 3- or 4-bayed façade (window alongside door 1st story), door with transom, 12/12-paned windows.

5   1½-story shingle, high brick basement, ridge chimney, 4-bayed façade, later 2/2-paned windows. (N. H. A. *Photo Albums*, Book 2, p. /7/)

6   1¾-story shingle on rock foundations, ridge chimney, 4-bayed façade, doorway with transom, 12/12- and 9/9-paned windows.

7   Built before 1768 for Christopher Swain, gambrel roof house. 1½-story shingle, ridge chimney, 3-bayed façade, door with transom, originally had 12/12-paned windows (now 9/9-paned windows) in front. Renovated in 1930s by Everett U. Crosby. (Worth-Palmer, *Photos*, p. 30; E. A. Stackpole, *Rambling*, p. 84)

8   1¾-story shingle. Much changed.

Fig. 125 37 Fair Street Showing Rear of Lean-To House in Tattle Court to Left.

Fayette Street

Fayette Street is outside the early eighteenth-century lot layouts, though its west end is near the junction of Fish Lots and West Monomoy. It was laid out in the section along the shore known as Consue Meadows, below the Ware House Lots. Fayette Street does not figure on the 1834 map of William Coffin but appears on the 1848 map of A. D. Bache. It remains nameless on the Henry Walling map of 1858. A block long, Fayette connects Union and Washington streets. The present sign at its east end lengthens the name to "Lafayette."

Historic Buildings

1 Greek Revival style. 1¾-story shingle, chimney at side, 3-bayed gabled façade, pilastered doorway, later 2/2-paned windows. (N. H. A. *Photo Albums*, Book 2, p. /8/)

6 2½-story shingle, high brick basement, ridge chimney, 3-bayed façade, pilastered Greek Revival doorway, 12/12-paned windows, lean-to added on rear.

Federal Street

When the Wescoe Acre Lots were laid out in 1678, their boundary on the shore was the site of the present Federal Street. The dunes to the east were leveled for the creation of Bocochico in 1743. Early buildings throughout this area were destroyed by the Great Fire of 1846, and all now extant postdate the catastrophe. Back of the Nickerson Brick Store (east corner of Main) stood Harmony Hall, in which the Roman Catholics worshiped prior to the construction of Saint Mary's Our Lady of the Isle Church on the same site in 1897.[1] Across Cambridge Street is the present Post Office (1936), successor to the one that had stood on Main facing Federal since the middle of the nineteenth century. The little shop building across the way (4 Federal) was demolished and rebuilt in the fall of 1970, with errors in the details and the much later angle door that mutilates the southeast corner pilaster included in the rebuilding. The structure at the southwest intersection of India was a charming residence before conversion for commercial purposes *(Fig. 94)*. Diagonally opposite is the handsome Atheneum (1 India, *Figs. 105–106)*. The balance of the buildings are Greek Revival residences, up to the middle of the block between Oak and East Chestnut, beyond which the new civic center was built in 1964, including the Nantucket Town and County Building (facing Broad), information bureau, police station, and fire station (facing South Water), the last predating the others, having been constructed in 1929.

Note

1 Annie W. Bodfish, "A Few Facts Relating to Main Street," *Proceedings of the Nantucket Historical Association,* 1918, p. 33.

Historic Buildings

3 Built after 1846 Fire, ties in with 23–29 Main Street block. 2-story brick, 4-bayed on Federal, 3-bayed on Main with rounded corner entrance, 6/6-paned windows.

4 Copy of predecessor built after 1846 Fire, Greek Revival style, demolished Oct. 8, 1970. 2-story clapboard, pilasters at corners supporting frieze and cornice, 2-bayed façade, pediment with fan, 6/6-paned windows 2nd story. Southeast corner door later.

8 Built after 1846 Fire. 1¾-story shingle, gable facing street, pair 6/6-paned windows over shop front.

10 Built after 1846 Fire, Greek Revival style. 1¾-story, had clapboard front, shingle sides, pilasters at corners supporting entablature on flanks, 3-bayed façade with gable, 6/6-paned windows, outer 2 in 2nd story had ¼-round heads. 1st floor dropped to street level and entire new commercial front added. (N. H. A. *Photo Albums,* Book 3, p. /8/)

12 Built after 1846 Fire, Greek Revival style. 2½-story clapboard on high brick basement, end chimneys, 5-bayed façade, pilasters at corners, full entablature, center doorway with sidelights sheltered by distyle Doric portico, 6/6-paned windows. No windows front of basement wall. (A. E. Poor, *Colonial Architecture,* pl. 90)

20	Built after 1846 Fire, Greek Revival style. 2½-story clapboard on brick basement, chimneys at sides, 3-bayed pedimented façade with shafts at corners, 6/6-paned windows, doorway on north side.
21	Built after 1846 Fire, Greek Revival style. 2½-story clapboard on brick basement, chimney on roof slope, roof walk, 3-bayed façade with pilasters at corners supporting full entablature all around, pediment at front with pair of ¼-round-headed windows, pilastered recessed doorway with sidelights, 6/6-paned windows. Later wing on north flank.
24	Built after 1846 Fire. 2½-story clapboard front, shingle sides, high brick basement, 3-bayed façade, 6/6-paned windows, entrance moved south side, sheltered by porch with Doric columns.

Flora Street

The lane next north of Mulberry, Flora connects Orange and Union Street and has an angle midway in the block. It is labeled Flora Street on the 1834 Coffin map.

Historic Buildings

2	Built 2nd quarter 19th century. 1¾-story shingle, stuccoed basement, ridge chimney, 3-bayed façade, 12/12-paned windows (new).
3	Built 2nd quarter 19th century. 1¾-story shingle on brick basement, end chimneys, 5-bayed façade, Greek Revival pilastered center doorway with stoop, 6/6-paned windows (8/8- and 8/12-paned in basement).
4	Federal style. 2½-story clapboard front, shingle sides, brick basement, ridge chimney, 3-bayed façade, pilastered doorway with sidelights and blind fan, 6/6-paned windows.

Gardner Street

A popular designation for streets in Nantucket, the name "Gardner" is applied to a court south of Main on the east side of Orange Street; it was given to two lanes, one connecting Pine and Fair—at present called Mott Lane—and the other branching westward from Pleasant—south of Moors' End (19)—and now obliterated. These were listed by Isaac Coffin as existing in 1799. Also listed is Gardner Street, beginning on Main at the "South-west corner house of Christopher Starbuck" and extending "north to Liberty." The Starbuck residence was the present 105 Main Street, opposite the Civil War monument. Gardner Street originated as a right-of-way conveyed by Ebenezer Gardner to Zaccheus Macy in 1763[1] The only street that cuts into Gardner is Howard, which initially was Macy Court. The fire house on the south corner was built in 1886 and now is an exhibition room for old fire equipment. Next door is a shop formerly rented as the Women's Christian Temperance Union headquarters, later a grocery, and now the Christian Science Church. The second stretch of Liberty Street would seem to be a continuation of Gardner, but such is not the case in nomenclature.

Note

1 Henry Barnard Worth, *Nantucket Lands and Land Owners*, Nantucket Historical Association, Vol. II, Bulletin No. 5, 1906 (reissued 1928), p. 256.

Historic Buildings

4	Built 1824 for Caleb Allen, typical Nantucket house. 2½-story shingle, ridge chimney, 4-bayed façade, later Greek Revival doorway, 6/6-paned windows. (Miss Edith Bartlett)
8	Greek Revival style. 1-story clapboard, pilasters at corners, pedimented façade. Moved from front of yard of 4 Howard. Was W. C. T. U. hall early 20th century. (Miss Edith Bartlett)
10	Typical Nantucket house, the basic structure said to have stood on Duke Street near Crooked or Long Lane, sold by Jonathan Coleman to son-in-law Samuel Riddell in 1771, later moved to present site and rebuilt. 2½-story shingle on stone basement, ridge chimney, 4-bayed façade,

door with transom, stoop (lengthened), 12/12- and 9/9-paned windows. (H. B. Worth, *Nantucket Lands*, p. 256; K. Duprey, *Old Houses*, pp. 87–89; *Guidebook*, p. 23; E. U. Crosby, *Ninety Five Per Cent*, photo p. 56)

13	Moved here from Ray's Court. 2½-story shingle, brick basement, 2 ridge chimneys, 5-bayed façade, pilastered doorway with transom, wood stoop with steps both sides, 6/6-paned windows. (E. A. Stackpole, *Rambling*, p. 29)
14	Typical Nantucket house. 2½-story shingle, brick basement, ridge chimney, 4-bayed façade, pilastered doorway with transom and 12/12-paned windows (modern).
15	Typical Nantucket house. 2½-story shingle, ridge chimney, 4-bayed façade, door with transom, 12/12-paned windows. Sidewalk paved with bluestone. (N. H. A. *Photo Albums*, Book 3, p. /9/)
16	Built 1831 for Reuben Coffin, Federal style. 2½-story shingle on brick basement, ridge chimney, 3-bayed façade, doorway with sidelights and blind fan, 6/6-paned windows. (E. A. Stackpole, *Rambling*, p. 29; E. U. Crosby, *Ninety Five Per Cent*, photo p. 56)
18	Built 1837 for Capt. Robert Joy, Greek Revival style. 2½-story shingle on high brick basement, 4 end chimneys, roof walk, 5-bayed façade, center pilastered doorway with sidelights, wood stoop with stairs both sides, 6/6-paned windows. (E. A. Stackpole, *Rambling*, p. 29)
19	Claimed to have been built in 1777. 2½-story shingle, many changes, originally faced Liberty Street. (N. H. A. *Photo Albums*, Book 3, p. /4/)

Gay Street

Situated on the slope of Academy Hill, Gay Street originally was called Coffin Court from the Joshua Coffin house at the corner of Centre (52). After the Atlantic Silk Company factory (10, 12 Gay) was built in 1835–36 at the opposite end of the block, the name was changed to honor Gamaliel Gay, the inventor who improved the machinery used in the mill. The looms are said to have been the second in the world powered by steam machinery, and the plant was the first and only one of its kind in Nantucket. Groves of mulberry trees, essential to the raising of silkworms, were planted back of the George Easton house on North Water and elsewhere but did not do well. The silk industry on Nantucket was short-lived, lasting only eight years. One of the heaviest investors, Samuel B. Tuck, reclaimed a fraction of his losses through building and selling the houses opposite the mill.[1]

Note

1 Alexander Starbuck, *The History of Nantucket*, Boston, 1924, pp. 330–335.

Historic Buildings

4	Originally a typical Nantucket house, stood at 1 Quince Street. 2½-story shingle, had ridge chimney, 4-bayed façade, 12/12-paned windows. Moved to present site at end of 19th century, enlarged into "Queen Anne" style house with roof walk. (N. H. A. *Photo Albums*, Book 5, p. /3/)
5	2½-story shingle on brick basement, 2 ridge chimneys, roof walk, 5-bayed façade, pilastered doorway with transom, 12/12-paned windows, quoins at corners. (E. U. Crosby, *Ninety Five Per Cent*, photo p. 57—mislabeled "6 Gay")
6	2-story clapboard on brick basement, end chimneys, 5-bayed façade, deeply recessed pilastered Greek Revival doorway with sidelights, 6/6-paned windows.
7	Built 1840s, Greek Revival style. 1¾-story shingle, very high brick basement, end chimneys, 5-bayed façade, center doorway with sidelights, stoop, 6/6-paned windows.
9	Built 1840s, Greek Revival style. 1¾-story shingle on high brick basement, chimneys at side, shafts at corners supporting entablature along flanks, 3-bayed façade with gable, pilastered doorway with sidelights, stoop, 6/6-paned windows. (N. H. A. *Photo Albums*, Book 2, p. 10)
10, 12	Originally ATLANTIC SILK COMPANY MILL, built 1835–36, Greek Revival style. Closed in 1844 and building converted into duplex. 2½-story clapboard on high brick basement, 4 end chimneys, low fan window in west pediment, pilasters at corners, entablature encircling building, 7-bayed façade,

	pilastered recessed doorways with sidelights, stoops, 6/6-paned windows, except double window in center. Early house appended southeast corner as wing. (*Historic Nantucket*, Oct. 1963, pp. 19–22; A. Starbuck, *History,* pp. 330–335; E. A. Stackpole, *Rambling,* p. 26)
11	Built 1840s, Greek Revival style. 1¾-story shingle, had ridge chimney, corner pilasters, entablature across front, 3-bayed façade, pilastered doorway with sidelights, stoop, 6/6-paned windows. Modern dormers on front.
15, 17	Built 1840s, twin houses, Greek Revival style. 2½-story shingle on high brick basements, end chimneys, each 3-bayed façade, pilastered doorway with sidelights, stoop, 6/6-paned windows. (N. H. A. *Photo Albums,* Book 2, p. /11/)

Gorham's Court

The uppermost of three dead-end lanes above Flora Street, branching from the east side of Orange, Gorham's Court takes its name from Captain N. D. Gorham, for whom was built the first and sole survivor of four houses that were here in the middle of the nineteenth century *(Fig. 58).*

Historic Buildings

2	Built 1824 for Capt. Nathaniel Davis Gorham, faced south, Federal style. 2½-story shingle on brick basement, ridge chimney, roof walk, 3-bayed façade, 12/12-paned windows. Entrance has been moved to west side of later rear extension. 2nd house placed at north end of extension and converted into small theater for Dr. Benjamin Sharp, who purchased property in 1881. (Notes by Virginia Sharp Newhouse, courtesy Mrs. Victor Sutro; E. U. Crosby, *Ninety Five Per Cent,* photo p. 57)

Green Lane

A unique instance, for Nantucket, in which a public way originally was called a street and later has become a lane is this offshoot from Milk Street, originating across from the intersection of New Mill. In the eighteenth century, according to the Isaac Coffin survey, Green Street turned and ran westward parallel to Prison Lane (Vestal) through to Grave Street (Quaker Road). It therefore extended near the site of the present Cooper Lane. On the William Coffin 1833–34 map, Silver Street—the predecessor of Copper Lane—was in existence, and a narrow passageway at the west end of Green connected with Vestal. Today the west end of Green Lane spills into the angle of Copper. The designation, "Lane," is of relatively recent date.

Gull Island Lane

The fifth radial at the intersection of Centre-North Centre and Chester-West Chester streets is a narrow country-like lane running westwardly back to a prominence called Gull Island. The term "island" may be applied to a piece of land surrounded by a marsh and does not necessarily mean that Lily Pond encircled the rise. However, the pond at one time overflowed into a stream on which the first mill was built (Chapter One), and so it was a body of water of some consequence. With the post-and-rail fence on the north side, abundant vegetation, and three interesting early houses, no more delightful spot is to be found in Nantucket than Gull Island Lane, and, despite its modern dormers and rear additions, there is no more appealing residence than that at the apex of the "island" *(Fig. 126).*

Historic Buildings

1	Typical Nantucket house, built *ca.* 1800. 2½-story shingle, ridge chimney, 4-bayed façade, 12/12- and 9/9-paned windows, later pilastered Greek Revival doorway. Modern wing southwest end.
2	Moved here from ridge on Gull Island (near 3). 1¾-story shingle, ridge chimney, 3-bayed façade,

door with transom, 12/12-paned windows, wood eaves gutter. (photo *ca.* 1900, *Inquirer & Mirror*, July 2, 1949)

3   Built 1739 for Thomas Gardner, original house southeast section (with ridge chimney), to which added southwest, later (early 19th century) doubled in size with center hall. 2½-story shingle, 4 end chimneys, 5-bayed façade 1st story, 3-bayed above, center pilastered doorway with sidelights, 12/12-paned windows. 2 modern dormers (12/8-paned windows) front slope of roof. (*Inquirer & Mirror*, May 7, 1910, p. 1; H. B. Worth, *Nantucket Lands*, pp. 245–246; G. A. Fowlkes, *Mirror of Nantucket*, pp. 111–112)

High Street

In 1799, Isaac Coffin described High Street as extending from "Pleasant street at south-west corner of the old Poor House, east to Pine street, between house of Reuben Coffin and land of the Town of Nantucket."[1] The old jail, as well as the poorhouse, stood on the public land adjacent to the north side of this first cross street south of Summer. At that time, a new poorhouse recently had been erected on Vestal Street (then called Prison Lane), and a jail soon was to be constructed there as well (1805). The lean-to house of Reuben Coffin at the east end of High Street fronted on Pine.

Note
1   Henry Barnard Worth, *Nantucket Lands and Land Owners,* Nantucket Historical Association, Vol. II, Bulletin No. 5, 1906 (reissued 1928), p. 258.

Historic Building
2   Lean-to house, built late 18th century for Reuben Coffin, originally faced Pine Street. 1¾-story shingle, ridge chimney, 3-bayed present front on High Street, later pilastered Greek Revival doorway, 6/6-paned windows. (N. H. A. *Photo Albums*, Book 4, /14/)

Hiller's Lane

Hiller's Lane belongs to the group dividing the west range of the Fish Lots (1717), a later eighteenth-century addition, here spaced about one lot apart. It figures in the 1799 survey of Isaac Coffin. Hiller's Lane connects Fair and Pine streets between Charter and Darling.

Howard Street

The stretch of Howard Street projected from Gardner originally was called Macy Court, after the home of Zaccheus Macy II (9) on the south side, and it was so listed in the Isaac Coffic Survey of 1799. By the time William Coffin drew and published his map of Nantucket (1833–34), its west end was connected with a lane extending northward from Main, and the combined elbow was called Howard Street. The building at the northwest angle was William Holland's pig and horse barn prior to renovation into a studio home for the Misses Gertrude and Hanna Darlington Monaghan during the 1930s. Its conversion made use of many reused parts from buildings in Philadelphia, New York, and as far afield as Italy. The square bounded by Howard Street constitutes the first important area parceled off "Crooked Record," the largest of land holdings in the vicinity of present Nantucket Town (*Fig. 2*), owned by Richard Gardner for two decades prior to his decease in 1688.

Historic Buildings
3   2½-story shingle, 3-bayed façade, parts of Federal enframement to doorway. Enlarged and altered, 2/2-paned windows.

6	1¾-story shingle on brick basement, ridge chimney, 3-bayed façade, pilastered Greek Revival doorway. Modern 12/12-paned windows, porch and dormer added.
9	Built before 1750, lean-to house, moved to present site 1790 for Zaccheus Macy II, faces south. 2½-story shingle, ridge chimney, originally 2-bayed façade (door was in place of west window and present front door is later addition), 12/12-paned windows of which upper had smaller panes. Later addition with shed roof and 2-story wing on west flank. Some mid-19th-century 6/6-paned windows. In 1866 the north slope of the roof was raised, making street side of house full 2 stories. Greek Revival doorway at northeast corner. (H. B. Worth, *Nantucket Lands*, pp. 262–263; E. A. Stackpole, *Rambling*, p. 77)

Hussey Street

The east section of Hussey Street was opened in 1758 and called Hussey Court. It ran from Centre as far as the widow Mary Barnard's lean-to house (19). The west end, which curves down to intersect with India and Liberty streets, came into existence as Bunker's Court just in time to be included in the Coffin survey of 1799. An intervening space of a few rods later was connected to create the present Hussey Street.[1] Westminster Street, which originates by the east flank of the Barnard house, also dates from the early years of the nineteenth century, coeval with the building of the academy. The three lean-to houses (19, 25 and 30—the last gambrel in front), the other early dwelling (11), and the pediment light of 22 are notable architectural features of Hussey Street (*Figs. 12, 41, 90–91).*

Note
1   Henry Barnard Worth, *Nantucket Lands and Land Owners*, Nantucket Historical Association, Vol. II, Bulletin No. 5, 1906 (reissued 1928), pp. 244, 258.

Historic Buildings

3	Greek Revival style. 1¾-story clapboard on high brick basement, ridge chimney, 4-bayed façade with pilasters at corners supporting full entablature all around, double pointed windows in front pediment, 6/6-paned windows, pilastered doorway on east flank.
5	Greek Revival style. 1¾-story shingle on brick basement, ridge chimney, shafts at corners, entablature on flanks, 3-bayed façade with gable, doorway with sidelights, 6/6-paned windows. Later dormers on sides. (N. H. A. *Photo Albums*, Book 2, p. /12/)
7	Typical Nantucket house. 2½-story shingle, ridge chimney, 4-bayed façade, later pilastered Greek Revival doorway (had been on east end with distyle Doric portico), 6/6-paned windows. (N. H. A. *Photo Albums*, Book 2, p. /12/)
10	Greek Revival. 2-story clapboard on brick basement, end chimneys, 5-bayed façade, pilastered center doorway, stoop with steps both sides, 6/6-paned windows. (N. H. A. *Photo Albums*, Book 2, p. /13/)
11	Built probably 3rd quarter 18th century, perhaps first as 2-bay half-house constituting west section of present building. 2½-story shingle, stone foundations, articulated chimney. East section added on stone basement, 2 windows 1st story and 1 in 2nd, all 12/12-paned sashes. (N. H. A. *Photo Albums*, Book 3, p. /13/)
12	2½-story shingle, ridge chimney. Façade fenestration changed including new studio window.
14	2½-story shingle, had ridge chimney, 3-bayed façade, 6/6-paned windows. Original house stifled by dormer and additions. (N. H. A. *Photo Albums*, Book 2, p. /14/)
19	Built 1758 for Timothy Barnard, lean-to house. 2½-story shingle, ridge chimney, 3-bayed façade (originally had 1 instead of 2 windows 2nd story over parlor windows), door trim and 6/6-paned windows 19th century. Early shed-roof addition west end. (E. A. Stackpole, *Rambling*, p. 28; H. B. Worth, *Nantucket Lands*, p. 258; N. H. A. *Photo Albums*, Book 2, p. /15/); *H. A. B. S.* #195)
20	1¾-story shingle on brick foundations, 4-bayed façade, 6/6-paned windows. Much changed, box dormer in front and entrance shifted to east side. (N. H. A. *Photo Albums*, Book 2, p. /15/)
22	Transitional Federal to Greek Revival. 2½-story clapboard front, shingle sides, end chimneys, pilas-

ters at corners, 3-bayed façade capped by pediment with fine leaded window, pilastered doorway with sidelights, 6/6-paned windows. Horizontal cornice to pediment improperly restored.

23   2nd quarter 19th century. 2-story shingle on high brick basement, end chimneys, 5-bayed façade, center doorway with transom and sidelights, 6/6-paned windows. Much later gingerbread porch. Had roof walk.

24   Similar to 22 Hussey. 2½-story clapboard front and sides on brick basement, inverted plan, different trim, later double window in pediment. (N. H. A. *Photo Albums*, Book 2, p. /16/)

25   Built 1733 for Caleb Gardner, 3-bayed lean-to house. East 2 bays later addition. 2½-story shingle, articulated ridge chimney, 5-bayed façade, center door, 12/12-paned windows, except originally had 8/12-paned windows west end 2nd story. Later shed-roof extension west flank. (Worth-Palmer, *Photos*, p. 26; E. A. Stackpole, *Rambling*, p. 28; K. Mixer, *Old Houses of New England*, pp. 232–233; N. H. A. *Photo Albums*, Book 3, p. /17/; H. B. Worth, *Nantucket Lands*, p. 245, 1881 photo facing p. 239)

26   2½-story shingle on brick basement, L-plan, end and ridge chimneys, 4-bayed façade, 6/6-paned windows, new doorway (originally had transom over door, no sidelights). (N. H. A. *Photo Albums*, Book 2, pp. /16/, /17/)

30   Built 1772 for Grindell Gardner, unusual gambrel roof treatment in front only, lean-to at rear. 1½-story shingle, ridge chimney, 4-bayed façade, door with transom, had 9/6-paned windows (at present 6/6). Dormers date from 1890s. (M. M. Coffin, *H. A. B. S.* #927; H. B. Worth, *Nantucket Lands,* p. 245, 1881 photo facing p. 271; E. A. Stackpole, *Rambling,* p. 28; K. Mixer, *Old Houses of New England*, pp. 233–234)

Fig. 126 Thomas Gardner House (1739 and later additions), 3 Gull Island Lane.

India Street

Provided for in the layout of Wescoe Acre Lots in 1678, the earliest name given the street was Pearl, by which it was designated in the Isaac Coffin survey at the end of the eighteenth century. Joseph Sansom, in the January, 1811, issue of *The Port Folio,* reported that it was called "India Row" from the "number of residents who lived in ease and affluence thereon." Perhaps it never was changed officially, as the street is lettered "Pearl" on the Coffin 1834 and Walling 1858 maps, and on the Stoner 1881 bird's-eye view. In the present century, although the stretch from South Water to Centre retained the name Pearl into the 1960s, the street otherwise has been called India, as on the Historic District Map of 1956.

The Atheneum, at Federal, is among the foremost architectural gems of Nantucket *(Figs. 105–106).* Greek Revival houses in the next block are reminders of the Great Fire of 1846, which they (like the Atheneum) postdate. An early fire cistern is under the street intersection at Centre. The building on the southwest corner was built as a handsome residence *(Fig. 115).* The Silas Paddock house (18) is a charming example of a New England eighteenth-century gambrel-roof dwelling *(Figs. 39–40).* In this block between Centre and Liberty is a notable array of typical Nantucket houses–15, 20, 21, 23, and 25 (altered), 27, 29, 31, 32 (slightly altered), 33, 35, 37, 41, 43, and 45. The three-bayed brick house (12), unique in the town, and the wide Greek Revival (28) with distyle portico, together with the Paddock house mentioned, make an interesting contrast to the preponderance of a unified type. The big clapboard house to the east of the Paddock is modern (1970). A good portion of the row on the north side (inclusive of 15–45) was recorded in a neighborhood study plan made under the auspices of the Historic American Buildings Survey and Nantucket Historical Trust in the summer of 1970.

Historic Buildings

1   ATHENEUM, built 1847 by Charles Wood after design of Frederick Brown Coleman, Greek Revival style. Somewhat reflects form of predecessor on same site, originally the Universalist Church (constructed 1825), acquired for the Atheneum in 1834. Earlier building had pedimented portico of 4 Ionic columns, pointed doorway and windows. It burned in the 1846 Fire. Present building 2-storied of flush boards on brick foundations, walls articulated by colossal pilasters supporting full entablature, 5 bays on flanks, 6/6-paned windows with hood molds, double-pedimented façade, recessed portico, distyle Ionic *in antis,* pilastered and pedimented main doorway. Railing-type fence with pedestal posts on brick retaining wall. Lecture hall on 2nd floor, 1st story was library and museum. Has been public library since 1900, children's reading room in basement since 1963. (Prof. George C. Wood; *Inquirer & Mirror,* April 21, 1900, p. 4; M. M. Coffin, *H. A. B. S.* #812; F. A. Fowlkes, *Mirror of Nantucket,* pp. 90–92; A. Starbuck, *History,* pp. 337, 579, 582, illus. p. 338; E. U. Crosby, *Ninety Five Per Cent,* photo p. 59)

2   Built after 1846 Fire, Greek Revival style. 2-story clapboard front, shingle sides, brick basement, end chimney, pilasters at corners, 4-bayed façade, doorway with sidelights sheltered by distyle Doric portico, 6/6-paned windows.

9   Built after 1846 Fire, Greek Revival style. 2½-story shingle on brick basement, 2 ridge chimneys (later), 5-bayed façade, pilastered doorway with sidelights, 6/6-paned windows.

11   Built after 1846 Fire, Greek Revival style. 2½-story clapboard on brick basement, ridge chimney, pilasters at corners and spaced across front supporting encompassing entablature, 3-bayed façade, fan window in pediment, pilastered doorway sheltered by Doric porch at corner, 6/6-paned windows. Now the Bayberry Inn. (E. U. Crosby, *Ninety Five Per Cent,* photo p. 60)

12   Transitional Federal to Greek Revival. 2½-story brick, had parapet and 2 chimneys west end, 3-bayed façade, deeply recessed doorway with sidelights, 6/6-paned windows, new brick steps.

15   Built 1810 for Capt. William Stubbs, typical Nantucket house. 2½-story clapboard front, shingle sides on brick (front) and rock (sides) foundations, ridge chimney, 4-bayed façade, pilastered doorway with transom, wood stoop, 12/12- and 9/9-paned windows. (M. M. Coffin, *H. A. B. S.* #1013; E. U. Crosby, *Ninety Five Per Cent,* photo p. 61; N. H. A. *Photo Albums,* Book 2, p. /18/)

17   Built 1789 for Obediah Wood. 2½-story clapboard front, shingle sides, brick basement (part stone on sides), ridge chimney, 5-bayed façade, later pilastered Greek Revival center door, 12/12-paned windows modern restoration. (M. M. Coffin, *H. A. B. S.* #1013)

18   Built 1767 for Silas Paddock, gambrel roof house. 1½-story, ridge chimney, 3-bayed façade, door with transom, 12/12-paned windows, extension on west end trapezoid shape covered by shed roof served as rum shop, once had 2nd door on India Street. New brick steps to main entrance. (H. B. Worth, *Nantucket Lands,* p. 272, 1881 photo facing p. 247; E. U. Crosby, *Ninety Five Per Cent,* photo p. 62)

19   Built 1809 for Zaccheus Hussey, frame with brick ends. 2-storied shingle front, end chimneys, brick basement, 5-bayed façade, center doorway in Federal style with transom and sidelights, restored porch on stoop of brick and brownstone, 6/6-paned windows. (M. M. Coffin, *H. A. B. S.* #1013)

20   Typical Nantucket house. 2½-story shingle on brick basement, ridge chimney, 4-bayed façade, 12/12- and 9/9-paned windows, later pilastered Greek Revival doorway. (N. H. A. *Photo Albums,* Book 2, p. /19/)

21   Built *ca.* 1800 for John Howland Swain, typical Nantucket house. 2½-story shingle on brick basement, ridge chimney, 4-bayed façade, later pilastered Greek Revival doorway, wood stoop, 6/6-paned windows. (M. M. Coffin, *H. A. B. S.* #1013)

23   Built *ca.* 1800 by John & Perez Jenkins, builders, sold to Capt. Reuben Baxter 1801, originally a typical Nantucket house. 2½-story shingle, had ridge chimney, 4-bayed street side with 6/6-paned windows, entrance moved to east end, pilastered Greek Revival doorway with sidelights. (M. M. Coffin, *H. A. B. S.* #1013)

25   Built *ca.* 1794 for Daniel Coffin, typical Nantucket house, remodeled in Greek Revival style. 2½-story shingle on brick foundations, ridge chimney, 4-bayed façade, entrance with sidelights sheltered by distyle Doric portico, later 2/2-paned windows. (M. M. Coffin, *H. A. B. S.* #1013)

27   Built 1794 for Robert Folger, typical Nantucket house. 2½-story shingle on brick basement, ridge chimney, 4-bayed façade, wood quoins at corners, stoop before doorway, 12/12-paned windows. (H. B. Worth, *Transcript of Books,* pp. 320–326; M. M. Coffin, *H. A. B. S.* #1013)

28   Built 2nd quarter 19th century probably for David Baxter, attributed to John Coleman, Greek Revival style. 2½-story clapboard on high brick basement (no windows in front), 4 end chimneys, roof walk, vertical panel shafts at corners, 5-bayed façade, center doorway sheltered by distyle Doric portico, wood stoop with stairs both sides. 6/6-paned windows, parapet over cornice. (G. A. Fowlkes, *Mirror of Nantucket,* p. 112; Worth-Palmer, *Photos,* p. 42; E. U. Crosby, *Ninety Five Per Cent,* photo p. 62)

29   Built 1795 for Benjamin Swift, typical Nantucket house. 2½-story shingle, ridge chimney, originally 4-bayed façade (front window nearest east corner closed), 12/12-paned windows. Later pilastered Greek Revival doorway, pediment atop front of wing added northeast corner, curved staircase installed in enlarged front hall. (Prof. George C. Wood; H. B. Worth, *Transcript of Books,* pp. 320–326; M. M. Coffin, *H. A. B. S.* #1013; N. H. A. *Photo Albums,* Book 2, p. /19/)

30   Late Federal style. 2½-story clapboard, high brick basement (no windows in front), 2 ridge chimneys, 5-bayed façade, pilastered doorway with sidelights, swirled meander in fascia, stoop, 6/6-paned windows.

31   Built *ca.* 1795 for Eliab Hussey, unusually wide typical Nantucket house. 2½-story shingle, ridge chimney, 4-bayed façade, later pilastered Greek Revival doorway, still later 2/2-paned windows and dormers. (M. M. Coffin, *H. A. B. S.* #1013)

32   Originally typical Nantucket house. 2½-story shingle on high brick basement, ridge chimney, 4-bayed façade, later pilastered Greek Revival doorway with sidelights occupying space of former 2 east openings, stoop, 12/12-paned windows.

33   Built probably for John Russell end 18th century, typical Nantucket house, exceptionally wide front. 2½-story shingle, ridge chimney (modern), 4-bayed façade, pilastered doorway with transom, 6/6-paned windows. After Civil War period fore-section of southeast room made into stairhall. Staircase afterward put back in original position using later railing. (M. M. Coffin, *H. A. B. S.* #1013)

34   Greek Revival style. 1¾-story clapboard, high brick basement (no windows in front), end chimneys, heavy pilasters at corners supporting entablature, 4-bayed façade with "Gothic" pointed windows in pediment, 6/6-paned windows, doorway with distyle square-piered portico on west side.

35   Built *ca.* 1786 for George Lawrence, typical Nantucket house. 2½-story shingle, ridge chimney,

4-bayed façade, 12/12-paned windows. Later extension east end with shed roof, much later dormers. (M. M. Coffin, *H. A. B. S.* #1013)

37   Built *ca.* 1804 for Charles F. Hussey, typical Nantucket house. 2½-story shingle, ridge chimney, 4-bayed façade, door with transom, 12/12-paned windows. (M. M. Coffin, *H. A. B. S.* #1013)

38   2½-story shingle on brick basement, ridge chimney, 3-bayed façade, late Federal doorway with transom and sidelights, 6/6-paned windows.

39   Built *ca.* 1836 for Gorham Macy for son George (1839), late Federal house. 2½-story shingle on high brick basement, end chimneys, 3-bayed façade with pediment, doorway with transom and sidelights, door and window trim with corner blocks, 6/6-paned windows. (M. M. Coffin, *H. A. B. S.* #1013)

41   Believed moved from old Sherburne *ca.* 1761, became Andrew Bunker house 1809 (when he married Nancy Colesworthy), typical Nantucket house with small 2nd-story windows. 2½-story shingle, ridge chimney, 4-bayed façade, pilastered door with transom, 12/12-paned windows 1st story, 9/6-paned windows 2nd story (all modern replacements). (M. M. Coffin, *H. A. B. S.* #1013)

42   2½-story clapboard front, shingle sides, ridge chimney, 3-bayed façade, pilastered Greek Revival doorway, 6/6-paned windows. (N. H. A. *Photo Albums,* Book 2, p. /20/)

43   Built *ca.* 1805 for Melatiah Nye, variation on typical Nantucket house. 2½-story shingle on brick basement, ridge chimney, wide pilastered doorway with transom and sidelights, 2 windows west of door and 4 windows 2nd story, 12/12-paned. New brick steps to entrance. (M. M. Coffin, *H. A. B. S.* #1013; E. U. Crosby, *Ninety Five Per Cent,* photo p. 63)

45   Built *ca.* 1804 for Rescom Taber, similar to 43 India, exceptions include 6/6-paned windows, wood stoop, overhanging eaves on end gables (modern). (M. M. Coffin, *H. A. B. S.* #1013)

Jefferson Lane

The Jefferson Lane of today is not the Jefferson's Lane of the William Coffin 1833–34 and Henry F. Walling 1858 maps of Nantucket, and it may not be the Jefferson Lane of the Isaac Coffin 1799 survey. The old designation applied to the present Eagle Lane, one block south. All connect Pine and Fair, and the west extension of the current Jefferson Lane continues to Pleasant. The old angle near the west end of the stretch between Fair and Pine was straightened to align with the section continuing to Pleasant. No building of historic vintage fronts it.

Joy Street

Joy Street drops perpendicularly from the lower side of Prospect Street between Mount Vernon and New Mill. Although indicated as having houses along it on the 1833–34 and other nineteenth-century maps, it remains anonymous on these documents. The name, Joy, is of a Nantucket family, made famous by Captain Reuben Joy, who was on the *Minerva,* first Salem ship to circumnavigate the earth.

Historic Building
3   Inscribed 1799, 1¾-story shingle, ridge chimney (new), 3-bayed façade, 8/12-paned windows.

Liberty Street

Liberty Street is the most confusing in Nantucket because of the promiscuous way it wanders. The first stretch seems quite normal. It was the south boundary of the deeper inland range of the Wescoe Acre Lots of 1678 *(Fig. 2);* but where Liberty meets Gardner Street, it turns sharply to the north and becomes what ought to be the con-

Fig. 127 19 Hussey Street at Turn of Century.

tinuation of Gardner. Liberty passes the convergence of India and Hussey Streets, and, at an equal distance beyond, it comes to a V-fork, where one would expect it to end. It does, yet does not. The right branch becomes Lily Street, but the left sector acquires the designation of North Liberty and meanders upward as far as Cliff Road. North Liberty itself is almost as long as Main Street, and the two Liberties together constitute the lengthiest street of one name within the limits of the island town.

Liberty begins between the flanks of the Pacific National Bank (1818) and the Methodist Church (1822–40) at the head of Centre. None of its houses is within a half-century as old as the street itself, though a number of interesting examples belong to the eighteenth century. Numbers 3, 5, 13, 15, 27, and 31 are early houses, the first (3) being the latest and dating from 1756. The other five were built as lean-to houses, although only 12 and 15 retain the saltbox form, and the latter lost three feet from its east side when rebuilt on the present narrow lot about 1740 *(Figs. 22–23)*. Typical Nantucket houses (4, 19, 21, 23, 26, 36, and 40) and a few Federal and Greek Revivals (14, 17, 33, 39, and 41) represent other phases of Nantucket architecture during the flourishing period *(Fig. 128)*.

Historic Buildings

3   Built *ca.* 1756 for Jonathan Barney. 2½-story shingle, rock foundations, 2 ridge chimneys, 5-bayed façade, center door with transom and 12/12-paned windows restored. (H. B. Worth, *Nantucket Lands,* p. 260; N. H. A. *Photo Albums,* Book 3, p. /1/)

4   Originally a typical Nantucket house. 2½-story shingle on brick basement, ridge chimney, at present

Fig. 128 19 Liberty Street at Turn of Century.

3-bayed façade with late 2/2-paned windows. Extension with shed roof on west end, later 2-story wing east end.

5   Built 1748 for Barnabas Pinkham, transitional lean-to house with rear wall later heightened to 2 full stories. 2½-story shingle, ridge chimney, roof walk, 5-bayed façade with added extension having shed room on east end, 12/12-paned windows. Pilastered Greek Revival center doorway, had later enclosed entrance porch. (H. B. Worth, *Nantucket Lands*, p. 260; G. A. Fowlkes, *Mirror of Nantucket*, p. 112)

9   Built *ca.* 1820. Cottle house moved from Pleasant Street here for Capt. Joy. 2½-story shingle, had ridge chimney, 3-bayed façade, later bracketed doorway and 6/6-paned windows. (E. A. Stackpole, *Rambling*, p. 33)

12   Built after 1723 for Thomas Macy, given to son Nathaniel in 1745, lean-to house. North section may originally have been house at old Sherburne moved here and enlarged. 2½-story clapboard front, shingle sides, articulated ridge chimney, 5-bayed façade, center door with transom, 12/12-paned windows, those of 2nd story smaller than below. (H. B. Worth, *Nantucket Lands*, p. 261, 1881 photo facing p. 255; M. M. Coffin, *H. A. B. S.* #1003; E. A. Stackpole, *Rambling*, pp. 32-33; K. Duprey, *Old Houses*, pp. 14-18: G. A. Fowlkes, *Mirror of Nantucket*, pp. 112-113; E. U. Crosby, *Ninety Five Per Cent*, photo p. 63)

14   Built mid-19th century, Greek Revival style. 2½-story clapboard on high brick basement, chimneys at outer sides, 3-bayed gabled façade with pilasters at corners, pilastered doorway with sidelights, wood stoop, 6/6-paned windows. Similar to 7 Winter Street. Later double window in front gable.

15   Lean-to house rebuilt here *ca.* 1740 for Thomas and William Starbuck and conveyed to their sister Jemima (Mrs. Silvanus Allen). About 3 feet removed from east end to fit building on restricted lot. 2½-story shingle, rock foundations, articulated ridge chimney, 5-bayed façade, doorway and 9/9-paned windows part of extensive Alfred F. Shurrocks restoration during early 1930s. (H. B. Worth, *Nantucket Lands*, p. 261, 1881 photo facing p. 363; G. A. Fowlkes, *Mirror of Nantucket*, p. 113; E. A. Stackpole, *Rambling*, p. 33; E. U. Crosby, *Ninety Five Per Cent*, photo p. 64)

17   Early Federal period. 2½-story shingle, 2 ridge chimneys, 5-bayed façade, doorway with transom, 12/12-paned windows (modern).

19   Typical Nantucket house. 2½-story clapboard front, shingle sides, ridge chimney, 4-bayed façade, 12/12-paned windows, raking cornices making pediment over doorway added turn of century. (N. H. A. *Photo Albums*, Book 3, p. /1/)

21   Typical Nantucket house. 2½-story shingle on brick basement, ridge chimney, 4-bayed façade, pilastered doorway, stoop, restored 12/12-paned windows. (N. H. A. *Photo Albums*, Book 3, p. /2/)

22   Later 18th-century type. 2½-story clapboard front, shingle sides, ridge chimney, 5-bayed façade, 6/6-paned windows later than house, projecting bay window much later.

23   Typical Nantucket house. 2½-story shingle, ridge chimney, 4-bayed façade, later door frame and 6/6-paned windows.

26   Built beginning 19th-century, typical Nantucket house. Capt. Benjamin Worth an early owner. 2½-story shingle, brick basement, ridge chimney, 4-bayed façade, door with transom, 12/12-paned windows. (E. A. Stackpole, *Rambling*, p. 30; K. Duprey, *Old Houses*, pp. 121-126; N. H. A. *Photo Albums*, Book 3, p. /3/; E. U. Crosby, *Ninety Five Per Cent*, photo p. 65)

27, 29 Built 1745 for Benjamin Fosdick, lean-to house. 2½-story shingle, articulated ridge chimney, 5-bayed façade. In 1801 divided into 2 houses for sons, west half given to Benjamin II and east to Reuben. Had 2 doors, 6/6-paned windows. In 1960 enclosed entrance porch added. (H. B. Worth, *Nantucket Lands*, pp. 259–60, 1881 photo facing p. 263; G. A. Fowlkes, *Mirror of Nantucket*, p. 113; E. A. Stackpole, *Rambling*, p. 32; E. U. Crosby, *Ninety Five Per Cent*, photo with 2 doors, p. 65)

31   Built *ca.* 1740, lean-to half-house. Rear heightened. 2½-story shingle, ridge chimney, 3-bayed façade, enclosed entrance porch, 12/12- and 9/9-paned windows. Modern wing west end.

33   Greek Revival style. 1¾-story clapboard, ridge chimney, pilasters at corners supporting entablature on flanks, 3-bayed façade with gable, pilastered doorway with sidelights, 6/6-paned windows, outer 2nd story windows have ¼-round heads. (E. U. Crosby, *Ninety Five Per Cent*, photo p. 66; N. H. A. *Photo Albums*, Book 3, p. /3/)

35	Typical Nantucket house. 2½-story shingle, ridge chimney, 4-bayed façade, new door frame, 6/6-paned windows.
36	Typical Nantucket house. 2½-story clapboard front, shingle sides, on concrete-block foundations, ridge chimney, roof walk, 4-bayed façade, 6/6-paned windows.
39	Greek Revival style. 2½-story shingle on high brick basement, 4 end chimneys, 5-bayed façade, pilastered doorway, stoop, 6/6- and later 2/1-paned windows.
40	Typical Nantucket house. 2½-story shingle, high brick basement, ridge chimney, 4-bayed façade, late 2/2-paned windows, doorway.
41	2½-story clapboard front, shingle sides, high brick basement, ridge chimney, 3-bayed façade, pilastered Greek Revival doorway, stoop, 6/6-paned windows. (N. H. A. *Photo Albums,* Book 3, p. /4/)

Lily Street

Lily Street is the east fork of the Y intersection of which North Liberty is the west fork and Liberty proper the stem. Lily proceeds to Centre Street, which curves into West Chester, which, in turn, intersects North Liberty. The triangle thus formed encloses Gull Island and old Lily Pond. The latter lends its name to its southeast boundary, the street under consideration. With the exception of the first two buildings at the lower end of Lily Street (1 and 2), the houses along the south half are cottages with upper rooms under sloping roofs (inclusive of 5 to 19), whereas those along the north segment (beginning with 22) are two-and-a-half-storied, mostly of the Federal period. Number 31 is an exception, being a lean-to half-house of the mid-eighteenth century. The doorway to 35 is especially handsome *(Fig. 129).*

Historic Buildings

1	Greek Revival style. 1¾-story clapboard front, shingle sides, ridge chimney, pilasters at corners supporting entablature along flanks, 3-bayed façade with gable, pilastered doorway with sidelights, 6/6-paned windows, outer upper windows have ¼-round heads.
2	2½-story shingle, ridge chimney, 4-bayed façade, pilastered doorway with sidelights, 6/6-paned windows. Has been altered.
5	1¾-story clapboard front, shingle sides, had ridge chimney, 5-bayed façade, pilastered Greek Revival doorway, 6/6-paned windows.
7	1½-story clapboard front, shingle sides, ridge chimney, 3-bayed façade, 6/6-paned windows. Modern box dormer in front.
8	1¾-story shingle, had ridge chimney, 4-bayed façade, Federal doorway with heavy enframement and corner blocks, 6/6-paned windows. Late 19th-century wing south side.
9	1½-story clapboard front, shingle sides, ridge chimney, 3-bayed façade, 6/6-paned windows. Plan is an inversion of 7 Lily Street. Modern box dormer in front.
11	Federal style. Originally 1½-story shingle, had 2 end chimneys, 4-bayed façade, 6/6-paned windows. Front wall has been heightened to 2 full stories. (N. H. A. *Photo Albums,* Book 3, p. /5/)
12	Late Federal or Greek Revival period. 1¾-story clapboard front, shingle sides, end chimneys, 4-bayed façade, pilastered doorway with sidelights, 6/6-paned windows. (N. H. A. *Photo Albums,* Book 3, p. /6/)
14	Greek Revival style. 1¾-story clapboard front, shingle sides, end chimneys, 3-bayed façade, pilastered doorway, 6/6-paned windows.
15	Late Federal Style. 1¾-story shingle, end chimneys, 4-bayed façade, doorway with sidelights, 6/6-paned windows.
19	Federal style. 1¾-story clapboard front, shingle sides, high brick basement, end chimneys, 4-bayed façade, doorway with sidelights, 6/6-paned windows. Plan is an inversion of 15 Lily Street. Modern front dormers, wing south end.
22	Inscribed 1795, typical Nantucket house. 2½-story shingle, ridge chimney, 4-bayed façade, pilastered doorway with transom (modern), had 12/12- and 9/9-paned windows. Chimney rebuilt 1971.

27	2½-story shingle on high brick basement, ridge chimney, 3-bayed façade, 12/12- and 9/9-paned windows. (N. H. A. *Photo Albums,* Book 3, p. /6/)
28	Originally typical Nantucket house. 2½-story shingle, brick basement, ridge chimney, roof walk, had 4-bayed façade, extended 1 bay north end, later pilastered Greek Revival center doorway with sidelights, 6/6-paned windows.
31	Built on Fair Street for Benjamin Chase mid-18th-century, lean-to house. Moved to present site 1810 and altered for James F. Chase. 2½-story clapboard front, shingle sides, brick basement, ridge chimney, 3-bayed façade, later Greek Revival doorway, 6/6-paned windows. (*Inquirer & Mirror,* July 15, 1971, p. 20; E. U. Crosby, *Ninety Five Per Cent,* photo p. 66)
32	2½-story shingle, brick basement, ridge chimney, 3-bayed façade, entrance on north side sheltered by Greek Revival porch and enclosed vestibule, 6/6-paned windows.
35	2½-story clapboard front, shingle sides, brick basement, ridge chimney, 3-bayed façade, Federal pilastered doorway with triglyphs in frieze, inner frame with corner blocks, 6/6-paned windows. Modern porch south end.

Lyon Street

Isaac Coffin described Lyon Street in 1799 as connecting Orange and Pine. The continuation between Pine and Pleasant was called Barton's Lane. Both are shown on the William Coffin 1834 map though not named. By the time A. D. Bache had rendered his map in 1848, Lyon had been extended to Union. Lyon lies between Twin and Jefferson. The six old houses listed are between Fair and Pine. They are early nineteenth-century examples, and none of this period face the street in the outermost blocks, which are quite short.

Historic Buildings

1	2½-story shingle, ridge chimney, 3-bayed façade, 6/6-paned windows.
3	1¾-story shingle, ridge chimney (new), 3-bayed façade, late doorway and 2/1-paned windows.
4	2-story shingle on high brick basement, hip roof, had end chimneys, 5-bayed façade, pilastered Greek Revival center doorway with sidelights, 6/6-paned windows.
5	1¾-story shingle, ridge chimney, 3-bayed façade, Federal enframed doorway, 6/6-paned windows.
6	2½-story shingle, ridge chimney, 3-bayed façade, pilastered Greek Revival doorway, later 2/2-paned windows.
8	1¾-story shingle, ridge chimney, 3-bayed façade, 6/6-paned windows. Front porch modern.

Madaket Road

At the upper end of Main Street, Madaket Road veers to the left at Caton Circle, running alongside the old Friends' burying ground, while Main itself continues straight ahead for a short distance and makes a right turn into New Lane. An extension of New Lane continues across to Madaket Road.

Historic Building

X	(house at east corner of New Lane) 1¾-story shingle, ridge chimney, 4-bayed façade, pilastered doorway, 6/6-paned windows.

Martin's Lane

Connecting Fair and Orange streets, between Main and Plumb, Martin's Lane was opened in 1756 as one of the later modifications to the Fish Lots layout.[1] It is listed in the Isaac Coffin Survey of 1799. Except for Main, in the vicinity of and beyond the Civil War monument, Martin's Lane is Nantucket's one street paved in brick.

Note

1 Edouard A. Stackpole, *Rambling Through the Streets and Lanes of Nantucket*, New Bedford, Mass., 1969, pp. 89–90.

Historic Buildings

2   2½-story clapboard front (on Orange Street), shingle sides, ridge chimney, roof walk, 3-bayed façade, 6/6-paned windows. Projecting bay window replaces original doorway, entrance now on north side.

6   1¾-story shingle, ridge chimney, 3-bayed façade, pilastered Greek Revival doorway, 6/6-paned windows. New box dormer.

10   Probably built soon after lane laid out in 1756, lean-to house. 1¾-story shingle, ridge chimney, 5-bayed façade with center door, 12/12-paned windows, smaller upper window to hall. Unusual for smaller lean-to in having winder stairs in front of chimney, 2nd-story fireplace in west chamber. (E. A. Stackpole, *Rambling*, pp. 89–90)

Milk Street

Isaac Coffin's survey of 1799 describes Milk Street as beginning on "Main street at Town House" and running southwest "to south of Abraham Hoeg's house to the north of the Ropewalk, to William Ellis in Uppertown." The Town House was the 1716 building moved from West Chester Street in 1783 that remained opposite the site of the later Civil War monument for eighty years (Chapter One). Abraham Hoeg's house is 27 Milk Street. The ropewalk was at the summit of what now is Prospect Hill Cemetery, and the William Ellis house stood southeast of the Elihu Coleman dwelling on Hummock Pond, Uppertown being an indefinite location nearby.[1] Beyond the first block of Milk Street, many of the houses of the time of the survey are still standing, some built as lean-tos (9, 14, 23, 27, and 39), some as typical Nantucket houses (10, 11 as rebuilt, 12, 18, 26, and 33). Number 21 was built after the Revolution as a center-chimney, two-story house (*Fig. 130*). Number 35 had been a boat-building shop on Quaker Road, later converted into a residence and meeting house, moved here in the 1880s.

Note

1 Henry Barnard Worth, *Nantucket Lands and Land Owners*, Nantucket Historical Association, Vol. II, Bulletin No. 5, 1906 (reissued 1928), pp. 266–267.

Historic Buildings

1   Typical Nantucket house. 2½-story shingle on brick basement, ridge chimney, 4-bayed façade, later pilastered Greek Revival doorway, 6/6-paned windows.

5   2½-story clapboard, brick basement, 2 ridge chimneys, 5-bayed façade (south 2 bays only half depth, perhaps added), 6/6-paned windows, new doorway with sidelights identical to that of 4 Milk Street (which is a new house).

7   Built early 19th century for Thomas Coffin, Federal style. 2½-story shingle, 2 ridge chimneys, 5-bayed façade, center pilastered doorway with transom and sidelights, wood stoop with stairs both sides, 6/6-paned windows. Now the Hinckman House (Natural Science Museum), owned by Nantucket Maria Mitchell Association. (K. Duprey, *Old Houses*, pp. 157–160; *Guidebook*, p. 19)

9   Originally lean-to house, said to have been built at old Sherburne in 1740s, moved here soon after. 2½-story shingle, ridge chimney, 5-bayed façade, pilastered center doorway with transom, 12/12-paned windows. (G. A. Fowlkes, *Mirror of Nantucket*, p. 115; E. A. Stackpole, *Rambling*, p. 72; E. U. Crosby, *Ninety Five Per Cent*, photo p. 82)

10   Originally a typical Nantucket house. 2½-story clapboard front, shingle sides, ridge chimney, had

Fig. 129 Entrance Detail of 35 Lily Street.

4-bayed façade, later Federal-manner doorway with transom and sidelights, 6/6-paned windows. Late 19th century bay window.

11 Part of double house said built *ca.* 1761 at Capaum Pond for Thomas Starbuck. Son, Thomas Starbuck II, moved this section here about 1790, converted into typical Nantucket house. 2½-story shingle, ridge chimney, 4-bayed façade, door with transom, 12/12-paned windows. Ell added 1913, restored 1931. (M. M. Coffin, *H. A. B. S.* #942; H. B. Worth, *Nantucket Lands,* p. 257; K. Duprey, *Old Houses,* pp. /85/–86; E. A. Stackpole, *Rambling,* p. 72; E. U. Crosby, *Ninety Five Per Cent,* photo p. 82)

12 Built before 1784 for Tristram Starbuck or soon after for and perhaps by John Coleman, mason, typical Nantucket house. Has extension south side. 2½-story shingle, ridge chimney, originally 4-bayed. Has 6/6-paned windows. *(Inquirer & Mirror,* July 15, 1971, pp. 1, 20; N. H. A. *Photo Albums,* Book 3, p. /11/)

14 Built mid-eighteenth century, originally lean-to half-house. Probably moved here for Matthew Myrick shortly after Revolution. 2½-story shingle, ridge chimney, 3-bayed façade, 12/12-paned windows 1st story, and smaller 12/12- and (over door) 9/9-paned windows 2nd story. (H. B. Worth, *Nantucket Lands,* p. 267; E. A. Stackpole, *Rambling,* p. 71; N. H. A. *Photo Albums,* Book 3, p. /11/; E. U. Crosby, *Ninety Five Per Cent,* photo p. 83)

18 Built late 18th century, typical Nantucket house. 2½-story shingle, ridge chimney, 4-bayed façade, doorway with transom, had 12/12-paned windows, all now 6/6-paned. (E. A. Stackpole, *Rambling,* p. 71; K. Duprey, *Old Houses,* pp. 109–110)

21 Built after 1780 for Silas Gardner, frame may have come from old Sherburne. 2½-story shingle, ridge chimney, 3–4-bayed façade, center door with 1 window west and 2 on east side, 12/12-paned, 3 windows 2nd story 8/12-paned. Brick stoop modern. (M. M. Coffin, *H. A. B. S.* #928; K. Duprey, *Old Houses,* pp. 46–48; E. U. Crosby, *Ninety Five Per Cent,* photo p. 83)

23 Built *ca.* 1740, lean-to house. 1¾-story shingle, ridge chimney, 4-bayed façade, door with transom, restored 12/12-paned windows. Moved here *ca.* 1800 from Matthew Myrick lot at Milk and New Mill Street. (H. B. Worth, *Nantucket Lands,* p. 250; N. H. A. *Photo Albums,* Book 3, p. /14/; *Guidebook,* p. 30, /captioned "26 Milk"/; Kenneth Duprey)

26 Built end of 18th century, typical Nantucket house. 2½-story shingle, ridge chimney, 4-bayed façade, 12/12-paned windows (modern). (E. A. Stackpole, *Rambling,* pp. 70–71; K. Duprey, *Old Houses,* pp. 102–108, 216–217, 221–226)

27 Built before 1798 for William Hoeg, lean-to house. 1¾-story shingle, ridge chimney, 4-bayed façade, 12/12-paned windows (modern). (Worth-Palmer, *Photos,* p. 34)

28 1¾-story clapboard, high brick basement, blind fan in gable facing street, 3-bayed façade, Greek Revival pilastered doorway, 6/6- and later 1/1-paned windows. (N. H. A. *Photo Albums,* Book 3, p. /12/)

30 2½-story shingle, ridge chimney, 3-bayed façade, Greek Revival doorway with sidelights, 6/6-paned windows.

32 Built *ca.* 1841 for Capt. Calvin Worth, Greek Revival style. 2½-story shingle, ridge chimney, 3-bayed façade with gable, pilastered doorway with sidelights, 6/6-paned windows. (K. Duprey, *Old Houses,* p. 183)

33 Built 1820 for George Coffin, typical Nantucket house. 2½-story shingle, ridge chimney, 4-bayed façade, pilastered doorway with transom, 12/12-paned windows. (M. M. Coffin, *H. A. B. S.* #854; K. Duprey, *Old Houses,* pp. 134–/138/, 228; E. A. Stackpole, *Rambling,* p. 69; G. A. Fowlkes, *Mirror of Nantucket,* pp. 63–65, 117; E. U. Crosby, *Ninety Five Per Cent,* photo p. 84)

35 Before 1800, boat-building shop of Charles and Hiram Folger, stood on Quaker Road near Vestal. In 1848 south half converted into dwelling and north half used as meeting hall. Moved here 1880s to site of Hiram Folger's 2-story house that was taken off-island 1865. Remodeled 1903, again 1946–47. (M. M. Coffin, *H. A. B. S.* #923; *Proceedings,* 1916, pp. 35–43, photo before removal facing p. 40; E. A. Stackpole, *Rambling,* p. 69)

39 Lean-to house. 1¾-story shingle, ridge chimney, 4-bayed façade, pilastered doorway, later 2/2-paned windows.

Fig. 130 Silas Gardner House (1780s), 21 Milk Street.

Mill Street

Mill Street projects from the west side of Pleasant Street adjacent to the north flank of Moors' End (19). Beyond its staggered intersection with North Mill and New Dollar, Mill Street bends and continues southwest, originally to the Charles Bunker mill, which stood where Mill and New Mill would have converged *(Fig. 2)*. Mill Street then bore directly west to the ropewalk, which was on the site of Prospect Hill Cemetery, but this last stretch was abandoned during the first third of the nineteenth century. Of the ten old houses on Mill Street, five (5, 6, 9, 11, and 19) are excellent examples of the typical Nantucket type *(Figs. 46–47)*, and one (4) is a two-storied center-chimney type now serving as a museum. The street bend, vacant lot enclosed by post-and-rail fence on the south side below North Mill, and the ample grounds and homeness of the houses give the impression of a tiny New England village of long ago. The only discordant notes are the electric wires and poles *(Fig. 131)*.

Historic Buildings

4　　　　Built 1801 by Richard L. Coleman, sold to Jeremiah Lawrence. 2½-story shingle on high stone foundations, ridge chimney, 5-bayed façade with center doorway. Had 12/12-paned windows, now replaced by later 6/6-paned windows (one 6/9-paned window still in 2nd story of west flank). Called "The 1800 House," owned by Nantucket Historical Association. Rear wing is old house moved to site and attached for service ell. (K. Duprey, *Old Houses*, pp. 147–151; G. A. Fowlkes, *Mirror of Nantucket*, p. 117; E. U. Crosby, *Ninety Five Per Cent*, photo p. 84)

5　　　　Typical Nantucket house, built before or soon after American Revolution. At end of 18th century occupied by Alexander Ray. 2½-story shingle, ridge chimney, 4-bayed façade, door with transom, 12/12- and 9/9-paned windows. Complex addition on east end. (H. B. Worth, *Nantucket Lands*, p. 267; E. A. Stackpole, *Rambling*, p. 67; E. U. Crosby, *Ninety Five Per Cent*, photo p. 85; N. H. A. *Photo Albums*, Book 3, p. /13/)

8　　　　Typical Nantucket house. 2½-story shingle, ridge chimney, 4-bayed façade, 12/12- and 9/9-paned windows, shed-roof extension east side. (E. U. Crosby, *Ninety Five Per Cent*, photo p. 85)

9　　　　Built last quarter 18th century, typical Nantucket house. 2½-story shingle, ridge chimney, 4-bayed façade, door with transom, 12/12- and 9/9-paned windows. Lean-to house east wing may have come from old Sherburne, has batten door, 9/9-paned windows. (E. U. Crosby, *Ninety Five Per Cent*, photo p. 86; N. H. A. *Photo Albums*, Book 3, p. /13/)

11　　　 Built 1790 by and for Job Macy, typical Nantucket house. 2½-story shingle, ridge chimney, 4-bayed façade, restored 12/12- and 9/9-paned windows 1st story and 8/12- and 6/9-paned windows 2nd story. Later rear ell. (M. M. Coffin, *H. A. B. S.* #1002; K. Duprey, *Old Houses*, pp. 78–83; E. A. Stackpole, *Rambling*, p. 67; N. H. A. *Photo Albums*, Book 3, p. /14/; H. B. Worth, *Nantucket Lands*, p. 232)

15　　　 Built 2nd quarter 19th century. 2½-story shingle, ridge chimney, 3-bayed façade, new replaced doorway and 12/12-paned windows. (N. H. A. *Photo Albums*, Book 3, p. /14/)

17　　　 Built early 19th century, 2-story shingle, ridge chimney, 3-bayed façade, Greek Revival doorway, 6/6-paned windows

19　　　 Typical Nantucket house, faces east. 2½-story shingle, ridge chimney, 4-bayed façade, door with transom, later 6/6-paned windows. 9/9-paned windows in south gable and some in rear.

21　　　 Small lean-to house. 1¾-story shingle, ridge chimney (new, 3-bayed façade, 12/12-paned windows (modern).

24　　　 Inscribed 1834. 1¾-story clapboard front, shingle sides, ridge chimney, Greek Revival pilastered doorway with sidelights, 6/6-paned windows. Pilasters and entablature enframe façade.

Mooer's Lane

This little alley below Main Street, connecting Pine and Fair streets, was called Moose Lane at the time of the Isaac Coffin Survey of 1799. By the middle of the nineteenth century, it had become Moore's Lane, perhaps because of the family living in the house south of the Episcopal church (predecessor of present building on the same site) across on the east side of Fair Street. The inversion of the last two letters is twentieth century, and it constitutes another Nantucket family name. The orientation of the old lean-to house here (7) indicates that the building predates the street.

Historic Building

7   Built 1745 for Capt. Joseph Chase, lean-to house, faces south (not aligned to lane). 2½-story shingle, articulated ridge chimney, 3-bayed façade. Doorway and 6/6-paned windows later. Appendage on west end with shed roof of early date, later additions on left flank and rear. (E. A. Stackpole, *Rambling*, p. 50)

Mott Lane

The next lane south of Mooer's Lane, this alley takes its name from Lucretia Coffin Mott, daughter of Captain Thomas Coffin (for whom 15 Fair was built, on the south side of the lane) and wife of the Quaker teacher, James Mott. The way originally was called Gardner Lane.

Fig. 131 View of Mill Street.

Mount Vernon Street

Prospect Hill Cemetery is shown as only a fraction of its present size on the Walling 1858 map, a truncated L-shape at the foot of Mount Vernon Street on Joy. Mount Vernon Street branches south from Milk Street a short distance west of the Prospect Street intersection. It first appears on the Bache 1848 map, the frame cottages on its east side having probably been built about a decade earlier. A couple of contemporary buildings were standing then on the site of the later enlarged cemetery.

Historic Buildings

12   Was 1¾-story shingle, ridge chimney (new), 3-bayed façade, later door, 2/2-paned windows, façade heightened.

14   1½-story shingle, ridge chimney, 3-bayed façade, pilastered doorway, front windows reduced in height, now with 6/6-paned sashes.

16   1¾-story shingle on high brick basement, ridge chimney (new), 3-bayed façade, pilastered doorway, 12/12-paned windows. (N. H. A. *Photo Albums*, Book 3, p. /17/)

18   1½-story shingle, ridge chimney (replaced), 3-bayed façade, pilastered doorway, had 6/6-paned windows (now 6/1). Had roof walk.

Mulberry Lane

On the division line between the Fish Lots (1717) and West Monomoy (1726) subdivisions, Mulberry Lane post-dates the latter. Isaac Coffin, in 1799, described it as connecting Orange and "Union street under Quanaty Bank," the last being the name of the cliff that was the original east boundary of the Fish Lots.[1] In spite of any resemblance it may have to an old house, 2 Mulberry Lane is a twentieth-century Sears-Roebuck building. Number 3 had a roof walk and lattice railing to its stoop *(Fig. 132)*.

Note
1   Henry Barnard Worth, *Nantucket Lands and Land Owners*, Nantucket Historical Association, Vol. II, Bulletin No. 5, 1906 (reissued 1928), p. 268.

Historic Buildings

3   Faces east, typical Nantucket house. 2½-story shingle, brick basement, ridge chimney, 4-bayed façade, pilastered doorway with transom, 6/6-paned windows. Had roof walk. (N. H. A. *Photo Albums*, Book 3, p. /18/)

4   Federal period. 2½-story shingle, ridge chimney (new), 3-bayed façade, pilastered doorway, 6/6-paned windows.

5   Typical Nantucket house. 2½-story shingle, ridge chimney (replaced), 4-bayed façade, 12/12- and over door), later pilastered Greek Revival doorway, 12/12-paned windows.

New Dollar Lane

Although so designated in the Isaac Coffin survey and on the 1858 Walling map, New Dollar Lane was called Risdale Street during the last quarter of the nineteenth and early in the twentieth century. It connects Milk and Mill streets. Behind 4 were the Starbuck oil house and candle factory.

Historic Buildings

4   Built 1809 for Joseph Starbuck. 2½-story clapboard front, shingle sides, brick basement, 2 ridge chimneys, 5-bayed façade, later pilastered Greek Revival doorway with sidelights, 6/6-paned windows.

Later wing south end. The Starbuck oil house and candle factory were behind. (M. M. Coffin, *H. A. B. S.* #940; G. A. Fowlkes, *Mirror of Nantucket*, pp. 58–59)

5   Typical Nantucket house. 2½-story shingle, ridge chimney (replaced), 4-bayed façade, 12/12- and 9/9-paned windows. Later pilastered Greek Revival doorway. New kitchen on north end. (N. H. A. *Photo Albums,* Book 3, p. /19/)

New Lane

The west extremity of Main Street makes an abrupt turn, and the road extending due north is called New Lane. Isaac Coffin described it in 1799 as passing "through the Gardner Burying Ground . . . to Chester street," the latter now called West Chester. On the 1833–34 William Coffin map, the "Burying Ground" is shown only on the west side of the lane, and the old round-topped mill (then over a century old) is situated on the rise above present Brush Road. This windmill stood through the 1840s, after which the east section of the cemetery expanded over its site. There are quaint carvings and inscriptions on the tombstones in the early burying ground across the way.

New Mill Street

Physically New Mill Street is a continuation of the first stretch of Milk, originating at the Civil War monument on Main, continuing in a straight line down past Prospect to a hypothetical meeting with Mill Street at the site of the old Charles Bunker mill. The second stretch of Milk Street angles off to the west, creating a triangle with New Mill and Prospect Street. On New Mill, three typical Nantucket houses (2, 5, and 7) are noteworthy. The house at the northwest corner of Prospect (9 New Mill) has had an interesting architectural career, the first section (southeast corner) having been built as a lean-to half-house oriented southward, later enlarged to a full-house, and then extended, so as to have two façades.

Historic Buildings

2   Built *ca.* 1790 for Matthew Myrick, typical Nantucket house. 2½-story shingle, ridge chimney, 4-bayed façade, doorway with transom, stoop, later 6/6-paned windows. (Worth-Palmer, *Photos*, p. 36; E. U. Crosby, *Ninety Five Per Cent*, photo p. 86—labeled "4 New Mill St.")

5   Built late 18th century for Tristram Folger II, typical Nantucket house. 2½-story shingle, ridge chimney, 4-bayed façade, 12/12-paned windows. (E. A. Stackpole, *Rambling*, pp. 71–72; K. Duprey, *Old Houses*, pp. 117–119; H. B. Worth, *Nantucket Lands*, p. 269)

7   Built early 19th century, typical Nantucket house. 2½-story shingle, ridge chimney, 4-bayed façade, had 12/12- and 9/9-paned windows, now all 6/6-paned windows. (K. Duprey, *Old Houses*, p. 120; N. H. A. *Photo Albums,* Book 4, p. /2/)

9   Original house built *ca.* 1740, lean-to half-house at southeast corner, said to have been brought from old Sherburne. Enlarged to full-house facing Prospect Street. Later extended into L-shaped residence facing New Mill. 2½-story shingle, brick basement, ridge and end chimneys, 5-bayed façade, center doorway with high stoop, late 18th century 2/2-paned windows. Back wall of original newel stairway in oldest part convex, practically ¼ circle.

10   Early 19th century. 1¾-story shingle, ridge chimney, 4-bayed façade, pilastered doorway, 12/12-paned windows. Modern box dormer in front. (N. H. A. *Photo Albums,* Book 4, p. /2/)

11   1¾-story shingle, ridge chimney, 3-bayed façade, Greek Revival pilastered doorway, 6/6-paned windows.

14   1¾-story clapboard front, shingle sides, ridge chimney (new), 3-bayed façade, 6/6-paned windows.

Fig. 132 3 Mulberry Lane.

New Street

During the late eighteenth and through the first three decades of the nineteenth century, only the west half of the south side of New Street existed and faced a widened section of Warren Street off Pleasant. The 1848 Bache map shows the east half of New cut through to Orange. A single dwelling (17) on the north side stood on a solitary lot rescued from the Warren plaza. Within a decade (according to the Walling 1858 map), New Street had become a normal lane, though its upper face remained bare of buildings.

Historic Buildings

2	1¾-story clapboard, ridge chimney (new), 3-bayed façade, pilastered doorway, 6/6-paned windows. (N. H. A. *Photo Albums*, Book 3, p. /20/)
4	1½-story shingle, ridge chimney, 3-bayed façade, pilastered doorway, later 2/2-paned windows, box dormer.
6	1¾-story shingle, ridge chimney, 3-bayed façade, 6/6-paned windows. (N. H. A. *Photo Albums*, Book 3, p. /20/)
8	1¾-story shingle, ridge chimney, 3-bayed façade, pilastered doorway, later 2/2-paned windows.
12	1¾-story shingle, had end chimney, 4-bayed façade, pilastered doorway, 6/6-paned windows.
14	1¾-story shingle, had ridge chimney, 3-bayed façade, 6/6-paned windows, later box dormer on front.
17	2-story shingle, ridge chimney (new), probably had 3-bayed façade, later 6/1-paned windows, doorway west side.
18	1¾-story shingle, ridge chimney (new), 3-bayed façade, pilastered doorway, later 2/2-paned windows, shed-roof extension west end.

20	Now 2-storied shingle, ridge chimney (new), much altered. (N. H. A. *Photo Albums*, Book 4, p. /1/)
22	1¾-story shingle, ridge chimney, gabled 3-bayed façade, later bracketed hood over doorway, 2/2-paned windows. (N. H. A. *Photo Albums*, Book 4, p. /1/)
24	1¾-story shingle, ridge chimney (later), 3-bayed façade, entrance pent, 6/6-paned windows.

North Avenue

"Court" would be more appropriate than the prepossessing "Avenue" for this little street that branches northward from the intersection of Cliff Road and Chester-Easton streets. Its name obviously derives from North Street, the former designation for Cliff Road.

Historic Building

| X | Built during 1840s, Greek Revival style. 1¾-story clapboard on brick foundations, pilasters at corners, entablature on flanks, 5-bayed gabled façade, pilastered doorway with sidelights, 6/6-paned windows. Much altered. |

North Liberty Street

Originally considered the upper stretch of Liberty Street (see above), North Liberty constitutes the west boundary of the Lily Pond area and extends northward beyond. Except for two examples at the Cliff Road end, all of the old houses on North Liberty are below the West Chester intersection. Number 10 is so altered one can hardly believe it was originally a lean-to house. By far the most unusual building is 6, having a typical Nantucket house plan, and a gambrel plus lean-to roof (*Fig. 45*). The chimney and foundations have been rebuilt in modern times. With a Cliff Road address (60), the Josiah Coffin house at the upper extremity is one of the handsomest of early houses in Nantucket (*Figs. 19–20*).

Historic Buildings

47	Typical Nantucket house. 2½-story clapboard front, shingle sides, ridge chimney, 4-bayed façade, pilastered Federal doorway with transom, 6/6-paned windows. Originally had 12/12-paned windows. (N. H. A. *Photo Albums*, Book 4, p. /3/); E. U. Crosby, *Ninety Five Per Cent*, photo p. 87 — labeled "47 North Liberty St.")
50	2-story clapboard front, shingle sides, end chimneys, 4-bayed façade, Federal doorway with sidelights, heavy enframement with corner blocks, 6/6-paned windows. New entrance porch.
10	Originally lean-to house, stood across the street to northwest, had been completely altered inside before being moved to present site in 1912. 2½-story clapboard on concrete-block foundations, ridge chimney (modern), 3-bayed façade, pilastered Greek Revival doorway with sidelights, 6/6-paned windows. Addition at rear. (Photo before removal in N. H. A. picture collection, copy hanging in house, owned by Robert B. Blair)
X	(west side) 1¾-story shingle, ridge chimney (new), 3-bayed façade, 6/6-paned windows. (N. H. A. *Photo Albums*, Book 4, p. /4/)
6	Built *ca.* 1798 for Seth Ray, combination of typical Nantucket house, gambrel roof and lean-to. 2½-story shingle on concrete block (modern) foundations, chimney (new) on rear slope of roof, 4-bayed façade, door with transom, 12/12- and 9/9-paned windows. (H. B. Worth, *Nantucket Lands*, p. 260, 1881 photo facing p. 271)
16	1¾-story shingle on brick basement, ridge chimney, 3-bayed façade, pilastered Greek Revival doorway, 6/6-paned windows, wing north end.
61	1¾-story clapboard front, shingle sides, ridge chimney, 3-bayed façade, pilastered Greek Revival doorway, 6/6-paned windows. Modern dormers.

North Mill Lane

Although shown on Nantucket maps, North Mill Lane seldom is identified. It should not be confused with the lower stretch of Mill Street proper (below the bend), labeled "North Mill Street" on the William Coffin 1834 town plan. Despite its name, the one tangible end of North Mill Lane branches south from Mill Street slightly east of the corner of New Dollar Lane. After passing the house on the west side, North Mill Lane becomes little more than a trail ascending the hill back of the old mill. It corresponds roughly to what was known earlier as Brimstone Lane, which led directly to Brimstone Mill,[1] just west of the existing Nathan Wilbur mill, both located on Prospect (then called Copper) Street.

Note
1 Edouard A. Stackpole, *Rambling Through the Streets and Lanes of Nantucket*, New Bedford, Mass., 1969, p. 66.

Historic Buildings
1   1¾-story shingle, ridge chimney, 3-bayed façade, pilastered Greek Revival doorway, 6/6-paned windows.

2   Late-18th- or early-19th-century lean-to house, built for Benjamin Hussey. 1¾-story shingle, ridge chimney (new), 3-bayed façade, later 6/6-paned windows, addition and alterations at rear. (E. A. Stackpole, *Rambling*, p. 66)

North Water Street

Despite the jog at Broad Street, what now are North and South Water streets were listed simply as Water in the Isaac Coffin 1799 survey, They are separated, as now, on the 1834 Coffin map. On the Walling 1858 map (notable for its errors in street names), South Water is labeled as the upper stretch of Washington; but this cannot be regarded as official. All the area below Sea Street fell victim to the Great Fire of 1846, and present buildings here postdate the catastrophe. The house that stood at the northeast corner of Broad and North Water (site of the new historical museum) was moved to 2 South Beach Street in the 1920s (see below). Number 4 North Water is a bizarre combination of Greek and Gothic Revival elements *(Figs. 112–113)*. Number 5 also originally had pointed windows in the second story *(Fig. 115)*. Number 8, a pure Greek Revival example, had a small south wing preceded by a pretty arched portico, now confused by fenestration *(Fig. 133)*. The house at the southeast corner of Sea is a Victorian Gothic with Eastlake details. A notable array of typical Nantucket houses line the street northward (15, 17, 22, 23, 24, 25, 26, and 28).

Historic Buildings
4   Built after 1846 Fire for E. F. Easton, afterward acquired and altered for Obed H. Joy, Greek-Gothic eclectic style. 1¾-story clapboard on high brick basement, chimney on roof slope, 3-bayed façade and flanks, curious 12-sided wood piers on tall brick plinths support entablature, steep pediment-gable in front with corbel-arch "Gothic" windows, recessed doorway with sidelights, stoop, 6/6-paned windows. Later dormers on sides, bay window south flank. (M. M. Coffin, *H. A. B. S.* #957; T. F. Hamlin, *Greek Revival*, pl. XLI)

5   Built after 1846 Fire, Greek Revival style. 1¾-story clapboard on high brick basement, chimney on roof slope, pilasters at corners supporting entablature on flanks, 3-bayed façade with gable, recessed doorway with sidelights, 6/6-paned windows, originally had "Gothic" corbel-arch windows 2nd story. New wing south end. (N. H. A. *Photo Albums*, Book 4, p. /5/)

7   Built after 1846 Fire, Greek Revival style. 1¾-story clapboard front, shingle sides, brick basement, chimney on roof slope, shafts at corners, 4-bayed façade, pilastered doorway with sidelights, later 2/2-paned windows 1st story, windows in front gable changed.

8   Built after 1846 Fire, Greek Revival style. 2½-story clapboard on brick basement, ridge chimney, 3-bayed pilastered façade with entablature, triple window in front pediment, recessed doorway with

Fig. 133 8 North Water Street at Turn of Century.

          sidelights, 6/6-paned windows. Small wing south flank had arched portico, now glassed-in sun room. (N. H. A. *Photo Albums*, Book 4, p. /5/)

9   Built after 1846 Fire, Greek Revival style. 2½-story clapboard on brick basement, chimney on roof slope, shafts at corners, 3-bayed façade, pointed window in front pediment, pilastered doorway with sidelights, 6/6-paned windows. Originally had cupola.

10   Built after 1846 Fire, Greek Revival style. 1¾-story clapboard on high brick basement, side chimneys, shafts at corners supporting entablature on flanks, 3-bayed façade with gable, doorway with sidelights, stoop, 6/6-paned windows, outer windows 2nd story have ¼-round heads.

11   Built after 1846 Fire, Greek Revival style. 2½-story clapboard on brick basement, chimney on roof slope, pilasters at corners supporting entablature, 3-bayed façade with pediment, pilastered doorway with sidelights, 6/6-paned windows. New dormers.

12   Built after 1846 Fire, Greek Revival style. 1¾-story shingle on brick basement, ridge chimney, pilasters at corners with entablature on flanks, 3-bayed façade with gable, pilastered doorway with sidelights, stoop, 6/6-paned windows.

14   2½-story shingle on brick basement, 2 ridge chimneys, 5-bayed façade, center doorway. Greatly altered.

15   Built 1795 for Robert Brayton, typical Nantucket house. 2½-story shingle on stone foundations, ridge chimney, 4-bayed façade, 12/12-paned windows. Later pilastered Greek Revival doorway. (H. B. Worth, *Nantucket Lands,* p. 276; E. U. Crosby, *Ninety Five Per Cent,* photo p. 88)

17	Typical Nantucket house, built 1812. 2½-story shingle on stuccoed basement, ridge chimney, roof walk, 4-bayed façade, door with transom, 12/12-paned windows. Modern dormers.
19	Originally 2-storied clapboard on high brick basement, 5-bayed façade with center doorway. Greatly enlarged for hotel, Springfield House, late 19th century. Now is Harbor House. (J. F. Murphy, *65 Views*, pl. /12/)
20	Built *ca.* 1830, late Federal style. 2½-story clapboard front, shingle sides, on high brick basement, had 4 end chimneys, 5-bayed façade, columned doorway with transom and sidelights (door itself late 19th century), 6/6-paned windows. In early 1880s connected to Veranda House (now Overlook Hotel). Later front box dormer.
21	2½-story shingle, had ridge chimney, 3-bayed façade. Much altered. Front structure on street part of covered gallery connecting this building to Springfield House, 19 North Water.
22	Typical Nantucket house. 2½-story shingle on high stone basement, ridge chimney, 4-bayed façade, 2nd story windows 12/12- and 9/9-paned, 1st story changed to 6/6-paned windows.
23	Typical Nantucket house. 2½-story shingle, ridge chimney, 4-bayed façade, door with transom, 12/12- and 9/9-paned windows. (E. U. Crosby, *Ninety Five Per Cent,* p. 88)
24	Built early 19th century, wide typical Nantucket house. 2½-story shingle on high brick basement, ridge chimney, pilastered door with transom, 12/12-paned windows, later colored glass in top sashes.
25	Typical Nantucket house. 2½-story clapboard front, shingle sides, ridge chimney, 4-bayed façade, 6/6-paned windows. Altered.
26	Built *ca.* 1765 for Richard Swain, typical Nantucket house. 2½-story shingle on high brick basement, ridge chimney, 4-bayed façade. Late 18th century 2/2-paned windows, more recent box dormer. (H. B. Worth, *Nantucket Lands*, p. 281)
27	2-story clapboard on high brick basement, had 2 ridge chimneys, 5-bayed façade, doorway with sidelights, 6/6-paned windows. Later mansard roof.
28	Typical Nantucket house. 2½-story on very high brick basement, ridge chimney, 4-bayed façade, late 2/1-paned windows.

Oak Street

Below Chestnut and above India, connecting Federal and South Water streets, Oak Street is in the Bocochico area laid out in 1744. Its architectural assets face neighboring streets. Foremost of these is the rear of the Atheneum, which has its portico on India.

Orange Street

Orange Street came into being in 1726 with the parceling of West Monomoy, as it separated the east from the west lots in this subdivision, extending from Pleasant eastward to Union Street, and from about Silver down to Bear. Of necessity, Orange Street was made to cut through the middle of the east range of the earlier Fish Lots, which lay between West Monomoy and Main Street. Orange Street proceeded southwest to the first milestone, near which was Newtown Gate, a sheep barrier that remained in use as late as 1840, and beyond which branched the separate Polpis and Siasconset roads.[1] After the evacuation of old Sherburne, Orange Street was the most frequented way into Nantucket Town.

Briefly, after 1885, the fountain now in the Lower Square was placed at the head of Orange Street on Main. The Philip H. Folger house (now commercial) stands at the west corner *(Fig. 134),* and farther along on the same side of the street is The Block (15, 17, 19, 21, and 23), also built for Folger, Nantucket's only example of row (actually duplex) houses *(Figs. 72–73).* Folger's brick residence and five frame tenements date from 1831. Between these buildings, at 5 Orange, is the town's most notable gambrel-roof house, erected just before or soon after the American Revolution as a frame house with brick chimney ends *(Fig. 42).* The front was rebuilt in brick during the second quarter of the nineteenth century. A little beyond is the Second Congregational Church, constructed in 1809 and becoming Unitarian fifteen years later *(Figs. 79–80)*. Also known as South Tower, its bell tolls the hours and emphasizes reveille (7:00 A.M.), noon, and curfew (9:00 P.M.) with an additional fifty-two strokes. The fancy house on the other side of the street (6) was built for James Easton in 1885 and is now the rectory of Saint Mary's Catholic Church. Farther south (14) is a house dressed in heavy Greek Revival formality, conceived in 1838 by the builder, William M. Andrews, as a speculative venture, and sold to Levi Starbuck *(Figs. 97–98)*. Later it was the home of James Codd, master mariner. Orange Street has been the address of 126 sea captains over the span of a century, believed to be a record unsurpassed by any other street in America.[2]

During the last quarter of the eighteen-hundreds, when Nantucket's paramount industry had shifted from whaling to playing host to off-islanders, Orange was the street of hostelries. Operating here at the time were: American House, northwest corner of Martin's Lane; Sherburne House, diagonally across the street; and Bay View House (38). American House is gone, and Sherburne House was moved on the lot and rebuilt into the home of William Barnes (30) in 1900. Bay View House was a converted Greek Revival residence, and it still wears the Reconstruction-era hotel dormers. Two half-lean-to houses are on the west side (33 and 53), the first with enlarged windowpanes, the second with an extra set of windows in its façade *(Fig. 14)*. Midway between them (43) is a full lean-to house, though much altered. Orange Street makes two slight bends. Beyond the first, where Quanaty Bank becomes less steep, a number of lanes connect with Union, and a few run westward. Four blocks beyond the second, at Consue Spring, Orange Street is joined by Union. Immediately south of where the old railroad (1881–1917) crossed at Bear Street stands the Christopher Baxter saltbox house (Number 114, 1756), now the Old Spouter Pottery Shop *(Figs. 28–29)*.

Notes

1   Henry Barnard Worth, *Nantucket Lands and Land Owners*, Nantucket Historical Association Vol. II, Bulletin No. 5, 1906 (reissued 1928), p. 271.

2   Edouard A. Stackpole, *Rambling Through the Streets and Lanes of Nantucket*, New Bedford, Mass., 1969, p. 36.

Historic Buildings

5   Variously ascribed to dates from 1772 to 1793 (the last under the ownership of Capt. Silas Jones), the character of the original parts tends to favor the earlier period. Gambrel roof. 2-story frame with common-bond chimney ends having belt courses at 2nd- and 3rd-floor levels, originally clapboard façade, 5-bayed, with center doorway. Present unbonded brick front wall constructed early 1830s, when 1st-story stairhall and front rooms remodeled, and probably at that time rear ell attached. Doorway has transom and sidelights, wood stoop, 6/6-paned windows. (M. M. Coffin, *H. A. B. S.* #956; K. Duprey, *Old Houses*, pp. 152–156; E. A. Stackpole, *Rambling*, p. 36; G. A. Fowlkes, *Mirror of Nantucket*, p. 55; E. U. Crosby, *Ninety Five Per Cent*, photo p. 89; A. E. Poor, *Colonial Architecture*, pl. 24)

8   Built *ca.* 1836 for Benjamin Coggeshall, Greek Revival style. 2½-story clapboard on brick basement, chimneys at side, 3-bayed pedimented façade with vertical ribbed shafts at corners, fan in tympanum, pilastered doorway with sidelights, 6/6-paned windows. (M. M. Coffin, *H. A. B. S.* #1014)

9   Earlier house remodeled in Greek Revival style. 2½-story shingle, ridge chimney, 3-bayed façade with pilasters at corners, pilastered doorway with sidelights, 6/6-paned windows.

10   Built 1802 for Peleg Coggeshall. 2½-story shingle on brick basement, ridge chimney, originally had 3-bayed façade, later pilastered Greek Revival doorway with sidelights, 6/6-paned windows, much later 2-storied bay window on front. (M. M. Coffin, *H. A. B. S.* #1014)

11   SECOND CONGREGATIONAL CHURCH, built 1809 by Elisha Ramsdell, tower erected 1815, tower replaced 1830 by Perez Jenkins, Federal style. Church altered in 1844 by Frederick Brown Coleman, balcony removed and tall side windows installed, double stairs in vestibule, interior decorated by Carl Wendte. Clapboard auditorium-type church, 3-storied tower-entrance pavilion, double doorway with blind fanlight, clock in each face of square superstructure, railing over cornice, octagonal bell section, cupola and bonnet with weathervane. Erected by group of Congregationalists separating from First Church on Beacon Hill, becoming Unitarian in 1824. Bell cast in Lisbon, Portugal, 1810, hung and first rung 1815. Rehung in present belfry when heightened 1830, cupola above used for town fire watch. First town clock installed 1823, present clock gift of William Hadwen Starbuck,

Fig. 134 Orange Street Looking South from Main About 1874.

1881. Church also known as South Tower, the Unitarian-Universalist Church. (M. M. Coffin, *H. A. B. S.* #838; E. A. Stackpole, *Rambling,* pp. 34–35; *Historic Nantucket,* Jan. 1965, pp. 5–19; G. A. Fowlkes, *Mirror of Nantucket,* pp. 124–125; E. U. Crosby, *Ninety Five Per Cent,* photo p. 107; A. E. Poor, *Colonial Architecture,* doorway pl. 72)

12   North section was early lean-to house, 2-bayed south section added for home of Christopher Hussey II, 1788. 2½-story shingle, articulated ridge chimney, later pilastered Greek Revival doorway, 6/6-paned windows. 2-story bay window end of 19th century. (M. M. Coffin, *H. A. B. S.* #1014; K. Duprey, *Old Houses,* pp. 64–65)

13   Built *ca.* 1800 for Henry Pinkham, typical Nantucket house. 2½-story clapboard front, shingle sides on brick basement, ridge chimney, 4-bayed façade, later Greek Revival pilastered doorway with sidelights, 6/6-paned windows. Modern roof walk, parapet over front cornice. (M. M. Coffin, *H. A. B. S.* #1014)

14   Built 1838 by William M. Andrews, housewright, sold to Levi Starbuck. Greek Revival style. 2½-story flush boards, 4 chimneys on roof slope (2 lately removed), 3-bayed front and sides defined by colossal anta supporting entablature, pediment facing street, blind center window with glazed sashes and inside shutters, parapet over cornice on flanks, small distyle Ionic portico with parapet sheltering center doorway with sidelights on south front, 6/6-paned windows (those of 1st story with paneled apron). Later service wing east end. Sidewalk paved with bluestone. (M. M. Coffin, *H. A. B. S.* #912; E. A. Stackpole, *Rambling,* p. 36; K. Duprey, *Old Houses,* pp. 203–205; E. U. Crosby, *Ninety Five Per Cent,* photo of portico, p. 90; T. F. Hamlin, *Greek Revival,* pl. XL; A. E. Poor, *Colonial Architecture,* pl. 45)

14½   Built 1755 for Samuel Calder, original house constitutes south section of present building, faces east. 2½-story shingle, ridge chimney, 5-bayed façade, center door with transom, later 6/6-paned windows. (Miss B. Crichton)

15, 17, 19, 21, 23   THE BLOCK, five row (or duplex) houses built 1831 for Philip H. Folger and sold individually. Federal style. 2½-story clapboard on high brick basement, each has 3-bayed façade, pilastered doorway with transom and sidelights, 6/6-paned windows. Chimneys and dormers articulate roof. Originally had dining rooms and kitchens in basement, now have rear extensions. (M. M. Coffin, *H. A. B. S.* #947; E. A. Stackpole, *Rambling,* pp. 35–36; G. A. Fowlkes, *Mirror of Nantucket,* p. 107; *Inquirer & Mirror,* Oct. 9, 1965, p. 3; E. U. Crosby, *Ninety Five Per Cent,* photo p. 89; A. E. Poor, *Colonial Architecture,* doorways pl. 94)

16   Built *ca.* 1755 for Andrew Myrick. 2½-story clapboard front, shingle sides, ridge chimney, 3-bayed façade, later pilastered Greek Revival doorway, 6/6-paned windows. Modern dormers. (M. M. Coffin, *H. A. B. S.* #1014)

18   Built *ca.* 1770 probably for Matthew Beard, typical Nantucket house. 2½-story shingle, ridge chimney, 4-bayed façade, later pilastered Greek Revival doorway, 6/6-paned windows. Modern dormers. (M. M. Coffin, *H. A. B. S.* #1014)

20   Built *ca.* 1800 perhaps for John Beard, typical Nantucket house. 2½-story shingle, ridge chimney, roof walk, 4-bayed façade, doorway with sidelights, 6/6-paned windows. Modern dormers. (M. M. Coffin, *H. A. B. S.* #1014)

22   Built *ca.* 1760 for Nathaniel Woodbury, typical Nantucket house. Extended north end. 2½-story shingle, 2 ridge chimneys (modern), roof walk, 5-bayed façade, including 2 doors 1st story, 4 windows above (none over north door), 12/12-paned windows except 9/9 over center door. Dormers modern. (M. M. Coffin, *H. A. B. S.* #1014)

25   Built *ca.* 1819 by Isaiah Nicholson, housewright, sold to Joshua Bunker 1820, typical Nantucket house (remodeled). 2½-story shingle, ridge chimney, 4-bayed façade, Greek Revival doorway, 6/6-paned windows. Modern wing south side, front dormers, roof walk. (M. M. Coffin, *H. A. B. S.* #1014)

26   Built before 1755, Seth Folger early owner, center chimney house. 2½-story shingle, ridge chimney, 5-bayed façade (4 windows 2nd story), late 19th-century wing north end and entrance pent, 6/6-paned windows. (M. M. Coffin, *H. A. B. S.* #1014)

28   Original house (now rear wing, facing south) built after 1755 for George Hussey or Benjamin Tupper. Front block built 1833 for Charles Bunker. Greek Revival style. 2-story clapboard on high basement,

	end chimneys, parapet and cupola, 5-bayed façade, center doorway with sidelights sheltered by distyle Doric portico, 6/6-paned windows. (T. Bunker, *Research*, #51-18; M. M. Coffin, *H. A. B. S.* #1014; E. U. Crosby, *Ninety Five Per Cent,* photo p. 91)
29	Built *ca.* 1844 by Josiah Gorham, housewright; appears to be earlier house remodeled. 2½-story clapboard front, shingle sides on high brick basement, 2 ridge chimneys, 5-bayed façade, distyle Greek Doric portico sheltering center doorway, stoop with double steps, 6/6-paned windows, later wing south flank. (M. M. Coffin, *H. A. B. S.* #1014)
33	Built *ca.* 1766 for Robert Wyer, lean-to house. 2½-story with ridge chimney, 3-bayed façade. Later clapboard front, pilastered Greek Revival doorway with transom, 6/6-paned windows. Renovated in 1930s by Dr. Will Gardner. Modern roof walk. (M. M. Coffin, *H. A. B. S.* #946; K. Duprey, *Old Houses*, p. 59; E. U. Crosby, *Ninety Five Per Cent*, photo p. 93)
34	2½-story shingle on brick basement, end chimneys, 5-bayed façade, 6/6-paned windows. Entrance on south side.
36	2½-story clapboard on brick basement, end chimneys, 5-bayed façade, pilastered center doorway with transom and sidelights, stoop with double stairs, 12/12-paned windows (new—had 6/6-paned windows). Large rear addition. (E. U. Crosby, *Ninety Five Per Cent*, photo p. 96)
37	Built after 1753 for John Jackson, originally a gambrel-roof house, altered. 2½-story shingle, ridge chimney (replaced), 5-bayed façade, pilastered doorway with sidelights and blind fan (modern), 6/6-paned windows. (M. M. Coffin; A. E. Poor, *Colonial Architecture*, doorway pl. 81)
38	Built *ca.* 1840, Greek Revival style. 2½-story clapboard front, shingle sides, high brick basement, 4 end chimneys with stepped parapets, cupola on roof, 5-bayed façade, colossal pilasters at corners supporting full entablature, may have had parapet, deeply recessed doorway with sidelights enframed by pair of Ionic colonnettes, 6/6-paned windows, those of 1st story with cornice hood molds. Dormers much later, when building was hostelry called Bay View House. (E. A. Stackpole, *Rambling*, 1880 view of Orange Street, p. 24; A. E. Poor, *Colonial Architecture,* doorway, pl. 86)
38½	2½-story shingle, ridge chimney, roof walk, 3-bayed façade, 12/12-paned windows, door on east side.
39	Built *ca.* 1830 for Edward Hammond, Greek Revival style. 1¾-story shingle, pilasters at corners, guttae in entablature, 5-bayed façade, recessed center doorway with pilasters and sidelights, wood stoop, 6/6-paned windows, roof platform. Originally had end chimneys, present brick foundations entirely rebuilt, dormers and other changes date from turn of century. (Hammond-Coffin family *Bible* preserved by present owner, Mrs. W. P. Constable II; house shown center of photo of Orange Street in 1880, reproduced E. A. Stackpole, *Rambling*, p. 24)
40	Originally typical Nantucket house. 2-story shingle, ridge chimney (new), 3-bayed façade, pilastered doorway with transom, 6/6-paned windows. (E. U. Crosby, *Ninety Five Per Cent*, photo p. 94)
41	Built early 19th century, typical Nantucket house. 2½-story shingle on brick basement, ridge chimney (new), had roof walk and parapet over cornice, 4-bayed façade, pilastered Greek Revival doorway, much later projecting bay window in front, 6/1-paned windows. (appears 1880 photo Orange Street, E. A. Stackpole, *Rambling*, p. 24)
43	Built mid-18th century, lean-to house. Moved to site and set on high basement; stairhall replaces original chimney. 2½-story shingle, ridge chimney (new), 5-bayed façade, center doorway, late 2/2-paned windows. (N. H. A. *Photo Albums*, Book 4, p. /6/)
45	Typical Nantucket house. 2½-story clapboard front, shingle sides, brick basement, ridge chimney, 4-bayed façade, pilastered doorway with transom, 6/6-paned windows. Had 2-story bay windows; restored 1970–71. (2nd house from left, 1880 view of Orange Street, E. A. Stackpole, *Rambling,* p. 24)
47	2½-story shingle, brick basement, ridge chimney (changed), 3-bayed façade, later pilastered Greek Revival doorway, 6/6-paned windows. Interior staircase has been reversed. Detached building to northwest was old carpenter shop. (house appears extreme left 1880 view of Orange Street, E. A. Stackpole, *Rambling*, p. 24; N. H. A. *Photo Albums*, Book 4, p. /6/)
48	Greek Revival style. 2½-story shingle on brick basement, end chimneys, 3-bayed façade with front gable, two ¼-round windows to garret, pilastered doorway, 6/6-paned windows, later 2-story projecting bay window.

49	2½-story shingle, ridge chimney, 3-bayed façade, pilastered doorway with transom, 6/6-paned windows. (N. H. A. *Photo Albums*, Book 4, p. /7/)
50	Similar to 48 Orange, inverted plan, fenestration intact except for 2/1-paned sashes.
51	Typical Nantucket house with Greek Revival changes. 2½-story shingle, ridge chimney, 4-bayed façade, pilastered Greek Revival doorway, 6/6-paned windows.
52	Typical Nantucket house. 2½-story shingle, ridge chimney (new), 4-bayed façade, later pilastered Greek Revival doorway, 6/6-paned windows. (N. H. A. *Photo Albums*, Book 4, p. /9/)
53	Built mid-18th century, at end of century owned by Seth Coffin, lean-to house. 2½-story shingle, ridge chimney, originally 2-bayed façade, door with transom. Restored 12/12-paned windows (6/9 over door) as 3-bayed façade. (M. M. Coffin, *H. A. B. S.* #837; H. B. Worth, *Nantucket Lands*, p. 271, 1881 photo facing p. 279; *Guidebook*, p. 16; K. Mixer, *Old Houses of New England*, pp. 11–12; E. U. Crosby, *Ninety Five Per Cent*, photos before and after "restoration," p. 95; N. H. A. *Photo Albums*, Book 4, p. /7/)
54	Built *ca.* 1835 for Edward Field, Greek Revival style. 2½-story clapboard on brick basement, end chimneys, pilasters at corners, 3-bayed façade with fan window in front pediment, doorway with sidelights sheltered by distyle Ionic portico, 6/6-paned windows. (H. Wade White; N. H. A. *Photo Albums*, Book 4, p. /10/)
55	Typical Nantucket house with Greek Revival changes. 2½-story shingle, ridge chimney, 4-bayed façade, pilastered Greek doorway, 6/6-paned windows, sidewalk paved with bluestone. (N. H. A. *Photo Albums*, book 4, p. /8/)
56	Typical Nantucket house, late Federal style. 2½-story shingle on brick basement, ridge chimney, 4-bayed façade, pilastered doorway, 6/6-paned windows.
57	Federal style. 2½-story shingle on high brick basement, ridge chimney, 3-bayed façade, channeled pilastered doorway with triglyphs on frieze and inner molding with corner blocks, later 2/2-paned windows.
61	Federal style. 2½-story shingle on high brick basement, ridge chimney, 3-bayed façade, cornice with guttae and modillions, double engaged colonette doorway with sidelights and leaded transom, door itself later, also 6/1-paned windows.
62	Was typical Nantucket house. 2½-story shingle, high basement, ridge chimney, 2/2-paned windows, projecting bay window on front.
65	Typical Nantucket house. 2½-story clapboard front, shingle sides, high brick basement, ridge chimney, 4-bayed façade, later pilastered Greek Revival doorway, modern 12/12-paned windows. Had roof walk.
66	Typical Nantucket house. 2½-story shingle, ridge chimney, 4-bayed façade, later pilastered Greek Revival doorway, 6/6-paned windows.
69	Federal style. 2½-story shingle on brick basement, ridge chimney, 3-bayed façade, doorway with whorled carving on fascia, leaded sidelights, distyle Tuscan portico, 6/6-paned windows.
70	1¾-story shingle, had ridge chimney, 4-bayed façade, pilastered Greek Revival doorway, late 19th-century gable and 2/2-paned windows.
71	Typical Nantucket house. 2½-story shingle, brick basement, ridge chimney, 4-bayed façade, pilastered doorway with transom, 6/6-paned windows.
72	2½-story shingle, brick basement, ridge chimney, 3-bayed façade, pilastered Greek Revival doorway, 6/6-paned windows.
73	2½-story shingle, ridge chimney (new), 3-bayed façade, late 2/2-paned windows, modern doorway.
74	Probably originally typical Nantucket house, late Federal style. 2½-story clapboard on high brick basement, ridge chimney, pilasters at corners, pilastered doorway with leaded sidelights, 6/6-paned windows.
75	Typical Nantucket house. 2½-story shingle, ridge chimney, 4-bayed façade, later pilastered Greek Revival doorway with sidelights, 6/6-paned windows. (N. H. A. *Photo Albums*, Book 4, p. /8/)
76	Typical Nantucket house. 2½-story shingle, ridge chimney, 4-bayed façade, boxed entrance pent (very late), 2/2- and 6/6-paned windows.

77	Typical Nantucket house. 2½-story clapboard front, shingle sides, ridge chimney, 4-bayed façade, pilastered doorway, 6/6-paned windows. (N. H. A. *Photo Albums*, Book 4, p. /9/)
78	Greek Revival style. 2½-story clapboard front, shingle sides, brick basement, chimneys at sides, pilasters at corners supporting entablature, 3-bayed façade with fan in pediment, pilastered doorway with sidelights, 6/6-paned windows. (N. H. A. *Photo Albums*, Book 4, p. /12/)
81	2½-story shingle and clapboard front, shingle sides, ridge chimney, 3-bayed façade, Federal pilastered doorway and cornice, 6/6-paned windows. Late 18-century porch.
82	Transitional Federal to Greek Revival style. 2½-story clapboard front, shingle sides, ridge chimney (new), 3-bayed façade, pilastered doorway with sidelights, 6/6-paned windows.
85	2½-story shingle, ridge chimney, originally 3-bayed façade, later 2/2-paned windows and new doorway, extension north end. (N. H. A. *Photo Albums*, Book 4, p. /11/)
88	Built early 19th century by Richard L. Coleman, housewright. 1¾-story shingle, ridge chimney, 5-bayed façade, door with transom, 6/6-paned windows (later frames). (Deed Book 20, p. 9)
89	2½-story shingle, high brick basement, ridge chimney, 3-bayed façade, Greek Revival pilastered doorway with sidelights, 6/6-paned windows.
90	2½-story shingle, ridge chimney, 3-bayed façade, late hood over doorway, 2/2-paned windows. (N. H. A. *Photo Albums*, Book 4, p. /13/)
91	2½-story shingle on high brick basement, ridge chimney, 3-bayed façade, Federal pilastered doorway, 6/6-paned windows.
93, 95	2½-story shingle, high brick basement, ridge chimney, 3-bayed façade, Greek Revival pilastered doorway, 6/6-paned windows.
94, 96	2½-story shingle, ridge chimney, 3-bayed façade, 94 has pilastered doorway with transom, 96 has 6/6-paned windows, other features later.
97	2½-story shingle, ridge chimney, 3-bayed façade, pilastered doorway, 6/6-paned windows, shed-roofed extension north side.
99	1¾-story shingle, ridge chimney, gable at front, 3-bayed façade, 6/6-paned windows. (N. H. A. *Photo Albums*, Book 4, p. /12/)
101	Originally similar to 88 Orange, chimney later, bay window and dormers added.
103	2½-story shingle, ridge chimney (later), 3-bayed façade, 6/6-paned windows.
109	Late Greek Revival bracketed style. 1¾-story shingle, ridge chimney, gabled 4-bayed façade (3 windows 2nd story), bracketed cornice, pilastered doorway with sidelights, 6/6-paned windows.
114	Built or moved here for Christopher Baxter in 1756, lean-to house. 2½-story shingle, ridge chimney, 2-bayed façade, 12/12- and 6/6-paned windows (entrance north end), extension on east flank. (H. B. Worth, *Nantucket Lands*, p. 272)
115	1½-story shingle, ridge chimney, gabled 3-bayed façade, later 2/2-paned windows.
118	1¾-story shingle, ridge chimney (new), 3-bayed façade, modern protruding vestibule in front of doorway, later 2/2-paned windows.
119	1¾-story shingle, high brick basement, ridge chimney, 4-bayed façade, pilastered doorway, later 2/1-paned windows.
120	1¾-story shingle, ridge chimney, 3-bayed façade, pilastered doorway, later 2/1-paned windows.
123	1¾-story shingle, ridge chimney, 3-bayed façade, Greek Revival pilastered doorway, later 1/1-paned windows.
152	(on west side of street) Lean-to house, 1¾-story shingle, had ridge chimney, originally 5-bayed façade, later protruding entrance vestibule, later 2/2-paned windows and dormers, raised on high basement.
156	(on west side of street) 1¾-story shingle, ridge chimney (new), 2-bayed façade, later 2/1-paned windows. Door on south side, box dormer in front.

Pine Street

Except for the slight angle at the north extremity, allowing it to meet more nearly perpendicularly with Main, Pine Street describes the west outline and extends the length of the Fish Lots, laid out in 1717. The street as such, however, originated later, as the Fish Lots all faced Fair. Pine Street probably came into existence a little before the middle of the eighteenth century, soon after the John Barnard house was built at 84 Main (east corner of Pine) and before the two oldest fronting Pine (5 and 8) were erected. The smaller of the two (8), dating from 1748, has a gambrel roof *(Figs. 37–38)*. Next door (10) is the late-seventeenth-century Starbuck dwelling moved from the Hummock Pond region, rebuilt and enlarged here early in the nineteenth century *(Figs. 6–7)*. One other house dating from soon after the street was opened is the lean-to of Micajah Coffin (14) at the corner of Charter Street. A number of lanes connect Pine with Fair, whereas only a few link it with closer Pleasant Street. The south half of Pine Street is lined with typical Nantucket and smaller houses of the Federal period, and a few Greek Revival examples. One of the last, the façade of which has been stripped of its architectural dress, is 32 Pine, presenting a sad contrast to its original appearance *(Fig. 92)*. A rare Cape Cod cottage on the island is 40 Pine, which is distinct from the more prevalent Nantucket small-house type next door *(Figs. 74–75)*.

Historic Buildings

4   Originally a typical Nantucket house. 2½-story shingle, ridge chimney, now has 3-bayed façade (space between door and north corner blank), 6/6-paned windows.

5   Built 1750 for John Pinkham. 2½-story shingle, ridge chimney, 3-bayed façade, 12/12-paned windows (except 9/9 over door), doorway modern. (E. A. Stackpole, *Rambling*, p. 50)

6   Greek Revival style. 1¾-story clapboard front, shingle sides, 3-bayed façade with pilasters at corners supporting front gable, pilastered doorway, 6/6-paned windows. (N. H. A. *Photo Albums*, Book 4, p. /13/)

8   Built 1748 for George Gardner, gambrel roof house, probably originally T-plan with ell longer than present. 1½-story shingle, originally center chimney behind ridge, 5-bayed façade, center door with transom, 9/9-paned windows. Current center chimney entirely new stack; remodeled early 1940s including addition of chimney at south end. (M. M. Coffin, *H. A. B. S.* #858; E. A. Stackpole, *Rambling*, p. 51; *Guidebook*, p. 18; Worth-Palmer, *Photos*, p. 56; E. U. Crosby, *Ninety Five Per Cent*, photo before addition of south chimney, p. 99)

9   Built early 1800s for Zenas Coffin, plain Federal style. 2½-story shingle, 2 ridge chimneys, 5-bayed façade, center doorway with transom, wood stoop with double stairs, 12/12-paned windows. (E. A. Stackpole, *Rambling*, p. 52)

10   Enlarged house, northwest section reused framing from Nathaniel Starbuck house (*ca.* 1676) near Hummock Pond, moved here in 1820 and incorporated into double house by John Folger, Quaker carpenter. 2½-story shingle on brick basement, ridge chimney, 5-bayed façade, center door with transom, 12/12-paned windows (upper smaller than lower). Called "Parliament House" because of Friends' meetings held in great room of Starbuck house. (E. A. Stackpole, *Rambling*, p. 51; *Proceedings*, 1904, p. 20; H. B. Worth, *Nantucket Lands*, 1881 photo facing p. 271; K. Duprey, *Old Houses*, pp. 53–56; E. U. Crosby, *Ninety Five Per Cent*, photo p. 99)

12   Early house remodeled mid-19th century. 2½-story shingle, 2 ridge chimneys, 5-bayed façade, center doorway with Greek Revival pilasters, wood stoop, 6/6-paned windows.

14   Built 1760 for Micajah Coffin, lean-to house. 2½-story shingle on stone foundations, ridge chimney (replaced), 3-bayed façade. Late 19th-century door and 2/2-paned windows. Upper and lower window nearer south corner moved outward about 18 inches by present owner. (H. B. Worth, *Nantucket Lands*, p. 247; E. A. Stackpole, *Rambling*, p. 52; Franklin C. Lamb)

15   Originally typical Nantucket house. 2½-story shingle, ridge chimney, now 3-bayed façade, 6/6-paned windows, wood stoop with double stairs to entrance. (E. A. Stackpole, *Rambling*, p. 52; N. H. A. *Photo Albums*, Book 4, p. /14/)

17   Built 2nd quarter 19th century. 2½-story shingle, ridge chimney, 3-bayed façade, pilastered Greek Revival doorway, 6/6-paned windows. New brick steps at entrance.

18   Typical Nantucket house. 2½-story shingle, ridge chimney, 4-bayed façade, 12/12- and 9/9-paned

26	windows. Extension with shed roof on north side. (E. U. Crosby, *Ninety Five Per Cent*, photo p. 100)
	Greek Revival style. 1¾-story shingle, chimneys side and rear, corner pilasters supporting entablature on flanks, 3-bayed façade with gable, doorway with sidelights (new), wood stoop, later 2/2-paned windows, outer upper windows have ¼-round heads. Stars from steam-sail Civil War battleship *Lancaster* applied to façade by William Devlan. (Samuel Burgess; N. H. A. *Photo Albums*, Book 4, p. /16/)
27	2½-story shingle, high brick basement, ridge chimney, 3-bayed façade, pilastered doorway with transom and sidelights, 12/12-paned windows, extension north side.
28	May originally have been small lean-to half-house 1¾-story shingle, chimney in front of ridge, 3-bayed façade, restored 12/12-paned windows. Much remodeled, including addition of box dormers.
30	1¾-story shingle on brick basement, ridge chimney, 3-bayed façade, pilastered doorway, 6/6-paned windows. Extension north end and box dormer modern.
31	2½-story shingle, ridge chimney (later), 3-bayed façade, 12/12-paned windows.
32	Greek Revival style. Originally 2-story clapboard on brick basement, ridge chimney, had pilasters at corners, 3-bayed façade, had front pediment, pilastered doorway, 6/6-paned windows. Façade now shingled, stripped of pilasters and pediment. (N. H. A. *Photo Albums*, Book 6, p. /4/)
33	Typical Nantucket house. 2½-story shingle, ridge chimney (new), 4-bayed façade, 12/12- and 9/9-paned windows, later pilastered Greek Revival doorway.
34	1¾-story shingle on high basement, ridge chimney, pilasters at corners, 3-bayed façade, pilastered Greek Revival doorway, stoop, altered 6/1-paned windows.
35	1¾-story shingle, ridge chimney (replaced), probably 3-bayed façade, additions south end and rear. Interior details *ca.* 1825–30.
36	1¾-story shingle, very high brick basement, ridge chimney, 4-bayed façade, pilastered Greek Revival doorway, later 2/2-paned windows. (N. H. A. *Photo Albums*, Book 4, p. /17/)
37	Originally typical Nantucket house. 2½-story clapboard front, shingle sides, ridge chimney, now 3-bayed façade. Altered, 2/1-paned windows.
38	1¾-story shingle on high brick basement, ridge chimney (new), 4-bayed façade, pilastered doorway with transom, 12/12- and 9/9-paned windows. This is a deep house with low-pitched roof. (N. H. A. *Photo Albums*, Book 4, p. /18/)
40	Cape Cod cottage. 1½-story shingle on high brick basement, ridge chimney, 3-bayed façade, later 2/2-paned windows.
42	2½-story shingle, ridge chimney (later), 3-bayed façade, pilastered Greek Revival doorway, had 6/6-paned windows (now 2/1). (N. H. A. *Photo Albums*, Book 4, p. /18/)
43	Originally typical Nantucket house. 2½-story shingle, ridge chimney, now 4-bayed 1st story, 3-bayed 2nd, 6/6- and 2/1-paned windows.
44	1¾-story shingle on high brick basement, had ridge chimney, 3-bayed façade, late 2/2-paned windows.

Pleasant Street

Pleasant Street must have been a road in the mid-1700s, when the Stephen Chase lean-to house (25) was built below the angle of South Mill Street. Pleasant was described by Isaac Coffin in 1799 as beginning on Main at the "Northeast corner Friends' Meeting House," running south, then "south and east to Newtown Gate."[1] The Quaker Meeting House stood on the west corner of Main from 1790 to 1834, after which the present Greek Revival residence (98 Main) was built. Number 1 Pleasant was constructed soon afterward, and in style it relates to the three nearby on Main (including 94–96) and 7 and 9 (and somewhat to 17) farther down Pleasant *(Figs. 99–100)*. Other buildings of interest are six typical Nantucket houses (3, 6, 8, 10, 11—with additions—and 16), the last, opposite Mill, being unique in having first-story flank walls of brick. Across the street is the stately Federal house of Jared Coffin (1829–34), Nantucket's first all-brick residence *(Fig. 70)*. It has been altered, and the garden wall dates from the end of the nineteenth century. Beginning at about Silver Street, Pleasant corresponds to the inland boundary of the West Monomoy Lots (1726) down to Cherry. A quarter of a mile south of here it curves eastward to meet Orange at the first milestone, near which was the Newtown Gate, an old sheep barrier.

Note

1 Henry Barnard Worth, *Nantucket Lands and Land Owners*, Nantucket Historical Association, Vol. II, Bulletin No. 5, 1906 (reissued 1928), p. 274.

Historic Buildings

1 Built 1837 by Henry Macy for William H. Crosby, Greek Revival style. 2½-story clapboard on high brick basement, side chimneys, square cupola on slate roof, 3-bayed pilastered façade with fan window in pediment, wood distyle Doric portico with parapet, granite stoop, steps and posts, 6/6-paned windows, those of parlors have 3 sashes, unique in Nantucket. Originally had iron balcony in front and iron fence along sidewalk. House had rectangular plan with dining room and kitchen in basement, double parlors 1st floor with gray "Gothic" marble mantels identical to those in 94 and 96 Main Street, similar woodwork. Later extension south flank and rear wing. (E. A. Stackpole, *Rambling*, p. 55; G. A. Fowlkes, *Mirror of Nantucket*, pp. 120–121; E. U. Crosby, *Ninety Five Per Cent*, photo p. 101; A. E. Poor, *Colonial Architecture,* doorway pl. 87)

3 Built 1804 for Reuben Dow, typical Nantucket house. 2½-story shingle, ridge chimney, 4-bayed façade, door with transom, 12/12-paned windows. (Mrs. James D. Mayer II, K. Duprey, *Old Houses,* pp. 111–/114/, 218, 220; E. A. Stackpole, *Rambling*, p. 55)

5 2½-story shingle, 5-bayed façade, much altered. Interior details Federal and Greek Revival.

6 Built about 1820, typical Nantucket house. 2½-story clapboard front, shingle sides, brick basement, ridge chimney, 4-bayed façade, doorway with transom, 6/6-paned windows. (E. A. Stackpole, *Rambling,* pp. 54–55)

7 Built 1820s by John Coleman for Isaac Macy, transitional Federal-Greek Revival style. 2½-story clapboard, 4 end chimneys, roof walk, 5-bayed façade, center doorway with sidelights sheltered by distyle Greek Ionic portico, 6/6-paned windows. Parapet over cornice with balustrade insets aligned to windows. Sidewalk paved with bluestone. (G. A. Fowlkes, *Mirror of Nantucket*, pp. 74–75; E. A. Stackpole, *Rambling*, pp. 56, 57; E. U. Crosby, *Ninety Five Per Cent*, photo p. 102)

8 Built 1785 for Walter Folger II, typical Nantucket house, 2½-story shingle, ridge chimney, 4-bayed façade, doorway with transom, curious narrow windows with 4/4-paned sashes—related to group on West Chester (3, 8, 11, and 21), though these have 6/6-paned windows in combination. (G. A. Fowlkes, *Mirror of Nantucket*, p. 121; E. A. Stackpole, *Rambling*, p. 54; E. U. Crosby, *Ninety Five Per Cent*, photo p. 102)

9 Built 1830s by John Coleman for Benjamin Easton. Greek Revival style. 2½-story clapboard on brick basement, end chimneys, 3-bayed façade, front door with sidelights sheltered by distyle Doric portico with parapet, 6/6-paned windows. Later wing on south flank attempts reconciliation with original architecture. Spike fence along sidewalk. (E. A. Stackpole, *Rambling*, pp. 56, 57; K. Duprey, *Old Houses*, pp. 211–213, 230)

10 Built late 18th century, originally a typical Nantucket house. 2½-story shingle, ridge chimney, 4-bayed façade (no window 2nd story near north corner), Federal doorway, 12/12-paned windows. (E. A. Stackpole, *Rambling*, p. 54)

11 Originally a typical Nantucket house. 2½-story shingle, ridge chimney, 5-bayed façade (including 1-bay 1-room deep addition south end), 6/6-paned windows, center door with modern portico.

12 Built 1828 for J. H. Gibbs. 2½-story clapboard front, shingle sides, 2 ridge chimneys, 5-bayed façade, center doorway with Greek Revival pilasters and entablature, 6/6-paned windows. Modern front and side porches. (E. A. Stackpole, *Rambling,* p. 54)

13 Built third quarter 18th century, probably originally 2-bayed. 2½-story shingle, ridge chimney, now 3-bayed façade, 12/12- and 9/9-paned windows. Later addition with shed roof south end. (E. A. Stackpole, *Rambling,* pp. 57–58; E. U. Crosby *Ninety Five Per Cent,* photo p. 103)

15 Built 1800 for Obed Macy. 2½-story shingle, 2 ridge chimneys, façade 4-bayed plus door, 12/12-paned windows. (E. A. Stackpole, *Rambling*, p. 58; E. U. Crosby, *Ninety Five Per Cent*, photo p. 103; N. H. A. *Photo Albums*, Book 4, p. /19)

16	Typical Nantucket house variation. 2½-story shingle, 1st story each flank wall of brick, ridge chimney, 4-bayed façade, enclosed entrance pent, 12/12-paned windows 1st story, 8/12-paned windows 2nd. (A. E. Poor, *Colonial Architecture*, pls. 26, 71)
17	Built 1847 for Peter Macy, Greek Revival style. 1¾-story clapboard with gable at front, pilasters at corners supporting entablature along sides. Ionic column to entrance portico on north flank. Similar to 123 Main Street. (E. A. Stackpole, *Rambling*, p. 59)
19	Built 1829–34 for Jared Coffin, Federal style. Called Moors' End because at edge of town, 1st all-brick house in Nantucket. 2½-story common-bond brick (including foundations), parapets connecting end chimneys, square cupola on roof, 5-bayed façade, center doorway with sidelights and semicircular blind fan with eagle (door itself later), brick stoop with brownstone steps both sides, iron railing (some modern), meander frieze below and parapet over front cornice with lattice insets (1925) aligned to windows. Brick ell on granite sill Mill Street side, new brick chimney and some window changes. 1890s 2-story porch south side, high brick screen wall along Pleasant Street, clairvoyée fence on Angora connecting altered barn at south angle of lot. (M. M. Coffin, *H. A. B. S.* #917; drawings for Fiske Kimball restorations, 1925, S. P. N. E. A. archives; F. Kimball article, *Architectural Record,* Sept. 1927, pp. 191–200; G. A. Fowlkes, *Mirror of Nantucket,* pp. 81–83; E. A. Stackpole, *Rambling*, pp. 59–60; E. U. Crosby, *Ninety Five Per Cent*, photos pp. 104–105; A. E. Poor, *Colonial Architecture*, pl. 42)
20	Greek Revival style. 2½-story shingle, high brick basement, had end chimneys, 5-bayed façade, deeply recessed doorway with sidelights, door itself late 19th century, 6/6-paned windows. New wing south side. (N. H. A. *Photo Albums*, Book 4, p. /20/)
25	Built after July 17, 1745, when Jonathan Folger conveyed land to son-in-law, Stephen Chase. Faces south, lean-to house. 2½-story shingle, ridge chimney, 3–4-bayed façade (1st story has 4 openings including door), probably originally had 12/12-paned windows. Lean-to shortened. Once had rear wing behind (not original). (Worth-Plamer, *Photos*, p. 60; H. B. Worth, *Nantucket Lands*, p. 277, 1881 photo facing p. 255; K. Duprey, *Old Houses*, pp. /66/-/69/; E. A. Stackpole, *Rambling*, p. 64)
34	Typical Nantucket house. 2½-story shingle, ridge chimney, 4-bayed façade (window north of doorway closed up), later Greek Revival doorway, much later 6/1-paned windows.
39	Built early 19th century. 2-story shingle, end chimneys, 5-bayed façade, pilastered doorway, 6/6-paned windows, rear extension with shed roof.
50	1¾-story shingle, ridge chimney, 3-bayed façade, pilastered doorway, 6/6-paned windows.
60	1¾-story shingle, ridge chimney, 5-bayed façade, later 2/2-paned windows, part lean-to at rear.
61	1¾-story shingle, ridge chimney, 3-bayed façade, pilastered doorway, 6/6-paned windows, later front gable.
63	1½-story shingle, ridge chimney (new), 4-bayed façade, pilastered doorway, 6/6-paned windows. Later box dormer.

Plumb Lane

This is one of three lanes that connect Fair and Orange Street. Plumb is the center one and was named after the Plumb family living in the vicinity. The lane dates back to the eighteenth century and was listed in the Isaac Coffin Survey of 1799. Number 3 is an attractive house with unusual architectural refinements for its modest size *(Fig. 135)*. It had become dilapidated, but at the time of writing (1971) the house is being renovated.

Historic Buildings

1	Built early 19th century. 2½-story shingle, L-plan with end chimneys, 4-bayed façade, 12/12-paned windows 1st story, 8/12-paned windows above, later pilastered Greek Revival doorway.
3	Early 19th century Federal style. 2½-story shingle, ridge chimney (replaced), 3-bayed façade, pilastered doorway with transom, 6/6-paned windows. Note dental course beneath cornice, ½-round urns near top of upright corner boards. Had roof walk. (N. H. A. *Photo Albums*, Book 4, p. /20/)

4   Built *ca.* 1842. 1¾-story shingle, had ridge chimney (?), 4-bayed façade, Greek Revival pilastered
     doorway, 6/6-paned windows. (Leon F. Moynihan)

Fig. 135 3 Plumb Lane at Turn of Century.

Prospect Street

Originally called Copper Street, this road was described in the Isaac Coffin survey at the close of the eighteenth century as extending from Milk Street "south through Allentown by Edward Allen's house, south and east by Wind Mills to the Cow Bars near James Johnson's Pond in Newtown."[1] Prospect Street is practically a continuation of Quaker Road, which drops from the end of Main Street down to Milk, Prospect continuing in a slightly more easterly direction. Edward Allen built a series of small houses at the upper end of Prospect (hence the "Allentown"), and his own home is Number 21 *(Figs. 30–31)*. At the time of the survey, the road passed between the two eastern-most of the original four mills here on the ridge, only one of which is still standing, that built by Nathan Wilbur in 1746 at the corner of South Mill Street *(Figs. 2–3)*. At this point the present Prospect Street turns into West York, which runs directly to Pleasant. Old Copper Street followed the course of what now is South Prospect and projected beyond to the "Cow Bars" in Newtown, presumably below Orange. The name "Copper Street" should not be confused with little "Copper Lane" joining Quaker Road with Milk Street, a modern designation. On the Walling map of 1858, Prospect Street is labeled "Cooper," and as such it reappears in the fold-out map in E. K. Godfrey's *The Island of Nantucket*, 1882. However, on the J. J. Stoner *Bird's-Eye View* of the previous year, the street already has its current name of Prospect.

The large lean-to house near Milk (6) was moved here about 1800 *(Figs. 17–18)*. Its smaller neighbors date from the following decades. Beyond Mill Street stands another transplanted structure (30), a post-depression-era house that was assembled from parts of three early buildings. Prospect Street veers into South Prospect (see below) at Nantucket's most picturesque monument, the ancient windmill.

Note

1   Henry Barnard Worth, *Nantucket Lands and Land Owners*, Nantucket Historical Association, Vol. II, Bulletin No. 5, 1906 (reissued 1928), p. 250.

Historic Buildings

2	Greek Revival style. 1¾-story shingle, ridge chimney (late), pilasters at corners supporting front entablature, 3-bayed façade, pilastered doorway with sidelights, 6/6-paned windows. (N. H. A. *Photo Albums*, Book 5, p. /1/)
3	1¾-story clapboard front, shingle sides, ridge chimney, 3-bayed façade, pilastered Greek Revival doorway, 6/6-paned windows. (N. H. A. *Photo Albums*, Book 5, p. /1/)
5	1¾-story shingle, ridge chimney, 3-bayed façade, modern 12/12-paned windows. (N. H. A. *Photo Albums*, Book 5, p. /2/)
6	Built 2nd quarter 18th century for Matthew Myrick, originally on Milk near New Mill and moved here *ca.* 1800. Lean-to house, faces south. 2½-story shingle, ridge chimney, façade with 3 windows 2nd story, center door with transom flanked by 2 windows each side 1st story. Early house may have been west section, which has 9/9-paned windows, east section has 12/12-paned windows. (H. B. Worth, *Nantucket Lands*, p. 250; E. A. Stackpole, *Rambling*, p. 68)
7	1¾-story shingle, ridge chimney, 3-bayed façade. Late 19th-century bracketed doorway, 2/2-paned windows.
9	1¾-story shingle, ridge chimney, 3-bayed façade, 12/12-paned windows. At turn of century had 6/6-paned windows. (N. H. A. *Photo Albums*, Book 5, p. /2/)
11	Greek Revival style. 1¾-story shingle on high brick basement, had ridge chimney, pilasters at corners, 3-bayed façade with gable, 6/6-paned windows, entrance with sidelights east side.
16	Greek Revival style. 1¾-story shingle, ridge chimney, shafts at corners supporting front entablature, 3-bayed façade, doorway with sidelights, 6/6-paned windows.
17	West section original lean-to house. 1¾-story clapboard front, shingle sides, ridge chimney, 5-bayed façade (including 2-bay east addition), pilastered doorway with transom, 6/6-paned windows.
21	Built 1763 by and for Edward Allen, lean-to house. 1¾-story shingle, ridge chimney, 5-bayed façade, 12/12-paned windows, later pilastered Federal doorway. (Rev. & Mrs. James Kennedy; *Guidebook*, p. 29)
23	1½-story shingle on high brick basement, ridge chimney, 3-bayed façade, new pilastered doorway

	with sidelights, 6/6-paned windows.
26	Originally Greek Revival style. 1¾-story shingle, ridge chimney, front gable, 2 windows over 3-bayed 1st story, doorway with sidelights, 6/6-paned windows.
30	Assembled from parts of 3 old buildings in 1934 by and for Richard Emerson. 2½-story shingle, articulated ridge chimney, 5-bayed façade, center entrance pent, leaded casement windows. Timbers came from Jeremiah Coleman 1745 house on Warren Street and 2 houses converted into barns, one on upper Main and the other from the Hamblin property on Cliff Road. (E. A. Stackpole, *Rambling*, p. 66; K. Duprey, *Old Houses,* pp. 24–/30/)
X	(east of 30) Built *ca.* 1811–12 for George Brown. 1¾-story clapboard, end chimney, 5-bayed façade, center doorway with sidelights, 6/6-paned windows, early extension west side. House raised on high basement and porch added encircling front, 1925. (Note from Grace Brown Gardner to Mrs. Frederick L. Ackerman, July 16, 1945: courtesy Mr. & Mrs. C. H. Hecker)
X	WINDMILL see South Mill

Quaker Road

Bounding the old Friends' cemetery on its east side, Quaker Road is appropriately named. It was called Grave Street through the nineteenth century, and, briefly, Saratoga prior to becoming Quaker Road. It connects Main at Caton Circle with Milk Street, continuing southward as Prospect Street.

Quarter Mile Hill

Located in Richard Gardner's early parcel called "Crooked Record" *(Fig. 2)*, Quarter Mile Hill is north of Main Street and reached by a narrow lane west of Number 123. The old mid-eighteenth-century house now on Quarter Mile Hill originally stood east of 153 Main *(Fig. 118)*.

Historic Building

X	Built 1740s for Joseph Gardner, given to son Charles, was lean-to house, faces south (both before and after removal). 2½-story shingle, ridge chimney, 3-bayed façade, door with transom, 12/12-paned windows (present 8/12-paned windows 2nd story changed after transplanted), extension with shed roof west flank. Later wing east side. Moved to present location 2nd quarter 20th century. (H. B. Worth, *Nantucket Lands*, p. 265, 1881 photo facing p. 279; K. Duprey, *Old Houses*, pp. 42–45; E. A. Stackpole, *Rambling*, p. 75; old photo Miller R. Hutchison II Collection, N. H. A.)

Quince Street

An alteration made in 1719 to the Wescoe Acre Lots of 1678 consisted of opening a street west from Centre, above Hussey Court, and calling it Crown Court. Isaac Coffin described Crown Court in 1799 as extending to the house of Jonathan Myrick II.[1] This building (15) had been purchased by Myrick two years earlier from Mrs. Ann Gelston, for whom it was built in 1795. Westminster Street was cut alongside this house, perpendicular to Crown Court, at the time of the building of the Academy, early in the nineteenth century. Now being accessible from both ends, the court should have become a street, as had Hussey Street on the Coffin maps of 1833–34. Crown Court acquired a more radical name change later, becoming Quince Street by the time of the Walling map of 1858. Of special interest is the old Quaker schoolhouse (8) moved here from Fair Street. Number 9 has one of the finest doorways in Nantucket *(Fig. 49)*, to which the new shingle façade of 1970 hardly does justice. Number 14 was a lean-to house facing south *(Fig. 136)*, the street side now heightened to two full stories.

Note

1 Henry Barnard Worth, *Nantucket Lands and Land Owners*, Nantucket Historical Association, Vol. II, Bulletin No. 5, 1906 (reissued 1928), p. 250.

Fig. 136 14 Quince Street Before Remodeling.

222   THE ARCHITECTURE OF HISTORIC NANTUCKET

Historic Buildings

2	Built before 1782 by and for Theophilus Pinkham (house carpenter). 1¾-story shingle, ridge chimney, 3-bayed façade, door on east end, some 6/9-paned windows, later 6/6-paned windows. (T. Bunker, *Research*, #3165)
3	Federal style. 2½-story shingle on brick basement, ridge chimney, 3-bayed façade, pilastered doorway with sidelights, 6/6-paned windows.
4	Built before 1834. 2½-story shingle on brick basement, ridge chimney, 3-bayed façade, pilastered Greek Revival doorway, 6/6-paned windows.
5	Built before the American Revolution for David Hussey. 2½-story shingle, ridge chimney (smaller replacement), roof walk, 5-bayed façade, later Greek Revival doorway with sidelights, 6/6-paned windows. (E. A. Stackpole, *Rambling*, p. 28)
8	Originally Friends' School on Fair Street, built 2nd quarter 19th century, conducted by Hepzibeth Hussey. 1¾-story shingle, pilasters at corners, frieze and cornice across front. Placed here before 1900.
9	Federal style, typical Nantucket house. 2½-story clapboard until shingled in 1970, high brick basement, ridge chimney, 4-bayed façade, fine pilastered doorway with shuttered fan and sidelights, stoop with stairs both sides, 6/6-paned windows. Rear half of west flank has 12/12-paned windows. (E. U. Crosby, *Ninety Five Per Cent*, photo p. 106; N. H. A. *Photo Albums*, Book 5, p. /4/)
10	Typical Nantucket house. 2½-story shingle, ridge chimney, doorway and 6/6-paned windows new.
14	Built mid-18th century, lean-to house, faces south. Originally 2½-story shingle, ridge chimney, 3-bayed façade, had 12/12-paned windows (smaller over door). Shed-roofed extension added east flank. House enlarged after 1895, including street side built up to full 2 stories. Retains projecting bay window of that period but mostly remodeled to resemble early character. (H. S. Wyer, *Nantucket: Old and New*, plate /5/ shows house before 1895)
15	Built *ca.* 1795 for Mrs. Ann Gelston. 2½-story shingle on brick basement, ridge chimney, 3-bayed façade, later Greek Revival doorway and stoop, much later 2/2-paned windows. Extension east end. (H. B. Worth, *Nantucket Lands*, p. 250)
16	Early Greek Revival. 2½-story clapboard on brick basement, chimneys at side, 3-bayed façade, pilasters at corners, polygonal fan window in front gable, recessed doorway, 6/6-paned windows. Late 19th-century gingerbread porch added.

Ray's Court

The original Ray's Court is the stretch branching west from Fair Street, named for John Ray, whose mid-eighteenth-century house (8) stands on the south side, much enlarged and altered. The other section of the court, at right angles, connecting with Main, was called Turner's Alley. Both are described in the Isaac Coffin Survey of 1799.[1] They were joined before 1830.

Note

1 Henry Barnard Worth, *Nantucket Lands and Land Owners*, Nantucket Historical Association, Vol. II, Bulletin No. 5, 1906 (reissued 1928), pp. 275, 278.

Historic Buildings

2A	Built 2nd quarter 19th century. 1¾-story shingle, ridge chimney, 3-bayed façade, 6/6-paned windows. Additions west end and rear.
8	Built 1748 for John Ray, northeast section original lean-to half-house facing east. Altered and extensive additions south side and west end (roof completely changed) by 4th quarter 19th century. 2½-story shingle, ridge and end chimneys. Further changes around 1900, including porch on east end, bay window and tall west extension. (Rachel S. Carpenter; E. A. Stackpole, *Rambling*, p. 50)

Rose Lane

Listed as being in existence in 1799 by Isaac Coffin, Rose Lane runs from Centre Street along the north flank of the Methodist Church.

Historic Building

5   Believed built as counting house for Paul West after 1815, when he became owner of 5 Liberty Street. 2-story shingle, 3-bayed façade, 12/12-paned windows 1st story, 8/12-paned windows above. In 1940s moved from site 100 feet or so to the east. (Charles P. Flanagan)

Saratoga Lane

Next west of Quaker Road, connecting Milk and the extension of Vestal, Saratoga Lane takes the early nineteenth-century name for Quaker Road, Saratoga Street, formerly called Grave Street. Saratoga Lane is hardly more than a trail.

School Street

Located between Charter and Mott Lane, School Street is one of the series later cut through the west range of the Fish Lots connecting Fair with Pine Street. Its name derives from the Benjamin Coffin house and school formerly about opposite the street on Pine.[1] All six buildings listed below are shown on the 1833–34 Coffin map.

Note

1   Information courtesy Charles Clark Coffin, great- great- great-grandson of the schoolmaster, Benjamin Coffin.

Historic Buildings

1   Originally typical Nantucket house. 2½-story shingle, ridge chimney, now has 3-bayed façade, pilastered Greek Revival doorway, 6/6-paned windows. Modern porch.

3   Later typical Nantucket house. 2½-story shingle, ridge chimney, 4-bayed façade, doorway with transom, 6/6-paned windows.

4   2½-story clapboard front, shingle sides, 2 chimneys on west end, 3-bayed façade, pilastered Greek Revival doorway, 6/6-paned windows.

6   1¾-story clapboard front, shingle sides, high brick basement, end chimneys, 5-bayed façade, center door with transom, wood stoop, 6/6-paned windows.

7   Late 18th-century type. 2½-story shingle, ridge chimney, center doorway flanked by 2 windows each side, 3 windows 2nd story, 12/12-paned windows (modern).

9   Late 18th-century or early 19th-century house with addition. 2½-story shingle, ridge chimney. Original house 3-bayed west section, 2 rooms deep; single room attached east end, making 5-bayed façade with center doorway, 12/12-paned windows (modern).

Sea Street

Once a more important street than at present, in the eighteenth century, according to the Isaac Coffin survey, it extended eastward to the lighthouse on Brant Point. On the William Coffin map of 1833-34, Sea Street is reduced to a short stretch off North Water, terminating against a house facing north on a court branching inland from South Beach Street. The house burned in the Great Fire of 1846, and Sea Street was lengthened to South Beach. It is virtually a continuation of Step Lane, which ascends the bank to Centre Street.

Silver Street

The Silver Street listed in the Isaac Coffin 1799 survey is what now is Copper Lane, connecting Milk and Quaker Road. The present Silver Street must have come into existence soon afterward to connect the dangling end of Pine with Pleasant and Orange. Throughout most of the nineteenth century, Nantucket had two Silver streets, or until the name of the other was changed to Copper.

Historic Buildings

4	Greek Revival period. 1¾-story clapboard front, shingle sides, rock foundations, 3-bayed gabled façade, pilastered doorway, later 2/1-paned windows.
7	Built *ca.* 1820. 1¾-story shingle on brick basement full story above ground in front, ridge chimney, 3-bayed façade, late 19th-century 2/2-paned windows.
8	Shingled building, built before 1834 as barn. Converted into modern residence.
14	Lean-to house. 1¾-story shingle, ridge chimney (new), 5-bayed façade, center door with enclosed entrance pent, much later 2/2-paned windows.

South Beach Street

South Beach Street dates from the early part of the nineteenth century and is shown on the William Coffin 1833–34 maps as North Beach, the present North Beach similarly designated. Perhaps the broken, unlabeled continuation below Broad was meant to be called South Beach. Today's South Beach is east of North Water and connects Broad to Easton Street.

Historic Buildings

2	Moved from northeast corner Broad and North Water in 1920s, main block of house faces south. 2½-story clapboard, presumably had 2 ridge chimneys, 5-bayed façade, Greek Revival doorway with sidelights and distyle portico (columns modern), 6/6-paned windows. Later addition fronting on South Beach Street. (Robert L. White; N. H. A. *Photo Albums*, Book 1, p. /2/)

South Mill Street

South Mill bears southwest from Pleasant Street across from and a little above the end of Lyon Street. It begins to the rear of the Stephen Chase house and extends to the old mill, at the junction of Prospect and South Prospect streets, both structures built about 1746. South Mill Street dates from this period.

Historic Building

X	WINDMILL, built 1746 by Nathan Wilbur. Shingled octagonal battered form on rock foundations. Said to have been constructed of timbers of wrecked ships. Lone survivor of 5 windmills serving Nantucket Town, easternmost of 4 on Popsquatchett Hills. Purchased by Caroline French in 1897 and presented to Nantucket Historical Association. Subsequently repaired in 1913–14, 1935–36, 1949–50, and 1952 (after main shaft and 4 vanes destroyed). Still occasionally used for grinding corn. Museum open to public. (E. A. Stackpole, *Rambling*, pp. 63–64, illus. p. 65; *Proceedings*, 1940, p. 20, illus. facing p. 20; *Historic Nantucket*, July 1953, p. 59; *ibid.*, Oct. 1970, pp. 12–15; G. A. Fowlkes, *Mirror of Nantucket*, p. 119; H. Morrison, *Early American Architecture*, photo p. 93; E. U. Crosby, *Ninety Five Per Cent*, photo p. 116; A. E. Poor, *Colonial Architecture*, pl. 54; *H. A. B. S.* #141)

South Prospect Street

South Prospect Street begins at the mill, where Prospect Street proper ends (see above). It curves down to Atlantic Avenue, roughly following an old route but redeemed in relatively modern times.

Historic Building

61   1¾-story shingle, ridge chimney, had 3-bayed façade, enveloped by additions.

South Water Street

Originally South and North Water streets were called simply Water Street. See above, North Water Street.

Historic Buildings

17   DREAMLAND THEATRE. Built 1829 as Friends Meeting House that stood at site of 76 Main Street. In 1852 sold to Atlantic Straw Company and served as hat factory. Later became Atlantic Hall. In 1883 taken to Brant Point area and incorporated into Nantucket Hotel. Procured 1905 and removed to present location, 2nd story became Red Men's Hall. Extended at rear. Front added later when 1st floor became movie house. (G. A. Fowlkes, *Mirror of Nantucket*, p. 109; H. Turner, *Nantucket Argument Settlers*; A. Starbuck, *History,* pp. 513–14)

21   Built after 1846 Fire, Greek Revival style. 1¾-story shingle, gabled façade, pilasters at corners supporting entablature on flanks, new chimney south side and fenestration changes, said formerly to have been used as fire house.

Spring Street

Called Fish Lane from the late eighteenth to the early twentieth century, Spring Street is a continuation of Back Street, lying between Orange and Union, one block above their junction *(Fig. 137).*

Historic Building

5   Built early 19th century for David Wyer, lean-to house. 1¾-story shingle, ridge chimney, 5-bayed façade, pilastered doorway, modern windows with 6/6-paned sashes. (Deed Book 22, pp. 459–469)

Starbuck Court

Today a spur off Pleasant Street above Mill, on the 1833–34 Coffin map Starbuck Court (unlabeled) is shown running through to New Dollar Lane. The west end was closed before the issuance of the 1848 Bache map. The court derives its name from the Starbuck Oil and Candle Warehouse in the interior of the block.

Historic Buildings

X   Mid-19th-century shop. 2-story shingle, end chimney, 3-bayed façade, 12/12-paned windows. All details are modern. (E. A. Stackpole, *Rambling*, p. 57)

X   STARBUCK OIL AND CANDLE WAREHOUSE, built early 19th century, changed and enlarged from time to time. Building completely altered into guest houses.

Fig. 137 5 Spring Street Around Turn of Century.

Step Lane

Next above Ash Street and Ash Lane, Step Lane also connects Centre with North Water Street. Formerly called Chapman Avenue, its present name derives from its precipitous incline.

Historic Buildings

3   First structure here said to have been built from parts of William Gayer house (1684), that was demolished to make way for Peter Folger II house (*ca.* 1765) on adjoining property to north (51 Centre). Façade features are Greek Revival. 2½-story shingle on high brick basement, ridge chimneys, 3-bayed façade, pilastered doorway with sidelights. Building enlarged after 1881 into hostelry called Veranda House; since 1945 known as Overlook Hotel. (leaflet: T. J. Devine, *Overlook*)

4   Typical Nantucket house. 2½-story shingle, ridge chimney, 4-bayed façade, 12/12- and 9/9-paned windows, entrance moved to east side.

5   Greek Revival style. 2½-story shingle on brick basement, ridge chimney, 3-bayed façade, ribbed piers at corners, fanlight in front pediment, pilastered doorway with sidelights, 6/6-paned windows.

Stone Alley

Called Gunter on the Coffin map of 1833–34 and the Walling map of 1858, Stone Alley connects Orange and Union streets below Main. The cobblestoned east stretch, on the slope of Quanaty Bank, is restricted to pedestrians *(Fig. 138)*.

Historic Building

1, 3   Double lean-to house. Number 1 built 1720 or before by Solomon Gardner, who added west portion (3) *ca.* 1750, occupied by Paul Gardner in 1755. Faces south. Both 2½-story shingle on high brick basement. East section L-plan (hip at southeast corner of roof), due to enlargement, 3-bayed façade, 6/6-paned windows. West section retains lean-to form with chimney back of ridge, 2-bayed façade plus door, 6/6-paned windows. (M. M. Coffin, *H. A. B. S.* #1014; H. B. Worth, *Nantucket Lands*, p. 255; E. U. Crosby, *Ninety Five Per Cent*, photo of rear p. 106)

Summer Street

Referred to in Isaac Coffin's survey of 1799, Summer Street connects Pleasant and Pine below Main Street and in turn is joined to Main by Trader's Lane. The street is dominated by the First Baptist Church *(Fig. 104)*. A later building worth noting is the two-storied coach house (3) next to the church. Its pyramid roof originally was capped by a cupola, which shows in the J. J. Stoner *Bird's-Eye View* of 1881.

Historic Buildings

1   FIRST BAPTIST CHURCH, built 1840 by Frederick Brown Coleman, Greek Revival style. Frame for building came from Maine. Portico planned but curtailed because of cost. White clapboard on brick basement, pilastered and pedimented façade, 3-bayed flanks with pilasters at rear corners. Square stepped steeple with octagonal spire added in 1841. Bell installed in 1854. Late 19th-century colored glass windows. Steeple replaced 1962. (G. A. Fowlkes, *Mirror of Nantucket*, pp. 105–106; E. A. Stackpole, *Rambling*, pp. 51–52; *Historic Nantucket*, July 1962, pp. 5–7; E. U. Crosby, *Ninety Five Per Cent*, photo p. 109)

4   Originally typical Nantucket house. 2½-story clapboard front, shingle sides, ridge chimney, now 3-bayed façade. Later bracketed door and trim, 2/2-paned windows.

7   Built *ca.* 1790, typical Nantucket house. 2½-story shingle, ridge chimney, 4-bayed façade, 12/12- and 9/9-paned windows, later pilastered Greek Revival doorway, extension east end and rear with shed roofs. House depicted in Phebe Folger's watercolor *ca.* 1797. (*Historic Nantucket*, Oct. 1966, p. 16; E. U. Crosby, *Ninety Five Per Cent*, photo p. 109; A. E. Poor, *Colonial Architecture*, pl. 26)

Sunset Hill Lane

North of West Chester and east of North Liberty, Sunset Hill Lane, one of the newest streets in Nantucket Town, was opened about 1920 to the oldest house, that of Jethro Coffin (1686). The Nathaniel Paddock lean-to was built alongside it after 1708, but now the Coffin house stands alone. It is a public museum *(Figs. 9–11)*.

Historic Building

1   Built *ca.* 1686 for Jethro Coffin of timbers brought from Exeter, N.H., medieval or "English" style house. 1¾-story (with garret) shingle, ridge chimney ornamented with inverted U (Jacobean arch) in projecting brickwork, 3-bayed façade, center batten door with strap hinges, restored leaded casement windows. Original house contained 2 rooms on each floor (parlor and hall below, chambers above), separated by stairs and chimney. Had 2 front gables with windows lighting chambers. Rear lean-to (with kitchen, borning room, and milk room) added later, gables removed. On display since 1886. Restored partly to 1st and partly to 2nd period (thus making a 3rd) by William S. Appleton and

Alfred E. Shurrocks 1925–29. (M. M. Coffin, *H. A. B. S.* #919; H. B. Worth, *Nantucket Lands*, pp. 225–227; H. C. Forman, *Early Nantucket*, pp. /230/–/236/ incl. illus.; A. Starbuck, *History*, p. 616; *Proceedings*, 1927, pp. 26–28; *Ibid.*, 1943 photo frontispiece; /Mrs. Worron/, *"Trustum" and His Grandchildren*, pp. 55–58; G. A. Fowlkes, *Mirror of Nantucket*, pp. 28–31; K. Mixer, *Old Houses of New England*, pp. 8–10; K. Duprey, *Old Houses*, pp. 6–/9/; E. U. Crosby, *Ninety Five Per Cent*, photo p. 110; A. E. Poor, *Colonial Architecture*, pl. 1; H. Morrison, *Early American Architecture*, photo p. 67; H. E. Ripley, *Journal A. I. A.*, June 1928, pp. 218–223)

Fig. 138 Stone Alley (lower right) Viewed from Unitarian Church Tower About 1874.

Tattle Court

Tattle Court, which branches off the west side of Fair Street between Darling and Farmer, is all that is left of old Macy Lane, which once extended through to Pine. The early name was appropriate, since here stands the Thomas Macy house, erected soon after the Fish Lots were laid out in 1717 *(Figs. 15–16)*.

Historic Building

1 Built after 1717 on Fish Lot 19 for Thomas Macy, lean-to house. It is said that, during restoration, evidence was found of preexisting casement windows, which would give credence to the tradition that the late 17th-century house by Reed Pond, old Sherburne, "was moved to town after 1730" and rebuilt as this house. Worth says the house in question was re-erected nearby. 2½-story shingle, ridge chimney, 2-bayed façade, front door with transom, 12/12-paned windows. Shed-roof extension added east end 2nd quarter 18th century. Used as carpentry shop 1st half 20th century. Restored 1949–50 by Earl S. Ray and Mr. & Mrs. Stewart Mooney. (H. B. Worth, *Nantucket Lands*, p. 263; H. C. Forman, *Early Nantucket*, pp. 245–249 incl. illus.; E. A. Stackpole, *Rambling*, p. 89)

Trader's Lane

Described by Isaac Coffin in 1799, Trader's Lane connects Main with Summer Street, between Pine and Pleasant. It may have been named for the occupation of Peleg Bunker, who built 4 *(Fig. 139)*.

Historic Buildings

3 Built mid-18th century, originally lean-to house. 2½-story shingle, ridge chimney, 3-bayed façade with added south section, late 19th century. 2/2-paned windows.

4 Claimed built 1750 for Peleg Bunker but probably later, typical Nantucket house. 2½-story shingle, ridge chimney, roof walk, 4-bayed façade, door with transom, 12/12- and 9/9-paned windows, 2-story wing on southeast corner later. (H. B. Worth, *Nantucket Lands*, p. 278; E. A. Stackpole, *Rambling*, p. 52; G. A. Fowlkes, *Mirror of Nantucket*, pp. 50–51; N. H. A. *Photo Albums*, Book 5, p. /5/)

Twin Street

Twin Street connects Pine and Fair Street below Farmer and above Lyon.

Historic Building

1 2½-story shingle, high brick basement, ridge chimney, 3-bayed façade, later bracketed doorway, 2/2-paned windows.

Union Street

Excluded from the Fish Lots of 1717 (which extended eastward only to the crest of Quanaty Bank), Union Street was opened to become most of the harbor-side boundary of West Monomoy nine years later, curving into Orange at Consue Spring or the Newtown Bridge and connecting to Main *(Fig. 2)*. Near the north end stands the old brick Town House (2), built originally as two stores during the early 1830s. Several houses of the Federal period face Union immediately to the south; then begins an array of twenty-three typical Nantucket houses showing great variety, one being a wide version (15), one having a gambrel roof (21—*Fig. 44*), and one being both wide and having a gambrel roof (32). As Union approaches the bend above York, one finds a scattering of Greek Revival houses less than two stories in height among the "typicals." Flanking Coon Lane are two lean-to houses, a low full-house and taller half-house (59, 61), the latter greatly altered. The area between Union and Orange Street, south of Stone Alley, was measured and a plan made by the Historic American Buildings Survey team working in Nantucket during the summer of 1970. This area has changed little over the years *(Fig. 140)*.

Historic Buildings

2   OLD TOWN BUILDING, south section built *ca.* 1830 for Thomas Coffin, purchased for Town House 1836. North section built *ca.* 1830 for James Athearn, purchased by town for occupancy 1889. 2½-story brick, chimneys on roof slope, 6-bayed (altogether) façade, 6/6-paned windows, had parapets above roof line. Brick cornices and windows with brownstone lintels and sills are reconstructions after 1846 Fire. Most lintels and sills replaced with pink granite in 1969–70 restoration. (M. M. Coffin, *H. A. B. S.* #906; J. H. Robinson, *106 Views*, p. /25/)

6   Built 2nd quarter 19th century. 2-story shingle, hip roof, 4 end chimneys, 5-bayed façade, center doorway with transom and sidelights, 6/6-paned windows. (A. E. Poor, *Colonial Architecture*, pl. 31)

7   Originally double house, combined into one, Federal period. 2½-story shingle on brick basement, 2 ridge chimneys, 6-bayed façade except wide pilastered center doorway with sidelights spans 2 bays, column in middle of stairhall replaces earlier partition, 6/6-paned windows. Doorway modern replacement.

8   Federal style house. 2-storied, clapboard front, shingle sides, had 2 ridge chimneys, pediment in front with fan window, 3-bayed façade, 6/6-paned windows (had blind window center 2nd story, now obliterated). (N. H. A. *Photo Albums*, Book 5, p. /6/)

9   Built *ca.* 1820 for Elisha Green, typical Nantucket house. 2½-story clapboard front, shingle sides, brick foundations, ridge chimney, 4-bayed façade, 12/12-paned windows except 6/6-paned in 2 parlor windows. (M. M. Coffin, *H. A. B. S.* #1014; G. A. Fowlkes, *Mirror of Nantucket*, pp. 52–53; N. H. A. *Photo Albums*, Book 5, p. /5/)

11   Built 1802 for Nathan Beebe, typical Nantucket house. 2½-story shingle, brick foundations, ridge chimney (now gone), 4-bayed façade, 12/12-paned windows. (M. M. Coffin, *H. A. B. S.* #1014)

13   Built *ca.* 1796 for Francis Barker, typical Nantucket house. 2½-story shingle on high stone basement, ridge chimney, 4-bayed façade, later pilastered Greek Revival doorway, 6/6-paned windows. (M. M. Coffin, *H. A. B. S.* #1014)

14   Later variation of typical Nantucket house. 2½-story shingle, ridge chimney, 4-bayed façade (except no window 1st story north of door), pilastered Greek Revival doorway, 6/6-paned windows.

15   Built *ca.* 1800 by Richard Lake Coleman, house carpenter, sold to Timothy C. Clapp, wide typical Nantucket house. 2½-story shingle on high brick basement, ridge chimney, 4-bayed façade, pilastered doorway with transom, wood stoop, 12/12-paned windows. Kitchen in basement. Restored 1930s, roof walk added. (M. M. Coffin, *H. A. B. S.* #1014; Scott W. Stearns II; G. A. Fowlkes, *Mirror of Nantucket*, pp. 44–46)

16   Another variation on typical Nantucket house. 2½-story clapboard front, shingle sides, ridge chimney, 4-bayed façade (no window 2nd story north corner), 6/6-paned windows, restored doorway.

17   Built *ca.* 1802 for Joseph West, typical Nantucket house. 2½-story clapboard front, shingle sides, brick basement, ridge chimney, 4-bayed façade, Federal doorway with transom, 12/12-paned windows. (M. M. Coffin, *H. A. B. S.* #1014; N. H. A. *Photo Albums*, Book 5, p. /6/)

18   Built early 19th century, Federal style. Moved here from site of present Pacific National Bank, Main at Centre, *ca.* 1817. 2½-story clapboard on brick basement, 2 ridge chimneys, 5-bayed façade, pilastered doorway with transom, brownstone and brick stoop with wrought-iron railing (said to have come from Nantucket's 1st bank building of 1795), 12/12-paned windows, wood quoins at corners. (*Proceedings*, 1917, p. 32; G. A. Fowlkes, *Mirror of Nantucket*, p. 123; E. U. Crosby, *Ninety Five Per Cent*, photo of doorway p. 110; A. E. Poor, *Colonial Architecture*, pls. 36, 60, 93)

19   Built *ca.* 1803 by Nathan Nye, house carpenter, sold to Silvanus Ewer, typical Nantucket house. 2½-story shingle on stuccoed basement, ridge chimney, 4-bayed façade, 12/12- and 9/9-paned windows, later pilastered Greek Revival doorway. (M. M. Coffin, *H. A. B. S.* #1014)

20   Built early 1830s, Federal style. 2½-story clapboard front, shingle sides, on high brick basement

Fig. 139 4 Trader's Lane.

21 (no windows in front), 4 end chimneys, 5-bayed façade, pilastered doorway with transom, wood stoop with steps both sides, 6/6-paned windows. (K. Duprey, *Old Houses*, pp. 184–185)

21 Built after 1796 by Richard Lake Coleman, housewright, sold to William Nichols, 1803, typical Nantucket house with gambrel roof. 2½-story shingle on stone basement, ridge chimney, 4-bayed façade, pilastered doorway with transom, 12/12- and 9/9-paned windows. Restored 1970. (M. M. Coffin, *H. A. B. S.* #904; H. B. Worth, *Nantucket Lands*, p. 279; E. U. Crosby, *Ninety Five Per Cent*, photo of side p. 111; N. H. A. *Photo Albums*, Book 5, p. /7/)

22 Presently faces north, an early house with additions, the center section being the oldest, the west appended, then the east. 2½-story clapboard, ridge chimney, 6-bayed façade, enclosed entrance porch, 12/12- and 9/9-paned windows and others. (K. Duprey, *Old Houses*, p. 71)

24 Original house 3-bayed south section, to which 2-bayed north added. 2½-story shingle, chimney back of ridge, 5-bayed façade, center door with transom, restored 12/12-paned windows.

25 Typical Nantucket house. 2½-story clapboard front, shingle sides, brick basement, ridge chimney, 4-bayed façade, pilastered doorway with transom, stoop, 12/12- and 9/9-paned windows. (N. H. A. *Photo Albums*, Book 5, p. /8/)

26 Typical Nantucket house. 2½-story clapboard, ridge chimney, 3-bayed façade (originally 4-bayed?), later pilastered doorway, 12/12-paned windows, addition north end.

27 Originally typical Nantucket house. 2½-story shingle, stuccoed basement, ridge chimney, now 3-bayed façade, doorway with sidelights, stoop with steps both sides, 12/12-paned windows. Wing on south end.

28 Typical Nantucket house. 2½-story clapboard front, shingle sides, ridge chimney (new), 4-bayed façade, doorway with transom, 12/12-paned windows.

29 Originally similar to 27 Union. Has later bracketed doorway, 2/2-paned windows, wing with porch south side. (N. H. A. *Photo Albums*, Book 5, p. /10/)

30 Modified typical Nantucket house, built 1807–08. 2½-story shingle, ridge chimney, 3–4-bayed façade (1 window crowded beside doorway, only 3 windows in front above), doorway with transom, 12/12-paned windows.

31 Typical Nantucket house. 2½-story shingle on high brick basement, ridge chimney (new), 4-bayed façade, later pilastered Greek Revival doorway with sidelights, stoop, 6/6-paned windows.

32 Built soon after American Revolution for William Coffin, gambrel-roof house with resemblance to "typical" plan. 2½-story clapboard front, shingle sides, ridge chimney, 4-bayed façade (2 lower windows north of doorway modern, replacing earlier shop alteration), 12/12-paned windows, later pilastered doorway. (H. B. Worth, *Nantucket Lands*, p. 279)

33 2½-story shingle, very high basement, had 3-bayed façade, later 2-story bay window, entrance on south side.

34 Greek Revival style. 2-story shingle, ridge chimney, 2-3-bayed façade with gable, shafts at corners, pilastered doorway, 6/6-paned windows. Extension south side.

35 Typical Nantucket house. 2½-story shingle, stone basement, ridge chimney, 4-bayed façade, 12/12- and 9/9-paned windows 1st story, 8/12- and 6/9-paned 2nd story, later pilastered Greek Revival doorway.

37 Typical Nantucket house. 2½-story shingle on high brick basement, ridge chimney, 4-bayed façade, pilastered doorway, had 6/6-paned windows (now 2/1). (N. H. A. *Photo Albums*, Book 5, p. /9/)

38 Typical Nantucket house. 2½-story shingle, ridge chimney, 4-bayed façade, 12/12-paned windows. (N. H. A. *Photo Albums*, Book 5, p. /11/)

40 Greek Revival style. 2½-story shingle, chimney on roof slope, pilasters at corners, 3-bayed pedimented façade with fan in tympanum, pilastered doorway, later 2/2-paned windows and bay windows.

41 Built late 18th century, typical Nantucket house. 2½-story shingle on high brick basement, ridge chimney, roof walk, 4-bayed façade, wood stoop, restored 12/12-paned windows. (K. Duprey, *Old Houses*, p. 116; N. H. A. *Photo Albums*, Book 5, p. /11/)

43 Greek Revival period. 1¾-story clapboard front, shingle sides, brick basement, ridge chimney, pilasters at corners, 3-bayed gabled façade, window pattern changed, entrance on south side.

44   2½-story shingle on brick basement, ridge chimney, 3-bayed façade, pilastered Greek Revival door-
      way, stoop, 6/6-paned windows 2nd story, later 2/2-paned windows 1st story.

47   Original section faces south. 2½-story shingle on high granite basement, ridge chimney, 2-bayed
      façade, 12/12- and 9/9-paned windows, extension on west flank with shed roof, late bay window on
      east end and additions on north.

Fig. 140 17 Union Street (center) About Turn of Century.

48	Greek Revival style. 1¾-story shingle, chimney on roof slope, pilasters at corners, 4-bayed façade with gable, pilastered doorway, 6/6-paned windows, upper outer (of 3) windows have ¼-round heads.
49	Inscribed 1821. 1½-story shingle on brick and concrete block basement, was 4-bayed, parts of Greek Revival doorway, 6/6-paned windows. Enlarged.
51	(Handover Lane) 1¾-story shingle on brick basement, ridge chimney, 3-bayed façade, Greek Revival pilastered doorway, later 2/1-paned windows.
53	1¾-story shingle on brick basement, ridge chimney (new), pilasters at corners, 3-bayed façade with entablature, pilastered Greek Revival doorway, 6/6-paned windows.
55	Typical Nantucket house, Federal style. 2½-story shingle on brick basement, ridge chimney, 4-bayed façade with embellished cornice and similar entablature on pilastered doorway, 6/6-paned windows (orginally 12/12-paned). (N. H. A. *Photo Albums*, Book 5, p. /13/)
57	Typical Nantucket house. 2½-story shingle on stone basement, ridge chimney, 4-bayed façade, 12/12-paned windows.
59	1¾-story shingle, ridge chimney, 4-bayed façade, 6/6-paned windows, lean-to across ¾ of rear.
60	Greek Revival style. 1¾-story clapboard, brick basement, chimney at side, pilasters at corners, supporting entablature on flanks, 3-bayed gabled façade, pilastered doorway with sidelights, 6/6-paned windows, outer upper windows have ¼-round heads.
61	Lean-to house. 2½-story shingle, had ridge chimney (space inside now occupied by stairway), 3-bayed façade, later 6/6-paned windows, box dormer at rear.
64	1¾-story shingle, ridge chimney, 3-bayed façade, later front door and 2/2-paned windows, front dormer. (N. H. A. *Photo Albums*, Book 6, p. /9/)

Vestal Street

At the close of the eighteenth century, when Isaac Coffin's survey of Nantucket was being made, the town's institutions were in the process of being moved from the old site north of High Street to the block south of Main and east of Grave Street (now Quaker Road). The new poor house had been built. Although the jail was comtemplated, it was not to be ready for use for several years. Nevertheless, the street to the south, from which access was gained to the lot, already—in 1799—was called Prison Lane.[1] The name was changed to Vestal Street before publication of the William Coffin map in 1834. Its eastern terminus is Milk Street.

Three historic monuments on Vestal Street worthy of special note are: 1, the Swain house of 1790, now a museum, which has become famous as the birthplace and home of astronomer Maria Mitchell; 8, the Starbuck cooper shop of the second quarter of the nineteenth century; and 17, the sturdy, shingle-covered log jail of 1805, also a museum open to the public *(Figs. 48, 141, 5)*.

Note

1 Henry Barnard Worth, *Nantucket Lands and Land Owners*, Nantucket Historical Association, Vol. II, Bulletin No. 5, 1906 (reissued 1928), p. 274.

Historic Buildings

1	Built 1790 for Hezekiah Swain and brother, typical Nantucket house. 2½-story shingle, ridge chimney, roof walk, 4-bayed façade, 12/12- and 9/9-paned windows. Addition on northwest corner built *ca.* 1850 for Peleg Mitchell. In 1818, house owned by William Mitchell and here born daughter Maria, who became distinguished astronomer. House purchased by Maria Mitchell Association 1902. Brick observatory built on west end 1908. (M. M. Coffin, *H. A. B. S.* #901; K. Duprey, *Old Houses*, pp. 90–101, 214–215, 229; G. A. Fowlkes, *Mirror of Nantucket*, pp. 51–53; E. A. Stackpole, *Rambling*, p. 72; *Inquirer & Mirror*, Dec. 2, 1965, p. 3)
3	Originally 1¾-story shingle lean-to half-house, ridge chimney (new), 3-bayed façade, walls heightened front and back, changing roof line, later 6/6-paned windows. Much renovated inside. (E. U. Crosby, *Ninety Five Per Cent,* photo p. 111)
5	1¾-story shingle, ridge chimney, 4-bayed façade, entrance on east end, shed-roof extension at rear.

	Greek Revival window details. (N. H. A. *Photo Albums,* Book 5, p. /14/)
7	1¾-story shingle, ridge chimney, 3-bayed façade, 12/12-paned windows, pilastered Greek Revival doorway, modern 12/12-paned windows.
8	STARBUCK COOPER SHOP, built 2nd quarter 19th century. 2-story shingle on high brick and stone basement, 12/12-paned windows 1st story, 8/12-paned windows 2nd story (modern replacements). First Nantucket steam engine set up here. (E. A. Stackpole, *Rambling,* p. 74; N. H. A. *Photo Albums,* Book 5, p. /14/)
9	1¾-story shingle, brick basement, ridge chimney, 3-bayed façade, pilastered Greek Revival doorway, 6/6-paned windows.
11	Typical Nantucket house. 2½-story shingle, ridge chimney, 4-bayed façade, restored 12/12-paned windows. Had roof walk. (N. H. A. *Photo Albums,* Book 5, p. /15/)
13	Built for Gorham Hussey *ca.* 1820. 2½-story shingle, ridge chimney, lengthened west end (about 8′), now 4-bayed façade, 6/6-paned windows, modern false-fan doorway with sidelights, parapet over cornice. (John W. McCalley; E. U. Crosby, *Ninety Five Per Cent,* photo p. 112)
16	Built *ca.* 1825–35, Federal style. 1¾-story shingle, ridge chimney, 3-bayed façade, pilastered doorway on east side, 6/6-paned windows. (K. Duprey, *Old Houses,* pp. /179/–183; N. H. A. *Photo Albums,* Book 5, p. /15/)
17	OLD JAIL, may date from Revolutionary times, has stood on this site since 1805. 2-story shingle, end chimneys, 3-bayed front with iron-barred windows, center doors 2 levels with outside stairway to 2nd story. Constructed of squared horizontal logs with lapped corners, vertical iron straps applied inside. Later east addition removed in 1920 restoration. Opened as public museum 1948. Adjoining house of detention (1826) moved here from town farm at Quaise 1854, demolished 1954. Jail itself badly defaced by fire summer 1970, stairs rebuilt. (G. A. Fowlkes, *Mirror of Nantucket,* p. 118; E. A. Stackpole, *Rambling,* p. 74; photo frontispiece, *Proceedings,* 1919; caption and photo frontispiece, *Ibid.,* 1946; *Historic Nantucket,* July 1953, pp. 63–64; *Ibid.,* July 1955, p. 40; Starbuck, *History,* photo jail and house of correction, p. 277; *H. A. B. S.* #120; E. U. Crosby, *Ninety Five Per Cent,* photo p. 113)
19	Originally 1¾-story shingle lean-to half-house, ridge chimney (new), 3-bayed façade, modern 1/1-paned windows. Shed-roof extension east end.

Walnut Lane

Connecting Main and Liberty streets west of Centre, Walnut Lane goes back to the first half of the eighteenth century. Probably no house faced it prior to modern times, although the old Francis Macy dwelling (1790s) was turned toward it in becoming the ell to 77 Main, when the new front mass was built in the 1830s.

Warren Street

Listed in the Isaac Coffin Survey of 1799 as connecting Orange and Pleasant streets, and shown with a number of houses facing it on all of the nineteenth-century maps, Warren Street lately has deteriorated to a gravel trail branching eastward from a little above the west end of New Street.

Washington Street

Washington Street follows the same course today as it did in the eighteenth century, originating at the lower end of Market Square, bending toward the head of Commercial (Swain's) Wharf, then continuing southeast a short distance in from the shore of the Great Harbor to a little below the level of the south end of the Fish Lots. The

Fig. 141 Cooper Shop at 8 Vestal Street.

difference is that three streets (developed in the late 1830s) connect the nether stretch with Union Street, these being Fayette, Meader, and Franklin. The Walling 1858 map indicates that South Water Street, above Main, also was called Washington Street, but other liberties taken with street names on this document tend to discredit this one as having official sanction. The railroad tracks ran along Washington from 1881 to 1918.

Historic Buildings

17   1¾-story shingle, stuccoed foundations, ridge chimney, 3-bayed façade, Federal pilastered doorway, later 2/2-paned windows. Box dormer added 1971.

19   2-story shingle, ridge chimney (new), 4 openings 1st story and 2 in 2nd, 6/6-paned windows.

21   CHARLES G. & HENRY COFFIN WAREHOUSE, built mid-19th century. 2½-story brick, much altered, now American Legion headquarters.

39   1½-story shingle on concrete block foundations, ridge chimney, 3-bayed façade, Greek Revival pilastered doorway, later 2/2-paned windows, front dormers, extension on north end.

41   1½-story shingle, ridge chimney, 3-bayed façade, pilastered doorway, 6/6-paned windows, super-structure added. (N. H. A. *Photo Albums*, Book 5, p. /16/)

43   1½-story shingle, ridge chimney, 3-bayed façade, pilastered Greek Revival doorway, 6/6-paned windows.

45   1¾-story shingle, high stuccoed basement, ridge chimney, 3-bayed façade, pilastered doorway, 6/6-paned windows, new box dormers front and rear.

Fig. 142 House Formerly at 11 Cliff Road, Moved to 19 West Chester Street.

West Chester Street

The original Chester Street is probably the oldest road on the island, connecting Capaum with the Great Harbor. Its present namesake is only the short easternmost block between Centre and North Water, whereas the longer stretch, extending inland from the intersection of Centre, is now called West Chester Street. On it were built the first Meeting House and Town House, and many of the dwellings of the early settlers. They were located in old Sherburne, outside of the present limits of Nantucket Town, of which nothing survives *in situ* except for the Elihu Coleman house at the head of Hummock Pond. The Richard Gardner III lean-to house (32—1722–24) stands below West Chester in the Lily Pond region, facing south, its back to the road *(Fig. 21)*. Directly above, at the summit of Sunset Hill, the earlier Jethro Coffin house (1686) looks down upon old Chester Street, though in modern times a road (Sunset Hill Lane) has been opened nearer to the historic dwelling *(Figs. 9–11)*. Several typical Nantucket houses (3, 8, 9, 11, and 21) and a pretty Federal cottage with a blind fan doorway (19—*Fig. 142*) are other architectural attractions of West Chester. The last was moved here from Cliff Road and served as part of the group converted into Cottage Hospital, which was organized in 1911 and opened for patients in 1914.[1] To the east of 8 West Chester is a privet alley leading at right angles up the rise to the back of the main house on Gull Island *(Fig. 126)*. For a while, at the turn of the century, West Chester was known as West Centre Street.

Note

1 Information courtesy Mrs. Marie M. Coffin.

Historic Buildings

1   Greek Revival style, 1¾-story shingle on brick basement, chimney on roof slope, 3-bayed gabled façade, pilastered doorway, 6/6-paned windows. (N. H. A. *Photo Albums,* Book 5, p. /16/)

3   Typical Nantucket house. 2½-story shingle, brick basement, ridge chimney, roof walk, 4-bayed façade, pilastered Greek Revival doorway, 6/6- and 4/4-paned windows. (E. U. Crosby, *Ninety Five Per Cent,* photo p. 115)

8   Mate to 11 West Chester Street. Modern roof walk and new brick front steps. (N. H. A. *Photo Albums,* Book 5, p. /18/)

9   Originally typical Nantucket house. 2½-story shingle, brick basement, ridge chimney, at present 3-bayed façade, later 2/1-paned windows.

11   Typical Nantucket house. Inversion of 3 West Chester Street. Has stone foundations.

17   Greek Revival style. 1¾-story shingle on brick basement, ridge chimney, pilasters at corners support entablature on flanks, 3-bayed façade with gable, pilastered doorway with sidelights, 6/6-paned windows. (N. H. A. *Photo Albums*, Book 5, p. /19/)

19   Built 1820s, Federal style. 1¾-story shingle, brick basement, ridge chimney (new), 4-bayed façade, doorway with sidelights and blind fan, 6/6-paned windows. Originally stood at 11 Cliff Road, moved to West Chester and became part of and lent its name to first Cottage Hospital, served as nurses' home, later separated for private residence. Had parapet over cornice with baluster insets above openings. (Old photo Miller R. Hutchison II Collection, N. H. A.)

21   Typical Nantucket house. 2½-story shingle, stuccoed foundations, ridge chimney, 4-bayed façade, Greek Revival doorway with transom, 6/6- and 4/4-paned windows.

23   2½-story shingle, articulated ridge chimney, 5-bayed façade, later pilastered Greek Revival doorway with sidelights, stoop with double steps, 6/6-paned windows. (A. E. Poor, *Colonial Architecture,* pl. 24—labeled "Nantucket, West Center Street")

25   2-story shingle, high stuccoed basement, end chimneys, 4-bayed façade, doorway with sidelights, 6/6-paned windows.

27   1¾-story shingle, had ridge chimney, 4-bayed façade, door with transom, 8/12-paned windows.

32   Built 1722–24 for Richard Gardner III, lean-to house, faces south. 2½-story shingle on rock foundations, articulated ridge chimney, 3-bayed façade, slightly off-center batten door with transom, 12/12-paned windows. (M. M. Coffin, *H. A. B. S.* #839; K. Duprey, *Old Houses,* pp. /29/-35; H. B. Worth, *Nantucket Lands,* p. 249, 1881 photo facing p. 263; *Guidebook,* p. 15; G. A. Fowlkes, *Mirror of Nantucket,* p. 125; E. U. Crosby, *Ninety Five Per Cent,* photo of rear p. 115)

41   1¾-story shingle, end chimney (1880s), 4-bayed façade, restored 12/12-paned windows (old photo at N. H. A. shows 6/6-paned sashes), new doorway.

42   1¾-story shingle, ridge chimney (replaced), 3-bayed façade, later door and 2/2-paned windows.

52   Greek Revival style. 1¾-story shingle, ridge chimney (replaced), 3-bayed façade, pilastered doorway with sidelights and 6/6-paned windows. House moved and features transposed.

West Dover Street

Situated one block north of York, West Dover is a continuation of Dover proper, which was the name of the entire length until relatively recent times. The western section extends from Orange to Pleasant. Its older houses all are on the south side, on the left as one faces toward the mill *(Fig. 143)*.

Historic Buildings

2	Typical Nantucket house. 2½-story clapboard front, shingle sides, ridge chimney, 4-bayed façade, doorway with transom, 12/12- and 9/9-paned windows.
6	1¾-story shingle, ridge chimney, 5-bayed façade, later 2/1-paned windows, box dormer in front.
12	1¾-story shingle, ridge chimney, had 3-bayed façade, extension built on front.
14	Late 18th- or early 19th-century lean-to house. 1¾-story shingle, 3-bayed façade, door was nearest east corner and chimney directly behind. House has been completely altered but original form shows in 1st floor framing from present basement.

West York Lane

West York Lane drops perpendicularly from West York Street, a block west of Atlantic Avenue, and terminates at South Prospect.

Historic Building

4	(west side) 1¾-story shingle, ridge chimney (replaced), had 3-bayed façade, later front addition and dormer.

West York Street

A continuation of York Street running west of Pleasant, West York connects with Prospect at the old mill, corner of South Mill Street.

Historic Buildings

3	House faces east. 1¾-story shingle, ridge chimney, 3-bayed façade, 6/6-paned windows. Modern box dormer in front. (N. H. A. *Photo Albums,* Book 6, p. /7/)
4	1¾-story shingle, ridge chimney (new), 3-bayed façade, 2/2-paned windows.
5	1¾-story clapboard front, shingle sides, ridge chimney (new), 3-bayed façade, 6/9-paned windows.
7	1¾-story shingle, ridge chimney (later), 3-bayed façade, pilastered doorway, 6/6-paned windows.

Westminster Street

Connecting the west ends of Gay and Quince streets with Academy to the north and Hussey at the south, Westminster Street came into being early in the nineteenth century at the time of the building of the Academy, which stood on its west side near the upper extremity.

Historic Buildings

8	2½-story shingle on brick basement, ridge chimney, 3-bayed façade, pilastered Greek Revival doorway, 6/6-paned windows. (N. H. A. *Photo Albums,* Book 5, p. /20/)
12	Typical Nantucket house. 2½-story shingle on brick basement, ridge chimney, 4-bayed façade, pilastered Greek Revival doorway, 6/6-paned windows. Extension with shed roof on south flank has 12/12-paned windows. (K. Duprey, *Old Houses,* p. 115)

Weymouth Lane

Between Mulberry and Dover, Weymouth Lane connects Orange with Union Street and likewise dates from the eighteenth century. The Richard Swain lean-to house (3) is thought to have been built about 1755.

Historic Buildings

1   Typical Nantucket house, faces east. 2½-story shingle on stone basement, ridge chimney, 4-bayed façade, pilastered doorway, 12/12-paned windows.

3   Built for Richard Swain before 1767 (assumed *ca.* 1755), lean-to house. 2½-story shingle, ridge chimney, 3-bayed façade, 12/12-paned windows. (T. Bunker, *Research*, #3152)

4   Greek Revival style. 1¾-story clapboard front, shingle sides, ridge chimney, 3-bayed façade, pilastered doorway, 6/6-paned windows.

5   Built early 19th century. 1¾-story shingle, ridge chimney (new), 3-bayed façade, pilastered doorway, 6/6-paned windows.

6   Greek Revival period. 1¾-story clapboard façade, shingle sides, ridge chimney, 3-bayed façade, pilastered doorway, modern 12/12-paned windows.

10   Greek Revival period. 1¾-story shingle, ridge chimney (new), had 3-bayed façade, pilastered doorway, modern 12/12-paned double window.

Whaler's Lane

Whaler's Lane, connecting North Water and South Beach, a block above Broad Street, is in the section of Nantucket denuded by the ravenous fire of 1846. Its one pre-Civil War building is a notable attempt to surpass the architectural grandeur of the earlier pure Greek Revival style *(Fig. 114).*

Historic Building

3   Built after 1846 Fire for W. Whippy, Greek Revival Eclectic style. 1¾-story clapboard on high brick basement (no windows in front), had chimneys at sides, pilasters at corners support entablature on flanks, 5-bayed façade with gable, center doorway with sidelights, was sheltered by distyle Doric portico, wood stoop, 6/6-paned windows, battered window enframements with Greek ears, "Gothic" corbel-arch double window over doorway. Present porch is modern. (N. H. A. *Photo Albums*, Book 5, p. /20/)

William's Lane and William's Street

William's Lane is listed in the Isaac Coffin 1799 survey and depicted on the William Coffin 1833–34 map, connecting Orange and Pleasant streets, but neither document indicates a respectable residence facing it. Today called William's Street, no building of the historic period is to be found on it. Present William's Lane sweeps westward from Pleasant Street, opposite from a point between William's Street and Cherry, and it, too, is innocent of any historic building.

Winter Street

Winter Street connects Main with Liberty. It was opened in 1738, at which time the area between it and Walnut Lane was called the Clay Pits.[1] The notable building on Winter Street is the brick Greek Revival Coffin School (1852—*Fig. 109*).

Note

1   Henry Barnard Worth, *Nantucket Lands and Land Owners*, Nantucket Historical Association, Vol. II, Bulletin No. 5, 1906 (reissued 1928), p. 282.

Historic Buildings

4   COFFIN SCHOOL, built 1852, Greek Revival style. Red brick on high limestone (front) and granite (sides and rear) podium. Recessed portico with wood colossal Doric columns *in antis*, false doorway (entrances are in sides of recess), brick dentils and moldings in entablature and pediment. Open belfry on roof. Cast-iron front fence in halberd (or harpoon?) design. Isaac Coffin, Baronet, of the British Navy, endowed the Nantucket Lancastrian School in 1827, the Legislature thereafter incorporating it as the Admiral Sir Isaac Coffin Lancastrian School. All Coffin descendants were eligible to attend. Classes were conducted in 1823 in a building on the east side of Fair Street, north of Lyon, until completion of the building on Winter Street. West extension added in 1918. (H. B. Worth, *Nantucket Lands*, p. 254; E. A. Stackpole, *Rambling*, p. 32; G. A. Fowlkes, *Mirror of Nantucket*, p. 108)

6   Mid-19th century, Greek Revival style. 1¾-story shingle, gable at front, pilasters at corners supporting entablature along sides, 3-bayed façade, pilastered doorway with wood stoop, 6/6-paned windows, corbel-arch windows 2nd story. Later dormer on south side.

7   Built 1850s for Capt. Calvin Worth, Greek Revival style. 2½-story clapboard on high brick basement, chimneys at outer sides, fan in front gable, 3-bayed façade with pilasters at corners, pilastered doorway with sidelights, wood stoop, 6/6-paned windows. Similar to 14 Liberty Street. (E. A. Stackpole, *Rambling*, p. 32)

8   2½-story clapboard front, shingle sides, brick basement, ridge chimney (replaced), 3-bayed façade, pilastered Greek Revival doorway with sidelights, 6/6-paned windows. Originally had roof walk. (Worth-Palmer, *Photos*, p. 11)

York Street

In the eighteenth century, York Street connected Pleasant and Orange streets, south of Dover, and the extension that continues to Union was called Maiden Lane. By the close of the nineteenth century, the east stretch had begun to be called Lower York, as it is today.[1] The present West York (beyond Pleasant—see above) was just developing on the A. D. Bache 1848 map, and on the Henry Walling 1858 map is labeled "Cooper"—probably never so designated officially. With only one exception (16), the old dwellings on York are less than two-storied, and among them 22 is typical *(Fig. 144)*. Especially noteworthy is the little African School (29), built at the corner of Pleasant about 1825 to serve the colored colony to the west. Its interior has a coved ceiling. This historic monument has been converted into a garage and shamefully allowed to deteriorate.

Note

1   Henry Barnard Worth, *Nantucket Lands and Land Owners*, Nantucket Historical Association, Vol. II, Bulletin No. 5, 1906 (reissued 1928), pp. 264, 282.

Historic Buildings

1   1¾-story shingle on brick basement, ridge chimney, 3-bayed façade, pilastered Greek Revival door-

Fig. 143 View of West Dover Street Looking Toward the Old Mill.

way, later 2/1-paned windows.

2   1¾-story shingle on brick basement, ridge chimney, had 3-bayed façade, now late 19th-century bay window and bracketed doorway.

4   1¾-story shingle on brick basement, ridge chimney, 3-bayed façade, pilastered doorway, later 2/2-paned windows. (N. H. A. *Photo Albums*, Book 6, p. /1/)

5   Built *ca.* 1796 for Benjamin and Silvanus Folger. 1¾-story shingle, ridge chimney, 5-bayed façade, later bracketed doorway, 6/6-paned windows, modern box dormer in front. (Mrs. Augustus W. Roche)

6   1¾-story clapboard on brick basement, ridge chimney, 3-bayed façade, pilastered doorway (door later), later 2/2-paned windows.

8   1¾-story shingle on brick basement, ridge chimney (rebuilt), had 3-bayed façade, late 19th-century bay window, new doorway. (N. H. A. *Photo Albums*, Book 6, p. /1/)

15   1¾-story shingle, originally had ridge chimney, 3-bayed façade, late 2/1-paned windows. (N. H. A. *Photo Albums*, Book 6, p. /2/)

16   2½-story shingle, ridge chimney, 3-bayed façade, 6/6-paned windows.

22   1¾-story shingle, ridge chimney, 3-bayed façade, had doorway with transom, 12/12-paned windows (now 2/2). Entrance has been moved to east side. (N. H. A. *Photo Albums*, Book 6, p. /2/)

29   AFRICAN SCHOOL, built after 1825. 1-story shingle, hip roof, 12/12-paned windows on sides. Originally had wide center door flanked by single 6/9-paned windows in façade. Later became the Colored Baptist Church. Chandelier from the Masonic Hall at 63 Main Street was hung from coved ceiling until 1922, when building was converted into garage. (*Proceedings*, 1941, photo and caption facing p. 34; H. B. Worth, *Transcript of Books*, p. 188; M. M. Coffin, *H. A. B. S.* #909; *Union Lodge, F. & A. M. Nantucket, Mass.*, p. 31)

Fig. 144 22 York Street

Part Three

Appendices

Categories of Buildings and Architectural Features in Nantucket Town

A. **EARLY "ENGLISH HOUSES"**—*last quarter 17th century*

Jethro Coffin (1 Sunset Hill)—1686 (additions and renovations)
Richard Gardner or Richard Gardner II—(139 Main)—before 1688 (moved, additions and renovations)
Nathaniel Starbuck (10 Pine)—*ca.* 1676 (moved, rebuilt 1820, additions)
Southwest corner section 107 Main—late 17th century (additions)

B. **LEAN-TO HOUSES**—(s) signifies building faces south

1. "ENGLISH HOUSES" BECOME LEAN-TOS BY ADDITION
   - (s) 107 Main—(made full-house)
   - (s) 139 Main—(Gardner, see above A)
   - (s) 1 Sunset Hill Lane—(Coffin, see above A)
2. 2½-STORY INTEGRAL LEAN-TOS—*ca.* 1700–1760
   a. *Half-Houses*
   - (s) 5 Ash—(rear heightened and ell added)
   - (s) 3 Bear
   - 1 Bloom—(rear heightened and additions)
   - 12 Cliff—(rear heightened and additions)
   - (s) 20 Cliff—(narrow additions west end and rear)
   - 10 Fair—(rear heightened)
   - 29 Fair—(rear heightened when 31 Fair attached)
   - (s) 9 Howard—(rear heightened and addition northwest corner, 1866)
   - (s) 31 Liberty—(rear heightened)
   - 31 Lily—(rear additions)
   - (s) 151 Main—now Quarter Mile Hill—(early shed-roof extension west end, moved, later wing east end, rear heightened)
   - 14 Milk—(rear heightened)
   - (s) 7 Mooer's Lane—(shed-roof extension west end and later wing east end)
   - 33 Orange—(renovated)
   - 53 Orange—(façade fenestration pattern changed)
   - 14 Pine—(outer windows shifted)
   - (s) 14 Quince—(rear heightened, becoming front)
   - 8 Ray's Court—(altered and enlarged, roof completely changed)
   - (s) 1 Tattle Court—(shed-roof extension east end)
   - 61 Union—(much altered, stairway replaces chimney)

        (s)   3 Weymouth
- b. *Half-Houses Englarged to Full*
  - (s)   10 Ash—(east section original)
  - (s)   25 Hussey—(east section original)
  - (s)   89 Main—(east section thought original)
  - (s)   105 Main—(east section original)
  - (s)   9 New Mill—(southwest section original)
  -      12 Orange—(north section original)
  - (s)   25 Pleasant—(west section original)
  - (s)   6 Prospect—(west section original)
  - (s)   1 Stone—(east section original)
  -      3 Trader's Lane—(south section original)
- c. *Full-Houses*
  - (s)   60 Cliff Road
  - (s)   Elihu Coleman house, Hawthorne Lane (Hummock Pond)
  - (s)   5 Liberty
  -      12 Liberty
  - (s)   15 Liberty—(rebuilt and east end cut back)
  - (s)   27 Liberty
  - (s)   111 Main
  - (s)   153 Main
  - (s)   9 Milk
  -      43 Orange
  - (s)   32 West Chester
- d. *2½ Story Irregulars*
  - (s)   3 Beaver—(affinities to 84 Main)
  -      84 Main—(transitional house, plan anticipates that of typical Nantucket house, rear heightened, extension west side)
  - (s)   9 Mill—(west wing is lean-to)
  -      6 North Liberty—(4-bayed, gambrel roof, built 1798)
  -      10 North Liberty—(interior rebuilt mid-19th century, moved, modern addition on back)
  - (s)   114 Orange—(curious plan)

3. 1¾-STORY LEAN-TOS—last half 18th century into early 19th century
   - a. *3-Bay Houses*
     - (s)   86 Centre—shed-roof extension on west flank
     - (s)   9 Eagle Lane
     - (s)   21 Mill
     -      2 North Mill
     - (s)   3 Vestal—(walls heightened and roof changed)
     - (s)   19 Vestal
     -      14 West Dover—(greatly altered)
   - b. *4-Bay Houses*
     -      67 (North) Centre
     -      2 Copper Lane
     - (s)   23 Milk
     - (s)   39 Milk
     -      59 Union—(lean-to across ¾ of rear)
   - c. *5-Bay Houses*
     -      53 Atlantic
     - (s)   9 Beaver
     -      2 High—(entrance shifted to side, front fenestration on High changed)
     -      30 Hussey—(semi-gambrel roof)
     -      10 Martin's Lane
     -      152 Orange
     -      17 Prospect—(west section original, 5-bayed by addition)

```
                    21 Prospect
                    14 Silver
               (s)  5 Spring
```

C. GAMBREL-ROOF HOUSES—1748–1798

```
 7 Farmer—before 1768
30 Hussey—1772—(½ gambrel)
18 India—1767
 6 North Liberty—1798—(with rear lean-to)
 5 Orange—last quarter 18th century—(with brick ends)
37 Orange—mid 1750s—later altered to have 2 full stories
 8 Pine—1748
21 Union—after 1796
32 Union—after 1780
Rotch Market at foot of Main—ca. 1775—commercial building, brick
```

D. TYPICAL NANTUCKET HOUSE EXAMPLES—1760s to 1830s

Academy Hill (Church Lane)— addition and altered	23 India—altered	1 Milk
4 Academy Lane	25 India—altered	10 Milk
11 Academy Lane—altered	27 India—wide version	11 Milk
37 Centre—altered	29 India	12 Milk
46 Centre—through conversion	31 India	18 Milk
47 Centre	32 India—modified	26 Milk
49 Centre	33 India—wide version	33 Milk
60 Centre	35 India	5 Mill
65 Centre	37 India	8 Mill
68 Centre	41 India—variation	9 Mill
78 Centre	43 India—variation	11 Mill
2 Chester	45 India—variation	19 Mill
6 Chester—modified	4 Liberty—altered	3 Mulberry
9 Cliff—altered	19 Liberty	5 Mulberry—modified
16 Cliff	21 Liberty	5 New Dollar
17 Cliff—modified	23 Liberty	2 New Mill
24 Cliff	26 Liberty	5 New Mill
3 Darling	35 Liberty	7 New Mill
11 Darling—altered	36 Liberty	47 North Liberty
8 Fair	40 Liberty	6 North Liberty—gambrel roof and lean-to
30 Fair	22 Lily	15 North Water
40 Fair	28 Lily	17 North Water
43 Fair—enlarged and altered	81 Main	22 North Water
47 Fair—altered	87 Main	23 North Water
49 Fair	91 Main	24 North Water
54 Fair	99 Main—altered and enlarged	25 North Water
4 Gardner	102 Main	26 North Water
10 Gardner	109 Main	28 North Water
14 Gardner	118 Main	13 Orange
15 Gardner	120 Main	18 Orange
4 Gay—altered	122 Main	20 Orange
1 Gull Island Lane	126 Main	22 Orange—enlarged
7 Hussey	127 Main	25 Orange—altered
15 India	129 Main	40 Orange
20 India	145 Main	41 Orange
21 India	148 Main	45 Orange—altered
	154 Main	

51 Orange—modified	11 Pleasant—altered	27 Union
52 Orange	16 Pleasant—modified	28 Union
55 Orange—modified	34 Pleasant	29 Union
56 Orange	9 Quince	30 Union—modified
62 Orange—altered	10 Quince	31 Union
65 Orange	1 School—variation	32 Union—gambrel roof,
66 Orange	3 School	wide version
71 Orange	4 Step Lane—altered	35 Union
74 Orange—altered	4 Summer	37 Union
75 Orange	7 Summer	38 Union
76 Orange	4 Trader's Lane	41 Union
77 Orange	9 Union	55 Union
4 Pine—modified	11 Union	57 Union
15 Pine	13 Union	1 Vestal
18 Pine	14 Union—variation	11 Vestal
33 Pine	15 Union—wide version	3 West Chester
37 Pine	16 Union—variation	9 West Chester—modified
43 Pine	17 Union	11 West Chester
3 Pleasant	19 Union	21 West Chester
6 Pleasant	21 Union—gambrel roof	2 West Dover
8 Pleasant—modified	25 Union	12 Westminster
10 Pleasant—modified	26 Union	1 Weymouth

E. **LATE COLONIAL AND EARLY FEDERAL 2½-STORY 3-BAYED HOUSES WITH RIDGE CHIMNEY**—*ca.* 1750–1830s

5 Ash Lane	6 Fayette	73 Orange
7 Beaver	4 Flora	81 Orange
61 Centre	19 Gardner	90 Orange
64 Centre	2 Gorham's Court	91 Orange
74, 76 Centre (double house)	3 Howard	93 Orange
3 Charter	14 Hussey	94 Orange
5 Chester	38 India	95 Orange
2 Cliff	9 Liberty	96 Orange
6 Cliff—enlarged	27 Lily	97 Orange
5 Coon	36 Lily	103 Orange
8 Darling	1 Lyon	5 Pine
25 Fair	134 Main	17 Pine
36 Fair	156 Main	27 Pine
38 Fair	2 Martin's Lane	31 Pine
41 Fair	15 Mill	13 Pleasant (perhaps 2-bayed)
46 Fair	4 Mulberry	3 Plumb Lane
48 Fair	10 Orange	3 Quince
54 Fair	38½ Orange	15 Quince
57 Fair	47 Orange	1 Twin
58 Fair	49 Orange	7 Union (double house)
59 Fair	57 Orange	47 Union (2-bayed)
60 Fair	61 Orange	16 York
4 Farmer	69 Orange	

F. **2½-STORY HOUSES WITH CENTER CHIMNEY**—*ca.* 1750– early 1800s

3 Academy Lane	55 Centre	22 Fair
43 Centre	3 Cliff	34 Fair—4-bayed
51 Centre—3-storied	10 Darling	11 Hussey
52 Centre—rebuilt 1756	14 Fair	22 Liberty

9 Milk
21 Milk—4-3-bayed
4 Mill
14½ Orange
26 Orange

37 Orange
5 Pleasant
5 Quince
7 School—5-3-bayed
9 School—extension west end

22 Union—half-house (?)
24 Union—half-house (?)
23 West Chester

G. 2½-STORY HOUSES WITH TWIN CHIMNEYS—late 18th century through 1830s

48 Centre—altered
54 Centre
66 Centre
1 Chester
6 Darling
5 Fair
13 Fair—3-story—hip roof
15 Fair
33 Fair—additions
50 Fair
13 Gardner

5 Gay
30 India
3 Liberty
85 Main
90 Main
99 Main—additions
100 Main
117 Main—hip roof
5 Milk
4 New Dollar
14 North Water

19 North Water (?)
27 North Water (?)
29 Orange—remodeled mid-19th century
9 Pine—remodeled mid-19th century
12 Pleasant
15 Pleasant
18 Union

H. OTHER FEDERAL HOUSE TYPES—1780s to 1830s
1. 2-STORY OR MORE
   a. *With End Gables and End Chimneys*
      10 Academy Lane—4-bayed
      3 Atlantic—5-bayed
      1 Blackberry Lane—5-bayed
      45 Centre—5-bayed
      21 Cliff—5-bayed
      9 Darling—5-bayed
      17 Fair—4-bayed
      24 Fair—remodeled into 6-bayed
      18 Gardner—5-bayed
      3 Gull Island Lane—remodeled into 5-bayed
      23 Hussey—5-bayed
      26 Hussey—4-bayed
      12 India—3-bayed brick
      19 India—5-bayed
      69 Main—5-bayed brick
      75 Main—5-bayed brick
      82 Main—5-bayed
      88 Main—5-bayed
      50 North Liberty—4-bayed
      20 North Water—5-bayed
      15, 17, 19, 21, 23 Orange—each 3-bayed
      34 Orange—5-bayed
      36 Orange—5-bayed
      7 Pleasant—5-bayed
      19 Pleasant—5-bayed brick
      39 Pleasant—5-bayed
      1 Plumb Lane—4-bayed
      4 School—3-bayed
      20 Union—5-bayed
      25 West Chester—4-bayed
   b. *With Gabled or Pedimented Front*

      3 Howard
      22 Hussey—transitional Federal to Greek Revival
      24 Hussey—transitional Federal to Greek Revival
      39 India
      8 Union
   c. *Hip-roofed*
      54 Centre—3-bayed
      58, 60 Main—5-bayed brick (originally single residence)
      72 Main—5-bayed with end chimneys
      117 Main—5-bayed with twin ridge chimneys
      6 Union—5-bayed
2. LESS THAN 2-STORY
   a. *With Center Chimney*
      6 Academy Lane—4-bayed
      8 Academy Lane—4-bayed
      5 Atlantic—4-bayed
      6 Atlantic—5-bayed
      8 Atlantic—3-bayed
      9 Atlantic—3-bayed
      9 Back—3-bayed
      1 Beaver—3-bayed
      6 Beaver—3-bayed
      8 Charter—3-bayed
      3 Cherry—3-bayed
      7 Cherry—3-bayed
      8 Cherry—4-bayed
      10 Cherry—4-bayed
      5 Cliff—3-bayed with extension
      18 Cliff—4-bayed
      22 Cliff—3-bayed

30 Cliff—probably 3-bayed
2 Coon—4-bayed
7 Coon—3-bayed
1 Cottage—3-bayed
2 Cottage—3-bayed
3 Cottage—3-bayed—altered
2 Dover—3-bayed
4 Dover—3-bayed
5 Dover—3-bayed
8 Dover—3-bayed
3 Eagle Lane—3-bayed
4 Eagle Lane—3-bayed
42 Fair—4-bayed
2 Farmer—3-bayed
5 Farmer—4-bayed
6 Farmer—4-bayed
2 Flora—3-bayed
2 Gull Island Lane—3-bayed
6 Howard—3-bayed
20 Hussey—4-bayed
3 Joy—3-bayed
7 Lily—3-bayed
8 Lily—4-bayed
9 Lily—3-bayed
3 Lyon—3-bayed
5 Lyon—3-bayed
8 Lyon—3-bayed
Madaket Road at New Lane—4-bayed
140 Main—3-bayed
144 Main—3-bayed
152 Main—3-bayed
160 Main—was 3-bayed
162 Main—4-bayed
12 Mount Vernon—3-bayed
14 Mount Vernon—3-bayed
16 Mount Vernon—3-bayed
18 Mount Vernon—3-bayed
2 New Street—3-bayed
4 New Street—3-bayed
6 New Street—3-bayed
8 New Street—3-bayed
12 New Street—4-bayed
14 New Street—3-bayed
17 New Street—3-bayed (?)
18 New Street—3-bayed
22 New Street—3-bayed
24 New Street—3-bayed
10 New Mill—4-bayed

14 New Mill—3-bayed
X North Liberty—3-bayed
88 Orange—4-bayed
101 Orange—4-bayed
115 Orange—3-bayed
118 Orange—3-bayed
119 Orange—4-bayed
120 Orange—3-bayed
156 Orange—2-bayed
30 Pine—3-bayed
36 Pine—4-bayed
38 Pine—4-bayed
40 Pine—3-bayed
50 Pleasant—3-bayed
60 Pleasant—5-bayed
61 Pleasant—3-bayed
63 Pleasant—4-bayed
5 Prospect—3-bayed
7 Prospect—3-bayed
9 Prospect—3-bayed
61 (South) Prospect—3-bayed
2 Quince—3-bayed
7 Silver—3-bayed
64 Union—3-bayed
16 Vestal—3-bayed
17 Washington—3-bayed
41 Washington—3-bayed
45 Washington—3-bayed
19 West Chester—4-bayed
27 West Chester—4-bayed
42 West Chester—3-bayed
3 West York—3-bayed
4 West York—3-bayed
5 West York—3-bayed
5 Weymouth—3-bayed
1 York—3-bayed
2 York—3-bayed
4 York—3-bayed
5 York—5-bayed
6 York—3-bayed
8 York—3-bayed
15 York—3-bayed

b. *With End Chimneys*
11 Lily—4-bayed—front heightened
15 Lily—4-bayed
19 Lily—4-bayed
141 Main—5-bayed

I. GREEK REVIVAL PERIOD HOUSES—1830s to 1860
1. 2-STORY OR MORE
a. *With End Gables or Pediments*
8 Ash Street
5 Beaver
22 Broad

24 Centre
53 Centre
56 Centre

1 Chestnut
2 Chestnut
5 Chestnut
15 Fair—remodeled twin chimney
17 Fair—remodeled
27 Fair
37 Fair
1 Farmer
12 Federal
24 Federal
18 Gardner
6 Gay
10, 12 Gay
15 Gay
17 Gay
10 Hussey
9 India
28 India
42 India
39 Liberty
41 Liberty
32 Lily
75 Main
77 Main
78 Main—brick
92 Main
93, 95, 97 Main—brick
98 Main
100 Main—remodeled twin chimney
112 Main
113 Main
119 Main
121 Main
124 Main
128 Main
30 Milk
17 Mill
14 Orange
28 Orange
72 Orange
82 Orange
85 Orange
89 Orange
9 Pleasant
20 Pleasant
4 Quince
4 School
2 South Beach
3 Step Lane—enlarged for hotel
8 Westminster
8 Winter

b. *With Gabled or Pedimented Front*
4 Ash
23 Broad
24 Broad

20 Centre
28 Centre
31 Centre
33 Centre
34 Centre
38 Centre
4 Darling
9 Fair
4 Federal
20 Federal
21 Federal
11 India
14 Liberty
86 Main
94 Main—colossal portico
32 Milk
8 North Water
9 North Water
11 North Water
8 Orange
48 Orange
50 Orange
54 Orange
78 Orange
1 Pleasant
16 Quince
5 Step Lane
40 Union
7 Winter

c. *Hip-roofed*
29 Broad—3-story brick
10 Cliff Road
4 Lyon
96 Main—colossal portico

2. LESS THAN 2-STORY
a. *With End Gables or Pediments*
12 Academy Lane
1 Ash
8 Back
11 Back
4 Bloom
57 Centre
59 Centre
29 Cliff Road
51 Cliff Road
12 Darling
14 Darling
39 Fair
3 Flora
7 Gay
11 Gay
5 Lily
12 Lily
14 Lily
6 Lyon

138 Main
150 Main
158 Main
6 Martin's Lane
24 Mill
11 New Mill
16 North Liberty
61 North Liberty
1 North Mill
39 Orange
123 Orange
34 Pine
4 Plumb
2 Prospect
3 Prospect
16 Prospect
4 Silver
53 Union
7 Vestal
9 Vestal
39 Washington
43 Washington
52 West Chester
7 West York
4 Weymouth
6 Weymouth
10 Weymouth

b. *With Gabled or Pedimental Front—*
    *(examples followed by * have upper*
    outer windows with ¼- round heads)

2 Ash
16 Back
2 Beaver*
17 Broad
18 Broad
20 Broad
36 Centre
70 Centre*
72 Centre*
3 Chestnut
28 Cliff Road

36 Cliff Road
41 Cliff Road—enlarged and altered
49 Cliff Road
3 Coon* (until 1971)
1 Fayette
8 Federal
10 Federal* (originally)
9 Gay
3 Hussey
5 Hussey
34 India
33 Liberty*
1 Lily*
110 Main
114 Main
123 Main
28 Milk
22 New
X North Avenue
4 North Water
5 North Water
7 North Water
10 North Water
12 North Water
99 Orange
109 Orange
6 Pine
26 Pine*
17 Pleasant
11 Prospect
26 Prospect
4 Silver
21 South Water
43 Union
48 Union*
60 Union
1 West Chester
17 West Chester
1 Whaler's Lane
6 Winter

J. **HOUSES SHOWING GOTHIC REVIVAL INFLUENCE — 1850s**

4 Darling—pair tympanum windows with blind pointed arches
3 Hussey—pair pointed windows in pediment
34 India—pointed windows in pediment
86 Main—pointed window in pediment
123 Main—corbel-arch window front east wing
4 North Water—piers, gables, corbel-arch windows
5 North Water—had corbel-arch windows 2nd story
9 North Water—pointed lunette in pediment
13 (37) North Water—Eastlake bargeboards
3 Whaler's Lane—double corbel-arch window over portico
6 Winter—corbel-arch windows 2nd story
cast-iron front fence of 97 Main

K. SOME OUTSTANDING POST-CIVIL-WAR HOUSES—1860 to 1900

19 Broad—bracketed mansard—*ca.* 1872-75
21 Broad—bracketed mansard—1872
30 Centre—bracketed Italianate—late 1860s
8 Chester—bracketed mansard—*ca.* 1885
33 Cliff, Sea Cliff Inn—"Queen Anne"—1890s
34 Easton—"Queen Anne"—*ca.* 1890
37 Easton—Richardsonian shingle gambrel—*ca.* 1900
26 Fair—bracketed villa—*ca.* 1875
73 Main—bracketed Second Empire, built for Eliza Barney 1871
74 Main—"Queen Anne"—*ca.* 1885-90
76 Main—originally mansard-roof house—*ca.* 1885-90—note stable at rear on Ray's Court
13 (37) North Water—Eastlake Gothic—1870s
6 Orange—bracketed mansard, built for James Easton *ca.* 1880
30 Orange—Colonial Revival, built for William Barnes *ca.* 1900

L. NANTUCKET CHURCHES

CONGREGATIONAL:

Old North Vestry (rear of First Congregational)—*ca.* 1725, moved to Beacon Hill 1765, to present site 1834
First Congregational Church (62 Centre)—1834, enlarged 1840, remodeled 1868, present steeple 1968

UNITARIAN-UNIVERSALIST:

Second Congregational Church (11 Orange)—1809, tower 1815, tower replaced 1830, church altered 1844—has been Unitarian since 1824

METHODIST:

Methodist Church (2 Centre)—1822-23, portico added 1840

SOCIETY OF FRIENDS:

Quaker Meeting House (7 Fair)—1838, originally school, became church after 1863
former Quaker Meeting House (29 Centre)—1850, later became Baptist church, now annex of Bayberry Inn

BAPTIST:

First Baptist Church (1 Summer)—1840, steeple replaced 1962

CATHOLIC:

Saint Mary's Our Lady of the Isle (Federal at Cambridge)—1897

EPISCOPALIAN:

Saint Paul's Church (16 Fair)—1901

CHRISTIAN SCIENCE:

former Women's Christian Temperance Union headquarters (8 Gardner)

M. BRICK BUILDINGS

1. PUBLIC BUILDINGS

11 Broad—Richard Mitchell & Sons Candle Factory—1847
1 Main—Rotch Market—1775
23, 25, 27, 29 Main—stores—after 1846
33, 35, 37, 43, 45, 51, 55, 57 Main—stores—after 1846
54, 56 Main—stores—after 1846
61 Main—Pacific National Bank—1818 with additions
X Straight Wharf—Thomas Macy Warehouse—1846
2 Union—Thomas Coffin and James Athearn stores—*ca.* 1830—Town House after 1836, 1884
21 Washington—Charles G. and Henry Coffin Warehouse—mid-19th century
4 Winter—Coffin School—1852

2. RESIDENCES

29 Broad—1845

12 India—1830s
58, 60 Main—1831
69 Main—1834
75 Main—1832-33
78 Main—1831-33
93 Main—1836-38
95 Main—1836-38
97 Main—1836-38
19 Pleasant—1829-34

3. FRAME HOUSES WITH BRICK ENDS
19 India—1809
5 Orange—before or after American Revolution
16 Pleasant (1 story only)—late 18th century

N. BUILDINGS THAT HAVE BEEN MOVED OR ARE REPUTED TO HAVE BEEN MOVED
(NOTE: Those said to have come from "Old Sherburne" are to be accepted with reservation)
10 Ash—east section from "Old Sherburne"
53 Atlantic—from across road
3 Bear—original location unknown
34 Centre—from Howard
43 Centre—from "Old Sherburne"
52 Centre—southeast section from "Old Sherburne"
60 Centre—from adjoining lot on south
62 Centre—Old North Vestry—moved from site about 1 mile to west
6 Chester—rear wing from somewhere
5-7 Eagle Lane—shack between placed here recently
9 Eagle Lane—original location unknown
7 Fair—Friends' School moved onto new foundations
9 Fair—1850 type house on site of Friends' Meeting House moved to Cape Cod in 1863
10 Fair—from "Old Sherburne"
formerly 11 Fair—Levi Starbuck house—moved to west side Surfside Road
8 Gardner—from front yard of 4 Gardner
10 Gardner—said to have come from Duke Street, near Crooked Lane
13 Gardner—from Ray's Court
4 Gay—from behind on Quince
2 Gorham's Court—pavilion attached north end of extension moved here and converted into small theater
2 Gull Island Lane—from ridge on Gull Island
9 Howard—from "Old Sherburne"
9 Liberty—from Pleasant
12 Liberty—north section from "Old Sherburne"
15 Liberty—moved from somewhere and cut down to fit lot
31 Lily—moved from Fair Street
77 Main—rear wing originally at front of lot
105 Main—east section from "Old Sherburne"
107 Main—west section from "Old Sherburne"
111 Main—rear section from "Old Sherburne"
126 Main—from "Old Sherburne"
139 Main—from site to rear of house on west
151 Main (Quarter Mile Hill)—moved from east of 153 Main back to Quarter Mile Hill
9 Milk—from "Old Sherburne"
11 Milk—from "Old Sherburne"
14 Milk—earlier than when attributed to erection on site
23 Milk—from corner Milk and New Mill

35 Milk—from Quaker Road near Vestal
4 Mill—rear wing moved from somewhere
9 Mill—east wing from somewhere
9 New Mill—from "Old Sherburne"
10 North Liberty—from across street
5 Orange—rear wing may be old house attached
26 Orange—from "Old Sherburne"
30 Orange—from front of lot, rebuilt
43 Orange—moved forward on site
114 Orange—possibly moved from elsewhere
10 Pine—north section from site near north head Hummock Pond
6 Prospect—from corner Milk and New Mill (see 23 Milk above)
30 Prospect—assembled from parts of houses on Warren, upper Main, and Cliff Road
8 Quince—from Fair Street
3 Rose Lane—from site to east
2 South Beach—from corner Broad and North Water
17 South Water—from Main to Brant Point, finally here
3 Step Lane—from site 51 Centre
1 Tattle Court—from "Old Sherburne"
18 Union—from Main at Centre, site of Pacific National Bank
61 Union—original location unknown
17 Vestal—Old Jail—said to date from time of American Revolution, elsewhere prior to being located here
        in 1805
19 West Chester—from Cliff Road
52 West Chester—original location unknown

O. SPECIAL EARLY FEATURES
   1. ARTICULATED CHIMNEY STACKS—1686–1765
      43 Centre—*ca.* 1765—flanges on sides
      60 Cliff—*ca.* 1723–24—5-flanged front
      11 Hussey—3-flanged front
      25 Hussey—1733—3-flanged front
      12 Liberty—3-flanged front
      15 Liberty—*ca.* 1740—modern restoration
      27 Liberty—1745—3-flanged front
      105 Main—*ca.* 1757—3-flanged front
      139 Main—before 1688—modern restoration
      7 Mooer's Lane—1745—3-flanged front
      12 Orange—3-flanged front
      1 Sunset Hill—1686—"horseshoe" motif
      23 West Chester—3-flanged front
      32 West Chester—1722–24—3-flanged front
      Elihu Coleman house, Hawthorne Lane, on Hummock Pond—1722—3-flanged front—outside town
   2. HOUSES WITH CHAMFERED BEAMS
      60 Cliff—*ca.* 1724—east room
      107 Main—perhaps late 17th-century—southwest room
      139 Main—before 1688
      153 Main—after 1723
      12 Orange
      10 Pine—*ca.* 1676—northwest room
      30 Prospect—assembled from 3 old buildings (see Appendix N)
      1 Tattle Court—after 1717
      1 Sunset Hill—1686
      Elihu Coleman house on Hummock Pond—1722—outside town

P. **PORTICOES**
   1. FEDERAL
      a. *Public Building*
         61 Main—Pacific National Bank
      b. *Residences*
         Academy Hill (Church Lane) house
         19 India—restored
         72 Main—transitional Federal Greek
            Revival
         69 Orange—Tuscan order
   2. GREEK REVIVAL
      a. *Public Buildings*
         2 Centre—Methodist Church
         1 India—Atheneum—recessed portico
         4 Winter—Coffin School—recessed
            portico
      b. *Residences*
         1 Ash
         29 Broad
         53 Centre—on side
         56 Centre
         1 Chestnut
         5 Fair
         9 Fair
         17 Fair—on side
         12 Federal
         24 Federal—on side
         2 India
         11 India
         25 India
         48 India
         32 Lily
         77 Main
         93 Main
         94 Main—colossal order
         95 Main
         96 Main—colossal order
         97 Main
         123 Main—on side
         14 Orange—on south façade
         28 Orange
         29 Orange
         38 Orange—portal with colonnettes
         54 Orange
         1 Pleasant
         7 Pleasant
         9 Pleasant
         17 Pleasant—on side
         3 Whaler's Lane—inappropriate
            replacement
   3. MODERN
      a. *Public Building*
         13 Broad—Nantucket Historical
         Association Museum

      b. *Residences*
         141 Main
         11 Pleasant
         12 Pleasant

Q. **FAN DOORWAYS**
   1. WITH GLAZED FAN
      a. *Public Buildings*
         62 Centre—First Congregational
            Church (pointed)
         61 Main—Pacific National Bank
      b. *Residences*
         Academy Hill (Church Lane) house
         49 Fair—modern
         69 Main—restored
         30 Orange—modern
         13 Vestal—modern
   2. WITH BLIND FAN
      a. *Public Buildings*
         11 Broad—Mitchell Candle Factory
            (Whaling Museum)—modern
         11 Orange—Second Congregational
            Church
      b. *Residences*
         45 Centre
         54 Cliff—modern
         58 Fair
         4 Flora
         16 Gardner
         16 India—modern
         89 Main—modern
         90 Main
         92 Main—modern
         99 Main
         37 Orange—modern
         19 Pleasant
         9 Quince

R. **HIP ROOFS**
   1. *Public Buildings*
         7 Fair—Friends' School (Quaker
            Meeting House)
         61 Main—Pacific National Bank
         63 Main—Masonic Lodge Hall
         29 York—African School
         formerly on Methodist Church, 2
            Centre, before 1840 renovation
   2. *Residences*
         29 Broad
         54 Centre
         10 Cliff Road
         13 Fair
         4 Lyon
         58, 60 Main—truncated
         72 Main

96 Main
117 Main
6 Union

S. SLATE ROOFS

11 Broad
29 Broad
23–29 Main
69 Main
75 Main
78 Main
93, 95, 97 Main
94 Main
1 Pleasant
19 Pleasant
Thomas Macy Warehouse, Straight Wharf (slate roof removed 1944)

T. HOUSES WITH CUPOLAS

29 Broad
53 Centre
69 Main
72 Main
75 Main
86 Main
93 Main
94 Main
95 Main
96 Main
97 Main
110 Main—removed
123 Main
9 North Water—removed
28 Orange
38 Orange
1 Pleasant
19 Pleasant

U. NANTUCKET BUILDERS AND ARCHITECTS AND KNOWN WORKS

Edward Allen
built and lived at 21 Prospect (1763); perhaps built 17 Prospect, 2 Copper

William M. Andrews
built 14 Orange (1838), sold to Levi Starbuck

John Bishop
from Newbury, in Nantucket briefly during early 1660s (E. F. Guba, *Nantucket Odyssey,* p. 32)

Christopher Capen
head mason for 75 and 78 Main (1831–33) for Henry and Charles G. Coffin, and for 93, 95, and 97 Main (1836–38) for William, Matthew, and George Starbuck

James Childs
built 93, 95, and 97 Main (1836–38)

Elihu Coleman
built own home (1722) on Hummock Pond (Hawthorne Lane), repaired original Friends Meeting House in 1728

Frederick Brown Coleman
designed and added portico to Methodist Church (1840); designed First Baptist Church (1840); altered Second

Congregational Church (1844); designed Atheneum (1847); thought to have designed 94 and 96 Main (1844–45) for William Hadwen

John Coleman
said to have built 72 Main (1820) for John Wendell Barrett; believed to have built 7 Pleasant (1820s) for Isaac Macy, and 9 Pleasant (1830s) for Benjamin Easton; perhaps built 28 India

Richard Lake Coleman
built 21 Union (after 1796), sold to William Nichols (1803); built 15 Union (*ca.* 1800), sold to Timothy C. Clapp; perhaps built 88 Orange and similar house at 101 Orange; built 4 Mill (1801), sold to Jeremiah Lawrence

James Field
built 75 and 78 Main (1831–33) for Henry and Charles G. Coffin

John Folger
using frame of Nathaniel Starbuck house (*ca.* 1676), which stood near Hummock Pond, built 10 Pine (1820) as double house

Peter Folger
among 14 mechanics who came from Salisbury in early 1660s, worked as joiner, miller, interpreter, and surveyor (E. F. Guba, *Nantucket Odyssey,* p. 32)

Josiah Gorham
built (or rebuilt) 29 Orange (*ca.* 1844)

Jethro Hussey
built 51 Centre (*ca.* 1765) for Peter Folger II

Silvanus Hussey
built first Quaker Meeting House (1711) that stood on rise west and little north of Elihu Coleman house (*Proceedings,* 1950, p. 26)

Perez Jenkins
replaced tower of Second Congregational Church (1830); with John Jenkins built 23 India (*ca.* 1800), sold to Capt. Reuben Baxter

Henry Macy
built 1 Pleasant (1837) for William H. Crosby

Job Macy
built own home at 11 Mill (1790)

John Macy II
built first Town House (1716) near first Meeting House (*Proceedings,* 1950, p. 28)

Richard Macy
built first Long Wharf (1723) (*Proceedings,* 1950, p. 28)

Isaiah Nicholson
built 25 Orange (*ca.* 1819), sold to Joshua Bunker

Nathan Nye
built 19 Union (*ca.* 1803), sold to Silvanus Ewer

Theophilus Pinkham
built and lived at 2 Quince (before 1782)

Elisha Ramsdell
built Second Congregational Church (1809), 11 Orange

"Mr. Waldron, Boston"
probably Samuel Waldron, listed in 1834 Boston City Directory as "housewright, 20 Vine St."; built First Congregational Church (1834), 62 Centre

James Weeks
built Friends' School (1838) on Fair at Ray's Court

Charles Wood
built Atheneum after F. B. Coleman design; went to California and built San Francisco Custom House (Prof. George C. Wood)

Bibliography

A Bibliography of Nantucket Architectural and Related Subjects

(Books, articles, albums, photograph and picture collections, etc.)

I.   BOOKS ON NANTUCKET ARCHITECTURE

Kenneth Duprey, *Old Houses on Nantucket,* New York, 1959

George Allen Fowlkes, *A Mirror of Nantucket, An Architectural History of the Island, 1686–1850,* Nantucket, 1959

Everett U. Crosby, *Ninety Five Per Cent Perfect,* Nantucket, 1953 (1st edition 1937, 2nd 1940, 3rd enlarged 1953)

Henry Chandlee Forman, *Early Nantucket and Its Whale Houses,* New York, 1966

II.   NANTUCKET BUILDINGS IN RELATION TO STREETS

Henry Barnard Worth, *Nantucket Lands and Land Owners,* Vol. II, Bulletin No. 4, Nantucket Historical Association, 1904 (Chapters IX–X, pp. /183/–216; Vol. II, Bulletin No. 5, 1906, reissued 1928 (illustrated with photographs by Henry S. Wyer made in 1881)—(Chapters XI–XII, pp. /220/–283)

III.   BOOKS ON AMERICAN ARCHITECTURE INCLUDING SECTIONS PERTAINING TO NANTUCKET

Alfred Easton Poor, *Colonial Architecture of Cape Cod, Nantucket and Martha's Vineyard,* New York, 1932; reprinted Dover paperback, New York, 1970 (photographs and drawings only)

Knowlton Mixer, *Old Houses of New England,* New York, 1927

Talbot Faulkner Hamlin, *Greek Revival Architecture in America,* New York, London & Toronto, 1944; reprinted Dover paperback, New York, 1964 (pp. 168–171, Plates XXXIX–XLI)

Richard Pratt, *The Golden Treasury of Early American Houses,* New York, 1967 (pp. 134–139)

Dorothy & Richard Pratt, *A Guide to Early American Homes, North and South,* New York, 1956 (Vol. I, pp. 42–44)

IV.   RÉSUMÉS ON HISTORIC NANTUCKET BUILDINGS (see also XVII below)

Compiled by Marie M. Coffin for Historic American Buildings Survey (Washington) and Nantucket Historical Trust, 1966–70

Address	Historic Building	Listing in Original Ms.: copies N. H. A. Library and N. H. T.	Official H. A. B. S. Number under *MASS*
Academy Hill	R. R. Bunker house	47	#916
3 Bear	Tristram Bunker house	48	#900
11 Broad	Mitchell Candle Factory	59	#907
29 Broad	Jared Coffin house	24	#918
2 Centre	Methodist Church	14	#1007
5–21 Centre	Sherburne Hall	60	#908
51 Centre	Peter Folger II house	19	#924
52 Centre	Joshua Coffin house	32	#1004
62 Centre	First Congregational Church	50	#902
60 Cliff	Josiah Coffin house	29	#911
Hawthorne Lane	Elihu Coleman house	25	#2-86
30 Hussey	Grindell Gardner house	46	#927

1 India	Atheneum	10	#812
15–45 India	16 houses north side—India Street Neighborhood Study		#1013
12 Liberty	Thomas Macy house	38	#1003
1 Main	Rotch Market	8	#836
12 Main	commercial building	56	#954
14–16 Main	commercial building	64	#951
25–57 Main	13 commercial buildings	63	#952
58–60 Main	Philip H. Folger house	65	#949
61 Main	Pacific National Bank	41	#938
63 Main	Old Masonic Lodge Hall	54	#899
69 Main	Frederick Mitchell house	34	#936
72 Main	John Wendell Barrett house	18	#915
75 Main	Henry Coffin house	9	#811
77 Main	John H. Shaw house	43	#931
89 Main	Jared Coffin house	36	#921
93, 95, 97 Main	Starbuck "Three Bricks"	33	#941
94 Main	Mary G. Swain house	52	#905
96 Main	William Hadwen house	35	#929
99 Main	Thomas Macy house	17	#944
105 Main	Christopher Starbuck house	16	#939
107 Main	Zaccheus Macy house	26	#934
111 Main	Ebenezer Gardner house	30	#922
117 Main	Edward Cary house	3	#855
139 Main	Richard Gardner house	15	#955
153 Main	Barnabus Gardner house	28	#925
11 Milk	Thomas Starbuck house	40	#942
21 Milk	Silas Gardner house	38	#928
33 Milk	George Coffin house	7	#854
35 Milk	Folger boat-building shop	42	#923
11 Mill	Job Macy house	45	#1002
4 New Dollar	Joseph Starbuck house	3	#940
4 North Water	E. F. Easton house	66	#957
5 Orange	Silas Jones house	21	#956
11 Orange	Second Congregational Church	2	#838
14 Orange	Levi Starbuck house	27	#912
15–23 Orange	"The Block"	20	#947
			(also #1014)
16–31 Orange	10 houses both sides—Orange-Union Streets Neighborhood Study		#1014
33 Orange	Robert Wyer house	44	#946
53 Orange	Seth Coffin house	5	#837
8 Pine	George Gardner house	6	#858
19 Pleasant	Jared Coffin house	37	#917
Siasconset	Auld Lang Syne	13	#857
Siasconset	Shanunga	12	#610
1, 3 Stone	Solomon Gardner houses—Orange-Union Streets Neighborhood Study		#1014
Straight Wharf	Gardner Store	58	#913

Straight Wharf	Macy Warehouse	57	#914
1 Sunset Hill	Jethro Coffin house	23	#919
2 Union	Old Town House	55	#906
9–19 Union	6 houses west side—Orange-Union Streets Neighborhood Study		#1014
21 Union	Richard L. Coleman house	49	#904
1 Vestal	Swain-Mitchell house	22	#901
32 West Chester	Richard Gardner III house	11	#839
29 York	African School	61	#709

V.   ARTICLES ON NANTUCKET ARCHITECTURE (Architecture, home & art magazines)

J. A. Schweinfurth, "The Early Dwellings of Nantucket," *The White Pine Series of Architectural Monographs,* Vol. III, No. 6, December 1917

Talbot Hamlin, "Nantucket," *The Architectural Review,* Vol. CII, No. 608, August 1947, pp. 54–57

Helen G. Mackay, "The Houses of Nantucket and a Bit of Its History," *The House Beautiful,* Vol. LII, No. 3, September 1922, pp. 220–221, 250, 252

Joseph Downs, "Water Colors of Early American Houses" (of Nantucket, by Edgar Whitfield Jenney), *Bulletin of the Metropolitan Museum of Art,* Vol. XXXV, No. 11, November 1940, pp. 220–223

Hubert G. Ripley, "Under the Trees, Summer Sketches of Nantucket," *Pencil Points,* Vol. VIII, No. 1, January 1927, pp. 26–34

Hubert Ripley, "The Jethro Coffin House on Sunset Hill Sometimes Called the Horseshoe House," *Journal of the American Institute of Architects,* Vol. XVI, No. 6, June 1928, pp. 218–223

Fiske Kimball, "Moors' End, Nantucket, Massachusetts," *The Architectural Record,* Vol. 62, No. 3, September 1927, pp. 191–200

VI.   ARTICLES PERTAINING TO NANTUCKET BUILDINGS (*Proceedings of the N. H. A., Historic Nantucket,* and *Historic Preservation*)

1. *Proceedings of the Nantucket Historical Association*

   1903   Emily Weeks, "Development of Schools in Nantucket," pp. 11–22

   1904   Henry B. Worth, "Early Houses at Nantucket," pp. 19–24

   1906   Henry B. Worth, "The Colonial Church and Nantucket," pp. /26/–31

   1907   Allen Coffin, "The Courts of Nantucket—The Law and Lawyers from an Early Period," pp. 30–42

   1917   Annie W. Bodfish, "A Few Facts Relating to Main Street," pp. 36–38; 1918, pp. 32–33; 1919, pp. 25–27; 1920, pp. 57–61

   1926   Merle E. Turner, "The Development of Nantucket," pp. 39–42

   1927   Fred V. Fuller, "The Restoration of the 'Oldest House,'" pp. 26–28

   1929   Merle E. Turner, "Nantucket Streets and Lanes," pp. 48–53

   1931   Catherine Jones, "Wharves of Nantucket," pp. 23–28

   1932   Elizabeth Sylvia, "Notable Old Nantucket Buildings," pp. 12–16

   1938   David Wood, "Nantucket's Architectural Heritage," pp. 19–21

   1940   "Report on the Old Mill," p. 20

   1941   Edouard A. Stackpole, "'Angola Street' and Arthur Cooper," pp. 31–35

   1946   Edouard A. Stackpole, "The 'Great Fire of 1846,'" pp. 35–45

   1946   E. A. S., "The Old Mill," pp. 46–47

   1948   Edouard A. Stackpole, "A View of Nantucket Early in the Last Century," pp. /31/–/32/ (copper-plate engraving by Benjamin Tanner in *The Port Folio,* Philadelphia, 1811)

1950   Robert M. Waggaman, "'The Town of Sherburne,' an Oil Painting by Thomas Birch," pp. 16–17, illustration facing p. 32

1950   Robert J. Leach, "The First Two Quaker Meeting-Houses on Nantucket," pp. 24–33

2. *Historic Nantucket*

1956   (April) George W. Jones, "The Nantucket Historic Districts Commission," pp. 6–13

1962   (April) H. Errol Coffin, "The Jared Coffin House," pp. 40–55

1962   (July) Merle T. Orleans, "Dedication of the Baptist Church Steeple," pp. 5–7

1963   (October) Rev. Myron S. Dudley, "Silk Industry in Nantucket," pp. 19–22 (mill on Gay Street)

1964   (April) H. Errol Coffin, "65–67–69 Main Street," pp. 4–8

1965   (January) H. Errol Coffin, "The Second Congregational Meeting House," pp. 5–19

1965   (October) Myles Reis, Jr., "The Oldest House," pp. 19–21

1966   (October) Katherine Seeler, "Phebe Folger's Watercolor Drawings of Nantucket Made About 1797," pp. 13–18

1967   (April) Bassett Jones, "Was Nantucket Ever Forested?" pp. 5–22

1967   (October) H. Errol Coffin, "Nantucket Street Lighting," pp. 17–19

1969   (January) "A Steeple Comes Back to an Old Church," pp. 4–/21/

1969   (October) Edouard A. Stackpole, "The 'Oldest House' Becomes a National Historic Landmark," pp. 33–36

1970   (October) Sally Lamb, "Mills on Nantucket," pp. 12–15

3. *Historic Preservation* (Quarterly of the National Trust, Washington)

1966   (July–August) George W. Jones, "Whalers and Quakers—Historic Nantucket Island," pp. 157–159

1969   (October–December) Walter Beinecke II, "Nantucket, Massachusetts," pp. 27–/29/

VII.   MONOGRAPHS ON NANTUCKET BUILDINGS

/Harriet B. Worron/, *"Trustum" and His Grandchildren, by One of Them*, Nantucket 1881 (Jethro Coffin house, pp. 55–58)

Gardner Coffin, *The Oldest House on Nantucket*, New York, 1905

/Tristram Coffin, ed./, *The Oldest House on Nantucket Island*, in 2 parts, Poughkeepsie, N.Y., *ca.* 1911

Will Gardner, *Three Bricks and Three Brothers*, Nantucket, 1945 (93, 95, 97 Main)

Florence Bennett Anderson, *Through the Hawse-Hole*, New York, 1932 (40 Fair, pp. 172–176)

Mary Eliza Starbuck, *My House and I*, Cambridge, Mass., 1927 (the "house" is 8 Pleasant Street, but it is not described)

VIII.   GUIDEBOOKS TO NANTUCKET (see also XII, second item, below)

Edouard A. Stackpole, *Rambling Through the Streets and Lanes of Nantucket*, New Bedford, Mass., 1947, 1951

Nantucket Historic Districts Commission, *Guidebook for the Old and Historic Districts of Nantucket and Siasconset*, Nantucket, 1967

The Champion Coated Paper Company, "Nantucket," *Champion Monographs*, Vol. IV, No. 3, April 26, 1921, New York

Walter Pritchard Eaton, *Nantucket*, New York-New Haven & Hartford Railroad, New York, 1925

George W. Richardson, *Nantucket and Its Attractions Including Siasconset, Mass.*, New York, 1914

John H. Robinson, *Guide To Nantucket*, Nantucket 1905 (7th ed. *ca.* 1948)

Edward Kelly Godfrey, *The Island of Nantucket, What It Was and What It Is*, New York, 1882

Isaac H. Folger, *Hand-Book of the Island of Nantucket,* Nantucket, 1874, 1875, 1878

J. A. & R. A. Reid, *Reid's Sea Side Souvenir. A Guide to New Bedford, Martha's Vineyard and Nantucket,* Vol. II, No. 1, Providence, R.I., 1883

Richard Luce Pease, *A Guide to Martha's Vineyard and Nantucket,* Boston, 1878

John F. Murphy, *The Tourist Guide, Nantucket and Martha's Vineyard,* pub. by author, n. d.

IX. WALKING GUIDE LEAFLETS

Nantucket Historical Association, *Main Street . . . from the Head of the Square to the Monument,* Nantucket, 1964

William E. Gardner, *Rambles Through the Historic Nantucket District,* Nantucket, 1959

X. NANTUCKET: HISTORIES

Obed Macy, *The History of Nantucket,* Boston, 1835; 2nd ed., Mansfield, 1880

R. A. Douglas-Lithgow, *Nantucket, A History,* New York & London, 1914

Alexander Starbuck, *The History of Nantucket, County, Island, and Town, Including Genealogies of First Settlers,* Boston, 1924; reprint by Charles E. Tuttle, Rutland, Vermont, 1969

William F. Macy, *The Story of Old Nantucket,* Boston & New York, 1928

Emil Frederick Guba, *Nantucket Odyssey, A Journey Into the History of Nantucket,* Waltham, Mass., 2nd ed. 1965

Harry B. Turner, *Nantucket Argument Settlers,* Nantucket, 1917, 1920, 1924, 1926, 1936, 1944, 1946, 1959, and 1966

XI. NANTUCKET: PHYSICAL HISTORY AND ECOLOGY

Ervin H. Zube & Carl A. Carlozzi, editors, *An Inventory and Interpretation, Selected Resources of the Island of Nantucket,* Nantucket & Amherst, Mass., 1966

Michael Hugo-Brunt, *An Historical Survey of the Physical Development of Nantucket: A Brief Narrative History and Documentary Source Material,* Ithaca, N.Y., 1969 (not published for public consumption)

XII. NANTUCKET: BIBLIOGRAPHIES

Marie M. Coffin, *The History of Nantucket Island: A Bibliography of Source Material with Index and Inventory,* Nantucket, 1970

Everett U. Crosby, *Nantucket in Print,* Nantucket, 1946 (reprints early descriptions)

XIII. UNPUBLISHED SOURCE MATERIALS ON NANTUCKET BUILDINGS (see also IV above)

Henry Barnard Worth, *Transcript of Books One and Two Registry of Deeds,* 1946 (manuscript, Nantucket Historical Association)

Grace Brown Gardner, *Scrapbook* (59 volumes on 7 microfilm reels, Atheneum); Vols. I–II on Churches, Vol. III on Architecture

Theodore Bunker, *Research on Nantucket Houses, ca.* 1948–51 (Nantucket Historical Association)

William S. Appleton & A. E. Shurrocks: Notes, drawings and photographs of Jethro Coffin House made during 1925–29 renovations (Society for the Preservation of New England Antiquities, 141 Cambridge St., Boston, Mass.)

XIV. NANTUCKET: PICTURE BOOKS

John F. Murphy, *Fifty Glimpses of Nantucket Island from Photos,* Chicago & New York, 1897

John F. Murphy, *65 Views of Nantucket Reproduced from Recent Photographs,* Boston, n. d.

John F. Murphy, *Souvenir of Nantucket,* Boston, n. d. (fold-out of 2-tone woodcut views, *ca.* 1890)

Henry Sherman Wyer, *Nantucket in Picture and Verse,* Nantucket, 1892

Henry Sherman Wyer, *Nantucket: Old and New, Centennial Edition,* New York, 1895

Henry Sherman Wyer, *Nantucket, Picturesque and Historic,* published by the author, 1901

J. H. Robinson, *100 Views of Nantucket,* Nantucket, 1911

Samuel Chamberlain, *Nantucket, A Camera Impression,* New York, 1939

XV. NANTUCKET: HISTORIC VIEWS AND MAPS

The Town of Sherburne in the Island of Nantucket (actually a view of Nantucket Town), copperplate engraving by Benjamin Tanner. Illustration to article by Joseph Sansom, "A Description of Nantucket," *The Port Folio,* Philadelphia & New York, Vol. V, January 1811. (See *Proceedings,* 1948, pp. /31/–32)

John Warner Barber, *Historical Collections Related to the History and Antiquities of Every Town in Massachusetts,* Worcester, 1839. "South-Eastern View of Nantucket, Mass." facing p. 444.

Bird's Eye View of Nantucket in the State of Massachusetts Looking Southwest, 1881, Copyright Secured by J. J. Stoner, Madison, Wis., Beck & Paul: Lith., Milwaukee, Wis.

Henry Lang, *Aerial Views of Nantucket,* Island Service Company, 1926

Map of the Town of Nantucket in the State of Massachusetts Surveyed by Wm. Coffin, Jr., 1833 (Original Drawing, Nantucket Historical Association)

Map of Town of Nantucket, by William Coffin, Jr., Published by H. Clapp, Nantucket, 1834 (Printed edition of preceding item)

Nantucket Harbor, Detail of the Town and Harbor at the Base, by A. D. Bache, assisted by C. M. Eakin, Survey of the Coast of the United States, Chart 343, 1848. Street names are not designated.

Nantucket Town, Section of a Large Map of the Counties of Barnstable, Dukes and Nantucket, Massachusetts. Surveyed under Henry F. Walling, Supt. of State Maps, 1858

Historical Map of Nantucket Surveyed and Drawn by the Rev. F. C. Ewer, DD., 1869. Nantucket Historical Association owns copy mounted by Nantucket Literary Union with photos by J. Freeman forming border. It was displayed at the Philadelphia Centennial, 1876.

Nantucket Historical Study. Includes a series of maps prepared in the summer of 1968 by an urban history research team, sponsored by Cornell University, the Nantucket Historical Trust, and the Historic American Buildings Survey. Copies are deposited with the Historic American Buildings Survey material in the Library of Congress and with the Nantucket Historical Association. Maps 5 through 12 are of special interest for showing the development of Nantucket Town.

Number	Map Series	Title
1	Reference	County and Town Reference Map
2	Island 1	Natural Factors
3	Island 2	Historic Road Systems
4	Island 3	Historical Points of Interest (summary)
5	Town 1	Reconstruction of Sherburne—1673–1805
6	Town 2	Historical Period 1834
7	Town 3	Historical Period 1848
8	Town 4	Historical Period 1858
9	Town 5	Historical Period 1890
10	Town 6	Historical Period 1914
11	Town 7	Historical Period 1939
12	Town 8	Historical Period 1965
13	Town 9	Sewage Systems
14	Town 10	Wannacomet Water Co. 1890–1968
15	Town 11	Gas Systems 1907–1968
16	Town 12	Historical Areas, Districts and Buildings
17	Detail 1	1968 Structure Survey
18	Detail 2	1968 Fire Services
19	Detail 3	1968 Spatial Survey
20	Detail 4	1968 Paving Survey
21	Miscellaneous	

XVI.   PHOTOGRAPH COLLECTIONS OF NANTUCKET BUILDINGS (Unpublished)

Nantucket Historical Association, *Photograph Albums,* each contains 10 double-faced acetate leaves for pictures, spiral binding

    Book 1—40 prints—Academy Lane to Fair
    Book 2—40 prints—Fair to Kite Hill
    Book 3—40 prints—Liberty to New
    Book 4—40 prints—New to Prospect
    Book 5—40 prints—Prospect to Whaler's Lane
    Book 6—29 prints—York and Misc.

Henry Barnard Worth and Fred W. Palmer, *Photos.* Entitled, *Some of the Old Houses of Nantucket.* Album with notes by Worth. Photos taken in August 1905 by Fred W. Palmer of New Bedford. Acquired by Nantucket Historical Association in 1946.

Nantucket Historical Association, *Stereopticon Collection,* views of Nantucket

Nantucket Historical Association, *Postcard Collection,* views of Nantucket

Harry B. Turner Collection of about 400 Glass Slides, views from *ca.* 1845 to 1912, Nantucket Historical Association

Henry Sherman Wyer and Henry Platt Collections of Slides, Nantucket Historical Association

Alexander Starbuck Collection of Photo Post Cards, 10 Albums containing about 600 Items, Nantucket Historical Association

Miller R. Hutchison II Collection of Photographs, Nantucket Historical Association given copies, 1965

J. Freeman, Photograph Saloon, "For Sale, Stereoscopic Views [of Nantucket] . . . Allen's Block, Main Street," *Island Review,* Aug. 22, 1874 (Vol. I, No. 1), p. 1 (advertisement)

XVII.   NANTUCKET ARCHITECTURE: PHOTOGRAPHS AND GRAPHICS (see also IV above)

HISTORIC AMERICAN BUILDINGS SURVEY: Nantucket Items. Records preserved at Library of Congress, Washington, D.C., include historical data, photographs and measured drawings.

H. A. B. S. Number	Name of Structure	Address
MASS 2–86	Elihu Coleman house	Hawthorne Lane
MASS 120	Old Jail	17 Vestal Street
MASS 141	Old Windmill	South Mill at Prospect
MASS 162	Frederick C. Sanford formal garden	Federal Street at Broad
MASS 167	Henry Swift house	91 Main Street
MASS 183	Meridian Stones	Main Street, Fair Street
MASS 195	Timothy Barnard house	19 Hussey Street
MASS 610	Shanunga	Siasconset
MASS 614	some yards, fences and porch newels	
MASS 811	Henry Coffin house	75 Main Street
MASS 812	Atheneum	Pearl (India) Street
MASS 836	William Rotch Market	1 Main Street
MASS 837	Raymond-Coleman (Seth Coffin) house	53 Orange Street
MASS 838	Second Congregational Church	11 Orange Street
MASS 839	Richard Gardner house	32 West Chester Street
MASS 853	fish houses	Old South Wharf
MASS 854	Coffin-Gardner house	33 Milk Street
MASS 855	Edward Cary house	117 Main Street
MASS 856	early leaded-glass window details	unidentified house, now in N. H. A. Museum

MASS 857	Auld Lang Syne	Siasconset
MASS 858	George Gardner house	8 Pine Street
MASS 898	Easton-Wood-Athearn house	1 North Water Street (dem.)
MASS 899	Masonic Lodge Hall	63 Main Street
MASS 900	Tristram Bunker house	3 Bear Street
MASS 901	Swain-Mitchell house	1 Vestal Street
MASS 902	First Congregational Church	62 Centre Street
MASS 903	Old North Vestry	62 Centre Street
MASS 904	Richard Coleman house	21 Union Street
MASS 905	Hadwen-Wright mansion	94 Main Street
MASS 906	Coffin-Athearn Stores or Old Town Building	2 Union Street
MASS 907	Hadwen & Barney (Richard Mitchell & Sons) Candle House	11 Broad Street
MASS 908	Nantucket Lodge No. 66, I. O. O. F.	5–21 Centre Street
MASS 909	African Baptist Church (African School)	York at Pleasant Street
MASS 911	Major Josiah Coffin house	60 Cliff Road
MASS 912	James Codd (Levi Starbuck) house	14 Orange Street
MASS 913	Holmes and Wyer Carpenter Shop (Theatre Building)	Straight Wharf
MASS 914	Macy Warehouse (Kenneth Taylor Gallery)	Straight Wharf
MASS 915	John Wendell Barrett house	72 Main Street
MASS 916	Reuben R. Bunker house	Academy Hill
MASS 917	Moors' End	19 Pleasant Street
MASS 918	Jared Coffin house	29 Broad Street
MASS 919	Jethro Coffin house	Sunset Hill
MASS 921	Thaddeus Coffin (Jared Coffin) house	89 Main Street
MASS 922	Margaret Gardner Daggett (Ebenezer Gardner) house	111 Main Street
MASS 923	The Big Shop	35 Milk Street
MASS 924	Peter Folger II house	51 Centre Street
MASS 925	The Folger (Barnabus Gardner) house	153 Main Street
MASS 927	Grindell Gardner house	30 Hussey Street
MASS 928	Silas Gardner house	21 Milk Street
MASS 929	William Hadwen house	96 Main Street
MASS 930	Life Saving Station	Surfside
MASS 931	Francis Macy (John H. Shaw) house	77 Main Street
MASS 934	Reuben Joy, Zaccheus Macy house	107 Main Street
MASS 936	Frederick W. Mitchell house	69 Main Street
MASS 938	Pacific National Bank	Main Street
MASS 939	Christopher Starbuck house	105 Main Street

MASS 940	Joseph Starbuck house	4 New Dollar Lane
MASS 941	Three Bricks, Starbuck houses	93, 95, 97 Main Street
MASS 942	Thomas Starbuck house	11 Milk Street
MASS 943	Tashama Farm	Surfside Road
MASS 944	Swain-Macy house	99 Main Street
MASS 946	Robert Wyer house	33 Orange Street
MASS 947 (also MASS 1014)	The Block	15–23 Orange Street
MASS 949	The Folger Block	58–60 Main Street
MASS 950	commercial building	SE corner Main and Orange
MASS 951	Nantucket Looms building	14–16 Main Street
MASS 952	commercial buildings	north side Main (1 block east & west of Federal)
MASS 954	Frank F. Sylvia Antiques	12 Main Street
MASS 956	Capt. Silas Jones house	5 Orange Street
MASS 957	Obed Joy (E. F. Easton) house	4 North Water Street
MASS 966	Friends' Meeting House (school)	Fair Street at Ray's Court
MASS 967	Sea Cliff Inn	Cliff Road
MASS 968	Stiefel house (Sandanweed)	Hulbert Avenue
MASS 970	The Breakers	part of White Elephant, Easton Street
MASS 1002	Job Macy house	11 Mill Street
MASS 1003	Nathaniel (Thomas) Macy house	12 Liberty Street
MASS 1004	Joshua Coffin house	52 Centre Street
MASS 1006	Great Point Lighthouse	Great Point
MASS 1007	Methodist Church	Centre Street
MASS 1013	India Street Neighborhood Study	

includes: 15, 17, 19, 21, 23, 25, 27, 29, 31, 33, 35, 37, 39, 41, 43 and 45 India Street

| MASS 1014 | Orange and Union Streets Neighborhood Study | |

includes: 8, 10, 12, 13, 14½, 16, 17, 18, 20, 22, 25, 26, 28, 29 and 31 Orange Street
9, 11, 13, 15, 17 and 19 Union Street
1, 3 and 2 Stone Alley

XVIII. NANTUCKET: AN OUTSTANDING BOOK OF FICTION

Herman Melville, *Moby Dick,* Harper & Bros., New York, 1851. Rockwell Kent illustrations: Lakeside Press, Chicago, 3 vols. limited edition, 1930; Random House, New York, 1 vol. trade edition, 1930

Glossary

Glossary of Architectural Terms

ABACUS: the square uppermost element of the capital of a column

ACANTHUS: a prickly herb, the leaves of which the Greeks adapted for architectural ornament

ANTA (ANTAE, pl.): a heavy square engaged pier with all elements of a classic column

ANTEPODIUM (ANTEPODIA, pl.): a base or pedestal form projected forward from a basement (podium)

ANTHEMION: the Greek "honeysuckle" flower motif used as an ornament

APSE (APSIDAL, adj.): a vaulted semicircular end recess in a building

ARCHITRAVE: the first or lowest horizontal member of an entablature

ARCHIVOLT: the inner ornamental molding around an arch, the equivalent of an architrave in a straight entablature

ASHLAR: squared masonry or dressed stone

BANISTER: a slender upright shaft supporting the handrail of a staircase or platform

BALUSTER, BALUSTRADE: a shaped upright supporting a railing, the entire form; from *balustium* (Latin), "pomegranate"

BARGEBOARD: the decorated raking board of an overhanging gable

BASEBOARD: the plank or molding around the base of an interior wall

BATTEN: a strip of wood attached crosswise to a series of adjacent boards binding them together

BAY: a main division of an architectural structure

BAY WINDOW: a window structure projecting beyond a wall's outside surface

BEAD, BEADING: a small cylindrical molding

BEAM: a primary horizontal structural support

BELT COURSE: a flat, horizontal projection of exterior brickwork at an upper floor level

BELVEDERE: a pavilion affording a panorama, a cupola; from *belvedere* (Italian), "fine view"

BLIND ARCH: an arch structure applied to a wall

BLIND WINDOW: a false window for external effect only, not open

BRACKET: a projecting, shaped support to an architectural overhang, such as a cornice

BUTTRESS: an external shaft or mass integral with a wall for added support

CAPITAL: the top member or head of a column

CARTOUCHE: a raised plaque

CASEMENT: a window that swings or pivots open

CASING: the architectural framework around an opening

CENTERPIECE: a ceiling ornament from which the chandelier hangs

CHAIRRAIL: a protective molding placed horizontally on a wall at the height of a chair back

CHAMFER: a beveled edge cut where two planes meet at a right angle

CHANNEL: a vertical groove repeated around the shaft of a Doric column, somewhat wider than a flute and meeting its repeats at an edge or arris

CHIMNEYBREAST: the box-like projection of a chimney into a room

CLAPBOARD: a board applied horizontally to an exterior wall which overlaps the one below it

CLOSED STRINGER: see STRINGER

COLONNETTE: a small, slender column

COLOSSAL ORDER: the use of columns greater than one story in height

COLUMN: a classic support having base (except Doric), shaft, and capital

COMMON BOND: brickwork composed of several layers of bricks laid sidewise (stretchers) bonded by a row laid endwise (headers), repeated regularly

CONSOLE: a bracket of classic form, usually scrolled at top and bottom

COOL CELLAR: a dry circular well beneath a house for storing milk and vegetables

CORBEL: a bracket

CORBEL ARCH: a triangular opening, with point upward

CORINTHIAN: the classic order, distinguished by a campaniform capital ornamented with acanthus leaves

CORNICE: the topmost, projecting member of an entablature, sometimes used independently

CRADLE BOARD: a plank or plain dado set in the lower part of an interior wall for protection from thrusts of a rocking cradle

CUPOLA: a superstructure with windows on the sides for admitting light; a lantern

CURB ROOF: a gable roof with double slope, the lower being the steeper of the two; a gambrel

DENTIL: a small rectangular block used in a series beneath a cornice; a "tooth"

DISTYLE: having two columns

DORIC: the primary Greek order, distinguished by a heavy column without base, a channeled shaft, and a capital made up of a square abacus supported on a pillow-like echinus

DORMER: a roofed structure with a vertical window projecting from a sloping roof

DUTCH DORMER: one covered by a simple roof sloping outward, less steeply pitched than the roof of the building, differing from the English gabled dormer

EAVES: the overhanging lower edge of a roof

ECHINUS: the cushion form supporting the square abacus in the capital of a Doric column

ELL: an extension or wing, usually at the rear, containing full-size rooms

ENGLISH BOND: brickwork made up of alternating courses of headers and stretchers

ENTABLATURE: the full horizontal crowning of an architectural order, composed of architrave, frieze, and cornice

FAÇADE: the front or face of a building

FANLIGHT: a half-circular or half-elliptical window, usually over a door

FASCIA: a long, flat, horizontal architectural member or band

FLANGE: a projecting ridge, collar, or plane

FLANKER: a structure attached to the side or flank of a principal mass

FLEMISH BOND: brickwork composed of bricks laid alternately sidewise (stretchers) and endwise (headers) both horizontally and vertically

FLIGHT: a series of uniform steps in a staircase, whether straight or curved

FLUE: the throat or duct of a chimney

FLUSH: with exposed surfaces even or on the same plane

FLUTE, FLUTING: a groove or concave depression used decoratively, as in a column shaft

FOOTING: the bottom support of a wall or post

FRAME: a casing around an opening; a system of construction whereby the form is defined by timbers joined together

FRIEZE: the second member of an entablature, in classic architecture usually containing relief carvings

FRONTISPIECE: the portal or entrance elaboration

FULL-HOUSE: applied to "English" and lean-to houses and Cape Cod cottages that are complete with rooms on both sides of the chimney

GABLE: the triangular shape of an upper wall made by the sloping planes of a roof

GAMBREL: a double-pitched or curb roof with gable (see MANSARD)

GARRET: a room or space in a building just beneath the roof

GIRDER, GIRT: any of a number of primary horizontal beams in a timber framework

GREAT ROOM: the main living room in an early house

GUNSTOCK: the impost or thickened upper end of a post to increase the bearing surface for the girt or plate, so named because its shape resembles the stock of a gun

GUTTA (GUTTAE, pl.): one of a series of ornaments in the form of cone frustums used in an entablature; from the Latin for "drop"

HALF-HOUSE: early house that includes rooms only on one side of the chimney; see FULL-HOUSE

HALL: the main or great room in an early house; the chief passageway (usually with staircase) in a later house

HANDRAIL: the long, shaped upper member of a stairway railing

HEADER: a brick laid with short end exposed

HEXASTYLE: having six columns

HIP: the intersection of two sloping roof planes at an outer corner

HOOD: a projecting member over an opening to shed rainwater

IMPOST: a block at the top of a post or column providing a wider bearing surface

IN ANTIS: between ANTAE or piers, said of supporting columns in a doorway or portico

IONIC: the classic order, distinguished by volutes in the capital of the column

JAMB: an upright forming the side of an opening

JOIST: the horizontal support for a ceiling or floor subsidiary to beams and girts

KEYSTONE: the centermost voussoir of an arch, often given architectural treatment

LAMB'S TONGUE: a reverse-curve cut often found at either end of a chamfer

LANCET: pointed (as at the top of a Gothic arch)

LANDING: a platform between flights of a staircase

LATH: a thin, narrow wood strip nailed to rafters, joists, or studding as a base for plastering

LEAN-TO: a house that is tall in front with a long roof at the back sloping down to a low eaves level

LINTEL: the horizontal member bridging two vertical supports

LUNETTE: a half-moon window, a fan

MANSARD: a roof that is double-pitched on all four sides; named after the French architect Jules Hardouin Mansard

MIRROR BOARD: a vertical plank set in the interior wall between front windows of an early parlor to support a looking glass

MODILLION: a block in a series under a cornice somewhat larger than a dentil and smaller than a console

MULLION: a substantial support of stone or wood between window lights

MUNTIN: a slender window bar of wood or lead

NEWEL POST: the main upright support at the base or head of a stair railing

OBELISK: a tall, tapering upright square shaft capped by a small pyramid; an ancient Egyptian monument

OPEN NEWEL STAIRCASE: a curving flight of steps around an open well

OPEN STRINGER: see STRINGER

ORDER: a defined column and entablature combination constituting the unit of a classic style

PANEL: a flat member held within a framework

PARAPET: a wall section rising above a roof

PARLOR: a room set aside primarily for genteel conversation; from French, *parler,* "to speak"

PAVILION: a small building or single block of a building of complex form

PEDESTAL: a base or small foundation usually with moldings at top and bottom

PEDIMENT: the triangular form of a classic gable

PENT: a small attached room or pavilion with separate roof covering

PERISTYLE: a range of columns around a building or court

PIER: a plain upright support more pretentious than a post

PILASTER: a flat upright member applied to a wall and treated like a column, with base, shaft, and capital

PINNACLE: an ornamental peak or small spire

PLANK FRAME: a simple exterior casing for windows or doors, consisting of top lintel, upright sides, and bottom sill; used from the 17th to early 19th century

PLATE: the horizontal member in a house frame on which the eaves-end of the rafters rest

PLINTH: a square block at the base of a column

PODIUM: basement

PORCH: in early times the entry with staircase; later applied (in Nantucket) to the service ell, perhaps from Latin, *portus,* "storage spaces"

PORTICO: a classic porch

POST: a plain upright support

PROSTYLE: having columns across the front of a building

PURLIN: a horizontal member between rafters in early buildings to support the upright roofing boards

QUOIN: a slightly projecting block at the corner of a wall used decoratively

RAFTER: the sloping member in a roof frame

RAILING: a long horizontal or sloping member supported on uprights

RAKING: slanting, as at the edge of a roof gable or pediment

RAMP: a bend, slope, or curve where a handrail or coping changes its direction upward

REVETMENT: a slab applied for surface effect

RIDGE: the top horizontal meeting of two sloping roof planes

ROOF WALK: a platform with railing atop a house

ROSE WINDOW: a circular or wheel window of Romanesque or Gothic design

RUSTICATION: stonework in which individual blocks have beveled or rabbeted edges which make the joints more conspicuous

SALTBOX: a lean-to house

SASH: the window unit that raises or lowers

SEGMENTED ARCH: an arch that is less than half of a circle or ellipse, meeting the jambs at angles

SHAFT: an upright form, solid or hollow

SHED ROOF: a single-pitched roof over an extension, sloping away from the main pavilion

SIDELIGHTS: windows to either side of a door or center window

SILL: the base member of a house, door, or window frame

SPANDREL: the triangular space between the curve of an arch and its rectangular enframement

SPIRE: the tall, pointed topmost member of a steeple

STOOP: platform and steps before an entrance without covering

STRETCHER: a brick laid with side exposed

STRINGER: the board at the outer edge of a flight of steps; a CLOSED STRINGER retains its parallel sides, whereas an OPEN STRINGER is cut so as to show the profile of each step

STYLE: the architectural type or period characteristics of a building; derived from the Greek word for "column"

SUMMER BEAM: the principal spanning beam across a room, support for the joists that interlay it and the girders

TETRASTYLE: having four columns

TIE BEAM: a horizontal member bridging a space to check outward thrust

TRACERY: the open patternwork in a Gothic window

TRANSVERSE HALL: one that extends from front to back

TRIGLYPHS: the member in the Doric frieze alternating with metopes, essentially a rectangular block indented by two vertical grooves or glyphs, and having two chamfers or half grooves at the sides, together counting as a third glyph

TRUNCATED: with top removed

TUDOR ARCH: a broad, low-pitched pointed arch, technically four-centered

TUSCAN: the Etruscan or Roman version of the Greek Doric order; the column is more elongated, often with plain shaft and base

TYPICAL NANTUCKET HOUSE: a four-bayed, two-storied house with center chimney; see Chapter Five

UNBONDED: brickwork having all-stretcher (sidewise) bricks and no headers exposed

VOLUTE: a spiral form, as in an Ionic capital or at the base of some stair rails

WEATHERBOARD: an early type of feather-edge (triangular) plank used for outer wall covering, the thick edge of one weatherboard overhangs the thin edge of the next beneath; it differs from the rectangular clapboard of the later period

WINDER: the triangular step in a newel staircase, or wedge-shaped step used in turning the corner in a staircase with a straight flight

WITHE: strictly speaking, a thin stone slab set on edge dividing a chimney stack into separate flues; by extension, it is applied to the articulated planes of the front of a chimney stack exposed above the roof